One

Graham Priest presents an original exploration of philosophical questions concerning *the one and the many*. He covers a wide range of issues in metaphysics—including unity, identity, grounding, mereology, universals, being, intentionality, and nothingness—and deploys the techniques of paraconsistent logic in order to offer a radically new treatment of unity. Priest brings together traditions of Western and Asian thought that are usually kept separate in academic philosophy: he draws on ideas from Plato, Heidegger, and Nagarjuna, among other philosophers.

One

Being an Investigation into the Unity of Reality and of its Parts, including the Singular Object which is Nothingness

Graham Priest

OXFORD
UNIVERSITY PRESS

Great Clarendon Street, Oxford, OX2 6DP,
United Kingdom

Oxford University Press is a department of the University of Oxford.
It furthers the University's objective of excellence in research, scholarship,
and education by publishing worldwide. Oxford is a registered trade mark of
Oxford University Press in the UK and in certain other countries

© Graham Priest 2014

The moral rights of the author have been asserted

First published 2014
First published in paperback 2016

All rights reserved. No part of this publication may be reproduced, stored in
a retrieval system, or transmitted, in any form or by any means, without the
prior permission in writing of Oxford University Press, or as expressly permitted
by law, by licence, or under terms agreed with the appropriate reprographics
rights organization. Enquiries concerning reproduction outside the scope of the
above should be sent to the Rights Department, Oxford University Press, at the
address above

You must not circulate this work in any other form
and you must impose this same condition on any acquirer

Published in the United States of America by Oxford University Press
198 Madison Avenue, New York, NY 10016, United States of America

British Library Cataloguing in Publication Data
Data available

Library of Congress Cataloging in Publication Data
Data available

ISBN 978-0-19-968825-8 (Hbk.)
ISBN 978-0-19-877694-9 (Pbk.)

Links to third party websites are provided by Oxford in good faith and
for information only. Oxford disclaims any responsibility for the materials
contained in any third party website referenced in this work.

To the peace of all sentient beings

Contents

Preface: What One Needs to Know — xv
   P.1 Ways to be One — xv
   P.2 Wholes and their Parts — xvi
   P.3 The One of Parmenides and Plato — xvii
   P.4 All is One — xvii
   P.5 Paraconsistency — xviii
   P.6 Dialetheism and the Inclosure Schema — xx
   P.7 Noneism — xxi
   P.8 Characterization — xxii
   P.9 Buddhist Philosophy I: India — xxiii
   P.10 Buddhist Philosophy II: China — xxv
   P.11 And So... — xxvii

Part I. Unity

1. Gluons and their Wicked Ways — 5
   1.1 The Illusion of Simplicity — 5
   1.2 Frege and the Unity of the Proposition — 5
   1.3 Unities and their Parts — 8
   1.4 The Bradley Regress — 9
   1.5 Explaining Unity — 11
   1.6 The Aporia — 14

2. Identity and Gluons — 16
   2.1 How Gluons Glue — 16
   2.2 Breaking the Regress — 16
   2.3 Material Equivalence—Paraconsistent Style — 18
   2.4 Identity and Gluons — 19
   2.5 Gluons, Prime and Other — 21
   2.6 The Definition of Identity — 22
   2.7 Predicates and Properties — 24
   2.8 Objecthood Revisited — 26
   2.9 Looking Forwards — 27
   2.10 Technical Appendix: A Formal Semantics — 28

	2.10.1 Second-order *LP*	28
	2.10.2 Identity	30
	2.10.3 The substitutivity of identicals	30
	2.10.4 Gluon models	31
	2.10.5 World semantics	35
3.	Form, Universals, and Instantiation	38
	3.1 Aristotle into the Fray	38
	3.2 Aristotle Comes Unstuck	38
	3.3 Neo-Aristotelians	40
	3.4 Gluons and Form	42
	3.5 Universals	44
	3.6 Instantiation	45
4.	Being and Nothing	48
	4.1 Heidegger onto the Stage	48
	4.2 Simple Objects	48
	4.3 Being and Unity	49
	4.4 Heidegger's Aporia	51
	4.5 Being *an Sich*	53
	4.6 Everything and Nothing	54
5.	A Case of Mistaken Identity	57
	5.1 The Substitutivity of Identicals	57
	5.2 The History of SI	57
	5.3 The Ground for SI	59
	5.4 Intentionality	60
	5.5 Time	62
	5.6 Modality	64
	5.7 Fission	66
	5.8 Vagueness	68
	5.9 Looking Back	70
	5.10 When can SI be Applied?	70
	5.11 Object-Language Identity and Metalanguage Identity	71
	5.12 From Part I to Part II	73
	5.13 Technical Appendix: Second-Order *LPm*	73

Part II. In Plato's Trajectory

6.	Enter Parmenides: Mereological Sums	79
	6.1 The Muse of Plato	79
	6.2 All Wholes and No Parts	80

	6.3	The Way of Truth	80
	6.4	The Partlessness of Being	83
	6.5	Plato on Parmenides	84
	6.6	Refocusing the Argument	88
	6.7	Parthood	88
	6.8	Mereological Sums	90
	6.9	An Object and the Sum of its Parts	92
	6.10	Plural Reference	94
	6.11	An Object and its Parts	96
	6.12	The Bell for the End of Round One	97
	6.13	Interlude on Nothing	97
		6.13.1 The empty fusion	97
		6.13.2 A formal model	99
7.	Problems with the Forms—and their Solutions		101
	7.1	The *Parmenides*	101
	7.2	Background	101
	7.3	The Reply to Zeno (126a–130a)	104
	7.4	Parmenides' Attack, 1 (130a–131e)	107
	7.5	Parmenides' Attack, 2 (132a–133a)	109
	7.6	Parmenides' Attack, 3 (133b–135b)	112
	7.7	Transition to Part Two (135c–137c)	114
	7.8	From Part One to Part Two	117
8.	The One—and the Others		118
	8.1	The Unity of the *Parmenides*	118
	8.2	Approaches to the Second Part of the *Parmenides*	118
	8.3	Deduction IA (137c–142a)	121
	8.4	Deduction IB (142a–155e)	123
	8.5	Deduction II (157b–160b)	125
	8.6	Deduction III (160b–164b)	128
	8.7	Deduction IV (164b–165d)	130
	8.8	Deduction IC (155e–157b)	134
	8.9	The Big Picture	137
9.	In Search of Falsity		140
	9.1	From the *Parmenides* to the *Sophist*	140
	9.2	The Unity of the Proposition Again	141
	9.3	Extending the Account	143
	9.4	Truth	144

	9.5 Falsity: the Problem	147
	9.6 Falsity: the Solution	150
	9.7 Negative Properties	151
	9.8 From Plato to Paraconsistency	153
10.	Perception, Intentionality, and Representation	154
	10.1 To Represent and be Represented	154
	10.2 From the *Sophist* to the *Theaetetus*	154
	10.3 Socrates' Story of Perception	155
	10.4 Noema and Object	157
	10.5 Intentionality	159
	10.6 Representation	160
	10.7 From Part II to Part III	161

Part III. Buddhist Themes

11.	Absence of Self, and the Net of Indra	167
	11.1 Identity Again	167
	11.2 Look for Your Self	168
	11.3 The Illusion of Self	170
	11.4 Relational Quiddity	171
	11.5 Emptiness	173
	11.6 Structural Trees	175
	11.7 Trans-Temporal "Identity"	177
	11.8 Interpenetration	178
	11.9 The Net of Indra	179
12.	Embracing the Groundlessness of Things	182
	12.1 Problems of Emptiness	182
	12.2 The Regress of Quiddities	182
	12.3 The History of this Kind of Objection	183
	12.4 Cosmological Arguments	184
	12.5 Viciousness	186
	12.6 The Regress of Relations	188
	12.7 Analysing Loci	189
	12.8 Nihilism Again	191
	12.9 Happy Anachronism	193
13.	The World, Language, and their Limits	194
	13.1 Concepts and the World	194
	13.2 Idealism and Realism	195

13.3	Realism, East and West	196
13.4	Idealism, East and West	197
13.5	Between the Horns	198
13.6	The *Tractatus*, Same and Different	199
13.7	Emptiness and Gluon Theory	201
13.8	Nāgārjuna's Paradox	202
13.9	*Tathātā*	203
13.10	The Preconditions of Representation	205
13.11	The Paradox of Nothingness	207
13.12	From Metaphysics to Ethics	209
14.	**Peace of Mind**	**210**
14.1	Appeals to Authority	210
14.2	The Four Noble Truths	211
14.3	Rebirth	212
14.4	Inner Peace	214
14.5	Other Goods	215
14.6	Goods Incompatible with Inner Peace	216
14.7	The Unrealistic Nature of the Ethics	219
14.8	Freedom for Life	220
15.	**Compassion**	**221**
15.1	Others	221
15.2	Interconnectedness	222
15.3	From the Net of Indra to Compassion	223
15.4	The Import of Metaphysics	225
15.5	Two Observations	226
15.6	Interlude on Buddhism	227
15.7	Making Others Suffer	230
15.8	Those who Cause Suffering	231
15.9	Why be Moral?	232
15.10	Matters Socio-Political	233
Bibliography		239
Index		249

A fish-trap is for catching fish; once you've caught the fish, you can forget about the trap. A rabbit-snare is for catching rabbits; once you've caught the rabbit, you can forget about the snare. Words are for catching ideas; once you've caught the idea, you can forget about the words. Where can I find a person who knows how to forget words so that I can have a few words with him?

Zuangzi. [Mair (1994), p. 277]

Preface: What One Needs to Know

P.1 Ways to be One

This book—as may be surmised from its title—is about what it is to be one. I do not mean what it is for two people to be married; nor do I mean anything about political solidarity (though this notion does appear towards the end of the book). Rather, I mean what it is for things to be one in a metaphysical sense. This may sound a rather trivial matter. It is not, as we will see.

It may also sound a rather arcane matter, relevant only to an esoteric little bit of metaphysics. Again, it is not. The notion of being one thing is, perhaps, our most fundamental notion. One cannot say anything, think anything, cognize anything, without presupposing it. Unsurprisingly, then, its behaviour infuses the things that presuppose it. The ramifications of the matter spread out in many directions in philosophy, and affect questions in metaphysics, the philosophy of language, the philosophy of mind, and even ethics. They are to be found lurking under many questions in the history of philosophy.

However, what it means to be one, metaphysically, can itself be many things. Corresponding to each sense of *one*, there is a corresponding sense of *many*. And each pair gives rise to a problem often referred to as a *problem of the one and the many*. Three such will concern us in the book. For a start, we may be concerned with what it means for an object to be numerically one; what constitutes its unity, as it were. When an object has parts (the many), how does their multiplicity produce a unity? This is the theme of Part I of the book. Alternatively, we may be concerned with the problem of universals: how can one property be located in many things? Perhaps the most crucial case of this concerns the universal of *oneness* itself. What exactly is this, and how does it behave? Part II of the book revolves around this question. Third, it is not uncommon to hear philosophers of a certain kind claim that all things (the many) are one. The copula here can hardly be the *is* of identity. No one of sound mind is likely to claim that my right foot is literally and numerically identical with my left. I am obviously not a monopod. Sometimes, the claim is cashed out as the thought that each thing (the many) is all things (the one). What on earth is going on here? That is the topic of Part III of the book. Although the three questions with which the book deals are distinct, the answers to them interact in important ways. The parts of the book themselves therefore cooperate to form a unity.

Let us look at the parts of each part a little more closely, so that the reader has a taste of things to come.

P.2 Wholes and their Parts

Every object—or at least, every object with parts—is both a one and a many. But being one and being many are contradictories, so how is this possible? This is not a serious puzzle: it is the thing that is one, and its parts that are many. But other problems are harder—much harder. How do the parts conspire to form a whole? What is the difference between a unity and a mere congeries? Something must, as it were, glue them together. But when one starts to examine this matter, that thing appears to have contradictory properties. (Frege's notorious problem of the concept *horse* is just a special case of this.) This might be thought of as a problem. But Part I of the book simply accepts this conclusion: these things—gluons, as they will be called in Chapter 1—do have contradictory properties.

Indeed, it not only accepts this fact, but puts it to constructive use. How do gluons glue a unity together? When facing this question, one confronts the "Bradley regress". The regress is solved by a theory of identity according to which it is not transitive. The possibility of contradictory objects is integral to this. Chapter 2 elucidates, spelling out the required theory of identity, and how gluons fit into the picture. That such an account is available is crucial: without it, I am sure, the ideas of the book could not be taken seriously. The body of the chapter explains the ideas in relatively informal terms. Those with a taste for the techniques of formal logic will want to see how the ideas can be cashed out precisely. I relegate the details of this to a technical appendix to the chapter, Section 2.10. Those with no taste for such matters can skip the appendix without loss of understanding.

There is technical material in some other sections of the book, which may also be skipped without loss for those who are not formal logicians. These are Sections 5.13, 6.13.2, and 12.7–12.9.

The constructions of formal logic demonstrate that the notions employed are at least technically coherent. Philosophical coherence is, of course, another matter. And one may well suppose that any account of identity according to which the substitutivity of identicals is not valid is not philosophically coherent. (The transitivity of identity is a special case of such substitutivity.) That matter is taken up in Chapter 5.

The rest of Part I explores some of the immediate ramifications of gluons, such as their connection with tropes (or, as I will call them, *pins*—particular instantiations), with universals themselves, and with two very particular objects

nothing and **everything**. Lovers of Heidegger will be pleased to see that **nothing** is a quite coherent object. Indeed, it will play a significant role at crucial points in the book. We will see, moreover, that gluon theory provides a solution to Heidegger's notorious *Seinsfrage*—the question of Being.

P.3 The One of Parmenides and Plato

The problem of the one and the many around which Part I turns has often been overlooked as a serious problem. Where it has been taken very seriously is in Ancient Greek philosophy. Aristotle and Plato, in particular, were much concerned with it. Aristotle's solution is discussed in Part I. There is much more to be said about Plato's. This is the focus of Part II.

The behaviour of parts is intimately connected both with Parmenides' partless One, and with Plato's form of Oneness. Both come in for scrutiny in this part. In particular, both of these are involved in Plato's *Parmenides*. This dialogue is one of his most important and influential. It is also one of the most tantalizing and obscure. Many commentators despair of a coherent interpretation. The centrepiece of Part II is an interpretation based on gluon theory. This, it seems to me, provides just such an interpretation.[1]

These are not the only issues traversed in Part II, however. This part concerns itself with the application of gluon theory to questions of meaning, truth, intentionality, and formal mereology. (An interlude after Chapter 6 provides an account of the mereology of **nothing**.) These are, of course, central issues in contemporary philosophy. However, I have chosen to approach them through the lens of Plato. This gives the material a unity it might otherwise lack. More importantly, it will remind readers that contemporary problems sink deep into the history of the subject.

P.4 All is One

The key to understanding what it means for all things to be one—or at least one way of doing so—is to understand the notion of identity in question. Chapter 11 shows how this may be done in terms of the notion of interpenetration to be found in the Buddhist Huayan tradition. This, in turn, depends on an analysis and endorsement of the Buddhist—and specifically Madhyamaka—notion of emptiness. This chapter is no mere historical exegesis, however. In particular, it deploys

---

[1] A longer version of these chapters appears as Priest (2012). I am grateful to the editor of the *International Journal of Plato Studies* for permission to use this material here.

modern techniques of graph-theory (though not very heavy ones) to make sense of matters.

The doctrine of emptiness has always been controversial—even within Buddhism. Many have felt that it gives rise to a vicious regress. In Chapter 12 we see that it does not. In particular, we see why the regress in question, unlike the Bradley regress, is not vicious. Again, modern mathematical techniques are brought in at this point. This time, non-well-founded sets.

Ideas from Buddhist philosophy are also to be found in the other chapters in this part. Chapter 13 deals with the relationship between language (or our concepts) and the world. We will see how the notion of emptiness drives between the horns of idealism and realism. Buddhist philosophy often deals with the ineffable—and indeed, runs into paradox, since it talks about the ineffable. We will see how gluon theory makes sense of this. The final two chapters of this part concern ethics. Central to these is the view that persons, like all things, are empty, and the consequent ramifications of this concerning the virtue of compassion.

Evidently, this part of the book makes use, and I hope fruitful use, of ideas from Buddhist philosophy. That one may do this may be surprising news to many contemporary Western philosophers, whose conception of philosophy is myopically Eurocentric. If the book were to do nothing more than show this to be possible, it would serve a useful function.

P.5 Paraconsistency

So much for the preview. The material depends on ideas for which I have argued in other books. It seems otiose to argue for them again here; but I should at least spell out what I am presupposing. Chief amongst these ideas is dialetheism and the consequent paraconsistency.

Dialetheism is a metaphysical view: that some contradictions are true. That is, where $\neg$ is negation, there are sentences, propositions (or whatever one takes truth-bearers to be), A, such that A and $\neg A$ are both true. Given that A is false iff (if and only if) its negation is true, this is to say that there are some As which are both true and false.

Paraconsistency is a property of a relation of logical consequence. Explosion is the property of such a relation according to which any contradiction implies anything. That is, a relation of logical consequence, $\vdash$, is explosive iff for all A and B, $\{A, \neg A\} \vdash B$. A consequence relation is paraconsistent iff it is not explosive. There is, of course, a connection between dialetheism and paraconsistency. In particular, if one is a dialetheist, one had better hold that the appropriate logical consequence relation is paraconsistent, on pain of accepting everything: triviality.

Those who have never met dialetheism and paraconsistency before may well be puzzled by the views. Let me do at least a little to unpuzzle. In classical logic, any situation (interpretation) partitions all truth-bearers into two classes: the true ($\mathfrak{T}$) and the false ($\mathfrak{F}$). The two classes are mutually exclusive and exhaustive. Given that negation is a functor which toggles a sentence between truth and falsity, a sentence is in $\mathfrak{T}$ iff its negation is in $\mathfrak{F}$, and *vice versa*. Thus, we have the following:

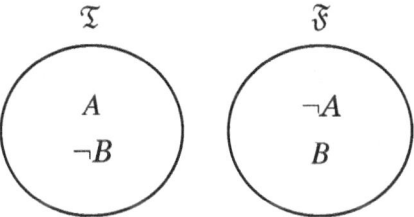

A standard definition of validity is to the effect that an inference is valid if there is no situation where all the premises are true and the conclusion is not true. Given the above set-up, there is no situation where, for any A, both A and $\neg A$ are true. *A fortiori*, there is no situation where A and $\neg A$ are true, and B is not—whatever B you choose. That is, Explosion is valid.

But now suppose that $\mathfrak{T}$ and $\mathfrak{F}$ may actually overlap in some situations. Given that negation works in the same way, it follows that if C is in the overlap, so is its negation. Thus, we have the following:

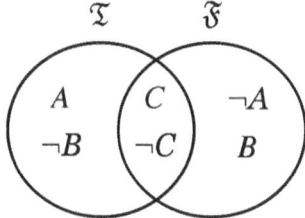

For a situation of this kind, both C and $\neg C$ are true (and false as well; but at least true). But B is false only (not true). Given exactly the same definition of validity as before, it follows that Explosion is not valid.

There is much more to be said about paraconsistent logic, though this is unnecessary here.[2] What I have said serves to indicate the most fundamental idea.

---

[2] There is, in fact, a wide variety of paraconsistent logics. A full discussion can be found in Priest (2002). What I have just described is the basic idea if the logic is characterized semantically. The basic idea can, however, be articulated in a number of different ways. The way that will be pursued in this book is that of the logic *LP*. Further details can be found in Chapter 2 (esp. Section 2.10.1).

Most of the other machinery of a formal logic may be taken to behave as it does in classical logic, though the following is worth noting. In first-order logic, a predicate has an extension—the set of things of which it is true—and an anti-extension—the set of things of which it is false. In classical logic, the anti-extension need not be mentioned explicitly, since it is simply the complement of the extension. However, in a paraconsistent logic, the extension of a predicate does not determine the anti-extension. It therefore needs a separate specification.

P.6 Dialetheism and the Inclosure Schema

Note that validity is defined as truth-preservation over *all* situations of a certain kind. These do not all have to be actual (that is, where everything that holds in the situation is actually true). One can reason correctly, not just about actual situations, but about ones that are hypothetical, conjectural, and so on. Moreover, not all situations may be expected to be such that $\mathfrak{T}$ and $\mathfrak{F}$ have a proper overlap. There will be consistent situations in which they are exclusive and exhaustive—and so where things behave *exactly* as in classical logic. So one does not have to be a dialetheist to hold that a paraconsistent logic gives the right (or a right) notion of logical consequence. One might hold that *actual* situations are of the consistent kind. Inconsistency, when it arises, occurs in merely hypothetical situations, such as the one we consider when we think what it would be like if someone squared the circle, or as described by some inconsistent (and untrue) scientific theory, such as Bohr's theory of the atom.

Dialetheism is, however, the view that some *actual* situations are such that, in them, $\mathfrak{T}$ and $\mathfrak{F}$ have a proper overlap. One may naturally, at this point, ask for examples of things in such an overlap. There are, in fact, many such—albeit controversial—examples.[3] A standard example is provided by sentences delivered by the paradoxes of self-reference. Let us look more closely at these.

An *inclosure-paradox* is a paradox that fits the inclosure schema. This arises when there is an operator, δ, and a totality, Ω, such that whenever δ is applied to any subset, x, of Ω, of a certain kind—that is, one which satisfies some condition ψ—it appears to deliver an object that is still in Ω, though it is not in x. A contradiction will then arise if Ω itself satisfies ψ. For applying δ to Ω will produce an object that is both within and without Ω. We may depict the situation as follows (φ is the defining condition of the set Ω, and × marks the contradictory spot—somewhere that is both within and without Ω):

---

[3] See Priest (1987).

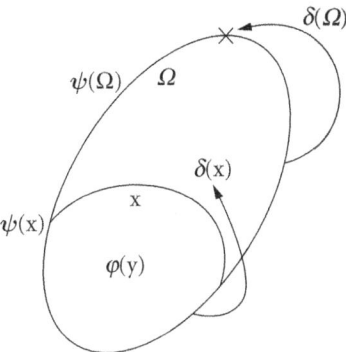

Now, all the standard paradoxes of self-reference are inclosure paradoxes.[4] Consider, for example, Russell's paradox. If x is any set, then the set of all its members which are not members of themselves is a set, and can easily be shown not to be a member of x. Applying this operation to the totality of all sets therefore gives a set that is both in and not in that totality. In this case, Ω is the set of all sets; $\delta(x) = \{y \in x : y \notin y\}$; and $\psi(x)$ is the vacuous condition, $x = x$.

Some of the paradoxes in question are paradoxes of definability. A paradigm of these is König's paradox. Something is *definable* if there is a (non-indexical) noun-phrase that refers to it. If a is a definable set of definable ordinals, then (since this is countable), there is a *least ordinal greater than all the members of a*. It is obviously not a member of a, but it is definable by the italicized phrase. Since the set of all definable ordinals is itself definable, we may apply this operator to it to obtain a set that cannot be referred to (defined), but which yet can. In this case, Ω is the set of all definable ordinals; $\psi(x)$ is 'x is definable'; and $\delta(x)$ is the least ordinal greater than all the members of x.

So much for some of the nuts and bolts of dialetheism. There is, of course, much more to be said about it. In particular, one might think that the view cannot be right, since it queers the pitch concerning truth, rationality, communication, or some such notion. It does not.[5]

Let us pass on to another important preliminary matter. This concerns noneism (the view that some objects do not exist).[6]

P.7 Noneism

Some objects do not exist: fictional characters, such as Sherlock Holmes; failed objects of scientific postulation, such as the mooted planet Vulcan; God (any one

---

[4] See Priest (1995), Part 3.   [5] See Priest (2006).
[6] What follows in the next two sections is spelled out in much greater detail in Priest (2005).

that you do not believe in). Yet we can think of them, fear them, admire them, just as we can existent objects. Indeed, we may not know whether an object to which we have an intentional relation of this kind exists or not. We may even be mistaken about its existential status. The domain of objects comprises, then, both existent and non-existent objects. There is a monadic existence predicate, *E*, whose extension is exactly the set of existent objects; and the extension of an intentional predicate, such as 'admire', is a set of ordered pairs, the first of which exists, and the second of which may or may not. How to understand the notion of existence, is, of course, a thorny issue. For the record, I take it to be to have the potential to enter into causal relations.

We can also quantify over the objects in the domain, whether or not they exist. Thus, if I admire Sherlock Holmes I admire *something*; and I might want to buy *something*, only to discover that it does not exist. I will write the particular and universal quantifiers as $\mathfrak{S}$ and $\mathfrak{A}$, respectively. Normally one would write them as $\exists$ and $\forall$, but given modern logical pedagogy the temptation to read $\exists$ as 'there exists' is just too strong. Better to change the symbol for the particular quantifier (and let the universal quantifier go along for the ride). Thus, one should read $\mathfrak{S}xPx$ as 'some *x* is such that *Px*' (and $\mathfrak{A}xPx$ as 'all *x* are such that *Px*'). It is not to be read as 'there *exists* an *x* such that *Px*'—nor even as 'there *is* an *x* such that *Px*', being (in this sense) and existence coming to the same thing. (To put it in Meinongian terms, some objects have *Nichtsein*—non-being.) If one wants to say that there *exists* something that is *P*, one needs to use the existence predicate explicitly, thus: $\mathfrak{S}x(Ex \wedge Px)$. Quantifiers, note, work in the absolutely standard fashion: $\mathfrak{S}xPx$ is true iff something in the domain of quantification satisfies *Px*; and $\mathfrak{A}xPx$ is true iff everything in the domain of quantification satisfies *Px*.

P.8 Characterization

So far so good. But more needs to be said about the properties of non-existent objects. Consider the first woman to land on the Moon in the twentieth century. Was this a woman; did they land on the Moon? A natural answer is yes: an object, characterized in a certain way, has those properties it is characterized as having (the Characterization Principle). That way, however, lies triviality, since one can characterize an object in any way one likes. In particular, we can characterize an object, *x*, by the condition that $x = x \wedge A$, where *A* is arbitrary. Given the Characterization Principle, *A* follows. We must take a different tack.

Worlds are many. Some of them are possible; some of them are impossible. The actual world, @, is one of the possible ones:

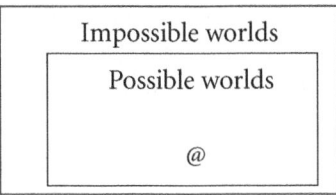

Given dialetheism, there are contradictions true at the actual world. One might wonder, therefore, what makes a world impossible. Answer: an impossible world is one where the laws of logic are different from those of the actual world (in the way that a physically impossible world is a world where the laws of physics are different from those of the actual world). Given the plurality of worlds, truth, truth conditions, and so on, must be relativized to each of these. That is a relatively routine matter.

What is not so routine is Characterization. If we characterise an object in a certain way, it does indeed have the properties it is characterized as having; not necessarily at the actual world, but at some world (maybe impossible). Specifically, suppose we characterize an object as one satisfying a certain condition, Px. We can write this using an indefinite description operator, ε, so that εxPx is 'an x such that Px'.[7] Given that we play our paraconsistent cards right, for *any* condition, Px, this is going to be satisfied at *some* worlds. If @ is one such, the description denotes an object that satisfies the condition there. If not, just take some other world where it is satisfied, and some object that satisfies it there. The description denotes that. Hence, we know that if $\mathfrak{S}xPx$ is true at @, so is $P(\varepsilon xPx)$; but if not, $P(\varepsilon xPx)$ is true at at least some world. Thus, consider the description $\varepsilon x(x$ is the first woman to land on the Moon in the twentieth century). Let us use 'Selene' as a shorthand for this. Then we can think about Selene, realize that Selene is non-existent, and so on. Moreover, Selene does indeed have the properties of being female and of landing on the Moon—but not at the actual world. (No existent woman was on the Moon in the twentieth century; and no non-existent woman either: to be on the Moon is to have a spatial location, and therefore to exist.) Selene has those properties at a (presumably possible) world where NASA decided to put a woman on one of its Moon flights.

P.9 Buddhist Philosophy I: India

One further topic is desirable by way of introduction. The final part of the book makes use of ideas from Buddhist philosophy. The ideas are explained, not taken

---

[7] To obtain a definite description, we just have to take the indefinite description 'an object uniquely satisfying Px'.

for granted. But in the process, reference is made to various Buddhist traditions, as well as to particular philosophers. In the contemporary philosophical climate, one must assume that most English-speaking philosophers will know little or nothing of these matters. In this and the next section I will provide an appropriate background. The material is not supposed to be a comprehensive account of the matter;[8] just enough for someone unfamiliar with the area to orient themselves.

The foundations of Buddhist philosophy were laid by the historical Buddha, the Indian thinker Siddhārtha Gautama.[9] (The word 'Buddha' itself is an honorific, like 'Christ', and simply means 'the awakened one'.) His exact dates are uncertain, but a traditional chronology gives them as 563 to 483 BC. He enunciated principles often called the *Four Noble Truths*. These diagnose what one might call the human condition: an unhappiness-causing attachment to things in a world of impermanence (*anitya*) and interdependence (*pratītyasamutpāda*); they then give a recipe for what to do about it. Buddhist thought developed for the next several hundred years, until a canon of writings emerged: the *Tripiṭaka* (Three Baskets).[10] One of these comprised the *sūtras*: discourses featuring the historical Buddha. Another was the *vinaya*, the rules for monastic living. The third was the *abhidharma* (higher teachings). A principal concern of this was to provide a taxonomy of things in the world and their parts. Thus, a person is just a collection of changing and interacting, mental and physical, parts (*skandhas*). Most objects of experience are of a similar kind, though this is not the way in which things appear. That is conventional reality (*saṃvṛti satya*), as opposed to the ultimate reality (*paramārtha satya*) of the way that things actually are. Naturally, a number of different schools of Buddhist thought developed in this period. Only one of these now survives: *Theravāda* (Doctrine of the Elders).

Around the turn of the Common Era, a new class of sūtras started to appear: the *Prajñāpāramitā* (Perfection of Wisdom) *Sūtras*. (These include the most famous, short and cryptic, *Heart Sūtra*.) They initiated a new kind of Buddhism: *Mahāyāna* (the Greater Vehicle). The new Buddhism differed from the old in ways both ethical and metaphysical. The older Buddhism was concerned with individuals liberating themselves from the human condition. Someone on this path was an *arhat* (worthy one). By contrast, according to Mahāyāna, the ethical path was to help *all* sentient creatures liberate themselves. People who had dedicated themselves to do this were said to be on the *Bodhisattva* (enlightened being) *Path*. In Mahāyāna, compassion (*karuṇā*) therefore became the central virtue.

[8] There are a number of books which provide this. See for example, Mitchell (2002).
[9] There are two languages of early Buddhism. One is the scholarly Sanskrit; the other is the vernacular Pali. Words, including proper names, may therefore be found written in both. I will stick with Sanskrit.
[10] The Pali version of this is often called the *Pali Canon*.

On the metaphysical front, the central concept became that of emptiness (śūnyatā). Not just the ordinary objects of our experience, but all things, are less substantial than they appear to be in conventional reality. Two different schools of Mahāyāna thought developed, which articulated this view in different ways. Historically the earlier was *Madhyamaka* (Middle Way). This was founded by perhaps the greatest of all Buddhist philosophers, Nāgārjuna. His dates are uncertain, but he flourished some time around 150–200 AD. His *Mūlamadhyamakakārikā* (Fundamental Verses on the Middle Way) was to exert a profound influence on all subsequent Buddhist thought. According to the Madhyamaka, to be empty is to be empty of self-existence (*svabhāva*). All things lack this. The historically later school was *Yogācāra* (Practice of Yoga), sometimes called by the more apt name *Cittamātra* (Consciousness-only). Traditionally, this is taken to have been founded by the half-brothers Vasubandhu and Asaṅga. Again, the dates are uncertain, but their period was around the fourth century AD. According to Yogācāra, to be empty is to be empty of mind-independence. All things are therefore mind-dependent.

Buddhist philosophy continued to develop in India until about the end of the millenium. Much of the development occurred in the great Buddhist university of Nālandā in Northern India (427–1197 AD). The university produced some thinkers, such as Śāntarakṣita, who tried to fuse the two Mahāyāna schools, as well as perhaps the greatest Mahāyāna ethicist, Śāntideva, who wrote the influential *Bodhicaryavatāra* (Guide to the Bodhisattva's way of Life). Both of these thinkers flourished in the eighth century AD. In this later period of Indian Buddhism, techniques of meditation were augmented with tantric practices.

Buddhism also spread outside the Indian sub-continent. Theravāda Buddhism went south-east, into countries such as Sri Lanka, Burma, and Thailand. Mahāyāna went north into modern-day Afghanistan, China, and, relatively late in the piece, Tibet (Śāntarakṣita playing an important role in this). It was virtually wiped out in Afghanistan and India by the waves of Moslem invasions late in the first millennium, Nālandā itself being sacked in 1197. A consequence of this is the fact that many Indian Buddhist texts are now lost, and exist only in Tibetan or Chinese translations.

P.10 Buddhist Philosophy II: China

Although the native Tibetan religion, Bön, did have some effect on Buddhism in Tibet, this was not enough for Buddhism to change its Indian heritage profoundly. Chinese Buddhism is a different matter.

Buddhist ideas began to enter China from Central Asia, across the Silk Route, around the beginning of the first century AD. There they encountered the two indigenous Chinese philosophies: Confucianism and Daoism.[11] Both of these originated at about the same time as Buddhism in India (and, for that matter, about the same time that Greek philosophy was hitting its straps). The former derived from the thought of Confucius—Kongfuzi; 'Confucius' is, of course, a Latinisation; 'zi', incidentally, is an honorific: a classy form of 'Mr'—(551–479 BC), and his intellectual descendants. His sayings are recorded in the *Lunyu* (Analects). The latter is derived principally from two texts: the *Dao De Jing* and the *Zhuangzi*. The former is traditionally attributed to Laozi, who is supposed to have flourished in the sixth century BC; but it may well be a compilation of sayings from different people. ('Laozi' can mean 'old masters'.) The second is an eponymously named text, Zhuangzi himself being dated at around 350–300 BC (though much of this is a compilation of various writers as well). Of Confucianism and Daoism, it was the latter that was to be the more important for Buddhism. According to Daoism, there is a principle behind the flow of events, the Dao; and the Daoist sage is someone who does not cling, but "goes with the flow" of the Dao.

Buddhism was not well understood when it entered China, and was taken to be an exotic form of Daoism. The Buddhist ultimate reality was (all too) easily identified with the Dao, and the enlightened Buddhist person was, again, easily identified with the Daoist sage. Things changed when good translations of the Buddhist texts became accessible, largely as a result of the translating work of the Kuchean missionary Kumārajīva (344–413 AD) and his students. After this, Chinese versions of the two major Indian Mahāyāna schools developed, *Sanlun* (Mādhyamaka) and *Weixin* (Yogācāra); but though they were influential, they soon disappeared in favour of the distinctively Chinese forms of (Mahāyāna) Buddhism.

Four of the most important of these were: *Qingtu* (Jap: *Jōdo*), *Tientai* (Jap: *Tendai*), *Huayan* (Jap: *Kegon*), and *Chan* (Jap: *Zen*). The first of these is notable for its devotionalism, but not for its philosophical developments.[12] The other three developed distinctive notions of ultimate reality (Buddha nature) and enlightenment, which bespeak not only Mādhyamaka and Yogācāra influences, but also a Doaist influence. Philosophically the most sophisticated was Huayan (Skt: *Avataṃsaka*; Eng: Flower Garland), named after the sūtra which it took to be most important. The founder of the school is traditionally taken to be Tuxun

---

[11] There are two ways of transliterating Chinese into English. One is the still common, but older, Wade Giles. The other is the more modern Pinyin. I will use the latter.

[12] In English this is called 'Pure Land Buddhism'. According to this, anyone who calls on the name of the Bodhisattva Amitābha (Chin: Amituofo), will, at death, be reborn in a Pure Land which will provide a fast-track to enlightenment.

(557–640 AD), but philosophically more important is Fazang (643–712 AD), who parlayed the Indian notion of emptiness into a picture of the world in which all phenomenal objects interpenetrate and mutually encode each other.

The Huayan school gradually faded out, and had all but disappeared by the ninth century AD (though it still exists in a minor way in Japan). But many of its ideas were incorporated in the Chan school. Legend has it that this school was founded by another missionary, Bodhidharma, who arrived in China some time in the fifth or sixth centuries AD. However, the most important person in the establishment of the school is arguably Huineng (638–713 AD), who wrote the most important early document of the school; the *Platform Sūtra*. The emphasis of the Chan school was practical, rather than theoretical (as may be surmised from its name, a Sinification of the Sanskrit *dhyāna*, meaning meditation). A distinctive feature of the school is that enlightenment can be sudden, and occurs with a conceptually unmediated, and therefore indescribable, encounter with ultimate reality (Buddha nature).

Buddhist ideas entered and took root in Japan around the eighth century AD, via the Korean peninsula. During the next centuries, nearly all the major Chinese Buddhisms were brought to Japan. Perhaps the most important period in Japanese Buddhism was the thirteenth century AD, when thinkers such as Dōgen (1200–1253 AD) imported Chan, or Zen, as it is called there. When it entered Japan, Buddhism encountered the indigenous animistic view, Shinto. Shinto certainly coloured Japanese Buddhism, but it did not have a profound impact in the way in which the indigenous Chinese ideas had done, the general perception being that Shinto and Buddhism are quite compatible.

P.11 And So...

These things, I hope, will help the reader to understand some of the ideas on which the book builds. Perhaps the book is unusual, in that it draws on ideas Ancient and Modern, Eastern and Western. But philosophy knows no boundaries of space and time.

As will also be clear, the book draws on two views that are contemporary heresies: dialetheism and noneism. Indeed, it adds a third to the picture, in the form of the non-transitivity of identity. Some may think that only ill can come from compounding heresy upon heresy. Personally, I do not see it that way. The orthodoxies on these matters were never as rationally grounded as their adherents like to pretend. Moreover, in the present context, the three heresies, far from adding to each others' woes, interlock and support each other in fundamental ways. And in doing so, they open up a perspective of the world that is forever closed to those with the blinkers of orthodoxy.

Finally, it is always a pleasure to say thank you. First: to my three academic communities during the period in which the book was written: the Departments of Philosophy of the University of Melbourne, the University of St Andrews, and the Graduate Center, City University of New York. Next: to the Australian Research Council, for a Professorial Fellowship (Grant No. DP0879972) which made it possible for the work to progress much faster than would otherwise have been the case. Third, and most importantly, to the people who have helped me. Writing philosophy is a solitary activity, done sitting in a study in front of a computer. But doing philosophy is a social activity: discussions occur in seminars, pubs, trains, by email. And no single person can claim credit for the final result. I have given material which fed into the book, not only at my home departments, but at numerous seminars and conferences at other places throughout the world in the last five years. I also presented the material in two series of seminars—one at the University of St Andrews in 2011 and 2012, and one at the Graduate Center, CUNY, in 2012. Thanks go to the many people who have made the thoughtful and helpful comments which I received in all this—especially to my students in the CUNY seminars, who subjected the material to intense criticism, much to its improvement.

Particular thanks are due to the following. Writing this book has taken me (again) into areas which involved a steep learning curve. For the material on Asian philosophy, Jay Garfield, Yasuo Deguchi, and Amber Carpenter helped me greatly; for the material on Plato, it was Sarah Brodie, Maureen Eckert, and Amber Carpenter (again). Throughout much of the time I was working on the book, Ricki Bliss was studying with me, writing her thesis on metaphysical grounding. Several ideas were clarified and steeled in the many fruitful and enjoyable discussions we had. Dave Ripley read a draft of the whole manuscript and made very helpful comments. He and Naoya Fujikawa cast discerning eyes over the formal material. Two anonymous referees for Oxford University Press provided a number of helpful comments and suggestions. Eric Steinhardt's expertise contributed to matters diagrammatic. Finally, many thanks go to Peter Momtchiloff at Oxford University Press for his sage judgement.

All these people helped to provide some parts of the jigsaw. The whole is, on this occasion I hope, greater than the sum of its parts. It has, I am sure, like any other philosophy book, its share of shortcomings. No doubt its ideas could have been improved with further thought. But if one waits for perfection, one will wait forever.

PART I
Unity

PART 1

Unity

> ... two things cannot rightly be put together without a third; there must be some bond of union between them. And the firmest bond is that which makes the most complete fusion of itself and the things it combines ...
>
> Plato *Timaeus* 31b–c [Hamilton and Cairns (1961)]

1
Gluons and their Wicked Ways

1.1 The Illusion of Simplicity

'One' is one of the simplest words in the English language, but the concept it expresses is of singular importance. Our most basic thoughts, perceptions, emotional reactions, are usually to, or of, something. That thing is a one thing. Such cognitive activity would, it would seem, not be possible unless we had a grasp of what it means to be one. And, it might be thought, such a grasp is almost trivial. What could be simpler than just being one thing? Appearances, here, are deceptive, though. We have many fundamental and apparently simple philosophical concepts, such as: being, existing through time, intentionality, identity—indeed being one is perhaps the most fundamental of all these, since it is embroiled in all of them. And like all of them, any simplicity it appears to have is illusory. Thought about it soon dissolves into knots. As Augustine said in a different context:[1] as long as no one asks me, I know what it is; but as soon as anyone asks me to explain, I do not.

Considering the question of what it means to be one reveals a number of interlocking problems, many of which will be our concern here. The first part of the book is about the problem of how, if an object has parts, these cooperate to produce a unity—one thing. I will provide an answer to the question, and explore some of its, perhaps surprising, implications. In this chapter, we will start with the problem itself.

1.2 Frege and the Unity of the Proposition

One of the hardest things in philosophy sometimes is to know the difference between a profound problem and a silly question. As with genius and insanity, the two can appear very similar. It might well be thought that the question with which we will be engaged is of the silly kind; one could be forgiven for thinking

---

[1] *Confessions*, bk. 11, ch. 14. The remark concerned time.

this. One way to see that it is not, is to see how some important philosophical projects have run aground on the matter; so let us start by doing this. Let us look at Frege's views on meaning and, in particular, his account of the unity of the proposition.

Consider the sentence 'Sortes homo est'. The sentence is constituted by a noun-phrase, 'Sortes', and a verb phrase, 'homo est'. According to Frege, the sentence has a sense. This is the proposition (thought) that it expresses: that Socrates is a person. The proposition is composed out of the senses of its two components, the sense of 'Sortes' (s), and the sense of 'Homo est' (h). But the proposition is not a plurality, a congeries of its two parts, s and h. Somehow these cooperate to form a unity. How?

For Frege, names (including definite descriptions) refer to objects, and predicates refer to concepts. He has no special names for the senses of the two grammatical categories, so let us just call them object-senses and concept-senses. Frege's answer was that concepts and concept-senses are radically different from objects and object-senses. Unlike objects and object-senses, they are "unsaturated", radically incomplete. The sense of 'homo est' has a "gap" in it, which is plugged by the sense of 'Sortes' to produce a single thing. Note the form of words here:

(*) The sense of 'homo est' has a "gap" in it.

The notions of being unsaturated, of having a gap, and so on, are of course metaphorical. This is not in itself a problem: literal explanation may well give out somewhere. What is a problem is that concept-senses are supposed to be unsaturated. But, the expression 'the sense of "homo est"' is a noun phrase, and so refers to an object(-sense); and these, according to Frege, are not unsaturated.

Frege was well aware of the matter. His solution was simply to reiterate the claim that the sense of 'homo est' is indeed saturated. But he was aware that this put him in a difficult situation. He says in the infamous *concept horse* passage:[2]

---

[2] Geach and Black (1952), p. 54. Frege actually addresses the matter for reference (*bedeutung*) rather than sense (*sinn*). However, he takes matters to be similar for sense. For our purposes, they are not. Frege takes a concept to be a function which applies to an object to form a truth value. Now, whatever a truth value is, the object is not part of it. (In the same way, the referent of 'John' is not a part of the referent of 'the father of John'.) Of course, there is a very good question about how one is to understand the relationship between an object and a concept (property) which applies to it. This is the question of how to understand instantiation; we will come to it in due course. Note that if Frege had taken the referent of a sentence, more naturally, to be a state of affairs (either existent or non-existent), of which the object and the concept are a part, the situation concerning reference would be exactly the same.

I admit that there is a quite peculiar obstacle in the way of an understanding with my reader. By a kind of necessity of language, my expressions, taken literally, sometimes miss my thoughts; I mention an object when what I intend is a concept[-sense]. I fully realize that in such cases I was relying on the reader who would be ready to meet me half-way—who does not begrudge me a pinch of salt.

But Frege underestimated (or understates) the problem. If he is right in his insistence that the description refers to an object, this undercuts his whole explanation of the unity of the proposition. Merely reflect for a moment on (*). This is now simply false. We seem forced into the view that concept-senses are objects, even though they cannot be.[3]

It is not just the unity of propositions which generates this situation for Frege.[4] In Fregean semantics, both the senses and referents of predicates are functions, and the same problem arises for normal cases of functional application. Thus, for Frege, 'the father of' refers to the function that maps each person to their father (and each non-person to something else), and has a corresponding sense. Call this a *function-sense*. So 'the father of Frege' refers to Herr Frege sr., and its sense is an object-sense—a unitary thing. It has this because the sense of 'Frege' fills the gap in the sense of 'father of'. But the sense of 'father of', according to Frege's criterion, is an object(-sense), and so it does not have a gap at all. The situation is exactly the same.

Frege's problem, then, is this. If concept-senses and function-senses are to play their role in accounting for the unity of complexes, they cannot be objects. But they are. One might avoid Frege's problem simply by rejecting his account of meaning. The situation in which Frege finds himself is, however, but an example of a much deeper problem which cannot be avoided in this way. At root, the problem is not about meaning at all. It is about how parts cooperate to form a unity of any kind. Let me spell this out.[5]

---

[3] See, further, Priest (1995a), ch. 12. The chapter shows how the problem gives rise to the distinction between saying and showing in Wittgenstein's *Tractatus*, together with its final spectacular self-destruction.

[4] Which makes any solution to the problem in terms of predication—such as that in Gaskin (1995)—beside the point.

[5] Frege's problem is, in fact, a version of a much older problem concerning properties (the traditional name for Frege's concepts). We say 'Socrates runs'. 'Runs' denotes the property of running. That is a thing. But 'Socrates runs' is not a congeries of two things. The two cooperate. In the sentence, one must understand 'runs' as essentially predicative, 'is running', which is not an object. Properties themselves are both objects and not objects. One can get around this to a certain extent, by taking it that there is only one lexical item with a predicative function: 'instantiates'. (As in 'Socrates instantiates the property of running'.) But one is still stuck with the phenomenon for the relation of instantiation. I will return to this matter in discussing Heidegger in Chapter 4.

1.3 Unities and their Parts

Things have parts. A computer has components, a country has regions, a history has epochs, a piece of music has notes, an argument has statements, and so on. (Whether all objects have parts is a matter to which we will come in due course.) What is the relationship between a thing and its parts? For a start, the parts can exist when a unity they compose does not. The bricks of a house, for example, can lie scattered around in a field before the house was built, or after it is destroyed.[6] Aristotle made the point this way (*Top.* 150^{a}15–21):[7]

> In general, too, all the ways of showing that the whole is not the same as the sum of its parts are useful in meeting the type . . . [of man who defines an object to be its parts]; for a man who defines in this way seems to assert that the parts are the same as the whole. The arguments are particularly appropriate in cases where the process of putting the parts together are obvious, as in a house and other things of that sort; for there, clearly, you may have the parts yet not have the whole, so that the parts and the whole cannot be the same.

The parts of the house are not sufficient: they have to be configured in a certain way. Similarly, a piece of music has to have its notes arranged in the right way. And an argument has to be structured into premises and conclusion.

A unity, then, is more than the simple sum of its parts.[8] What is this more? For the moment, and following Aristotle, let us call it the *form* of the object. Exactly how to understand the appropriate notion of form is a sensitive matter (and in due course, we will reject the claim that an Aristotelian form can do the required job). Conceivably, form is a different kind of thing in different kinds of case: what constitutes the unity of a house would seem to be different from what constitutes the unity of an argument. And what constitutes the unity of an object such as a house is, itself, by no means obvious: is it the geometric shape, or the causal interaction between the bricks, or the design in the mind of the architect, or is it something entirely *sui generis*? Never mind. I might add, also, that what the parts of an object are may also be a matter of dispute. Do the parts of a human body comprise, for example, its organs, the cells in these, the atoms in these, all of the above? For our purposes, it does not matter. Virtually nothing this book has to say will presuppose an answer to that question.

---

[6] Even if one takes the form of the house to be a part of it, one can still have all the parts without the house. If one takes universals to exist, the form of the house exists whether the bricks are scattered or together; and even if one takes universals to be non-existent objects, the form of a house was a perfectly good object before the bricks were brought together.

[7] Quotations from Aristotle through this book are taken from Barnes (1984), unless otherwise indicated.

[8] Well, its non-gluon parts, but this is to get ahead of ourselves.

Whatever the parts are, though, and whatever form is, the form is something that binds the parts into a whole. But now we have a contradiction. It is, after all, *something*, an object. (I have just spoken about *it*.) On the other hand, it cannot be an object. If it were, the collection of parts *plus* the form constitute a plurality, just as much the original. So the problem of binding would not be solved. In Frege, note, the role of binding is played by concept-senses; it is therefore these which occupy the contradictory role.

Here, then, is our problem of unity. Let me lay it out in abstract terms. Take any thing, object, entity, with parts, $p_1, \ldots, p_n$. (Suppose that there is a finite number of these; nothing hangs on this.) A thing is not merely a plurality of parts: it is a unity. There must, therefore, be something[9] which constitutes them as a single thing, a unity. Let us call it, neutrally (and with a nod in the direction of particle physics), the *gluon* of the object, g.[10] Now what of this gluon? Ask whether it itself is a thing, object, entity? It both is and is not. It is, since we have just talked about it, referred to it, thought about it. But it is not, since, if it is, $p_1, \ldots, p_n, g$, would appear to form a congeries, a plurality, just as much as the original one. If its behaviour is to provide an explanation of unity, it cannot simply be an object.

As is clear, the problem is posed by the contrast between an object, which has a unity, and a congeries, which is a plurality. It might be thought that when we refer to a plurality, we are referring to some one thing, in which case the supposed distinction disappears. But 'is a congeries' is not a predicate that applies to a single object. It is a predicate of a plurality, the parts of the object. I will return to the topic of plural reference in Section 6.10.[11]

1.4 The Bradley Regress

It will pay to become clearer about why a gluon cannot be an object. A vicious regress stands behind this.[12]

---

[9] Or some things; but it will turn out that there is only one.

[10] The name was coined, with essentially this meaning, in the Conclusion to Priest (1995a).

[11] Relatedly, one might be tempted to ask what it is in virtue of which a bunch of objects is a plurality. Are there anti-gluons? But such a question would make little sense. A gluon is whatever it is that answers the question about how parts cooperate to form a whole. If one asks how it is that objects cooperate to form a plurality, the answer is that they do not. No cooperation of any kind is necessary to be a disparate and disconnected bunch of things.

[12] This kind of regress argument is very old. In the form of the "third man argument" it is used in Plato's *Parmenides* as an argument against the theory of forms. Plato is there concerned with what makes all, for example, red things one (namely, red). Invoking a form of redness produces the regress. Being one by being red is not the same thing as being one by being parts of something, and Plato's form is not (obviously) a gluon. However, structurally, the situations are similar. We will come to the third man argument itself in Chapter 8.

Return to the matter of the unity of the proposition again. At one stage in his career, Russell was much concerned with this, and one possibility he considered was that it was the copula, 'is', that binds the constituents together. (So, in Fregean terms, there is just one concept, which is the copula.[13]) He then explains why the copula cannot be on a footing with the other constituents:[14]

> It might be thought that 'is', here, is a constant constituent. But this would be a mistake: 'x is a' is obtained from 'Socrates is human', which is to be regarded as a subject-predicate proposition, and such propositions, we said, have only two constituents [Socrates and humanity]. Thus 'is' represents merely the way in which the constituents are put together. This cannot be a new constituent, for if it were there would have to be a new way in which it and the two other constituents are put together, and if we take this way as again a constituent, we find ourselves embarked on an infinite regress.

Russell is using an argument used earlier to great effect by Bradley.[15] Again, addressing the problem of the unity of the proposition, Bradley starts by supposing that a proposition has components A and B. What constitutes them into a unity? A natural thought is that it is some relation between them, C. But, he continues:[16]

> [we] have made no progress. The relation C has been admitted different from A and B... Something, however, seems to be said of this relation C, and said, again, of A and B... [This] would appear to be another relation, D, in which C, on one side, and, on the other side, A and B, stand. But such a makeshift leads at once to the infinite process... [W]e must have recourse to a fresh relation, E, which comes between D and whatever we had before. But this must lead to another, F; and so on indefinitely... [The situation] either demands a new relation, and so on without end, or it leaves us where we were, entangled in difficulties.

And Bradley is, in fact, aware that this is not just a problem concerning the unity of the proposition. It is much more general. Thus, in discussing the unity of the mind, Bradley writes:[17]

> When we ask 'What is the composition of Mind,' we break up that state, which comes to us as a whole, into units of feeling. But since it is clear that these units, by themselves, are not all the 'composition', we are forced to recognize the existence of the relations... If units have to exist together, they must stand in relation to one another; and, if these relations are also units, it would seem that the second class must also stand in relation to the first. If A and B are feelings, and if C their relation is another feeling, you must either suppose

---

[13] A discussion of this view, in the context of its regress, is given in Gaskin (1995).
[14] Eames and Blackwell (1973), p. 98.
[15] In fact, it had been used some 600 years earlier by Jean Buridan in his *Questiones in Metaphysicam Aristotelis* (Bk V, q. 8). (See Normore (1985), p. 197f.) It should therefore be called the Buridan/Bradley regress.
[16] Allard and Stock (1994), p. 120.   [17] Allard and Stock (1994), pp. 78–9.

that component parts can exist without standing in relation to one another, or else that there is a *fresh* relation between C and AB. Let this be D, and once more we are launched off on the infinite process of finding a relation between D and C–AB; and so on forever. If relations are facts that exist *between* facts, then what comes between the relations and the other facts?

We can state the regress problem generally in terms of gluons. Suppose that we have a unity comprising the parts, a, b, c, d, for example. There must be something which, metaphysically speaking, binds them together. This is the object's gluon, g. But then there must be something which binds g and a, b, c, d together, a hyper-gluon, g'. There must, then, be something which binds g', g, and a, b, c, d together, a hyper-hyper-gluon, g''. Obviously we are off on an infinite regress. Moreover, it is a vicious one.

Perhaps it is not immediately obvious that this is so. Could there not just be a whole lot'a gluin' goin' on? To understand why this is not a valid response, we must come back to what is at issue here. Our original problem was how a unity of parts is possible. We need an *explanation*. Given a bunch of parts, simply invoking another object does not do this. We still have the original problem of how a unity of parts is possible. Thus is a new step triggered, and so on indefinitely. Even invoking an infinite regress of objects does not solve the problem. We still have no explanation of how a unity is constituted. If one is asked how to join two links of a chain together, it helps not one iota to say that one inserts an intervening link. (And adding that one might need an infinite number of such links merely makes the matter worse.) In vicious regresses of this kind (I do not think it is the only kind) the infinity has, in fact, precious little to do with matters. The point is that something has already gone wrong at the first step: a failure of explanation.[18]

As Frege realized, if something is to perform the role of explaining how it is that a unity of objects is achieved, it cannot just be another object.

1.5 Explaining Unity

A common thought at this point is that what accounts for the unity of the parts of an object, its gluon, is their configuration, arrangement, structure, or some such. Whatever you call it, it is a *relationship* between the parts, and relationships relate,

---

[18] '[I]t is the first step in the regress that counts, for we at once, in taking it, draw attention to the fact that the alleged explanation or justification has failed to advance matters; that if there was any difficulty in the original situation, it breaks out in exactly the same form in the alleged explanation. If this is so, the regress at once develops...' Passmore (1961), p. 31.

by definition. Call relationships objects if you wish; but they are a special *kind* of object; and they bind together the parts by their very nature.[19]

There is already a confusion at the heart of this thought—and not an uncommon one. The confusion is between relating and unifying. Relations do not, in general, unify. I am related to my mother by bearing the relationship of *child* to her. This may even be an internal relation (whatever, exactly, that means)—at least as far as I am concerned: I could not have been *me* had I not had that relation. But obviously the relation does not serve to render my mother and myself a unity in the appropriate sense.

Even setting aside the confusion, though, the thought still does not work. The fact that a gluon is a different *kind* of object does not solve the problem of unity. If anything, it simply makes it worse. Thus, what it is that joins the mind and body into a unity is a traditional and vexed problem in dualistic theories of mind. It is the very fact that they are different kinds of thing that seems to make the problem so intractable. In a similar way, suppose that it is the configuration of the bricks that binds them together to form a house. The bricks are physical objects; the configuration is, presumably, an abstract object. (Different sets of bricks can have the same configuration.) Any interaction between the bricks and the configuration would therefore seem just as problematic, perhaps even more so, as that in the mind/body case.

So it has to be the particular *nature* of the special object that is supposed to solve the problem. But how does it do so? To say that it just does do this—by its nature—is not to solve the problem; it is simply to name it. As Bradley puts it (speaking of the mind, but with considerations that apply quite generally):[20]

> When we ask 'What is the *composition* of [an object]', we break up [that object], which comes to us as a whole, into units ... But since it is clear that these units by themselves are not all the 'composition', we are forced to recognize the existence of relations. But this does not stagger us. We push on with the conceptions we have brought to the work, and which of course can not be false, and we say, Oh yes, we have there more units, naturally not quite the same as the others, and—*voilà tout*. But when a sceptical reader, whose mind has not been warped by a different education, attempts to form an idea of what is meant, he is somewhat at a loss.

For when one invokes the object in question, one simply adds an extra element to the melange. If one is puzzled by the unity in the first case, one should be equally puzzled by the supposed unity in the second. Thus, for example, instead

---

[19] We are not a million miles away here from Aristotle's proposed solution to the problem. We will look at the details of his account in Chapter 3.

[20] Bradley (1922), sect. 65. Here and throughout the book, all italics in quotations are original unless otherwise specified.

of a plurality of physical parts of an object, we now have a plurality of [parts plus configuration]. Or more generally, we have the parts plus the relationship between them (or the *action* of the relation, or the *fact* that they are so related). How is this any better? This is exactly what the Bradley regress highlights.

A quite different possibility for explaining the unity of an object is one which appeals to the notion of (ontological) dependence.[21] Consider a pile of stones and a person's body. The former, it might be suggested, is not a true unity; the latter is. And what makes the difference is that the identity of the pile depends on the identity of its parts, the stones; whereas in the case of the body, it is the other way around: the identity of the parts depends on the identity of the whole. (We would not have that hand unless it were part of that body.) Thus, the thought continues, what explains the oneness of a partite genuine unity is the dependence of its parts on the whole. There will be much to be said about dependence in Part III of the book. For the moment, let us grant the claims about what depends on what. Even given these, the suggestion will not work. The fact that in a unity the natures of the parts depend on the nature of the whole in no way explains how they cooperate to form a unity. For all their dependence, the parts are still parts; and facts about identity do not bear on cooperation. Granted, the parts would not be the parts they are unless they were parts of the whole. But that hardly explains how it is that the various parts do what they do to create the whole. We know, by their nature, that they are parts of that whole; but how is it that they have this nature?

One could, I suppose, be a quietist about the whole matter: one might just accept that one cannot provide an explanation. All one can say about the phenomenon is to aver, every time one walks past a united object, 'there it goes again'. Perhaps one has to be a philosophical quietist about some things. But giving up without a fight is an untoward defeatism. And if a perfectly good explanation can be found, as I shall argue that it can, unwarranted. Of course, explanations always come at a cost—some kind of commitment; and the explanation I shall offer is no exception. The cost in this case is revising how it is we currently think that certain things, and especially identity, work. But such is to be expected in any conceptual advance. Thus, for several hundred years scientists had no account of how gravitational effects are transmitted. Everything has an instantaneous effect on everything else, and that is that. No explanation. Since Einstein, we now have an explanation; but the explanation has caused major revisions in our conceptions of space, time, matter. The cost of a revision may be entirely warranted.

Alternatively, one might suggest that no explanation in the pertinent sense is called for. What constitutes the unity of a table? Simply that I take a piece of wood and nail four legs to it in appropriate places. There is nothing more to be

[21] This possibility was suggested to me by Jonathan Schaffer. It is hinted at in his (2010b).

said. This will not do, however. What we are being offered here is an explanation of how the unity came into being—the causal processes that brought it about. Now, explaining how something is brought about is not explaining what it is that has been brought about. To explain how to get married is not to explain what a marriage is. One who nails the legs to a table top in the appropriate way has indeed brought the table into existence by certain causal processes. But causal processes are going on all around us, and only some of them bring objects into existence. So what is it that one which does so, actually does? In any case, the suggestion, appealing as it does to causal processes, can account at best for the unity of things subject to such processes. It cannot account for the unity of abstract objects, such as propositions, pieces of music (types, not tokens), sets.

There are no easy roads here.

1.6 The Aporia

We have, then, an aporia. Whatever it is that constitutes the unity of an entity must itself both be and not be an entity. It *is* an entity since we are talking about *it*; it is *not* an entity since it is then part of the problem of a unity, not its solution. 'Aporia' is often glossed as 'puzzle' or 'uncertainly', but it literally means something like 'impasse'. An aporia is a source of puzzlement and uncertainty precisely because it seems to leave no way to go forward. In the present case, if we wish to go back, there are only three options:

1. We can say that there are no gluons.
2. We can reject the claim that a gluon is an object.
3. We can reject the claim that it is not an object.

Prospects look bleak.

Consider the first case. If there are no gluons, then we are bereft of an explanation as to the difference between a unity with parts and the plurality of the parts, which there certainly is. We could avoid this by supposing that there *are* no unities: the world is just a congeries of congeries. All parts, no unities. But this does not seem to help either. If there are no unities, there certainly appear to be; that is, there are unities in thought. This means that the mind constitutes unities— as, perhaps, for Kant. But in this case, there are gluons. These are mental entities, but they fall foul of the aporia in the usual way.[22]

---

[22] The view that there are no material wholes, only simples, is defended in Unger (1979). There are no tables: only atoms 'arranged table-wise' (as van Inwagen puts it (1990), p. 72ff). Sider (1993) points out that this commits the view to the (counterintuitive) necessity of the existence of physical simples (partless wholes). (Gluon theory is not so committed.) And Uzquiano (2004) argues that

At the other extreme, one might suppose that there are unities, but that they have no parts, and hence that there are no gluons. All unities, no parts. A very extreme form of this position is to the effect, not only that there are only unities, but there is only one of them. All else is appearance. The view is to be found in Parmenides and Bradley. Supposing that there are only unities with no parts is a desperate move. It flies in the face of common sense: if someone steals a wheel of my car then it is missing an essential part. And before one says that the car is not really a whole, but we only *think* of it in that way, recall that this means that there is a unity in intention, and we are back with intentional gluons.

In the second case, we must insist that the gluon is simply not an object. But this seems even more desperate: we can refer to it, quantify over it, talk about *it*. If this does not make something an object, I am at a loss to know what could. Anything we can think about is an object, a unity, a single thing (whether or not it exists). There seems little scope here.

Finally, in the third case, we may suppose that the gluon is simply an object. But we have seen that this just leaves us bereft of an explanation of the unity of an entity. How could we even have had the impression that any object *could* constitute the unity of another bunch of objects? Only because of taking the unity for granted. Thus, we write 'Socrates is a person' and the rest is obvious. But putting 'Socrates' and 'is a person' next to each other does not do the job; it just produces a plurality of two things. When we think of the two as cooperating, the magic has already occurred.

If we cannot go back, then we must go forward. What stands in the way? Evidently, the Principle of Non-Contradiction. If we accept that gluons both are and are not objects, then some contradictions are true. Whilst it must be agreed that *horror contradictionis* is orthodox in Western philosophy, at least since Aristotle's canonical—but fundamentally flawed—defence, the friends of consistency have done little as yet to establish that there is anything rational in this.[23] So let us go forward. Gluons are dialetheic: they have contradictory properties. Of course, if this were all there were to matters, the situation would not be particularly interesting. Going on means crossing the bridge of inconsistency;[24] and what is important is what lies on the other side.

---

attempts to paraphrase away talk of unities in the way suggested is problematic. In any case, the view hardly seems credible for abstract objects. A proposition is a single thing: one can believe *it*, express *it*. You can not do this to a plurality of meanings arranged proposition-wise, whatever that might be supposed to mean.

[23] See Priest (2006).
[24] Not that there are no other good reasons to do so. See Priest (1987) and (1995a).

2

Identity and Gluons

2.1 How Gluons Glue

In the previous chapter we saw that there must be something which accounts for a unity composed of parts where one exists—a gluon; and we saw that a gluon may be expected to have contradictory properties. But we have not yet faced the question of how the gluon does its job: how does it bind the parts (including itself) into a whole? Its having contradictory properties does not immediately address this question (though, one might suspect, it is going to play an important role). In this chapter, we look at the answer. The key is breaking the Bradley regress. We will start by seeing how.

This will immediately launch us into a discussion of identity. Identity cannot work in the way that orthodoxy takes it to if gluons are to do their job. In particular, it must be non-transitive. How so? The rest of the chapter explains, and articulates the nature of gluons more precisely in this theoretical context. The ideas are spelled out informally. Full technical details can be found in the technical appendix to the chapter, Section 2.10, which can be skipped without loss of continuity by those with no taste for such things.

2.2 Breaking the Regress

The problem of unity is to explain how it is that gluons glue. What stands in the way of an explanation is the Bradley regress. As we saw in Section 1.4, this is vicious, and so it must be broken. But how?

Suppose that an object has parts a, b, c, and d, and that these are held together by a gluon 中.[1] The Bradley regress is generated by the thought that 中 is distinct

---

[1] The character 中 (Chinese: *zhong*; Japanese: *chu*) means *centre*, which seems like a pretty good symbol for a gluon. (By coincidence, it is also sometimes used as part of one of the Chinese names for Madhyamaka Buddhism: *zhong dao zong*.) As the amount of logic increases, it also seems a good time for Western logicians to move to some less familiar languages in search of symbols. Unfortunately,

from each of the other parts. If this is the case, then there is room, as it were, for something to be inserted between 中 and a, and so on. Or to use another metaphor, there is a metaphysical space between 中 and a, and one requires something in the space to make the join. Thus, the regress will be broken if 中 is identical to a. There will then be no space, or need, for anything to be inserted.

Of course, 中 must be identical with b, c, d, for exactly the same reason. Thus, 中 is able to combine the parts into a unity by being identical with each one (including itself). The situation may be depicted thus:

$$a = 中 = c$$

with b above (= 中) and d below (= 中).

The explanation of how it is that the gluon manages to unite the disparate bunch is, then, that it is identical with each of them.[2] Consider, if it helps, an analogy. Suppose that one wants to join two physical bricks together with physical glue. The glue is inserted between the bricks. It bonds to each one, and so joins them. It does not make the two bricks one, but the molecules of the glue and each brick become physically indissoluble. In the metaphysical case, the parts of an object do not become identical either, but the gluon bonds with each part in the most intimate way, by being identical with it.

It should be immediately obvious that the relation of identity invoked here will not behave in the way that identity is often supposed to behave. In particular, the transitivity of identity will fail. We have $a = $ 中 and 中 $= c$, but we will not have $a = c$. Two bricks of a house are not identical. It might be doubted that there is any such coherent notion, or that, if there is, it is really one of identity. These concerns cannot be set aside lightly, and the only way to assuage them is to provide a precise theory of identity which delivers what is required. Let us turn to this.

I will use the character in this section only, due to the current difficulty of typesetting Chinese characters in heavily symbolic contexts.

[2] Of course, the parts of an object can themselves have parts. Thus, it could be the case that, for example, c has parts m and n. These will be joined by a gluon, 中′. So we will have $m = $ 中′ $= n$. If one takes the parthood relation to be transitive, m, 中′, and n, are also parts of the original object. So we will have 中 $= m$, 中 $= $ 中′, and so on.

2.3 Material Equivalence—Paraconsistent Style

For a start, gluons, we know, are contradictory objects, and so the account needs to be given in a paraconsistent logic, where contradictions do not explode. In Section P.5, we saw how negation works in a paraconsistent context. What we need to know now is how material equivalence (having the same truth value) works in this context.

Classically, every situation partitions sentences of the language into two zones, the truths ($\mathfrak{T}$) and the falsehoods ($\mathfrak{F}$), the two zones being mutually exclusive and exhaustive:

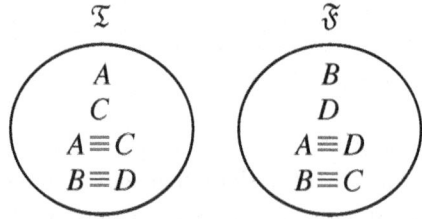

Sentences, $A, B, C, \ldots$ therefore find themselves in exactly one or other of the zones. If two sentences are both in the same zone, their material equivalence is in the $\mathfrak{T}$ zone; whilst if one is in one zone, and the other is in the other zone, their material equivalence is in the $\mathfrak{F}$ zone. (See the diagram above.)

In paraconsistent logic, everything is the same except that the $\mathfrak{T}$ and the $\mathfrak{F}$ zones may overlap.[3] Thus we have the following picture:

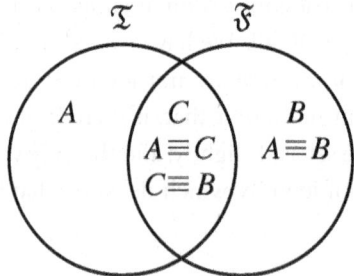

As before, the material equivalence of two sentences is in the $\mathfrak{T}$ zone if both are in the same zone ($\mathfrak{T}$ or $\mathfrak{F}$), and in the $\mathfrak{F}$ zone if they are in different zones, but now a sentence can be in both zones.

---

[3] In some logics, they may underlap as well, so that there are things that are in neither $\mathfrak{T}$ nor $\mathfrak{F}$; but in the logic we will be using, this is not the case.

$A \equiv A$ will always be in the $\mathfrak{T}$ zone, since A is always in the same zone as itself. If $A \equiv B$ is in the $\mathfrak{T}$ zone, then so is $B \equiv A$, since these are just ways of saying that A and B are in the same zone. So equivalence is reflexive and symmetric; but it is not transitive. A and C may be in the same zone, and C and B may be in the same zone, though A and B are not, because C is in the overlap. Hence, we may have $A \equiv C$ and $C \equiv B$ being in the $\mathfrak{T}$ zone, without $A \equiv B$ being so (see the diagram above). Note also that detachment for $\equiv$ may fail: we can have C and $C \equiv B$ in the $\mathfrak{T}$ zone without B being in it (same diagram).

For the record, here are some paraconsistent facts concerning negation, equivalence, and validity. As we noted in Section P.5, an inference is valid ($\models$) just if in every situation where all the premises are true (though they may be false as well), so is the conclusion. Bearing this in mind, and remembering that a formula is in the $\mathfrak{T}$ zone iff its negation is in the $\mathfrak{F}$ zone, it is easy to check the details.

- $\models A \equiv A$
- $A \equiv B \models B \equiv A$
- $A, B \models A \equiv B$
- $\neg A, \neg B \models A \equiv B$
- $A, \neg B \models \neg(A \equiv B)$
- $B, \neg B \models A \equiv B$
- $A \equiv B \models \neg A \equiv \neg B$
- $\neg A \equiv \neg B \models A \equiv B$
- $A \equiv B, B \equiv C \models (A \equiv C) \vee (B \wedge \neg B)$
- $A \equiv B, B \equiv C \not\models A \equiv C$

Of course, in a paraconsistent context, the truth of $\neg A$ is compatible with that of A. So even if it is the case that $\neg(A \equiv B)$ is true, it can still be the case that $A \equiv B$ is true as well.

2.4 Identity and Gluons

So much for the background. Against this, we can define identity. The definition is the standard Leibnizian one. Two objects are the same if one object has a property just if the other does. In the language of second-order logic, $a = b$ iff:

- $\mathfrak{A}X(Xa \equiv Xb)$

The second-order quantifiers here are to be taken as ranging over all properties. Whatever these are exactly (and we will come back to the matter later) the behaviour of identity is going to be inherited from the behaviour of $\equiv$.[4] In particular, it is going to be reflexive and symmetric, but, crucially, not transitive. Suppose, for the sake of illustration, that there is only one property in question, P, and that Pa, Pb and $\neg Pb$, and $\neg Pc$.[5] Then $Pa \equiv Pb$, $Pb \equiv Pc$, but not $Pa \equiv Pc$. Since P is the only property at issue, we have $a = b$ and $b = c$, but not $a = c$.[6]

It should be noted that though we do not have transitivity of identity in general, we do have it when the "middle" object is consistent, that is, has no contradictory properties. For suppose that $a = b = c$, and that b is consistent. Consider any property, P. Then $Pa \equiv Pb$ and $Pb \equiv Pc$. Hence, $(Pa \equiv Pc) \vee (Pb \wedge \neg Pb)$. Given that the second disjunct can be ruled out, we have $Pa \equiv Pc$. So $a = c$.

There is much more to be said about identity, but we may leave the matter for the moment. Given this understanding of identity, we may now define formally what a gluon is. Given a partite object, x, a gluon for x is an object which is identical to all and only the parts of x.[7] By being identical to each of the parts and to only those, it unifies them into one whole. Note that a gluon is identical to itself; it follows that it is a part of x. Note also that the gluon of an object is unique. For suppose that g and g' are gluons of an object, x, then, since g and g' are parts of x, $g = g'$ (and $g' = g$).

Let me illustrate a gluon structure with a simple example. Suppose that we have four objects, g, i, j, and k. g, i, and j are the parts of some object, x, and g is its gluon. Suppose that there are just three properties, P_1, P_2, and P_3, possessed as follows. '+' indicates that the object is in (just) the extension; '−' indicates that it is in (just) the anti-extension; and '±' indicates both.[8]

---

[4] I note that the property of being identical with something is normally ruled out in a Leibnizian definition of identity on pain of triviality. For given that $\mathfrak{A}X(Xa \equiv Xb)$, it would then follow that $a = b \equiv b = b$, and so $a = b$. This is not the case in the present context, due to the non-detachability of $\equiv$.

[5] For ease of the informal exposition, I collapse the notational distinction between properties and predicates in a harmless fashion.

[6] A consequence of this definition is that any object with contradictory properties is not self-identical. This consequence can be avoided by taking $\mathfrak{A}X(Xa \equiv Xb)$ to give the truth conditions for an identity statement, but giving different falsity conditions. One simple way to do this is to define $a = b$ as: $\langle a, b \rangle$ satisfies '$\mathfrak{A}X(Xx \equiv Xy)$'. Given the naive satisfaction scheme, this gives the appropriate truth conditions. But, arguably, negation does not commute with truth: $T \langle \neg A \rangle$ does not entail $\neg T \langle A \rangle$. (See Priest (1987), 4.9.) Similarly, it does not commute with satisfaction. So the fact that $\langle a, b \rangle$ satisfies '$\neg \mathfrak{A}X(Xx \equiv Xy)$' does not entail that $\langle a, b \rangle$ does not satisfy '$\mathfrak{A}X(Xx \equiv Xy)$'; that is that $\neg a = b$.

[7] To keep the account as general as possible, I leave it open here whether 'part' includes the improper part which is the whole.

[8] Recall, from Section P.5, that we need to specify both the places where P holds—the extension of P—and the places where $\neg P$ holds—the anti-extension of P—since, unlike the classical case, neither determines the other.

	P_1	P_2	P_3
i	+	−	+
g	±	±	+
j	−	+	+
k	+	+	−

It is easy to check that for each of the three properties, P, we have $Pi \equiv Pg$, and so $\mathfrak{A}X(Xi \equiv Xg)$, and similarly for g and j (and of course for g and g). Hence $i = g, g = g$, and $g = j$. However, we have none of the following: $P_3 i \equiv P_3 k, P_3 g \equiv P_3 k, P_3 j \equiv P_3 k$. Hence, none of $i = k$, $g = k$, and $j = k$ holds. g is identical to all and only the parts of x.[9] Note that $\neg(P_1 g \equiv P_1 g)$, so $\mathfrak{S}X(Xg \wedge \neg Xg)$, that is $\neg\mathfrak{A}X(Xg \equiv Xg)$; that is, $g \neq g$.[10]

2.5 Gluons, Prime and Other

In the example we have just looked at, the gluon, g, had all the properties of the (other) parts (but not *vice versa*). If a gluon is like this, having all the properties of every other part, I will call it a *prime gluon*.[11] If a is a consistent object (that is, has no contradictory properties) and $a = b$, then every property of a is a property of b. Hence, if g is the gluon of an object such that all its other parts are consistent, it

---

[9] Suppose that the object of our diagram had another part, l, which was in the anti-extension of P_1, P_2, and P_3. Then g would be in the anti-extension of P_3 too. Hence, k would be part of the object as well. This bespeaks a certain failure of atomism, but hardly a surprising one. If you build a room between a house and an out-house, and join them internally, the out-house becomes part of the house.

[10] A word, in this context, about counting sets which contain gluons. Let us define $[\mathfrak{S}x \leq n]x \in a$ (at most n things are in a) as:

- $\mathfrak{A}x_1 \in a \ldots \mathfrak{A}x_{n+1} \in a \bigvee_{1 \leq i < j \leq n+1} x_i = x_j$

Take as an example, the set $\gamma = \{a, b, g\}$, where g is gluon such that $g \neq g$. We have $[\mathfrak{S}x \leq n]x \in \gamma$ iff $n \geq 2$ (not 3, because $a = g$ and $b = g$). Now define $[\mathfrak{S}x \geq n]x \in a$ (at least n things are in a) as $\neg[\mathfrak{S}x \leq n - 1]x \in a$; that is:

- $\mathfrak{S}x_1 \in a \ldots \mathfrak{S}x_n \in a \bigwedge_{1 \leq i < j \leq n} x_i \neq x_j$

Then, for all n, $[\mathfrak{S}x \leq n]x \in \gamma$. (Simply take all the quantifiers to be instantiated by g!) Finally, define $[nx]A$ to be $[\mathfrak{S}x \leq n] \in a \wedge [\mathfrak{S}x \geq n] \in a$. Then it follows that $[nx]x \in \gamma$ iff $n \geq 2$. Hence, as expressed by quantifiers and identity, γ has every size greater than or equal to 2. This is hardly a surprise: if you count sets containing objects which are inconsistent in this way, what else would you expect?! (Whether there is a bijection between γ and 2, or γ and 3, where these numbers are defined in the standard von Neumann fashion, is another matter—to pursue which we would need to delve into the machinery of paraconsistent set theory.)

[11] Note that this does not rule out the possibility of its having other properties as well.

must be a prime gluon. It is not hard to show that if an object has a prime gluon, g, then g satisfies any (extensional) condition that any part satisfies. (In the technical appendix of Section 2.10.4, this is called the *Prime Gluon Corollary*.)

A gluon need not be prime, however. Suppose that we have two objects, x_1 and x_2, with gluons g_1 and g_2. Suppose that x_1 and x_2 have a part in common, p; and that p is consistent. Then we have that $g_1 = p = g_2$. Since p is consistent, $g_1 = g_2$, and so g_1 is a part of x_2 (and g_2 is a part of x_1). If the parts of x_1 and x_2 are not all the same, g_1 and g_2 cannot both be prime gluons though. If they were, g_1 and g_2 would have all the same properties, and so any part of x_1 would be a part of x_2, and *vice versa*. Here is a picture of a simple model which shows how neither g_1 nor g_2 may be prime. p, g_1, and g_2 are parts of x_1 and x_2. a_1 is a part of x_1 but not x_2; a_2 is a part of x_2, but not x_1. The only properties are P_1 and P_2. The properties of each part are listed below it.

	a_1	g_1	p	g_2	a_2
P_1	−	±	+	+	+
P_2	+	+	+	±	−

It is not the case that $g_1 = a_2$ because of P_2, and it is not the case that $g_2 = a_1$ because of P_1. And g_1 is not prime because g_2 is in the anti-extension of P_2, but g_1 is not. (Symmetrically for g_2.)

A final observation about prime gluons. Take an object with two distinct parts, a and b, and a prime gluon, g. Then $a = g = b$. But since a and b are distinct, for some property, P, we have Pa and $\neg Pb$ (or *vice versa*, which is similar). Hence we have Pg and $\neg Pg$, and hence $\neg(Pa \equiv Pg)$ and $\neg(Pb \equiv Pg)$. It follows that $a \neq g$ (and $b \neq g$). It might be thought that this non-identity would destroy the unity of the whole. But it should be remembered that the truth of $a \neq g$ does not *remove* the truth of $a = g$, and so the binding. But if g is distinct from a, do we not have the Bradley regress problem back? Why does there not need to be something between a and g which holds them together? There is!—g itself: $a = g$ and $g = g$. The regress terminates after one iteration, as it should.

2.6 The Definition of Identity

Let us now return to matters concerning identity. There can be no doubt that the Leibnizian definition of identity produces something naturally thought of as identity. The definition is not arbitrary. What might be doubted is whether the material biconditional does justice to the definition. For example, it might be thought that we need a detachable conditional—say the conditional of some relevant logic—for the definition to work. However, this would seem not to be the case. For example it is not clear that there is a relevant implication between, for example, 'Mary Ann Evans was a woman' and 'George Eliot was a woman'—at least, not without the suppressed information that Mary Ann Evans was George Eliot. What is required for the identity of a and b is that for every relevant predicate, P, Pa and Pb have the same truth value; and this is exactly what the material biconditional delivers.

It might still be objected that this is not the case, since $A \equiv B$ is true if A is true only but B is both true and false. But again, this is too fast. *True only* and *both true and false* are not truth values. There are only two truth values: *true* and *false*. It is just that sentences may have various combinations thereof. If A is true only and B is both true and false, *both* are true, hence one should expect the material biconditional to be true—and since one is true and the other is false, one should expect it to be false as well.

Of course, it remains the case that the transitivity of identity (TI), and so the substitutivity of identity (SI), of which this is a special case, fail. Since SI is often taken to be a defining characteristic of identity, this may well be thought to speak against the definition. This point is important enough to require a substantial discussion, and I will devote the whole of Chapter 5 to it.

One might also be concerned that a Leibnizian definition is itself inadequate; and specifically that there are counter-examples to it.[12] Putative counter-examples are of two kinds. The first concerns universes in which there are only symmetrically placed objects. Thus, for example, we might consider a universe where there are just two spheres of the same size, weight, colour, and so on. These are different objects, but each has exactly the same properties as the other. There are several ways in which one might address this putative counter-example.[13] However, the simplest reply to the objection would seem to be that the two objects *do not* have all the same properties. Thus, being distinct, they are made of different matter: so one is made of matter m_1, and the other is made of different matter, m_2. Moreover, they have different spatial locations. So, supposing that the space in which the spheres are located is three-dimensional, then for any coordinate system, their centres will be located at the distinct points $\langle x_1, y_1, z_1 \rangle$ and $\langle x_2, y_2, z_2 \rangle$. Of course, one could push the thought-experiment further. Not only are the spheres the same weight, colour, and so on, but they have the same matter, are located at the same spatial point, and so on. Now, however, the intuition pump ceases to function. The insistence that the spheres are nonetheless the distinct, starts to appear incoherent.

The second sort of counter-example concerns quantum particles. It has been argued that two particles may be distinct, even though any measurement on one

---

[12] For a survey and discussion, see Forrest (2010), French (2010).   [13] See Hawley (2009).

will yield exactly the same as a measurement on the other. Given that all properties are observationally determinable, we have a counter-example. This objection is harder to get to grips with, since it cannot be disentangled from interpretations of quantum mechanics. However, I am of the view that to talk of particles in this context is misguided. Any system (of one or more "particles") is determined by a state function, which maps points in space (and time) to complex values in a Hilbert space. (The state function determines the probabilities of the various outcomes which a measurement may produce.) The correct view, it seems to me, is to be a realist about, and only about, these state functions. They characterize what is really there. There are no particles in reality, though an observation may be described, for example, as a particle at a certain place.[14]

2.7 Predicates and Properties

We now need to address the question of what properties there are, over which the second-order quantifiers range. A simple assumption is that any condition which contains a single variable, x, specifies a property. This assumption is clearly problematic, however. The condition 'x is green and Paris is in France' applies to every green object, such as a deciduous tree in Melbourne. But it is hard to see that a tree in Melbourne has anything much to do with Paris. Similarly, the condition '$x = x$ or Caesar was a frog' applies to everything; but most things have little to do with Caesar or frogs. In the context of gluon theory, there are particular reasons to reject this assumption. If every condition specified a property, then every object would be distinct from itself. Let a be any object, P any one of its properties, and g any object such that $g = g$ and $g \neq g$. Then $Pa \wedge g = g$ and $\neg(Pa \wedge g = g)$. If '$Px \wedge g = g$' expresses a property of a, we have $\mathfrak{S}X(Xa \wedge \neg Xa)$, and so $\neg \mathfrak{A}X(Xa \equiv Xa)$. Gluons, we know, may be non-self-identical. But this should hardly be the case for everything.[15]

It would seem, then, that properties have to be what Lewis (1983) calls *sparse*, as opposed to *abundant* (the extension of an arbitrary condition with a free variable).[16] These have some robust kind of metaphysical reality; and it is this reality which has to do the heavy lifting. There is no guarantee that reality answers to

---

[14] The view is defended in Priest (1989).
[15] Here is another example. Take any partite object, y. Every part of y is an object. (Everything is an object.) Suppose that this condition were to specify a property of y, Py. Let g be the gluon of y. Then g is a part of y, and g not an object. So it is not the case that every part of y is an object, $\neg Py$. The condition, then, does not specify a property.
[16] For a defence of the distinction, see, for example, Armstrong (1989), esp. ch. 5, and the introduction to Mellor and Oliver (1997), pp. 24ff.

arbitrary conditions. (Actually, that claim is not really contentious. Most would agree that the condition 'John believes that x is happy' is not really a property of x.)

It would be nice, of course, to give some *a priori* criterion as to when a condition specifies such a property. I have nothing very interesting to offer in this regard, however, and I even doubt that such is possible. I suspect that what (sparse) properties are out there in the world is just as much a brute fact as what species there are out there in the world. Metaphysicians have to discover this, just as much as their zoological cousins.

It is possible to say more about what sorts of conditions do not specify properties, though. Suppose that $a_1 = a_2$; that is, $\mathfrak{A}X(Xa_1 \equiv Xa_2)$. If A is a condition with one free variable, x, and it specifies a property, it follows that $A_x(a_1) \equiv A_x(a_2)$, and so $A_x(a_1) \supset A_x(a_2)$. Given $A_x(a_1)$, one cannot validly infer $A_x(a_2)$, since the material conditional does not detach. The failure to preserve truth, however, arises only when the antecedent is contradictory; that is, when we have $A_x(a_1) \wedge \neg A_x(a_1)$.[17] Hence, provided that $A_x(a_1)$ is perfectly consistent, the inference will preserve truth. If, then, we have a case of the inference where $A_x(a_1)$ is consistent, but truth is *not* preserved, this must be due to the fact that the condition A does not express a property. Let us apply this observation. (I reserve a full discussion of the failure of SI for Chapter 5. The following merely serves to motivate the position taken up here with respect to the range of the second-order variables.)

By this test, intentional contexts, such as 'Mary believes that x is a famous novelist' do not specify a property. Mary can believe that George Eliot is a famous novelist, without believing that Mary Anne Evans is a famous novelist, even though the two are the same person. (Believing x to be a famous novelist is a perfectly consistent predicate.)

Another important class of contexts is that provided by modal operators, representing some kind of necessity or possibility, $\Box$ and $\Diamond$. There are many notions of necessity.[18] Epistemic necessity ('knows that') is one of these. Since this is an intentional operator, it has already been dealt with. But what if $\Box$ represents some sort of metaphysical necessity? Since Kripke (1972) it has been orthodox to maintain that SI *holds* within modal contexts of this kind.

But matters are not straightforward. Suppose that we have a lump of clay, l, made into a statue of the Buddha, b. Then $l = b$, $\Box b = b$, but it is not the case that $\Box b = l$: in a different world, the lump was made into a statue of Confucius, and b does not exist. (And there is nothing contradictory about the condition of necessarily being b.)

---

[17] See Priest (1987), ch. 8.   [18] See Priest (2008), 3.6.

Further failures of SI in modal contexts are provided by gluon theory itself. Suppose that, at one world, bricks $a, b, c, \ldots$ form a house, with gluon g. Then at that world $a = g$. But in another world, the bricks are just lying around in a field: there is no house. At that world, it is not true that $a = g$: g does not even exist. (The gluon of the house exists iff it does.) So it is not the case that $\Box a = g$ (even though $\Box a = a$). More generally, one should not expect a and g to satisfy the same modal conditions. For example if a is a brick of a house, it is possible for a to exist without the house, but it is not possible for g to exist without the house.

Hence, conditions where the free variable, x, occur within the scope of a modal operator do not specify a property. Properties are, in a certain sense, local. Being red, existing, and so on, are properties of objects; being red at world w, existing at world w, and so on, are not. For suppose that they were, and that $a = g$, then the definition of identity would give us: for all w, a exists at world $w \equiv g$ exists at world w. That is, $\Box(Ea \equiv Eg)$, which is wrong.

Matters are similar with respect to time.[19] Thus, consider l and b again. If l is to be refashioned into a statue of Confucius, then it will be the case that b ceases to exist, but it will not be the case that l ceases to exist. And if g is a gluon that glues together the bricks of a house, one of which is a, then while the house exists $g = a$, but after the house is demolished (but the bricks survive), it is not the case that $g = a$. Hence, properties are not only local to worlds, but, in the same sense, local to times: being red, existing, and so on, are properties of objects; being red at time t, existing at time t, and so on, are not.

What the preceding discussion indicates is that a condition with free variable x, whose truth conditions at an index of evaluation (world, time, and maybe other things) make reference to another index of evaluation, does not determine a property of x. Intentional operators, modal operators, tense operators, are all of this kind. All properties are, in the appropriate sense, local.

One consequence of this, note, is that identity is world-relative. Suppose that $a = b$ (actually, at this world); so $\mathfrak{A}X(Xa \equiv Xb)$. The properties in question are local. It is therefore quite possible for a and b to share all their properties at one world/time without sharing them at another. Hence, there is no reason why $a = b$ should hold at another world.

2.8 Objecthood Revisited

Let us finish by returning to the objecthood of gluons. We need two preliminary observations.

---

[19] Or, in the context of Special Relativity, spacetime.

Fact 1: a partite object has only one part, or its gluon is non-self-identical.

Proof: Let a be any object with parts. Suppose that (*):

- a has parts x and y such that for some P: x is not the extension of P and y is not in the anti-extension of P, or *vice versa*.

Then x is in the anti-extension of P and y is in the extension of P, or *vice versa*. If g is the gluon of a, then, in either case, since $g = x$ and $g = y$, $Pg \wedge \neg Pg$. So $\neg(Pg \equiv Pg)$, and $g \neq g$.

If (*) is not the case, then for every part, x and y, and for all P:

- if x is not in the extension of P, then y is in its anti-extension

and *vice versa*, that is: if y is not in the extension of P then x is in its anti-extension. By contraposition:

- if x is not in the anti-extension of P then y is in its extension.

Now, three cases. (i) If $Px \wedge \neg Px$, then $Px \equiv Py$. (Since $A \wedge \neg A \models A \equiv B$.) (ii) If x is not in the extension of P then x is in its anti-extension, and by the first conditional, y is in the anti-extension of P. So $Px \equiv Py$. (iii) Similarly, if x is not in the anti-extension of P then x is in the extension of P, and by the second conditional, y is in the extension of P. So $Px \equiv Py$. Hence, in all cases, $Px \equiv Py$. Since this is for all P, $x = y$. That is, a has just one part.

Fact 2: $x \neq x \models y \neq x$.

Proof: For the premise give us $\mathfrak{S}W(Wx \wedge \neg Wx)$. By the Principle of Excluded Middle, for this W, we have $Wy \vee \neg Wy$. Reasoning by cases, suppose that Wy. (The other case is similar.) Then Wy and $\neg Wx$, so $\neg(Wy \equiv Wx)$, so $\mathfrak{S}W\neg(Wy \equiv \neg Wx)$. That is, $y \neq x$.

Putting these facts together: Fact 1 tells us that any partite object, a, with gluon g has just one part, or $g \neq g$. Fact 2 tells us that in the second case, for all y, $y \neq x$; that is, $\neg \mathfrak{S}y\, y = g$. Now, to be an object is to be something. So, in the second case, g, not being anything, is not an object. We see that the solution to the problem of unity does indeed presuppose that a gluon may be both an object and not an object. Any gluon of a partite object is an object, since $g = g$ and so $\mathfrak{S}y\, y = g$; but $\neg \mathfrak{S}y\, y = g$ as well.

2.9 Looking Forwards

We now have the main elements of gluon theory before us. It is grounded by the considerations explained; but I do not expect it to recommend itself immediately to the reader. It asks a lot of them. In many ways, the rest of the book can be thought of as providing a number of applications of gluon theory, to a variety of problems—in metaphysics, the philosophy of mind and language, in the history of philosophy, and even in ethics. The power of the theory will speak in it favour.

As for the rest of this section, there remains the issue concerning SI to be dealt with. I will turn to this in Chapter 5. Before I do this, however, let us look at another couple of important philosophical issues: the connections between gluons, Aristotelian form, and being.

2.10 Technical Appendix: A Formal Semantics

In this appendix I will spell out the formal semantics of identity and gluons for those who wish to see them. Those who do not can safely skip the appendix. We will start with a simple extensional language, second-order *LP*. We will then look at identity in this language, and to what I will call gluon models. Finally, we will see how changing to a modal semantics affects matters.

2.10.1 Second-order LP

LP is a simple and natural paraconsistent logic.[20] The language has the connectives $\wedge$, $\vee$ and $\neg$, and the first- and second-order quantifiers $\mathfrak{A}$ and $\mathfrak{S}$. The material conditional and biconditional are defined in the usual way: $A \supset B$ is $\neg A \vee B$; $A \equiv B$ is $(A \supset B) \wedge (B \supset A)$. For simplicity, we suppose that all predicates are monadic, and that there are no function symbols. First-order variables are lower case, and monadic second-order variables are upper case.

There are various forms that the semantics of second-order *LP* may take; importantly, there are various possible constraints one may place on the range of the second-order variables. We will assume, for simplicity, that there are no constraints (other than that it be non-empty). Thus, it is natural to think of the second-order variables as ranging over properties of some fairly robust metaphysical kind.

An interpretation, *I*, for the language, is a triple $\langle \mathcal{D}_1, \mathcal{D}_2, \partial \rangle$. $\mathcal{D}_1$ is the non-empty domain of first-order quantification. $\mathcal{D}_2$ is the non-empty domain of second-order quantification. Members, *D*, of $\mathcal{D}_2$ are of the form $\langle D^+, D^- \rangle$, where $D^+, D^- \subseteq \mathcal{D}_1$, and $D^+ \cup D^- = \mathcal{D}_1$. ∂ assigns every individual constant a member of $\mathcal{D}_1$, and every predicate a member of $\mathcal{D}_2$. I will write $\partial(P)$ as $\langle \partial^+(P), \partial^-(P) \rangle$.

---

[20] See, for example, Priest (1987), ch. 5. For second-order *LP*, see section 7.2 of Priest (2002).

IDENTITY AND GLUONS   29

$\partial^+(P)$ and $\partial^-(P)$ are the *extension* and *anti-extension* of P (the set of objects of which P true and false, respectively).[21]

We now define what it is for a (closed) formula to be true, $\Vdash^+$, and false, $\Vdash^-$, in an interpretation. To state the truth and falsity conditions for the quantifiers, we augment the language, if necessary, to ensure that each member of $\mathcal{D}_1$ and $\mathcal{D}_2$ has a name. Thus, if $d \in \mathcal{D}_1$, we add an individual constant, k_d, to the language, such that $\partial(k_d) = d$; and if $D \in \mathcal{D}_2$, we add a predicate constant, P_D, to the language, such that $\partial(P_D) = D$. The extended language is called the *language of the interpretation*. If A is any formula, v_i ($1 \leq i \leq n$) any (first- or second-order) variables, and c_i any corresponding (individual or predicate) constants, then $A_{v_1,\ldots,v_n}(c_1,\ldots,c_n)$ will be the formula A with each free occurrence of v_i replaced by c_i, respectively.

The truth and falsity conditions for closed sentences in the language of the interpretation are as follows:[22]

- $\Vdash^+ Pc$ iff $\partial(c) \in \partial^+(P)$
- $\Vdash^- Pc$ iff $\partial(c) \in \partial^-(P)$
- $\Vdash^+ \neg A$ iff $\Vdash^- A$
- $\Vdash^- \neg A$ iff $\Vdash^+ A$
- $\Vdash^+ A \wedge B$ iff $\Vdash^+ A$ and $\Vdash^+ B$
- $\Vdash^- A \wedge B$ iff $\Vdash^- A$ or $\Vdash^- B$
- $\Vdash^+ A \vee B$ iff $\Vdash^+ A$ or $\Vdash^+ B$
- $\Vdash^- A \vee B$ iff $\Vdash^- A$ and $\Vdash^- B$
- $\Vdash^+ \mathfrak{S}xA$ iff for some $d \in \mathcal{D}_1$, $\Vdash^+ A_x(k_d)$
- $\Vdash^- \mathfrak{S}xA$ iff for all $d \in \mathcal{D}_1$, $\Vdash^- A_x(k_d)$
- $\Vdash^+ \mathfrak{A}xA$ iff for all $d \in \mathcal{D}_1$, $\Vdash^+ A_x(k_d)$
- $\Vdash^- \mathfrak{A}xA$ iff for some $d \in \mathcal{D}_1$, $\Vdash^- A_x(k_d)$
- $\Vdash^+ \mathfrak{S}XA$ iff for some $D \in \mathcal{D}_2$, $\Vdash^+ A_X(P_D)$
- $\Vdash^- \mathfrak{S}XA$ iff for all $D \in \mathcal{D}_2$, $\Vdash^- A_X(P_D)$
- $\Vdash^+ \mathfrak{A}XA$ iff for all $D \in \mathcal{D}_2$, $\Vdash^+ A_X(P_D)$
- $\Vdash^- \mathfrak{A}XA$ iff for some $D \in \mathcal{D}_2$, $\Vdash^- A_X(P_D)$

Finally, validity: If the members of $\Sigma \cup \{A\}$ are closed sentences, $\Sigma \vDash A$ iff in every interpretation in which every member of Σ is true, so is A.

---

[21] If the language contained n-adic predicates, for $n > 1$, we would need corresponding domains $\mathcal{D}_2^n$ (so that what I have written as $\mathcal{D}_2$ is $\mathcal{D}_2^1$). Each member of $\mathcal{D}_2^n$ would be a pair, $\langle X, Y \rangle$, where X and Y are subsets of $\mathcal{D}_1^n$ (the n-fold cartesian product of $\mathcal{D}_1$) such that $X \cup Y = \mathcal{D}_1^n$. ∂ then assigns each n-place predicate a member of $\mathcal{D}_2^n$.

[22] The generalization of the atomic truth/falsity conditions to n-adic predicates is the obvious one.

The first-order part of *LP* in the above semantics is entirely standard. The second-order part is a natural extrapolation. I leave it as an exercise to check the facts concerning $\equiv$ stated in Section 2.3.

2.10.2 Identity

Identity may now be defined in standard second-order fashion. $a_1 = a_2$ is: $\mathfrak{A}X(Xa_1 \equiv Xa_2)$.

Because the material biconditional is reflexive and symmetric, it follows that identity is too: $\vDash a = a$ and $a_1 = a_2 \vDash a_2 = a_1$. The material biconditional is not, however, transitive; identity inherits this property. Thus, consider an interpretation where:

- $\mathcal{D}_1 = \{1, 2, 3\}$
- $\partial(a_i) = i$ $(i = 1, 2, 3)$
- $\partial(P) = \langle\{1, 2\}, \{2, 3\}\rangle \in \mathcal{D}_2$
- For every other $D \in \mathcal{D}_2$, $D^- = \mathcal{D}_1$

Since $Pa_2 \wedge \neg Pa_2$ is true, so is $Pa_1 \equiv Pa_2$; and for every other predicate, Q, in the language of the interpretation Q, $\neg Qa_1 \wedge \neg Qa_2$ is true, so $Qa_1 \equiv Qa_2$. Hence, $\mathfrak{A}X(Xa_1 \equiv Xa_2)$, that is, $a_1 = a_2$ is true. Similarly, $a_2 = a_3$. But $Pa_1 \equiv Pa_3$ is not true; hence, neither is $\mathfrak{A}X(Xa_1 \equiv Xa_3)$; that is, $a_1 = a_3$ is not true. Thus, $a_1 = a_2, a_2 = a_3 \nvDash a_1 = a_3$.

Since transitivity of identity is a special case of substitutivity of identicals, this, too, fails. For another counter-example, note that $a_2 = a_3$, $Pa_2 \nvDash Pa_3$. In the above interpretation, the premises are true, but the conclusion is not. Finally, identity statements may not be consistent. Thus, in the above interpretation, since $Pa_2 \wedge \neg Pa_2$ is true, so is $\neg(Pa_2 \equiv Pa_2)$. It follows that $\mathfrak{S}X\neg(Xa_2 \equiv Xa_2)$, so $\neg\mathfrak{A}X(Xa_2 \equiv Xa_2)$; that is, $a_2 \neq a_2$.

2.10.3 The substitutivity of identicals

We can now establish some facts about substitutivity. First, note the following facts about *LP*. Given any interpretation, *I*:

- if $\Vdash^+ A \equiv B$ then $\Vdash^+ \neg A \equiv \neg B$
- if $\Vdash^+ A \equiv B$ and $\Vdash^+ C \equiv D$ then $\Vdash^+ (A \wedge C) \equiv (B \wedge D)$
- if $\Vdash^+ A_x(k_d) \equiv B_x(k_d)$ for all k_d in the language of the interpretation, then $\Vdash^+ \mathfrak{A}xA \equiv \mathfrak{A}xB$
- if $\Vdash^+ A_X(P_D) \equiv B_X(P_D)$ for all P_D in the language of the interpretation, $\Vdash^+ \mathfrak{A}XA \equiv \mathfrak{A}XB$

For the second of these, suppose that, in I, $(A \wedge C) \equiv (B \wedge D)$ is false only. Then $A \wedge C$ is true only and $B \wedge D$ is false only—or *vice versa*, the result of which is the same. Then A and C are true only, and at least one of B and D are false only. So either $A \equiv B$ or $C \equiv D$ is false only. For the third, suppose the antecedent. Then by the truth conditions of the universal quantifier, $\Vdash^+ \mathfrak{A}x(A \equiv B)$. But $\mathfrak{A}x(A \equiv B) \vDash \mathfrak{A}xA \equiv \mathfrak{A}xB$. (Suppose that in an interpretation the conclusion is false only. Then $\mathfrak{A}xA$ is true only and $\mathfrak{A}xB$ is false only—or *vice versa*, the result of which is the same. Hence every instance of A is true only, and some instance of B is false only. Hence, some instance of $A \equiv B$ is false only, and so is $\mathfrak{A}x(A \equiv B)$.) The result follows. The other two bullet points are similar.

Now, given any interpretation, if $\Vdash^+ \mathfrak{A}X(Xa \equiv Xb)$ then $\Vdash^+ P_D a \equiv P_D b$ for every P_D in the language of the interpretation.[23] It follows by induction that for any A, $\Vdash^+ A_x(a) \equiv A_x(b)$. In LP, $A \vee B$ can be defined in terms of negation and conjunction, and the particular quantifiers can be defined in terms of the corresponding universal quantifiers, in the usual way. Hence, it suffices to check the cases for negation, conjunction, and the two universal quantifiers. These are secured by the four facts above.

What we see, then, is that $a = b \vDash A_x(a) \equiv A_x(b)$. Hence, we have what we may call *material substitutivity*: $a = b \vDash A_x(a) \supset A_x(b)$.

2.10.4 Gluon models

The theory of identity allows us to construct interpretations in which there are objects which behave in a way appropriate for gluons. In this section I will show how.

First, a definition and lemma. Given an interpretation, $I = \langle \mathcal{D}_1, \mathcal{D}_2, \partial \rangle$ and $a \in \mathcal{D}_1$: $b \in \mathcal{D}_1$ *mimics* a iff for all $D \in \mathcal{D}_2$:

- if $a \in D^+$, $b \in D^+$
- if $a \in D^-$, $b \in D^-$

Mimicking Lemma: Given any interpretation, I, if b mimics a then for any formula, A, in the language of the interpretation with at most one free variable, x:

1. if $\Vdash^+ A_x(k_a)$ then $\Vdash^+ A_x(k_b)$
2. if $\Vdash^- A_x(k_a)$ then $\Vdash^- A_x(k_b)$

---

[23] If the language has n-ary predicates for $n > 1$, to establish that $P_D t_1 \ldots a \ldots t_{n-1} \equiv P_D t_1 \ldots b \ldots t_{n-1}$, we need the interpretation to be closed under projection, in the following sense: for any $\langle X, Y \rangle \in \mathcal{D}_2^n$, and $1 \leq i \leq n$, there is a $D \in \mathcal{D}_2$ such that the extension of D is exactly $\{x_i \in \mathcal{D}_1 : \text{for some } x_1, \ldots, x_{i-1}, x_{i+1}, \ldots, x_n, \langle x_1, \ldots, x_n \rangle \in X\}$.

Proof: This is proved by joint induction on the formation of A. If A is atomic, the result holds by definition. For the logical operators, there is a case for $+$, and a case for $-$. Here are the cases for $+$; those for $-$ are similar.

$$\begin{aligned}\Vdash^+ (B \wedge C)_x(k_a) &\Rightarrow \Vdash^+ B_x(k_a) \text{ and } \Vdash^+ C_x(k_a) \\ &\Rightarrow \Vdash^+ B_x(k_b) \text{ and } \Vdash^+ C_x(k_b) \text{ IH} \\ &\Rightarrow \Vdash^+ (B \wedge C)_x(k_b)\end{aligned}$$

The argument for $\vee$ is similar. For negation:

$$\begin{aligned}\Vdash^+ (\neg B)_x(k_a) &\Rightarrow \Vdash^- B_x(k_a) \\ &\Rightarrow \Vdash^- B_x(k_b) \text{ IH} \\ &\Rightarrow \Vdash^+ (\neg B)_x(k_b)\end{aligned}$$

For the second-order universal quantifier:

$$\begin{aligned}\Vdash^+ (\mathfrak{A}XB)_x(k_a) &\Rightarrow \text{for all } D \in \mathcal{D}_2, \Vdash^+ B_{x,X}(k_a,P_D) \\ &\Rightarrow \text{for all } D \in \mathcal{D}_2, \Vdash^+ B_{x,X}(k_b,P_D) \text{ IH} \\ &\Rightarrow \Vdash^+ (\mathfrak{A}XB)_x(k_b)\end{aligned}$$

The case for the particular quantifier is similar. For the first-order universal quantifier, let A be $\forall y B$. If x is y, there are no free occurrences of x in A, and hence the result is trivial. So suppose x and y are distinct.

$$\begin{aligned}\Vdash^+ (\mathfrak{A}yB)_x(k_a) &\Rightarrow \text{for all } d \in \mathcal{D}_1, \Vdash^+ B_{x,y}(k_a,k_d) \\ &\Rightarrow \text{for all } d \in \mathcal{D}_1, \Vdash^+ B_{x,y}(k_b,k_d) \text{ IH} \\ &\Rightarrow \Vdash^+ (\mathfrak{A}yB)_x(k_b)\end{aligned}$$

The case for the particular quantifier is similar. ∎

I note the *Prime Gluon Corollary*: If g is a prime gluon for an object a, then it mimics every part of a. Hence it satisfies any condition that any part of a satisfies.

Now let $\mathcal{D}_1$ be any set of objects. We will call these the *original objects*. We take a language, $\mathcal{L}$, which contains, amongst other things, a predicate P_a, for every $a \in \mathcal{D}_1$. Intuitively, $P_a x$ expresses the fact that x is a part of a.[24] Let $I = \langle \mathcal{D}_1, \mathcal{D}_2, \partial \rangle$ be an interpretation for this language, where the P_as are classical predicates. That is, $\partial^+(P_a) \cap \partial^-(P_a) = \emptyset$. Let Π_a be the set of objects in the extension of P_a.

We now construct an interpretation, $\hat{I} = \langle \hat{\mathcal{D}}_1, \hat{\mathcal{D}}_2, \hat{\partial} \rangle$ where all partite objects have gluons. I will call this the *gluon model for I*. We define the three components *seriatim*.

Take some set of new objects $G = \{g_a : a \in \mathcal{D}_1\}$. Call these the *gluons*. In the new model, if a has parts, g_a will be its gluon. $\hat{\mathcal{D}}_1 = \mathcal{D}_1 \cup G$.

---

[24] If we had two-place relations in the language, we could just use a binary relation, *part of*, but the monadic predicates will do for our purposes.

If $X \subseteq \mathcal{D}_1$, let $\hat{X} = X \cup \{g_a : a \in \mathcal{D}_1,$ and for some $d \in X, d \in \Pi_a\}$. Thus, the only original objects in $\hat{X}$ are those in X; and a gluon gets in iff some part of the object of which it is a gluon is already in. If $D = \langle X, Y \rangle \in \mathcal{D}_2$, $\hat{D} = \langle \hat{X}, \hat{Y} \cup \{g_a : \Pi_a = \emptyset\} \rangle$. (When $\Pi_a = \emptyset$, it does not matter, for the most part, whether g_a goes in the first component of $\hat{D}$ or the second. The only important thing is that it does not go into the extension of any P_b predicate.) $\hat{\mathcal{D}}_2 = \{\hat{D} : D \in \mathcal{D}_2\}$. (Note that if $D = \langle D^+, D^- \rangle \in \hat{\mathcal{D}}_2$ then $D^+ \cup D^- = \hat{\mathcal{D}}_1$. It is obvious that any original object, d, is in at least one of these sets. If $\Pi_a = \emptyset$, $g_a \in D^-$; and if not, g_a is in one of these sets, since some part of a is.) Note that, in $\hat{I}$, for every $a \in \mathcal{D}_1$ such that $\Pi_a \neq \emptyset$, g_a mimics each part of a.

For constants, c, $\hat{\partial}(c) = \partial(c)$. For predicates, P, $\hat{\partial}(P) = \hat{D}$, where $D = \partial(P)$.

We now show the following theorem:

Gluon Theorem: In $\hat{I}$ if $\Vdash^+ \mathfrak{S}xP_ax$ then for all $d \in \hat{\mathcal{D}}_1$, $\Vdash^+ P_ak_d$ iff $\Vdash^+ k_d = k_{g_a}$.

Proof: Assume that $\Vdash^+ \mathfrak{S}xP_ax$. First, suppose that $d \in \mathcal{D}_1$. If $\Vdash^+ P_ak_d$ then, by construction, g_a mimics d. Since $\Vdash^+ k_d = k_d$, $\Vdash^+ k_d = k_{g_a}$ by the Mimicking Lemma. Conversely, if it is not the case that $\Vdash^+ P_ak_d$, then $d \notin \hat{\partial}^+(P_a)$ and $d \in \hat{\partial}^-(P_a)$. Now, given that $\Vdash^+ \mathfrak{S}xP_ax$, there must be some $e \in \mathcal{D}_1$ such that $e \in \partial^+(P_a)$. (The only way for a gluon to be in the extension of P_a in $\hat{I}$ is for it to mimic one of the original objects.) Hence, $g_a \in \hat{\partial}^+(P_a)$. And for any original object, e, such that $e \in \partial^+(P_a)$, $e \notin \partial^-(P_a)$ (since P_a is a classical predicate). Hence, $g_a \notin \hat{\partial}^-(P_a)$. Thus, it is not the case that $\Vdash^+ P_ak_d \equiv P_ak_{g_a}$. So it is not the case that $\Vdash^+ \mathfrak{A}X(Xk_d \equiv Xk_{g_a})$; that is, that $\Vdash^+ k_d = k_{g_a}$.

Now suppose that d is a gluon, g_b. If $\Vdash^+ P_ak_{g_b}$ then there must be some original d which is in Π_a and Π_b. But since g_b mimics the parts of b, and $\Vdash^+ k_d = k_{g_a}$, $\Vdash^+ k_{g_b} = k_{g_a}$, by the Mimicking Lemma. Conversely, suppose that it is not the case that $\Vdash^+ P_ak_{g_b}$. Then there is no original object, $e \in \Pi_b$, such that $e \in \partial^+(P_a)$. All such objects are therefore in $\partial^-(P_a)$. Hence, whether or not Π_b is empty, $g_b \notin \hat{\partial}^+(P_a)$ and $g_b \in \hat{\partial}^-(P_a)$. But as we have already seen, $g_a \in \hat{\partial}^+(P_a)$ and $g_a \notin \hat{\partial}^-(P_a)$. Hence, it is not the case that $\Vdash^+ \mathfrak{A}X(Xk_{g_b} \equiv Xk_{g_a})$; that is, that $\Vdash^+ k_{g_b} = k_{g_a}$. ∎

Of course, $\hat{I}$ tells us nothing about the parts of gluons themselves. Let us add new predicates, P_g, to the language, for each gluon, $g \in G$. A very simple assumption is that all gluons are simplices; that is, that $\Pi_g = \emptyset$. If we extend $\hat{I}$ to make each P_g behave in this way, the Gluon Theorem then extends trivially to all predicates P_d for $d \in \hat{\mathcal{D}}_1$.

It is clear that one should not expect $\hat{I}$ to be conservative, in any sense, over I. Thus, if d and e are distinct parts of some original object, a, $\mathfrak{S}x(k_d = x \wedge x = k_e)$

will be true in $\hat{I}$, though it may not be true in I. However, there is a precise sense in which the extension of I to $\hat{I}$ does not disturb the facts about the original objects. To state this, extend the language for $\hat{I}$ with two new first-order quantifiers, $\mathfrak{A}^*$ and $\mathfrak{S}^*$, with the following truth/falsity conditions:

- $\Vdash^+ \mathfrak{A}^*xA$ iff for all $d \in \mathcal{D}_1$, $\Vdash^+ A_x(k_d)$
- $\Vdash^- \mathfrak{A}^*xA$ iff for some $d \in \mathcal{D}_1$, $\Vdash^- A_x(k_d)$
- $\Vdash^+ \mathfrak{S}^*xA$ iff for some $d \in \mathcal{D}_1$, $\Vdash^+ A_x(k_d)$
- $\Vdash^- \mathfrak{S}^*xA$ iff for all $d \in \mathcal{D}_1$, $\Vdash^- A_x(k_d)$

Now define a translation, t, from the language of I to the extended language of $\hat{I}$ by recursion, as follows—where P is any predicate of $\mathcal{L}$ (including one of the P_as) and c is any constant:

- $(Pc)^t = Pc$
- $(P_Dc)^t = P_{\hat{D}}c$
- $(\neg A)^t = \neg(A^t)$
- $(A \wedge B)^t = A^t \wedge B^t$

and similarly for the other connectives.

- $(\mathfrak{A}xA)^t = \mathfrak{A}^*x(A)^t$
- $(\mathfrak{S}xA)^t = \mathfrak{S}^*x(A)^t$
- $(\mathfrak{A}XA)^t = \mathfrak{A}X(A)^t$
- $(\mathfrak{S}XA)^t = \mathfrak{S}X(A)^t$

Thus, to translate a sentence, we simply replace every 'P_D' with '$P_{\hat{D}}$', and every first-order '$\mathfrak{A}$' and '$\mathfrak{S}$' with '$\mathfrak{A}^*$' and '$\mathfrak{S}^*$', respectively.

We can now state the following theorem:

Conservation Theorem: If A is a sentence in the language of I, then $I \Vdash A$ iff $\hat{I} \Vdash A^t$

Proof: The proof is by induction on the formation of A. There will be cases for $+$ and $-$, in every syntactic case. Here are the cases for $+$. The cases for $-$ are similar.

If A is an atomic sentence in the language of I, it is of the form Pc or P_Dc, where $\partial(c) \in \mathcal{D}_1$:

$$\begin{aligned} I \Vdash^+ Pc \text{ iff } & \partial(c) \in \partial^+(P) \\ \text{iff } & \hat{\partial}(c) \in \hat{\partial}^+(P) \text{ by construction} \\ \text{iff } & \hat{I} \Vdash^+ Pc \end{aligned}$$

$I \Vdash^+ P_D c$ iff $\partial(c) \in \partial^+(P_D)$
  iff $\partial(c) \in D^+$
  iff $\hat{\partial}(c) \in \hat{D}^+$ by construction
  iff $\hat{\partial}(c) \in \hat{\partial}^+(P_{\hat{D}})$
  iff $\hat{I} \Vdash^+ P_{\hat{D}} c$

For conjunction (the other connectives are similar):

$I \Vdash^+ A \wedge B$ iff $I \Vdash^+ A$ and $I \Vdash^+ B$
  iff $\hat{I} \Vdash^+ A^t$ and $\hat{I} \Vdash^+ B^t$ IH
  iff $\hat{I} \Vdash^+ (A \wedge B)^t$

Finally, the cases for the particular quantifiers (the universal quantifiers are similar):

$I \Vdash^+ \mathfrak{S} x A$ iff for some $d \in \mathcal{D}_1, I \Vdash^+ A_x(k_d)$
  iff for some $d \in \mathcal{D}_1, \hat{I} \Vdash^+ (A_x(k_d))^t$ IH
  iff for some $d \in \mathcal{D}_1, \hat{I} \Vdash^+ A_x^t(k_d)$
  iff $\hat{I} \Vdash^+ \mathfrak{S}^* x (A)^t$
  iff $\hat{I} \Vdash^+ (\mathfrak{S} x A)^t$

$I \Vdash^+ \mathfrak{S} X A$ iff for some $D \in \mathcal{D}_2, I \Vdash^+ A_X(P_D)$
  iff for some $D \in \mathcal{D}_2, \hat{I} \Vdash^+ (A_X(P_D))^t$ IH
  iff for some $D \in \mathcal{D}_2, \hat{I} \Vdash^+ A_X^t(P_{\hat{D}})$
  iff for some $\hat{D} \in \hat{\mathcal{D}}_2, \hat{I} \Vdash^+ A_X^t(P_{\hat{D}})$
  iff $\hat{I} \Vdash^+ (\mathfrak{S} X A)^t$

∎

2.10.5 World semantics

In this final section we consider how the above matters are changed when the language is extended to one in which there are operators whose truth conditions depend on an index-shift. I illustrate with respect to a language that contains a modal $\square$ and $\Diamond$ which behave in S5-like fashion.

If one were to go about generalizing the semantics of previous sections to a (constant domain) world-semantics, one would naturally come up with the following. An interpretation is a structure $\langle \mathcal{D}_1, \mathcal{D}_2, W, \partial \rangle$, where $\mathcal{D}_1$ and $\mathcal{D}_2$ are as before; W is a non-empty set of worlds; $\partial(c) \in \mathcal{D}_1$, and for every $w \in W$, $\partial_w(P) \in \mathcal{D}_2$. The truth/falsity conditions are the same, except for appropriate insertions of a 'w'. For example:

- $w \Vdash^+ Pc$ iff $\partial(c) \in \partial_w^+(P)$
- $w \Vdash^- Pc$ iff $\partial(c) \in \partial_w^-(P)$
- $w \Vdash^+ \neg A$ iff $w \Vdash^- A$
- $w \Vdash^- \neg A$ iff $w \Vdash^+ A$
- $w \Vdash^+ \mathfrak{S}xA$ iff for some $d \in \mathcal{D}_1$, $w \Vdash^+ A_x(k_d)$
- $w \Vdash^- \mathfrak{S}xA$ iff for all $d \in \mathcal{D}_1$, $w \Vdash^- A_x(k_d)$
- $w \Vdash^+ \mathfrak{S}XA$ iff for some $D \in \mathcal{D}_2$, $w \Vdash^+ A_X(P_D)$
- $w \Vdash^- \mathfrak{S}XA$ iff for all $D \in \mathcal{D}_2$, $w \Vdash^- A_X(P_D)$

For the modal operators:[25]

- $w \Vdash^+ \Box A$ iff for all $w' \in W$, $w' \Vdash^+ A$
- $w \Vdash^- \Box A$ iff for some $w' \in W$, $w' \Vdash^- A$
- $w \Vdash^+ \Diamond A$ iff for some $w' \in W$, $w' \Vdash^+ A$
- $w \Vdash^- \Diamond A$ iff for all $w' \in W$, $w' \Vdash^- A$

Validity is defined in terms of truth preservation at all worlds of all interpretations.

Natural as it is, this formulation hides a problem. To see what it is, examine the truth conditions of $a = b$ at a world. Unpacking the definition, we have:

$w \Vdash^+ a = b$ iff $w \Vdash^+ \mathfrak{A}X(Xa \equiv Xb)$
  iff for all $D \in \mathcal{D}_2$, $w \Vdash^+ P_D a \equiv P_D b$
  iff for all $D \in \mathcal{D}_2$ ($w \Vdash P_D a$ and $w \Vdash P_D b$, or ...)
  iff for all $D \in \mathcal{D}_2$ ($\partial(a) \in \partial_w^+(P_D)$ and $\partial(a) \in \partial_w^+(P_D)$, or ...)

How are we to understand $\partial_w^+(P_D)$? The only obvious understanding is that $\partial_w^+(P_D)$ is D; but then w drops out of the picture entirely, and identities are world-invariant, which, as we saw in Section 2.7, is to be avoided.

The solution is to take properties more seriously. We may think of properties as functions that map every world to an extension/anti-extension pair. (Natural, since one would expect the extension/anti-extension of a property to vary from world to world.) Predicates then refer (rigidly) to these.

The idea can be made precise by applying a second-order version of the techniques of contingent identity modal logics.[26] Let $H = \{\langle \alpha, \beta \rangle : \alpha \cup \beta = \mathcal{D}_1\}$. We will now take the second-order domain to be some set of functions from W to H, and call *this* $\mathcal{D}_2$. (This may seem perverse, but it will aid uniformity of notation.) Predicate constants denote members of *this* $\mathcal{D}_2$. If $D \in \mathcal{D}_2$, let us write $D(w)$ as D_w, $(\partial(P))_w$ as $\partial_w(P)$, its extension as $\partial_w^+(P)$, and similarly for its anti-extension. Then, with this notation, the truth/falsity conditions of atomic sentences may remain exactly as stated.

---

[25] See Priest (2008), 11a.4. [26] See Priest (2006), ch. 17.

And now, $\partial(P_D) = D$, so $\partial_w(P_D) = D_w$, which does depend on w. Here is a counter-model to the inference $a = b \models \Box a = b$ (even though $\models \Box a = a$). $W = \{w_0, w_1\}$; $\mathcal{D}_1 = \{i, j\}$, $\mathcal{D}_2 = \{f\}$; $f^+_{w_0} = \{i, j\}$, $f^-_{w_0} = \emptyset$, $f^+_{w_1} = \{i\}$, $f^-_{w_1} = \{j\}$; $\partial(a) = i$, $\partial(b) = j$. It is easy to check that $w_0 \Vdash^+ P_f a \equiv P_f b$, and so $w_0 \Vdash^+ \mathfrak{A}X(Xa \equiv Xb)$; but it is not the case that $w_1 \Vdash^+ P_f a \equiv P_f b$, or that $w_1 \Vdash^+ \mathfrak{A}X(Xa \equiv Xb)$, or that $w_0 \Vdash^+ \Box \mathfrak{A}X(Xa \equiv Xb)$.

I note that the inductive argument of Section 2.10.3 cannot be extended to arbitrary modal formulas. If I is an interpretation, and w a world in it, we do not have the required condition: if $w \Vdash A \equiv B$ then $w \Vdash \Box(A \equiv B)$.) So we do not even have material substitutivity for arbitrary contexts.

It is not difficult to extend the construction and proof of Section 2.10.4 to produce an interpretation in which the partite objects at all worlds have gluons. $\mathcal{D}_1$ is extended by the set of objects, G; then at each world g_a mimics the parts of a at that world. I leave the details as an exercise.

3
Form, Universals, and Instantiation

3.1 Aristotle into the Fray

So far, I have introduced the notion of a gluon, what it does, and how it does it—including a formal underpinnings for the story. In Section 1.3 I suggested—*pro tem*—calling gluons 'forms'. For Aristotle, the form of an object is that which unifies its parts, and makes it one; and so, of course, is its gluon. So could gluons be Aristotelian forms? This chapter investigates. The answer will be 'no'; but connections between gluons and Aristotelian forms—and, more generally, universals—will emerge. Let us start by looking at Aristotle's own account of the unity of an object.[1]

3.2 Aristotle Comes Unstuck

The problem of what it is that makes a bunch of things a unity is a venerable one in Western philosophy, and perhaps the earliest suggested solution is Aristotle's. The crucial discussion can be found in *Metaphysics* 7: 17. Here, the topic is the nature of substance. Aristotle commences the discussion as follows (1041^a6–14):

> We should say what, and of what sort of thing substance is, taking another starting-point: for perhaps from this we shall get a clearer view also of that substance which exists apart from sensible substances. Since, then, substance is a principle and a cause, let us attack it from this standpoint. The 'why' is always sought in this form—'why does one thing attach to another?' For to inquire why the musical man is a musical man is to inquire—as we have said—why the man is musical or it is something else.[2]

Here, Aristotle raises the question of how it is that some things are predicable of others; how is it that, for example, a man is musical?

---

[1] Aristotle's account of unity is a complex one. For a synopsis see Koslicki (2008), ch. 6. In what follows I will be concerned with the tightest kind of unity in Aristotle's taxonomy; namely, the kind of unity possessed by substances.

[2] The meaning of the last disjunct is obscure. Ross (1924), vol. 2, p. 222, suggests that the something else is the pointless question of why something is self-identical.

Aristotle sees this as a question of how parts fit together. He says (1041^{a}32–1041^{b}7):

> The object of the inquiry is most overlooked where one term is not expressly predicated of another (for example, when we inquire why man is), because we do not distinguish and do not say definitely 'why do these parts form this whole'? But we must distinguish the elements [that is, parts, GP] before we begin to inquire; if not it is not clear whether the inquiry is significant or unmeaning. Since we must know the existence of the thing and it must be given, clearly the question is *why* the matter is some individual thing, for example why are these materials a house? Because that which has the essence of a house is present.

Aristotle's answer to the question is hinted at in the very last sentence of this quotation. He goes on to spell it out. He starts by pointing out, as he did in the *Topics*—as we noted in Section 1.3—that a unity is different from a congeries of its parts (1041^{b}11–19):

> As regards that which is compounded out of something so that the whole is one—not like a heap, however, but like a syllable,—the syllable is not its elements, *ba* is not the same as *b* and *a*, nor is flesh fire and earth; for when they are dissolved the wholes, that is, the flesh and syllable no longer exist, but the elements of the syllable exist, and so do fire and earth. The syllable, then, is something—not only its elements (the vowel and the consonant) but also something else; and the flesh is not only fire and earth or the hot and the cold, but also something else.

Thus, the syllable *ba* is different from the syllable *ab*, though both have the same parts. The difference is in the structure—in this case, the order. And a congeries of *a* and *b* has no order. In the same way, a piece of flesh is not its elements (for Aristotle: earth, air, fire, and water). The elements have to be structured appropriately.

The question, then, is how to understand this notion of structure, this 'something else'. It cannot just be another part (1041^{b}19–25):

> Since, then, that something must be either an element or composed of elements, if it is an element, the same argument will again apply; for flesh will consist of this and fire and earth and something further, so that the process will go on to infinity; while if it is a compound, clearly it will be compounded not of one but of many (or else it will itself be that one), so that again in this case we can use the same argument as in the case of flesh or of the syllable.

Aristotle deploys what is, in effect, the regress argument. Whether this something is a simple or compound, if it were just another part, we would be faced with the same question of unity again. In other words, as we saw in Section 1.4, we have a vicious regress.

So what is this binding element? Aristotle tells us that it is the substance of the thing (1041^{b}25–33):

But it would seem that this is something, and not an element, and that it is the cause which makes *this* thing flesh and *that* a syllable. And similarly in other cases. And this is the substance of each thing; for this is the primary cause of its being; and since, while some things are not substances, as many as are substances are formed naturally and by nature, their substance would seem to be this nature, which is not an element but a principle. An element is that into which a thing is divided and which is present in it as matter, for example, *a* and *b* are the elements of the syllable.

Some care needs to exercised here. Aristotle operates with two notions of substance, often called 'primary' and 'secondary'. A primary substance, the substance of the *Categories*, is something like Aristotle and the Sun: a stand-alone entity, which can be the bearer of properties. Secondary substance, the substance of the *Metaphysics*, is, by contrast, the substance *of* something. It is whatever it is that makes the thing the (kind of) thing it is. So the substance of Aristotle is being a person, and the substance of the Sun is to be a star. This is the same thing as the essence or the form (*morphe*) of the object, which enforms its matter (*hyle*).[3] The substance we are concerned with in the present context is the second of these: form. It is this which, Aristotle thinks, "binds the parts together". Thus, it is the form of the syllable *ab* that binds *a* and *b* into that very syllable, and the form of flesh that binds fire and earth together to make meat.

Unfortunately, Aristotle forgets to tell us how the binding is done! He calls form 'a principle', to distinguish it from an element (part). But giving it a different name gets us nowhere (as we noted in Section 1.5). Moreover, it would seem that there is nothing stopping us running the regress argument with respect to this principle and the elements, just as much as we can run it for a bunch of elements. Finally, and in any case, both the form and the parts can exist without the object existing. (The form of the house exists just as much when the bricks are lying scattered around in a field.) Aristotle, then, though he is aware of the problem of unity, has not provided a solution to it.[4]

3.3 Neo-Aristotelians

In his 'Things and their Parts' Kit Fine launches an attack on the claim that an ordinary object is the mereological sum of its parts. (We will turn to the matter of whether or not he is right about this in Chapter 6.) In the process, he espouses a

---

[3] For a brief discussion, see Priest (2006), 1.7; for a longer discussion, see Dancy (1975), ch. 5.

[4] There were certainly medievals who were aware of this. Duns Scotus, for example, was clear that merely having matter and form—and even the relationship between them as well—did not secure a unity. He appears to think that the unity is brought about by a form of unity. But what, exactly, this is, and how it is supposed to create the unity, are unclear. See Cross (1995).

Neo-Aristotelian account of what an object is, in his theory of 'rigid embodiment'.[5] An object is a collection of parts-in-a-relation. The relation functions much as an Aristotelian form in this regard. Unfortunately, Fine explains no more than Aristotle how the relation does its unificatory job. He says (my italics):[6]

> I should like to suggest that we take the bold step of recognizing a new kind of whole. Given objects $a, b, c, \ldots$ and given a relation R that may hold or fail to hold between those objects at any given time, we suppose that there is a new object—what one may call "the objects $a, b, c, \ldots$ in the relation R." ... Intuitively, this new object is an amalgam or composite of the component objects $a, b, c, \ldots$ and the relation R. But it is a composite of a very different sort [from a mereological whole]. For the components and the relation do not come together as coequals, as in a regular mereological sum. Rather, the relation R preserves its predicative role and *somehow serves to modify or qualify the components*. However, the result of the modification is not a fact or state. It is a whole, whose components are linked by the relation, rather than the fact or state of the components being so linked.

Clearly, as far as an explanation of unity goes, we have no advance on Aristotle himself.

In her *The Structure of Objects* Kathrin Koslicki develops another Neo-Aristotelian account of the nature of objects.[7] According to her, unities with parts have a special sort of part, which she calls 'formal' (or 'structural'). Moreover, unlike Fine, she is quite explicit that this addresses the problem of unity. The account, she says,[8]

> provides the apparatus to solve the Problem of the One and the Many. For recall that ordinary material objects were taken to be both mereologically and ontologically complex, in the sense that they are composed of both material and formal components; the primary job of an object's formal components, moreover, is to act as a sort of *recipe* in specifying a range of selection requirements which must be satisfied by an object's material components, whose primary role was compared to the material *ingredients* called for in the recipe. In a successful case of composition, then, a plurality of objects in fact satisfies the requirements specified by some formal components associated with a particular kind, K; the result of this convergence is a new specimen of the kind in question, that is, an object that is *one* or *unified* relative to the measure supplied by the particular kind at hand.

But how, exactly, the form does this is left somewhat mysterious. You certainly don't make an omelette by throwing a recipe into the bowl with the eggs!

The quotation continues with an emphatic:

> Nothing more *needs* to be said or *could* be said to lay to rest the challenge contained in the Problem of the One and the many...

---

[5] This is extended to a theory about the persistence of objects over time in his theory of 'variable embodiment'. This need not concern us here.
[6] Fine (1999), p. 65.   [7] Ch. 4 of the book also contains a critique of Fine's position.
[8] Koslicki (2008), p. 197.

Objects have parts of a different kind from the material parts, whose job is to unify the parts. That is just the nature of the beasts; and that is that. At this point, Bradley must be rolling over in his grave (1.4).

And even Koslicki does not really believe that there is nothing more to be said. In a long footnote on the next page, she discusses the Bradley regress. She observes that to glue two parts of something together literally, one does not need something to glue the glue itself to the objects. The formal elements are supposed to be like *that*. But the analogy is a lame one. We know exactly why the glue does what it does: there is a chemical bond that joins molecules together. It is exactly the nature of the bonding that wants for an explanation in the metaphysical case.

3.4 Gluons and Form

As we have seen, then, both Aristotle and Neo-Aristotelians claim that it is the form of an object which accounts for its unity; but they provide no account of how it does this. Gluon theory, as we have seen, provides such an explanation. The two accounts could be reconciled if Aristotelian forms were gluons. Nice as this would be if this were true, it is not, for at least two reasons. The first is that, for Aristotle, form does (at least) two jobs. One is to explain the unity of a substance; the other is to answer the question of what something *is*. Gluons do only the first of these jobs. Secondly, and more importantly, the form of something, like *being a person* is something that many different objects (matters) can have in common; whilst gluons are particular to objects.[9]

Form is a notoriously tricky subject in Aristotle.[10] The form of something is, as I have noted, something, like *personhood*, which that thing can share with other things. But Aristotle seems to suggest—at least in some places—that, as well as personhood, there is such a thing as its occurrence in any particular object. Thus, we have the personhood of Socrates, the personhood of Hypatia, and so on. At *Categories* 1^a20–1^b2, he says:

Of things that are said, some involve combinations while others are said without combination. Examples of those involving combinations are: man runs, man wins; and of those without combination: man, ox, runs, wins.

Of things that are: (a) some are *said of* a subject but are not *in* any subject. For example, man is said of a subject, the individual man, but are not in any subject. (b) Some are in a subject, but not said of any subject. (By 'in a subject' I mean what is in something, not as a part, and cannot exist separately from what it is in.) For example, the individual knowledge-of-grammar is in a subject, the soul, but is not said of the subject; and the

---

[9] In fact, as we will see in the next chapter, they deliver the *being* of that object.
[10] For an overview, see Cohen (2008a).

individual white is in a subject, the body (for all colour is in a body), but is not said of any subject.

How to interpret the passage is contentious,[11] and I am happy to leave the matter of untangling it to Aristotle scholars. I will simply take it that he is suggesting that as well as personhood, which is said 'of', say, Socrates, there is the personhood of Socrates, which is 'in' him (and indeed could not exist without him—or, presumably, *vice versa*). The notion of something which is "in" an object in this way has a rich history; in the recent literature, things of this kind are usually called *tropes*. The name is a poor one, originating as it did as a sort of joke.[12] I shall call them by the more traditional name of *property instances*—or *pins* for short.

Given all this, we might simply take it that it is the pin of something's substance which accounts for its unity. That suggestion is no explanatory advance, however. True, one could not have the object without the pin of its substance (or *vice versa*); but the fact that the two always co-occur, in no way explains unity. You could not have the life of Socrates without Socrates, or *vice versa*; but neither explains the unity of the other.

But could the gluon of an object *be* the pin of its Aristotelian substance? It could, but objects have lots of pins. Why is the gluon *that* one? Perhaps, one might say, because the object could not be, if this pin were not. But that is equally true of other of its pins, such as the pin of unity. Indeed, this, as we shall see in the next chapter, is a more natural candidate for its gluon.

There is, however, a much more robust connection between form, its pins, and gluons. In that Socrates and Hypatia are both persons, they are the same one thing. Thus, we may suppose, the personhood of Socrates and the personhood of Hypatia, and so on, are parts of one thing. We may take the form of personhood itself to be the gluon of that one thing. It is this which makes the personhood of Socrates and the personhood of Hypatia the same: it is identical with both the one and the other. And since the universal would seem to be symmetrically related to all pins, it is natural to take the gluon in question to be a prime gluon.

Why not take the form to be the whole of which each pin is a part? Because, then, the form would not be wholly located where the object is. Only a part of it would be. So Socrates would be only partly human. The (prime) gluon of the unity, by contrast, having all the properties of the instances will be exactly where each trope is. (And yes, this is contradictory.) We are starting to trespass here on the topic of a later chapter. So let us leave matters at that for the time being. The form of something is the prime gluon of the unity whose parts are all and only the instances of the form.

[11] See Cohen (2008b).   [12] On these matters, see Bacon (2008).

3.5 Universals

Forms, like *being a person*, are naturally thought of as one kind of universal, that is, properties that can be shared by more than one thing. Sometimes Aristotle seems to say that they are; sometimes he seems to say they are not.[13] Again, I am happy to leave Aristotle scholars to sort out this tangle. I shall just assume that they are.[14] The account of forms we have arrived at makes no essential use of the fact that the properties in question are forms, as opposed to some other kind of universal. Indeed, in the quotation of the last section from the *Categories*, some of the properties that Aristotle mentions, such as whiteness, are not forms (that is, properties that give the *identity* of an object). The account of form naturally, therefore, extends to an account of universals.

Let me make the generalization explicit. Take, for example, a bunch of white things, $a, b, c, \ldots$ Consider a's whiteness, b's whiteness, and so on. One can think of these as the parts of a single totality. (They have a unity in a way that the whiteness of a, the roundness of b, the heaviness of c, do not.) What unifies them is the prime gluon of this totality, and this we may take to be the property of whiteness—or, to put a Platonic spin on matters, whiteness itself. This is what it is that makes them the same thing—white. Thus, we have the following picture; w is whiteness itself, and w_x is x's whiteness.[15]

$$
\begin{array}{c}
w_d \\
\| \\
w_a = w = w_c \\
\| \\
w_b
\end{array}
$$

Since w is a prime gluon, note, it has all the properties of each of the pins.

A universal, then, is the gluon of a bunch of pins. This means that a universal can change its properties over time (worlds). As the collection of white objects changes, so do the pins that constitute the bunch; so the gluon whiteness will be identical to different things at different times (worlds).[16]

---

[13] See Cohen (2008a), section 10.

[14] Halper (2009), 4.2.4, argues that forms are both universal and particular, though by making various disambiguations he renders the view consistent.

[15] In the technical semantics of Section 2.10.5, properties (universals by another name) are taken to be functions from worlds to extension/anti-extension pairs. That is quite compatible with their having parts that are pins. Abstract objects, like functions, can certainly have parts; and the *part of* relation is quite different from *value of* relation.

[16] If one does not like this, one could, instead, take the universal to be a function from times (worlds) to the gluons at those times (worlds). In the same way, in the semantics of Section 2.10.5, properties are taken as maps from worlds to extension/anti-extension pairs.

FORM, UNIVERSALS, AND INSTANTIATION

A final comment on uninstantiated universals. Aristotle held, famously against Plato, that there can be no uninstantiated universals (or at least, uninstantiated forms). Thus at *Metaphysics* 7: 13, he says ($1038^b 30$–34):

> And in general it follows, if man and such things are substances, that none of the elements of their formulae is the substance of anything, nor does it exist apart from the particular animals, nor do any other of the elements present in formulae exist apart.

On the present account, a gluon can also be uninstantiated at a world. No instances at that world, no totality, and no gluon. Some have found uninstantiated universals counter-intuitive. Is there not a universal of being a unicorn, even if there are none? From a noneist perspective, this is not a worry. It is a feature of noneist semantics that any characterization is realized at some world. Hence all universals are instantiated at some worlds.

3.6 Instantiation

Let us finish by returning to the passage from Aristotle with which we started the chapter. Aristotle, we saw, was concerned with the question of why one can predicate some things of others: why, for example, is it true of a certain man that he is musical. One way of understanding this question is as one concerning the nature of instantiation. What is it for the man in question to instantiate the universal *musical*?

An understanding of the instantiation relation naturally follows from our account of universals. *a* is white just if its whiteness is identical to whiteness itself. More precisely, *a* instantiates *U*-ness if, to a first approximation:

- *a* has a pin (the *U*-ness of *a*) which is identical with *U*-ness

We can illustrate this with respect to the object *a* and its whiteness, as follows. The circle contains *a*'s pins. (Note that I am not assuming that the pins are parts of the object.)[17]

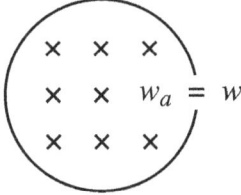

---

[17] w_a, being an object, may have parts of its own, and so its own gluon. Each of these parts, being an object, may have parts, and so on. Hence we will have a regress of gluons. But the regress is not vicious, since we are dealing with different objects in each case.

In fact, we cannot define instantiation in quite this way. For then it would follow that a does not instantiate U iff it has no pin that is identical with U. Any pin of a which is not a U-pin is not identical with U; and it may well be that the U-pin of a is also not identical with U either (as well as identical to it). In this case, every pin of a would be distinct from U, and so it would not be the case that a instantiates U. We have insufficient sensitivity. We may get around this problem by characterizing the anti-extension of I slightly differently. Let I be the instantiation relation, then:

- $\langle a, U \rangle$ is in the extension of I iff a has a pin that is identical with U
- $\langle a, U \rangle$ is in the anti-extension of I iff a has a pin that is identical with $\neg U$

(where $\neg U$ is the property of not being U). Then:

- a is U iff aIU
- a is not U iff $\neg aIU$

For the first, suppose that a is U. Then a has a U-pin, and this is identical with U. Hence aIU. Conversely, if aIU then a has a pin which is identical with U, and this must be the U-pin of a. (Indeed, we can define the U-pin of a to be the pin identical to U.) And so a is U. For the second, suppose that a is not U. Then a has a $\neg U$-pin, and this is identical with $\neg U$. Hence $\neg aIU$. Conversely, if $\neg aIU$, then a has a pin which is identical with $\neg U$, which must be the $\neg U$-pin of a. And so a is not U.

One of the worries often voiced about the instantiation relation is that it launches a Bradley-style regress. If instantiation relates an object, a, and a universal, U, what relates a, U, and instantiation? Some other relation; and, it might seem, we are off on a vicious regress. It is true that a instantiates U iff $\langle a, U \rangle$ instantiates instantiation. That is, we have aIU, $\langle a, U \rangle II$—and so on. But this regress is not vicious, any more than the truth regress: p, $T\langle p \rangle$, $T\langle T\langle p \rangle \rangle$, ...[18] (It does mean that the instantiation relation is non-well-founded. But non-well-founded relations are not a problem, given the resources of non-well-founded set theory.[19])

The matter is different if we are talking not about the relation between the object and the universal, but a *unity* that these form. (I have already observed that to relate and to unify are not the same thing (Section 1.5).) In particular, if one takes the instantiation relation to unify the two into a fact, then a vicious regress does loom. One might, of course, hold that there are no such things as facts. But if there are, their unity is explained exactly by gluon theory. The parts of the fact are

---

[18] As noted by Armstrong (1989), pp. 108ff. Here, T is the truth predicate, and $\langle . \rangle$ indicates some name-forming device.

[19] As in Aczel (1988).

the universal and the object that instantiates it (or the ordered *n*-tuple of objects, if it is a relation). And these are joined together by an appropriate gluon.[20] The solution to the problem of the unity of a fact is, then, just a special case of the general solution to the problem of unity we arrived at in Chapter 2.[21]

So much for universals and instantiation—for the time being: they will return in due course in the second part of the book. There are other things that need to be taken care of before that. One concerns the connection between gluons and a couple of very other important notions: being and nothingness. We turn to these in the next chapter.

---

[20] See, for comparison, the discussion of the unity of the proposition in Section 9.2.

[21] Armstrong's own account of the unity of a fact is quite different. For him, the unity is produced by a binding relation, one that is an internal relation, so that its elements cannot exist without the relation holding. (Armstrong (1989), p. 94f.) We have already seen that this does not work (Section 1.5).

4

Being and Nothing

4.1 Heidegger onto the Stage

The notions of being, totality (everything), and nothing(ness), have always been held to be puzzling philosophical notions. The writings of Heidegger are, of course, a fugue on the theme of wondering what being is. The theory of gluons has interesting applications for these notions—including an answer to Heidegger's question. In this chapter, we will explore these matters.

4.2 Simple Objects

Before we get to these things, however, we need to address the question of whether every object has a gluon. Something must account for the unity of any partite object. This, we know, is its gluon. But do all objects have gluons? Could an object have just one proper part (that is, one part distinct from the whole)? Arguably not. If x is a proper part of y then $y - x$ (the complement of x relative to y) is another. But what of simples—objects without proper parts?

It might be held that there are no simple objects: everything has proper parts. Thus, any physical object is extended. It therefore has a left and a right spatial part. But this will not provide the required argument. It could turn out in the end that space is quantized, and that its most minimal parts have no further spatial divisions, and so no left or right.[1] Less speculatively, the argument obviously applies only to physical objects. But many objects are not physical, such as numbers and other abstract objects.

In fact, by the end of this chapter we will see that at least some objects are simple. But simple as they are, they still have gluons. A gluon is what accounts for the unity of an object. What accounts for the unity of a simplex? It, itself—in virtue of the fact that it *is* a simplex. So we can take the simplex itself to be its own gluon. It is a sort of limit case (just as a set is a limiting case of its own subsets). In what

---

[1] And the same goes for time and temporal extension.

follows, where we need to distinguish this case, we will call these gluons *improper*. So a gluon of an object with multiple parts is a *proper gluon*. Note that for improper gluons, the argument of Section 2.8 to the effect that they are not objects fails. If any of them are not objects (as well as objects), the argument will therefore have to come from elsewhere. We will see that such is possible, later in the chapter.[2]

To summarize, then: every object, simple or complex, has a gluon. A gluon is what constitutes that object as a single object; that is, it is what it is that constitutes the unity of the object.

4.3 Being and Unity

Now let us turn to being; and let me start by explaining how this is to be understood in the present context. By 'being' I do not mean 'existence'. Noneism holds that not all objects exist: purely fictional objects, such as Sherlock Holmes, certain objects of fear, such as (we hope) the end of the Earth in a nuclear conflagration, impossible objects of dreams, such as the person who turns into a square, and so on. The being in question applies to all of these.

What I take *being* to mean here is *being an object*—that is (Section 2.7), being identical to something. Something is an object iff it has properties. For if it has properties, it is certainly an object; and if it is an object, it has properties—at least the property of being an object. Hence, being, in this sense, is equivalent to having *Sosein*, in Meinong's terms. This is quite different from what it means to exist, which, I take it, is the ability to enter into causal interactions.[3]

This is essentially Heidegger's understanding of being, too. Coming from the phenomenological tradition, Heidegger takes it that everything one can think about has being, not just what exists. Thus, he says:[4]

> Everything we talk about, mean, and are related to is in being in one way or another. What and how we ourselves are is also a being. Being is found in thatness and whatness, reality, the objective presence of things [*Vorhandenheit*], subsistence, validity, existence [*Da-sein*], and in the 'there is' [*es gibt*].

And he is clear that this being is the same as the being involved in *Sosein*. Thus, he says:[5]

---

[2] One might wonder whether proper gluons are themselves simples. Nothing we have seen so far settles that matter.

[3] See Priest (2009a), sec. 1.

[4] Heidegger (1996), p. 5. Some who translate Heidegger into English use a capital 'B' for being, and a lower case 'b' for beings. Though this has a certain point, it is entirely artifactual. In German, both words, being nouns, begin with capitals (*Sein, Seindes*). So I will not follow this practice.

[5] Heidegger (1997), p. 5.

Being is used in all knowledge and all predicating, in every relation to beings and in every relation to oneself, and the expression is understandable without 'further ado.' Everyone understands 'The sky is blue,' 'I am happy,' and similar statements.

I note, also, that there is no particular problem about non-existent objects having gluons. A unity with existent parts may have an existent gluon; a unity with non-existent parts may have a non-existent gluon. An existent object, such as a car, may go out of existence, say by falling apart. When it does so, its gluon becomes a non-existent object, and is no longer identical to the other parts (which may still exist).

On this understanding of being, it is clear that being and unity come to the same thing. If something is an object, it is one thing; and if it is one thing, it is certainly an object. The thought is, in fact, as old as Aristotle. As he puts it (*Met.* 1003^b 23–31):

> ... being and unity are the same and are one thing in the sense that they are implied by one another as principle and cause are ...; for one man and a man are the same thing and [man who is] and a man are the same thing, and the doubling of the words in 'one man' and 'one [man who is]' does not give any new meaning ...; and similarly with 'one', so that it is obvious that the addition in these cases means the same thing, and unity is nothing other than being ...[6]

And again (*Met.* 1054^a 13–19):

> And that in a sense unity means the same as being is clear from the fact that it follows the categories in as many ways, and is not comprised within any category, for example, neither in substance nor in quality, but is related to them just as being is; and from the fact that in 'one man' nothing more is predicated than in 'man', just as being is nothing apart from substance or quality or quantity; and to be one is just to be a particular thing.

The thought is echoed by Plotinus, at the beginning of *Ennead* VI, 9:[7]

> It is in virtue of unity that beings are beings.
>
> This is equally true of things whose existence is primal and of all those that are in any degree to be numbered among beings. What could exist at all except as one thing? Deprived of unity, a thing ceases to be what it is called: no army unless a unity: a chorus, a flock, must be one thing. Even house and ship demand unity, one house, one ship; unity gone, neither remains; thus even continuous magnitudes could not exist without inherent unity; break them apart and their very being is altered in the measure of the breach of unity.
>
> Take a plant and animal; the material form stands a unity; fallen from that into a litter of fragments, the things have lost their being; what was is no longer there; it is replaced by quite other things—as many others, precisely as possess unity.

---

[6] 'Man who is' is my rendering of the text's 'existent man'. This, I think, is more accurate.
[7] Translation from MacKenna (1991), pp 535–6.

To be, in the relevant sense, is *to be one*. Any world where an object is one (that is, any world) it is, and *vice versa*.

One might object. It would seem that we have plural forms of reference. Thus, we can say, for example, that Russell and Whitehead wrote *Principia Mathematica*, and that *they* were in Cambridge together at the time. The conjunctive noun phrase and pronoun appear to refer to objects that are inherently plural. Similarly, one can say that something is a square; but one also can say that *some things* have the same shape as each other. The italicized quantifier is plural, and refers to a plurality.[8] There are, then, objects that are, but are not one, being a plurality. *Russell and Whitehead*, for example, is (an object), but it is not one object.

The reply is simple, however. The machinery does not allow us to refer to objects which are plural, but to a plurality of objects. Thus, when we say that Russell and Whitehead wrote *Principia*, we are not referring to some strange object, *Russell and Whitehead*; we are referring to Russell and to Whitehead. (One cannot say: 'Russell and Whitehead wrote *Principia*, and *it* was in Cambridge at the time.) Similarly if we use plural pronouns and quantification we are referring to multiple objects. If something is, it is one, a unity; and if some things are, they are ones, unities. The machinery of plural reference does indeed enable one to refer to a plurality of objects, but each is one. So to be is still to be one.[9]

Let us now put all these thoughts together. The being of something is that in virtue of which it is. To be is to be one. So the being of something is that in virtue of which it is one. And what is it in virtue of which something is one? By definition, its gluon, g. The being of something is therefore its gluon. We have answered Heidegger's question as to the nature of being.

It is worth being clear about the exact form of this argument, lest one take it to be an application of SI. We have established that the conditions 'x is one thing' and 'x is' are coextensive (at every world). Hence, the inference: 'g makes it the case that x is one thing; hence g makes it the case that x is' is an application of the substitutivity of such equivalents.

4.4 Heidegger's Aporia

Let us look more closely at Heidegger.[10]

Heidegger asked, famously, what constitutes a thing's being: what is it for it to be? He says (p. 4f):

---

[8] See, for example, Yi (2005).
[9] I will return to the topic of plural reference in Chapter 6.
[10] For a more detailed discussion of some of these matters, see Priest (2001).

What is asked about in the question to be elaborated is being, that which determines beings as beings, that in terms of which beings have always been understood no matter how they are discussed.

Heidegger came to the conclusion that this question could not be answered. The being of something could only be shown, not said. But in the process, he contradicted himself.

This is precisely what one should expect given our answer to the question of being. As we have just established, the being of an object is its gluon. And gluons (at least, proper gluons), we know, are not objects. As Heidegger puts it (p. 5):

> The being of beings 'is' not itself a being. The first philosophical step in understanding the problem of being consists in avoiding telling the *mython tina diegeisthai*, in not 'telling a story', that is, not determining beings as beings by tracing them back in their origins to another being—as if being had the character of a possible being.

Heidegger infers that one cannot say what the being of something is. For to say anything of the form 'the being of such and such is so and so' is precisely to treat it as an object. Heidegger illustrates the problem at one place as follows:[11]

> If we painstakingly attend to the language in which we articulate what the principle of reason [*Satz vom Grund*] says as a principle of being, then it becomes clear we speak of being in an odd manner that is, in truth, inadmissible. We say: being and ground/reason [*Grund*] 'are' the same. Being 'is' the abyss [*Abgrund*]. When we say something 'is' and 'is such and so', then that something is, in such an utterance, represented as a being. Only a being 'is'; the 'is' itself—being—'is' not. The wall in front of you and behind me is. It immediately shows itself to us as something present. But where is its 'is'? Where should we seek the presencing of the wall? Probably these questions already run awry.

But the being of something, being its gluon, *is* a thing. Hence one can say things about it. I have just done so, and so does Heidegger. (See, for example, a number of the passages I have already quoted.) Even to ask the question 'what exactly is the being of something?' refers to it as a thing.

Heidegger, then, contradicts himself. But he does this precisely because what he is talking about is contradictory. The gluon of a partite object is and is not an object. So, it would seem, one can and cannot talk about it. Such is the contradictory nature of gluons.[12]

---

[11] Heidegger (1991), p. 51f.   [12] I will return to the matter of ineffability in Section 13.6.

4.5 Being *an Sich*

For Heidegger, being is always the being of a being (and so, in Aristotelian terms) a pin. Thus he says:[13]

> If we think of the matter just a bit more rigourously, if we take more heed of what is in contest in the matter, we see that *Being* means always and everywhere: the Being of *beings*.

Despite this, he also sometimes talks about what one might call *being an sich*. Thus, consider the following passage:[14]

> In as much as Being becomes present in the Being of beings ... Being grounds beings, and beings, as what *is* most of all account for Being.

The sentence draws an explicit contrast between *being* and the *being of beings*. It is natural to take being, when talked about in this way, as a reference to a universal (albeit an Aristotelian one). Indeed, in the same essay, he says:[15]

> The essential constitution of metaphysics is based on the unity of beings as such in the universal and highest.

This is obviously talking about being as universal in some sense. But what are we to make of this?

The gluon theory of universals of the last chapter suggests a way. The being of a being is, we know, its gluon. One might naturally take this to be its pin of being (unity). Possessing this is what makes the object be (be one).[16] The corresponding universal is the gluon of the object comprising these pins. Since this is a (proper) gluon, it is just as much an object and not an object as the individual pins; and all the considerations about effability and ineffability we have traversed still, then, apply.

There is then also a very close connection between Heidegger and the matter in Frege which we discussed in Chapter 1. For Heidegger, working as he was within traditional logic, there is only one predicate, the copula, 'is'. So in Fregean terms, there is only one concept (or concept-sense—the sense/reference distinction is not one with which Heidegger operates). And concepts are just universals by another name. So Heidegger's aporia concerning being (the universal) is just a special case of Frege's aporia concerning concepts.

---

[13] Heidegger (2002), p. 61. [14] Heidegger (2002), p. 69. [15] Heidegger (2002), p. 61.
[16] Though this is not mandatory. One might suppose that the object has this pin *because* it is (is one), that is, because it has a gluon.

4.6 Everything and Nothing

Heidegger arguably took being and nothing to be the same thing (at least at some times). We will not follow him down this path.[17] Nothing(ness) is, in fact, a curious thing in its own right. We will get to this in a moment. Let us start, not with nothing, but with everything.

The first thing to note about 'every' words and phrases is that they are ambiguous. One meaning—the one recognized in standard logic texts—is as quantifier phrases. So in 'everyone is descended from Adam', 'everyone' is a quantifier, and it means that for every person, x, x is descended from Adam. But 'every' words can also be noun phrases. Thus, consider: he found himself in the middle of everyone. This would not normally mean that for every person x, he found himself in the middle of x. That, indeed, would appear to be some kind of logical impossibility. It means that there was a totality of people, and he found himself in the middle of that. 'Everyone' names that totality. It is the noun-phrase, not the quantifier, that is our concern here.

Even as noun-phrases, 'every' words can be ambiguous, or at least context-dependent. So, 'he found himself in the middle of everyone' would normally refer to a particular totality of people, determined by the context of utterance. When I use the word 'everything' in what follows, I intend the range to be the broadest possible: 'everything' means absolutely *everything*, every object there is (whether or not it exists). 'Everything' means the totality of *every object*. To avoid confusion with the quantifier in what follows, I will write this 'everything' in boldface, thus: **everything**.

'Everything', like all noun-phrases, refers to an object. Some might wonder whether there is such a thing as **everything**. Completely unbounded totalities of this kind can lead one into contradiction. For example, Kant argued that what he called the cosmos, the totality of all things, was a contradictory entity, at least if it is taken to be a phenomenon. His solution was to say that it was not: it was a noumenon.[18] But there was still such a thing. In matters more contemporary, standard (ZF) set theory gets into trouble if there is a set of all sets; but in paraconsistent set theory, there is a set of *all* sets. It is contradictory, but not explosive.[19] And

---

[17] His central argument for this is to the effect that: (i) being is what it is that makes beings be; (ii) nothing is what it is that makes beings be; hence (iii) being is nothing. (See Priest (2001), section 5.) (ii) is the problematic premise. Heidegger says that this is true because something is able to be only because it "stands out" against nothingness. (More of this in Chapter 13.) This might show that there being nothing(ness) is a necessary condition for an object to be, but it does not show that nothingness is its being.

[18] See Priest (1995a), ch. 6.   [19] See Priest (1987), ch. 3, and Priest (2002), pp. 358–65.

quite generally, contradiction is obviously not a particular problem in the present context. Indeed, we should expect **everything** to be contradictory. Any gluon is an object, and so a part of the **everything**. But any proper gluon is not an object, and so is not a part of it. Gluon theory entails that **everything** has contradictory (abundant) properties. In any case, noneism assures us that '**everything**', like every noun phrase, refers to an object, which can be thought about—though it may be a non-existent object.

Is **everything** an existent object? It has, of course, existent parts, such as you and me. That does not settle the matter. The actual world is existent, but its domain comprises non-existent objects, such as Adam and Atlantis, just as much as Mozart and Melbourne. Neither does this mean that it is non-existent. Any world other than the actual world may be taken to be a non-existent object,[20] and such a world may contain objects that actually exist. Thus, there are worlds where Mozart lived to be 200, and composed some of his late operas in Melbourne.

We do not need to settle the matter here. All that is pertinent is that **everything** is an object—one thing. It therefore has a (proper) gluon. The gluon is a most distinctive object. **Everything** would seem to be symmetrically related to all other objects; hence we may take its gluon to be prime. This therefore has all the properties of any part (object). It is therefore red, not red, in Melbourne, not in Melbourne, existent and non-existent. It is close, in fact, to the trivial object—the object which has all properties.[21] Its contradictory nature does not impose spurious inconsistency on more ordinary objects, such as New York and Mount Fuji, however. Moreover, the gluon of **everything** is identical to all parts of **everything**. It is every thing. If we write g_e for the gluon of **everthing**, then we have $\mathfrak{A} y\, y = g_e$. In that sense, all things are one. There are other senses. We will come to them in Part 3 of the book.

Let us now turn to nothing. For a start, and obviously, 'no' words and phrases are frequently used as quantifier phrases too. When Alice says that she can see no one on the road, she means that for no person, x, can she see x on the road. But like 'every' words, they can also be noun phrases. We may say that Hegel and Heidegger both wrote about nothing. This does not mean that for no x did Hegel and Heidegger write about x. We can say that they said different things about *it*. *It* is also that out of which the Abrahamic God is supposed to have created the world. This nothing (noun phrase) is what will be our concern. And by nothing, I mean *absolutely nothing*. It is the complement of **everything**: the absence of every thing. Again, to avoid confusion with the quantifier, I will write this in boldface, thus: **nothing**.

---

[20] See Priest (2005), 7.3.   [21] See Priest (1998b).

Nothing is an object. We can, for example, think about it. (What things were like before God created the world.) Heidegger, indeed, claimed that one can have a direct phenomenological experience of **nothing** in a rather pessimistic way:[22]

> Does such an attachment, in which man is brought before the nothing itself, occur in human existence?
>
> This can and does occur, although rarely and only for a moment, in the fundamental mood of anxiety (*Angst*)...
>
> Anxiety reveals the nothing.

This does not, of course, entail that **nothing** exists. One can have direct phenomenological acquaintance with non-existent objects. (Try thinking of Zeus!) Indeed, **nothing** does not exist since, presumably, it is impossible for it to enter into causal interactions with things.

Of more importance is that **nothing** is a contradictory object. Since it is an object, it is something.[23] But it is the *absence* of all things too; so **nothing** is nothing. **Everything** is the mereological sum of the universal set. **Nothing** is the mereological sum of the empty set. (We will see how this idea can be articulated in the Interlude on Nothing, Section 6.13.) But there is nothing in the empty set, so **nothing** is absolute absence: the absence of all objects, all presences.[24] It is no thing, no object.

The Chinese/Japanese character for nothing is 無 (Chin: *wu*; Jap: *mu*). Using this for 'nothing', we therefore have: $\mathfrak{S}xx =$ 無 and $\neg \mathfrak{S}xx =$ 無. **Nothing** both is and is not an object. In this respect, it behaves exactly as does a proper gluon. In fact, it is a gluon. For **nothing** can have no parts (other than itself): if it did, it would not be the *absence* of every thing. Hence, it is a simplex, and so is its own gluon. **Nothing** is the gluon of **nothing**. In particular, then, improper gluons may be and not be objects.

There is much more to be said about **nothing** in later parts of the book. But before we even get to the second part, there is one final matter to be dealt with: the issue concerning SI, which I raised and set aside in Section 2.6. That is the topic of the next chapter.

---

[22] Heidegger (1977), p. 102f. I certainly do not endorse his pessimism.

[23] Philosophers often wonder why there is something rather than nothing. However, even if there were nothing—even if everything would be entirely absent—there would be something, namely **nothing**.

[24] And even all absences. The absence of an absence is not a presence!

5
A Case of Mistaken Identity

5.1 The Substitutivity of Identicals

In this chapter, I return to the matter left hanging in Section 2.6. There is, in current logic, a near-universal consensus about the relation of identity. Identity is an equivalence relation that satisfies substitution *salva veritate*. In the notation of first-order logic, it can be characterized by two principles, the "Law of Identity":

- $\vdash a = a$

and the Schema of the Substitutivity of Identicals (SI):

- $a = b, A_x(a) \vdash A(b)$

Clearly, the previous chapters fly in the face of this orthodoxy, since they deny SI. What to make of this? The chapter investigates.[1]

5.2 The History of SI

There are two noteworthy facts about SI. The first is that its emergence as a supposedly secure principle is an historically recent one—the second we will come to in the next section. Perhaps the first place one might think to find it articulated is in Euclid. And indeed, one does find something that looks like this in the Common Notions of Book 1. For example, the second of these states that if equals are added to equals, the wholes are equal.[2] But this is, at best, simply an *instance* of SI; and in any case, on closer inspection, it is not SI at all, but a principle about magnitudes. Let $a + b$ be the straight line obtained by adding the lines a and b end on, and let $\ell(a)$ be the magnitude of a. Then Euclid's principle tells us that:

- $\ell(a) = \ell(c), \ell(b) = \ell(d) \models \ell(a + b) = \ell(c + d)$

---

[1] Some of the material in this chapter comes from Priest (2010a).
[2] See, for example, Artmann (1999), p. 19.

which is not an instance of SI.

A few years earlier in the *Topics* (152^{a}30–38) Aristotle states what might be thought to be a version of SI:

> Again, look and see if, supposing the one to be the same as something, the other is also the same as it: for if they are not both the same as the same thing, clearly neither are they the same as each other.
>
> Moreover, examine them in the light of their accidents and of the things of which they are accidents: for any accident belonging to one must belong also to the other, and if the one belong to any as an accident, so must the other also. If in any of these respects there is a discrepancy, clearly they are not the same.

But the remark is a very casual one, and there is no attempt in Aristotle to articulate or defend the thought.[3]

Medieval logicians certainly endorsed things that look like instances of SI, but they denied others. Take Ockham, for example. He tells us:[4]

> For this is no fallacy 'You know Coriscus; Coriscus is coming; therefore you know the one coming', nor this 'You know Coriscus; Coriscus is hooded; therefore you know the hooded one'.

But he also tells us:[5]

> Because one essence is many persons, and those persons are mutually distinct, it is not necessary that every name of a person of which the name of the essence is predicated be predicated of the name of the other person... This is a fallacy of accident: 'This essence is the Father; this essence is the Son; hence, the Son is the Father.'

So Ockham did not endorse SI as a general principle.

One of the things which makes discussions of SI in the Aristotelian tradition murky is the fact that the distinction between the *is* of identity and the *is* of predication tends not to be made. Thus, for example, in the same discussions from which I have just quoted, we find Ockham worrying about fallacies such as: 'Socrates is a man; Plato is a man; hence, Socrates is Plato' and 'Socrates is a man; a man runs; hence Socrates runs'.[6]

---

[3] As Kneale and Kneale (1962), p. 42, put it: '[These principles of identity] were destined to be reformulated much later by other philosophers without reference to Aristotle's work. In his text, they occur without emphasis, and it is therefore not surprising that he does not generally get any credit for them.'

[4] Del Punta (1979), p. 231.   [5] Boehener *et al.* (1974), pp. 821–2.

[6] Interestingly, this is not true of Abelard, who clearly distinguishes numerical identity; and according to him this is, indeed, non-transitive. Each of God the father, God the son, and God the holy spirit, are identical with the Godhead, without being identical with each other. See King (2010), section 7.

The first clean appearance of SI in the history of philosophy would seem to be in Leibniz, whose account of numerical identity is as follows:[7]

Let us now try to explain *partial terms*, that is, relative terms, from which there also arise the particles which denote the relation of terms. The first of which occurs to me on inquiry is *the same*. That A is the same as B means that one can be substituted for the other in any proposition without loss of truth...For example Alexander the Great and the king of Macedonia who conquered Darius, and again triangle and trilateral, can be substituted for each other.

That is, two things are identical iff they are always inter-substitutable. In the notation of modern second-order logic:

$$\text{LL: } a = b \text{ iff } \forall X(Xa \equiv Xb)$$

The right-to-left direction of the definition is the identity of indiscernibles (II). The left-to-right direction quickly delivers SI, given second-order universal instantiation, and *modus ponens*. (Leibniz is not working in a paraconsistent context, of course. For him, the biconditional involved is a detachable one.)

Leibniz' logical ideas had precious little effect on succeeding generations, logic falling largely into oblivion. But two hundred years later, on its reinvention, the biconditional LL was endorsed by Frege in *Grundgesetze* (Vol. 1, Sect. 20), and Russell and Whitehead in *Principia Mathematica* (Vol. I, *13.01)[8]—though in Frege's case, not as a definition. Both logics had the resources of second-order quantification. When logic was stripped back to first-order by Hilbert and his school, these resources were no longer present to express II, but SI survived in the now familiar form.[9]

5.3 The Ground for SI

One might be happy to see the disappearance of II. As we saw in Section 2.6, a number of people have taken the principle to be false (though as we also saw there, the reasons are not decisive). SI, on the other hand, seems much more secure; indeed, it has seemed to many contemporary philosophers fundamental to our understanding of identity. This brings us to the second noteworthy fact about SI: it is so fundamental that it does not seem possible to give any independent argument for it. The natural way to justify SI invokes, in one way or another, SI itself:

---

[7] Leibniz (1686), pp. 52–3. Where the original text cited by Parkinson (Couturat (1961)) uses italics, Parkinson uses quotation marks. Parkinson's translation also inserts quotation marks where there are none in the text. I have restored the original punctuation. The context makes clear that the 'means that' is offering a definition. It does not mean 'implies that'.

[8] Frege (1893), and Whitehead and Russell (1910).

[9] See, for example, Hilbert and Ackermann (1928), ch. 3, sec. 11.

Suppose that $a = b$ and $A_x(a)$ are true. Then the denotation of 'a' and the denotation of 'b' are the same, and the denotation of 'a' satisfies A. Hence, the denotation of 'b' satisfies A, since they are the same (SI).

In this respect, SI is the same as a number of other logical principles—or mooted principles—which are so fundamental that there seems to be no non-circular way of justifying them. *Modus ponens* and the Principle of Non-Contradiction appear to be in the same camp.

This raises the question of how one might justify such principles. A plausible thought, articulated by Crispin Wright,[10] is that in such cases we have a rational entitlement to the principle, provided that there are no known counter-examples. The no-counter-example condition is necessary because of principles such as *modus morons* ($B, A \to B \vdash A$), which may be justified as follows. Suppose that $A \to B$ and B are true. Then if A is true, so is B. Hence, A is true (*modus morons*). The very virtue of such a principle is that there can be nothing more fundamental. Of course, if there are counter-examples, this fundamental status changes from a virtue to a vice. Defences then just beg the question.

5.4 Intentionality

And there are indeed counter-examples—certainly *prima facie* counter-examples. In the next few sections let us look at these. None of them is novel. Those familiar with the literature will recognize them all. Indeed, much ink has been spilled on these matters.[11] I shall make some comments about other possible treatments of the examples, but I shall make no attempt at a comprehensive discussion of the matter. Indeed, to do so would itself require a book-length essay. I will say just enough to remind the reader that there are no easy solutions to the problems at hand. The aim of the following discussion is to situate the examples in the account of identity endorsed in the book. Gluon theory itself also provides counter-examples to SI, of course. But I leave these aside in this chapter, so as not to be thought to beg any questions.

Let us start on safe ground. Consider the following instance of SI:

Sylvan = Routley
Sylvan was born 'Routley'
―――――――――――――――
Sylvan was born 'Sylvan'

---

[10] Wright (2004).
[11] Surveys can be found in the introduction to Rea (1997); Lowe (2002), chs. 2–5; and Wasserman (2009).

The premises are true; the conclusion is false. Richard Sylvan was born 'Richard Routley', and changed his family name only later in his adult life. The analysis of this example is entirely orthodox: 'Sylvan was born "Routley"' does not express a condition on Routley, the person, at all. It expresses a condition on his name. Hence, this is not an instance of SI at all. To make it so, the premise would have to be 'Sylvan'='Routley'.

A bit less orthodox, but still on relatively safe ground, there are examples involving intentionality (goal-directed cognitive states). Suppose that a hooded man enters the room. The man is, in fact, Coriscus, whom you know, but you have no idea who the hooded man is. Then the following would seem to be invalid:

Coriscus is the hooded man
You know Coriscus
———————————————
You know the hooded man

This apparent counter-example is less persuasive than it might at first appear, though. If the premises are true, then we may simply endorse the conclusion as true. You *do* know the hooded man; you just do not *realize* that you do.[12]

However, that merely shifts the problem. Consider:

Coriscus is the hooded man
You realize that you know Coriscus
———————————————
You realize that you know the hooded man

One can precisely not now say that this is valid.[13] SI must fail in the scope of intentional operators. But in the natural semantics for intentional operators, to evaluate something of the form 'you realize that you know x' at a world, w, we have to evaluate things of the form 'you know x' at worlds other than w.[14] And as we saw in Section 2.7, SI should be expected to fail for such contexts.[15]

---

[12] This was, in fact, Ockham's view, as we saw in Section 5.2. The view is defended in Priest (2005a). There, it is argued that SI is perfectly valid in the scope of intentional predicates—though not intentional operators.

[13] One might think that SI fails here because of the use of a definite description, 'the hooded man', since this may have different denotations in different worlds. However, one can set this consideration aside, since one can label the hooded man as he walks through the door with a rigid designator, say 'Nescio', and run the argument with this instead of the description. The situation is then exactly the same.

[14] This is argued in Priest (2005a). In the semantics given there, a rather different account of identity is provided from the one given in Section 2.6. In particular, the failure of SI in the context of intentional operators is obtained, technically, by the application of the techniques of contingent-identity semantics to objects. (The account in Section 2.10.5 applies them to properties.) The present account of identity provides, it seems to me, an explanation of the failure of SI for these contexts, which is just as good.

[15] A different solution is advocated by Frege (1892b). His analysis of the situation is analogous to the Routley example. In the context at hand, 'Coriscus' does not refer to the object the word refers

5.5 Time

Another swag of counter-examples to SI is posed by temporal considerations. With the following, we are still on relatively safe ground. Suppose that we have two photographs. The first is of a baby; call the baby b. The second is of an adult; call the adult a. It may well turn out that the second photograph was taken a lot later than the first, and that a and b are the same person. And if so, the following inference appears fallacious:

$a = b$
$\underline{b \text{ is a baby}}$
$a \text{ is a baby}$

However, it is not. One must remember that these statements are significantly tensed. One must therefore supply the times at which the statements are supposed true or not. Let t_1 and t_2 be the earlier and later times, respectively. The first premise is true at both times. At t_1 both the second premise and the conclusion are true; at t_2 both are false. We have no counter-example.

A very different sort of scenario poses a harder problem—or, actually, variety of problems.[16] Consider van Gogh, v, who cut off his ear at some time, t. Let s be the sum total of van Gogh's parts before he cut his ear off, and s^- the sum total of all the parts minus the ear. Furthermore, let us suppose the ear to be destroyed after it is cut off. So s then ceases to exist; s^- is all that is left. At first blush, one might take the following to be sound:

$v = s$
$\underline{s \text{ does not exist}}$
$v \text{ does not exist}$

Were it so, the conclusion would be absurd: it would mean that van Gogh could escape liability for his crimes simply by cutting off his ear.[17] But when we fill in the times at which the various statements are supposed to be true, the example

---

(*Bedeutung*) to, but to something else—the sense (*Sinn*) of 'Coriscus'. This strategy runs into trouble when quantifying in. Thus, suppose that Jesus really was the son of God, but that Nietzsche did not believe it. Then it would appear to follow that someone is such that he is the son of God, but Nietzsche did not believe him to be so:

$\exists x(x \text{ is the son of God} \wedge \text{Nietzsche did not believe that } x \text{ is the son of God})$

This is just false. If the x in question is something that truly (meaningfully?) fits in the context of the second conjunct, it is a linguistic sense, not something that could be the son of God at all.

[16] See van Inwagen (1981).
[17] This is sometimes called the Debtor's Paradox. (See Rea (1997), p. xv, or Wasserman (2009), section 1.)

disappears. The first premise is true before t, but the second premise is false then. The second premise is true after t, but the first premise is false then ($v = s^-$).

But for a variation, try:

$$v = s$$
$$\text{It will be the case after } t \text{ that } s \text{ does not exist}$$
$$\overline{\text{It will be the case after } t \text{ that } v \text{ does not exist}}$$

where all the statements are evaluated before t. Both premises are true, but the conclusion is false. We have a counter-example to SI; but this is to be expected on the present account, since we are substituting into the scope of a temporal operator, as noted in Section 2.7.

Matters are similar with yet a third variation of the problem. Consider the following inference, where the time of evaluation is before t:

$$v = s$$
$$\text{It will be the case after } t \text{ that } v = s^-$$
$$\overline{\text{It will be the case after } t \text{ that } s = s^-}$$

Both premises are true; the conclusion is false. Again, we have a counter-example to SI within the context of a temporal operator.[18]

A quite different sort of example is posed by the following situation.[19] Suppose that at a certain time, t_1, we form a lump of clay, l, into a statue, b, of George W. Bush. At a later time, t_2, we refashion it into a statue, o, of Barack Obama. Then the following inference would seem not to preserve truth, where all the sentences are considered at time t_1:

$$l = b$$
$$\text{It will be the case that } l = o$$
$$\overline{\text{It will be the case that } b = o}$$

---

[18] We are very close to another problem often styled "the one and the many" here. Before the ear-lopping, s^- would seem to be pretty much just as good a candidate as s for van Gogh himself—as would s minus the other ear, or his s minus the left index finger, and so on. How many van Goghs are there? One or many? There is only one. s^- and similar things are not van Gogh. They are proper parts of van Gogh—at least until the ear-lopping. It might be said that even though s^- is not van Gogh himself, it is still a person. So van Gogh himself seems to comprise a multitude of people. But one can simply deny this: they are *parts* of a person; and a part of a person is not a person. The problem is often illustrated with respect to an object such as a cloud, rather than a person. (See Weatherstone (2009).) This adds some extra complexity. First, we may still take the cloud to be the mereological whole of all the water droplets; but unlike van Gogh, the cloud is a vague object. This is not a relevant difference. A relevant difference is that a part of a cloud is still a cloud, in a way that a part of a person is not a person. So we do in fact have many clouds. The cloud itself, the mereological whole, and any proper part (of suitable size and connection), which is also a cloud.

[19] See Gibbard (1975).

The statues of Bush and Obama are not the same object—at t_1 or at any later time. When the statue of Obama comes into existence, the statue of Bush goes out of existence.[20]

On the present account of identity, the situation is explained in the simplest possible way: the inference is invalid. As we have seen, SI does not apply within the scope of temporal operators.[21]

5.6 Modality

Modal notions bring another crop of counter-examples to SI. Consider the following very familiar inference:

> The Morning Star = the Evening Star
> Necessarily, the Morning Star = the Morning Star
> ──────────────────────────────
> Necessarily, the Morning Star = the Evening Star

The notion of necessity is multiply ambiguous.[22] One important meaning is epistemic. To say that something is necessary in this sense is to say that it is known to be true. The inference is certainly invalid in this sense. When the sentences are evaluated at this world, from the epistemic perspective of the Ancient Babylonians, the first two premises are true, and the conclusion is false,[23] so we have a counter-example to SI. But we should now expect this: epistemic necessity is an intentional notion, and we have already noted that SI should be expected to fail in such contexts.

Matters appear to be different if we interpret the necessity in question as metaphysical necessity. As Kripke (1980) famously argued, premises and conclusion are both, then, true. In fact, he argued that SI is valid within contexts of metaphysical necessity. The reason for this, *au fond*, was that it is valid in standard Kripke semantics for first-order modal logic. On the present account, the inference is invalid, and it is shown to be so by the semantics of second-order modal logic, as we saw in Chapter 2. Of course, that does not mean that the premises and

---

[20] One way of attempting to solve the problem is by invoking "four-dimensionalism". *l*, *b*, and *o*, are objects extended over time. *b* and *o* are then parts of *l*. The identity $l = b$ is just, therefore, false. We will meet four-dimensionalism again in a moment, and I defer comments on it till then.

[21] It is sometimes suggested that the problem can arise with respect to non-temporal/modal contexts. Thus, *b* is a statue and *l* is not. But this can simply be denied. *l* *is* a statue (at this time). Of course, the creator of *b* did what they did to *l* because they wanted to produce *b*. They did not do what they did because they wanted to produce *l*. But we know that SI fails in intentional contexts.

[22] See Priest (2008), 3.6.

[23] Let us suppose; actually, I have no idea who it was that discovered the truth of the identity statement in question.

conclusion are not true. But true premises and conclusion do not a valid argument make.[24]

And the modal analogue of our statue example does provide a counter-example. Suppose that o had never been made, and through the whole of their temporal existence l and b coincide. None the less, where $\Box$ denotes metaphysical necessity, and the statements are evaluated at the actual world, the premises of the following argument are true. The conclusion is not:

$$l = b$$
$$\Box l = l$$
$$\overline{\Box l = b}$$

At another world, l was made into o, not b. We have a counter-example to SI. The inference fails, as we should expect it to, since we are substituting into the scope of a modal operator.

A commonly suggested solution is to deny that the relationship between the lump and the statue is one of identity. There are two objects present at t_1: l and b. And l is not identical to b: it *constitutes* it. But whatever one makes of the notion of constitution, and of two objects being in one place at the same time, this solution jars. I clear a table and sit you next to it. From out of a cupboard I take something. It is a lump of clay fashioned into a statue of the Buddha. I put it on the table. How many objects are there on the table? *Look carefully*. If you say 'two', I will have to assume that you are cross-eyed.[25]

SI can also fail when substituting into conditional contexts. Thus, the Morning Star is the Evening Star; and if the Morning Star is not the Evening Star, then modern astronomy is badly mistaken. But it does not follow that if the Morning Star is

---

[24] A word about another apparent counter-example to SI, made famous by Quine (1953): The number of planets $= 9$; $\Box$ $9 = 9$; hence $\Box$ the number of planets $= 9$. The inference is indeed invalid, as the present account has it. The orthodox explanation for this is to locate the invalidity of the inference in the fact that a definite description is employed. This may change its denotation from world to world. (See Priest (2008), 16.4.) Though I have not spelled out the semantics of descriptions in what has gone before, it is a routine matter to do so. And if one does, one can construct countermodels to the inference which depend precisely on this fact. The inference is then doubly invalid; that is, invalid for two quite distinct reasons. It might be wondered what, then, is the inferential difference between rigid designators and descriptions if they both behave the same way with respect to identity. The answer is that they behave in different ways with respect to quantifiers. Thus, if t is a rigid designator, we have $\models \mathfrak{S}x\Box x = t$, but if t is not a rigid designator, we do not.

[25] Rudder Baker (1997) argues that constitution is not identity as follows. Suppose it were, then since $l = b$ and b is essentially a statue, l is essentially a statue, which it is not. But to to say that x essentially F is to say that $\Box(x$ exists iff $Fx)$ (or something even stronger if not all necessary properties are essential properties). Hence, the argument deploys SI within a modal context, and so begs the question here. She also deploys what are, in effect, temporal versions of the argument (pp. 614 f.). If constitution is identity, we can have a situation in which $l = b$, but l will exist (at a certain time), and b will not; or b will cease to exist (under certain conditions), and l will not. The same comment applies to this.

not the Morning Star, then modern astronomy is badly mistaken—modern logic would be! (See Priest (2008), 19.5.4.) Given a worlds-analysis of conditionals, this is to be expected.[26]

5.7 Fission

We have now looked at a number of putative counter-examples to SI—including some real ones (namely, those which substitute into a context whose semantic evaluation requires an index-shift). The account of identity in this book invalidates a very particular instance of SI, however: the Transitivity of Identity (TI). And none of the counter-examples we have looked at so far target that. Let us move on to some that do.[27]

Suppose that we have an amoeba, a. At a certain time, t, it divides into two amoebas, b and c, and so becomes both of them. After t, $a = b$ (so $b = a$) and $a = c$. But clearly, it is not the case that $b = c$. Hence, $b = a, a = c \nvDash b = c$. One may make various moves at this point. One could say that a is b, but not c (or vice versa). But the situation is symmetrical, and there would seem to be nothing which could ground such an asymmetry. The only other symmetrical response is that a is neither b nor c. It would be crazy to assume that a has gone somewhere else (for example, that it has materialized on the Moon); so a must have gone out of existence. This seems implausible. Suppose that c were to die as soon as the split occurred. We would have no hesitation in saying that a was b. But whether or not some third party exists cannot affect the identity of an object. So even if c exists, a must still be b—and similarly c.[28]

Here, one might invoke "four dimensionalism" to solve the problem. Objects are stretched out over time, and are the sums of their temporal parts. Thus, one amoeba comprises the temporal stretch of a plus the temporal stretch of b. Another comprises the temporal stretch of a plus the temporal stretch of c.

---

[26] This delivers an answer to the following objection to gluon theory. Let us suppose that we have a device with two buttons, a and b. a is a dummy button, but if b were pressed the device would explode. As a matter of fact, a is being pressed and b is not. Suppose that the device has a prime gluon, g. If it has all the properties of a and b then it has the properties of being pressed and being such that if it were pressed the device would explode. Hence the device should explode, which it does not. However, one of these conditions—being such that if it were pressed the device would explode—contains a (counterfactual) conditional. Since the truth conditions of this involve a world-shift, it does not define a property of b or, therefore, a property of g. The corresponding material conditional may well do. However, for this, detachment fails.

[27] The following example comes from Prior (1968). The view taken here is defended at greater length in Priest (1995b).

[28] It might be suggested that there is another symmetric response: that $a = b \oplus c$, where the $\oplus$ indicates mereological fusion. But $b \oplus c$ is not an amoeba. Hence amoeba a has gone out of existence. Hence, a is *not* $b \oplus c$.

According to this, before the split, there were really two amoebas present.[29] This is odd. It means that two amoebas can occupy the same place at the same time. This is even worse than the statue and the lump of clay (Section 5.5): it would seem to violate the very way in which we individuate amoebas. More: suppose, that the world came to an end just before the split. Then we would have no hesitation in saying that there was just one amoeba there. How can the integrity of the amoeba (here now) depend on something that happens in the future? Suppose that it were not amoebas dividing, but people. It would seem bizarre to suppose that I was not a single person because of future events beyond my ken.

As one might expect, the temporal example has a world-analogue. Suppose that in another world, w, the zygote that was to become me, m, in this world, split to produce two identical twins, m_1 and m_2. Then, it would seem, $m_1 = m = m_2$, but it is not the case that $m_1 = m_2$. Analogous comments are applicable. In particular, supposing that m is neither m_1 nor m_2, seems wrong. If the embryo that was m_2 had died immediately after the split, we would have no hesitation in saying that $m = m_1$. m_1 would then, after all, be the only object with my essential properties (DNA structure).

One might try to solve this problem by the modal analogue of four-dimensionalism. Objects are spread out, not over time, but over worlds, with parts at each. Analogous points would then apply. But in any case, the strategy is much less plausible in the modal case than in the temporal case. The notion of a temporal part of an object is reasonably clear; the notion of a modal part, much less so.[30]

The account of identity of the book accounts nicely for the splitting example, since TI is not a valid inference. Indeed, given that account, we have a natural explanation of why the inference fails in these cases. Take the amoeba case. (The zygote case is similar.) After the split, b and c are located in different places, x_b, and x_c. We know that TI fails to be truth-preserving when the medial object, a in this case, has contradictory properties. Now, after the split, where is a? It is natural to suppose that it is located exactly where b is, and exactly where c is. It is therefore

---

[29] Matters can be made even stranger. Suppose that each of b and c itself splits at a later time, and that each of their descendants splits, and so on. Then, starting with a, there would be an infinite number, in fact $2^{\aleph_0}$, of future "amoeba lines" stemming from a; and before the split, there would be an uncountable number of amoebas present.

[30] One might think that Lewis' counterpart theory would help with the problem. (Lewis (1968).) According to this, objects in different worlds are always distinct, but an object may have counterparts (even more than one counterpart) in different worlds. It is not, then, true that $m = m_1$ (or that $m = m_2$). m_1 and m_2 are simply the counterparts of m at w. But whatever one thinks of counterpart theory, it plays havoc with the notion of identity in any case. In counterpart theory, $\Box A$ is true iff at every (accessible) world every counterpart of each of the objects mentioned by A satisfies it. This invalidates SI. Suppose that at this world $a = b$, and that there is just one other world, w, at which a (that is, b) has multiple counterparts, c_1 and c_2. Then $\Box a = a$ is true, since at w, $c_1 = c_1$ and $c_2 = c_2$. But $\Box a = b$ is false, since at w, c_1 is a counterpart of a, c_2 is a counterpart of b, and $c_1 \neq c_2$.

both at x_b and not at x_b (and both at x_c and not at x_c). Indeed, consider the object after the split, o, whose parts are exactly a, b, and c.[31] Then we may take a to be the prime gluon of this object, in which case it has exactly the properties of b and c.

The problems that arise in the case of fission arise in the case of fusion too, when two objects become one. Details can happily be left to the reader to symmetrize considerations.

5.8 Vagueness

Vagueness provides another counter-example to TI.[32] If I change the exhaust pipes of my bike, or any other of its parts, it is still numerically the same bike. So suppose that each day I replace a different part until, on the last day, n, every part has been changed. Let the bike on distinct days be $a_0, a_1, \ldots, a_n$. $a_0 = a_1 = \ldots = a_n$. But $a_0 \neq a_n$. After all, I can reassemble all the parts and stand a_0 next to a_n. Again, we have a violation of TI.

This is a version of the Sorites paradox, usually called 'the Ship of Theseus', and there are, of course, many suggested solutions to the Sorites paradoxes. Those who would endorse SI have to say that there is at least one i such that $a_i = a_{i+1}$ is not true. Should one say all i, or just some i? Those who advocate an epistemicist or a supervaluationist solution to the Sorites[33] say 'only some'. Whatever one thinks of such solutions, they all run up against considerations of symmetry. The relation between each pair, a_i and a_{i+1}, is exactly the same: one part has changed. Maybe one of the parts is the most important. The fuel-injector? No, that seems bizarre. In any case, whatever part we suppose, I can change that first. There is no part which is so important that changing just that makes a difference of identity to a_0. How come changing that part does not affect the identity of a_0, but it does affect the identity of a_i?

Perhaps, then, none of the identities is true. This seems extreme. In real life, everything is in a constant state of material change; if we go down this track, there would be no identity over time. That would play havoc with many of our common-sense notions. For example, moral and legal concepts such as ownership and responsibility would go out of the window.[34] The blow may be softened by

---

[31] This assumes that there is such an object. I will return to this matter in Section 6.8.
[32] The material in this section draws on Priest (2010c).
[33] For example, Williamson (1994) and Fine (1975), respectively.
[34] It could, I suppose, be suggested that these practices are not based on identity *in stricto sensu*, but on what Butler called identity in the "loose and popular sense". (Butler (1849), p. 305. See Baxter (1988).) The first thing to note about this, is that it concedes the fact that identity, in the pertinent sense, is non-transitive. It may be maintained that this is not *real* identity; but if one holds that *real*

those who advocate a fuzzy solution to the Sorites paradox.[35] A sentence has a degree of truth from 0, completely false, to 1, completely true. The premises of the Sorites may not be completely true, but they are near enough; and near enough is good enough for practical purposes. Whatever one thinks of such a solution, the important point to note here is that it effectively concedes the failure of TI anyway. Each of the identity premises is true enough, but $a_0 = a_n$ is completely false, and so not true enough.[36]

In fact, the theory of identity at hand solves the problem nicely. TI does indeed fail here, just as it would appear to do. The situation is, in fact, similar to the amoeba case, though more complicated. Take any object in the sequence, a_i. Then it would appear to be the case that a_i is identical with the things near enough to it (those a_j for which i is close to j), and distinct from (not identical with) those things far enough away. Let a_k be one such far-away object. The identity of the objects between a_i and a_k would themselves seem to form a Sorites sequence: things close to a_i are identical with a_i, and distinct from a_k; those close to a_k are identical with a_k, and distinct from a_i. In the middle there is the problematic area distinctive of Sorites transitions. What to say about this area is one of the *cruces* of Sorites paradoxes. Many philosophers have thought that statements about such borderline cases are neither true nor false. But what the Pure Light of Natural Reason tells us is that the middle is symmetrical with respect to the two ends. At the two ends we have clear cases of truth and falsity. Being neither true nor false is indeed symmetrical with respect to these, but so is being both true and false; and, as far as that goes, just as good.[37] However, there are reasons to suppose that the latter is a better answer.[38] Assuming this to be the case, then in the borderline cases there are going to be a_js which are both identical with, and distinct from, a_i and a_k.

Let me illustrate. Suppose that we have a sorites sequence of objects, $a_0, \ldots, a_6$, such that the ends are clearly distinct from each other. Then the behaviours of the predicates $a_0 = x$ and $x = a_6$ may be illustrated as follows:

$$a_0 = a_0 \quad a_0 = a_1 \quad a_0 = a_2 \quad a_0 = a_3 \quad a_0 = a_4$$
$$a_0 \neq a_2 \quad a_0 \neq a_3 \quad a_0 \neq a_4 \quad a_0 \neq a_5 \quad a_0 \neq a_6$$
$$a_0 \neq a_6 \quad a_1 \neq a_6 \quad a_2 \neq a_6 \quad a_3 \neq a_6 \quad a_4 \neq a_6$$
$$a_2 = a_6 \quad a_3 = a_6 \quad a_4 = a_6 \quad a_5 = a_6 \quad a_6 = a_6$$

identity is non-transitive, one does not need this gratuitous and apparently *ad hoc* distinction to deal with the case.

[35] For example, Machina (1976).
[36] Technically, if $|A|$ is the truth value of A, then $Min\{a_i = a_{i+1} : n > i \geq 0\} > |a_0 = a_n|$. So the inference is truth-value-*decreasing*.
[37] This was first observed by Hyde (1997).
[38] See Priest (2010c).

We clearly have a failure of TI, since $a_0 = a_3$ and $a_3 = a_6$, but we do not have $a_0 = a_6$. As we noted in Section 2.4, failures of transitivity may occur when and only when the middle object has some contradictory property. In this case, there must be a P such that: Pa_0, Pa_3, $\neg Pa_3$, $\neg P_6$. What is such a P? An obvious candidate is $a_0 = x$ itself. That is, $\mathfrak{A}X(Xa_0 \equiv Xx)$. We have already seen that this property satisfies exactly those conditions. In particular, for this P we have $Pa_3 \wedge \neg Pa_3$, and so $\mathfrak{S}X(Xa_3 \wedge \neg Xa_3)$. True, this P is itself something specified with a second-order quantifier. This is impredicative; but second-order logic is that kind of thing. There are also going to be more run-of-the-mill Ps. Thus, if a_0 is a Harley Road King, and a_6 is a Harley Soft Tail (and so not a Road King), then a_3 will be both a Road King and a Soft Tail. As in the amoeba case, we might even take a_3 to be the gluon of the object with parts a_0, a_3, and a_6.

5.9 Looking Back

What we have now seen is that the theory of identity which I have set out handles the paradoxes of identity (at least, the ones that are not relatively superficial) in a simple and natural way. Of course, one may argue that accepting the novel theory of identity is a cost, and that there are other ways in which one might try to solve the problems (as I have indicated, if all too briefly). But each of these ways, even if it works in its own terms, comes with its own costs: revisionary views in metaphysics, the philosophy of language, and even ethics. The standard strategies offered to solve each kind of paradox are also typically quite different. It is not at all clear that they are mutually compatible; and even if they are, they do not tell a uniform story. All too often, the paradoxes in question are treated in a piecemeal and disunified fashion. By contrast, the approach mooted here offers a single unified account. Such is, of course, a distinct methodological virtue.

5.10 When can SI be Applied?

What we have seen, then, is that SI—and TI—are not to be expected in general. But of course, we do apply SI sometimes, and get the right result. The inference is not valid, but it can be applied in a truth-preserving way under certain conditions. Let us look more closely at the matter.

SI is an inference of the following form: $\mathfrak{A}X(Xa \equiv Xb)$, $A_x(a) \vdash A_x(b)$. Clearly, $\mathfrak{A}X(Xa \equiv Xb) \vdash Pa \equiv Pb$. A simple induction shows that $\mathfrak{A}X(Xa \equiv Xb) \vdash A_x(a) \equiv A_x(b)$, where the x is not in the scope of a modal operator.[39]

---

[39] The proof is to be found in Section 2.9.4.

It follows that $a = b \vdash A_x(a) \supset A_x(b)$. We can call this *material substitutivity*. Given that $a = b$, to get from $A_x(a)$ to $A_x(b)$ we now need to apply the disjunctive syllogism. This is not valid; but it is, in the terminology of *In Contradiction*, quasi-valid.[40] That is, we can apply it in a truth-preserving fashion provided that we do not have $A_x(a)$ and $\neg A_x(a)$. This may be thought of as the "truth" behind (extensional) SI. It works, when it does, because the appropriate consistency obtains. Thus, if John is James, and John sees Mary, then it is quite correct to proceed to the conclusion that James sees Mary: *seeing Mary* is a quite consistent property. These ideas can be worked into a non-monotonic account of validity, according to which the standard (extensional) inferences concerning identity are valid in consistent situations. The details can be found in the technical appendix to this chapter.

In summary, then, SI is perfectly fine when we are substituting into a consistent extensional context; otherwise not. Thus, the account explains not only where SI fails, but also where its application does work.

The thought that identity delivers indiscriminability is certainly a well entrenched view in contemporary logic. However, like the view that contradictions cannot be true, it would appear that it cannot be defended without begging the question, as we noted. And like that view, both common sense and metaphysics may force us to reject it as an overhasty generalization. Indeed, the two views are closely connected. The definition of identity employs a material (bi)conditional. Substitutivity fails (in extensional contexts) because the material conditional fails to detach; but it fails to detach precisely because some contradictions are true. Given the definition of identity, then, the failure of substitutivity in extensional contexts and dialetheism come to the same thing.

5.11 Object-Language Identity and Metalanguage Identity

We can now confront a final important objection to the effect that the identity of gluon theory is not real identity. This goes as follows. The meaning of identity is spelled out by the semantics of the language (given, precisely, in the technical appendix 2.10). This is formalized in set-theoretic terms, and the natural assumption is that this is ZF set theory. In particular, the domain of objects is furnished with a notion of identity which appears to be the orthodox notion. (Thus, for example, in the interpretation depicted in Section 2.4, g, i, and j are distinct

---

[40] Priest (1987), ch. 8.

objects.) *This*, therefore, is the real notion of identity, and the notion of identity in our sights here ('gluon identity') is an impostor.

By way of reply, grant, for the moment, that the object language and metalanguage identity are indeed different. It does not follow that it is the identity relation of the metalanguage which is the real notion. Simply to claim so is to beg the question. As we have just seen, the ordinary (real) notion of identity appears to fail to satisfy substitutivity—including transitivity—in a number of ways. One might, of course, contest the examples I used, but they show that those who would claim that identity satisfies substitutivity, or even transitivity, across the board, cannot claim to have common-sense appearances on their side.

Notwithstanding, it remains the case that the identity relations of the object language and the metalanguage are out of kilter. There is therefore something *prima facie* awry in the situation. Someone who holds that it is the object-language notion that is the correct notion of identity would, it might seem, be better off specifying the semantics of the object language using *that* notion, homophonically: '$a = b$' is true iff $a = b$. This is too fast, however. Whilst a homophonic semantics is always an option, it is not always the best option. The standard semantics of modal languages, for example, do not specify the semantics of modal operators using modal operators: the specification is given in terms of quantification over worlds.

But in non-homophonic cases such as this, we should at least be clear about what the notions of the metalanguage are, and why we employ them in framing the semantics. In the modal case, the meaning of quantification over worlds is clear enough, and the machinery serves to explicate the properties of the modal operators in a transparent and well-understood way, something that a simple homophonic semantics would not do (at least before the advent of world semantics). In the case of identity, what is the metalinguistic relation standardly written as '=', if it is not identity? The answer is simple: it is the relationship of inter-substitutability: $a = b$ if, for all the contexts, A, provided by the language involved, $A_x(a)$ iff $A_x(b)$. And it is useful to deploy this notion in giving the semantics of identity for much the same reason that possible-world semantics is useful: because it explicates the properties of the notion in a transparent and well-understood way.

But there is a more fundamental problem with the objection. It takes the metalanguage to be classical; and this need not be the case. Let us grant that the metatheoretic reasoning is all correct when coded in Zermelo Frankel set theory (ZF). There is a way of understanding paraconsistent set theory in such a way that it is formulated with a material conditional, and yet anything established in ZF—and so using SI—also holds in this theory! (The details can be found in the second edition of Priest (1987), 18.4.) Of course, since the theory is inconsistent, various contradictions, including ones concerning identity, may hold as well; but the things established still stand. Moreover, we may formulate ZF (and so paraconsistent set theory) without an explicit identity predicate. As is well known, we can simply *define* $x = y$ as $\forall z(x \in z \equiv y \in z)$ (and take the extensionality axiom as $\forall z(z \in x \equiv z \in y) \supset \forall z(x \in z \equiv y \in z)$). This definition of identity is then essentially the first-order set-theoretic version of the second-order definition given in Section 2.4.

5.12 From Part I to Part II

This completes our discussion of the identity predicate, and with it the first part of the book. In this part we have confronted the problem of unity: how is it that a multitude of parts can constitute a unity? We have seen the need for gluons: objects with contradictory properties, and for an account of identity in which TI fails—as well as the reasonableness of both of these things. We have also had a first look at how gluons engage with questions concerning universals, nothingness, and other important philosophical notions. There are many more things to be said about these matters, as we will see in due course. Several of them will arise in the next part of the book. To give the investigations in this part themselves a unity, we will take Plato as our matrix.

5.13 Technical Appendix: Second-Order *LPm*

On the basis of first-order *LP*, one can define a non-monotonic logic, *LPm*, the inference relation of which coincides with classical validity when the premises are consistent.[41] In this section, we see how a similar construction can be performed on second-order (non-modal) *LP*, with its definition of identity.[42] In particular, provided that we are reasoning about consistent situations, identity may be taken to behave in the orthodox fashion in first-order contexts.[43] In what follows, the notation is the same as in the technical appendix 2.10.

Call a second-order *LP* interpretation *classical* iff for every $D \in \mathcal{D}_2$, $D^+ \cap D^- = \emptyset$. The classical interpretations are simply those where no atomic sentence—and hence no sentence at all—behaves inconsistently. If I is an

---

[41] See Priest (1987), second edition, ch. 16.
[42] How best to modify the idea so that it works in the second-order case is not obvious. The following strikes me as natural and plausible. A slightly different approach is given in Priest (2010b).
[43] In Priest (1987), 8.4, I argued that consistency should be taken as a default assumption. If this is right, then the classical properties of identity may be invoked unless and until that default assumption is revoked.

interpretation, let $I! = \{P_Dk_d : d \in \mathcal{D}_1, D \in \mathcal{D}_2, d \in D^+ \cap D^-\}$. $I!$ is the set of inconsistent atomic sentences in the language of I. If I_1 and I_2 are interpretations, define $I_1 \prec I_2$ (I_1 is more consistent than I_2) to mean that $I_1! \subsetneq I_2!$.[44] I is a *minimally inconsistent* (mi) model of Σ iff I is a model of Σ and there is no $J \prec I$ such that J is a model of Σ. Finally, *minimally inconsistent consequence* can be defined thus:

$\Sigma \vDash_m A$ iff every mi model of Σ is a model of A

If Σ is classically consistent, it has models, I, in which $I! = \emptyset$. These are its mi models. They are not necessarily models of classical second-order logic. There is no reason to suppose, for example, that for every $X \subseteq \mathcal{D}_1$, $\langle X, \mathcal{D}_1 - X \rangle \in \mathcal{D}_2$. Therefore Σ may have consequences in classical second-order logic which are not consequences in *LPm*. However, their first-order parts are classical. So if A is a first-order classical consequence of Σ, it is true in all these models. Hence $\Sigma \vDash_m A$. The converse is obvious. (Any classical counter-model can be turned into an *LPm* counter-model, since the second-order machinery is irrelevant.) Hence, the first-order *LPm* consequences of Σ are exactly its classical consequences.

Moreover, any model of Σ is a model of anything of the form $a = a$ and and $a = b \supset (A_x(a) \equiv A_x(b))$, where A is any first-order formula.[45] Now, the valid inferences in classical logic with identity are exactly the first-order consequences of these axioms. Hence, if Σ is consistent, any inference valid in classical first-order logic with identity is *LPm* valid. (In particular, since $\{a = b, b = c\}$ is consistent, $a = b, b = c \vDash_m a = c$.) Again, the converse is obvious.

Hence, *LPm* gives us a formal and precise account of the acceptability of the classical first-order inferences involving identity in consistent (and extensional) contexts.

---

[44] It is not required, note, that the first- and second-order domains of the two interpretations be the same. Crabbé (2011) shows that in the case of first-order *LPm* it makes good sense to require the domain of I_2 to be a subset of that of I_1. The same considerations apply to the first-order domain for second-order *LPm*. They appear to carry over naturally to the second-order domain as well.

[45] For the latter, see the argument in Section 2.10.3. In *LP*, if $A \vDash B$ then $\vDash A \supset B$.

PART II

In Plato's Trajectory

The safest general characterization of the European philosophical tradition is that it consists of a series of footnotes to Plato.

Alfred North Whitehead, *Process and Reality* [(1979), p. 39]

6

Enter Parmenides: Mereological Sums

6.1 The Muse of Plato

The previous part of the book laid the foundations of gluon theory. In this part of the book, we will look at various of its applications. We will be concerned, amongst other things, with mereology, falsity, intentionality—and universals again. These are, of course, some of the central notions of philosophy; and discussions of them go back to the origins of Western philosophy. It is therefore appropriate to take Plato as our muse. We will be concerned to untangle some of the knots he bequeathed philosophy.[1]

Aristotle, as we saw in Section 3.2, had an account of what makes the parts of something into a unity. Plato had no such explicit account. One has to try to piece together his view from various discussions. This is no easy matter, and I shall not attempt it here.[2] He was, however, much concerned with this question in many of

---

[1] I shall often quote Plato at length. Those who know their Plato may find this unnecessary, and can frequently skip the quotes. I give them so that those who are not so familiar with Plato do not need to go and dig them out.

[2] The most extended attempt to sort out the matter is in Harte (2002). She summarizes her take of Plato's considered view of the matter as follows (p. 268f):

> What emerges from ... [Plato's discussions] is a conception of wholes as contentful structures. Structure, according to this conception, is essential to the constitution of wholes. Indeed, wholes ... are here best thought of as being (instances) of structures and not as things that 'have' structure in a way that makes structure more or less detachable from the whole and its parts. In Plato's conception of wholes, structure is no less essential to the parts of such a whole than to the whole itself. The parts of such a whole are structure-laden; that is, the identity of the parts is determined only in the context of the whole they compose.

The view has some commonality with Aristotle's view: unity is provided by structure. But there is no connection of structure with form. Nor, in Aristotle, is there, in general, a suggestion that the identity of a part is dependent on the whole in which it finds itself: a brick is a brick, whether or not it is part of a house. Though he does suggest that this is true in certain cases, such as organic unities: a hand is not really a hand when it is cut off. (*Gen. Anim.*, 726^{b}22–24, *Met.* 1035^{b}24–25). The general

80   IN PLATO'S TRAJECTORY

its appearances. The one that will concern us in this chapter is a certain appearance in the *Sophist*. Considering it will take us into an extended discussion of matters mereological.

We start, however, not with Plato, but with Parmenides.

6.2 All Wholes and No Parts

In Section 1.6 we noted that one way of avoiding the need for (improper) gluons is by taking all objects to be partless unities. As we also noted there, an extreme form of the view takes there to be just *one* thing. Parmenides referred to it as 'what is'; Bradley called it 'the Absolute'. We might just call it 'the One'. Call it what you like; everything else must be relegated to the realm of appearances, as both Parmenides and Bradley did.[3] The view certainly appears an extreme one. In fact, however, one is easily driven to it once one goes down the partless route. For if **everything**, the totality of all that is, contains more than one unity, these would be distinguishable parts of it.

From the present perspective, the view cannot be right. For many things, including **everything**, have parts. In this chapter we will examine the view carefully. Even though it is wrong, we will see that considering the matter exposes important new considerations. We will start by looking at Parmenides' own case for his view; then we will look at Plato's critique of it. What will emerge in the process are crucial questions concerning the relationship between an object and its parts. These are addressed in the second part of the chapter.

6.3 The Way of Truth

Parmenides' arguments for his view are to be found in the poem he wrote, *On Nature*. The work no longer survives, but many parts of it were quoted by later writers, enough that we can, fortunately, reconstruct large parts of it, including the relevant ones. After a prologue, there is a part, 'The Way of Truth', telling us how things are; then there is a second part, 'The Way of Opinion', telling us how things are taken to be, but are not. It is the arguments in 'The Way of Truth' that concern us.

---

dependence of the identity of a part on the whole in Harte's take on Plato is more like the Huayan view of matters, which we will meet in due course.

[3] This, at any rate, is the orthodox view of Parmenides. There are dissenting voices, such as Curd (2004).

In the prologue of his poem, Parmenides announces his project as follows:[4]

> But come, I will tell you—preserve the account when you hear it—
> the only roads of enquiry there are to be thought of:
> one, that it is and cannot not be,
> is the path of persuasion (for truth accompanies it);
> another, that it is not and must not be—
> this I say to you is a trail devoid of all knowledge.
> For you could not recognize that which is not (for it is not to be done).
> nor could you mention it. For the same things can be thought of and can be.

Parmenides, then, will tell us about *what is*. He claims that *what is* is exactly the same as what can be thought/talked about. What to make of this claim depends on how one interprets 'is'. If it means to exist (have being in that sense), then the claim is just false, since many things that do not exist can be thought about. However, as I noted in Section 4.2, one may take 'is' to mean 'is an object', that is, 'has some property'. In that case, Parmenides' claim is much more plausible. For if something has (abundant) properties, it can be talked about—for example, one can say that it has those properties. And if one can talk about something, it has (abundant) properties—for example, whatever it is that one can say about it. Which of these two senses does Parmenides have in mind? Probably both. In fact, he, in common with many Greek philosophers, probably did not draw the crucial distinction.[5]

Soon after announcing his inquiry, Parmenides articulates its fundamental principle, a proto-statement of the Principle of Non-Contradiction:[6]

> Never will this prevail, that what is not is;
> restrain your thought from this road of inquiry
> and do not let custom, based on experience, force you along this road,
> directing unobservant eye and echoing ear
> and tongue; but judge by reason the battle-hardened proof
> which I have spoken.

This is perhaps the first statement of something like the Principle of Non-Contradiction in Western philosophy. It should go without saying that gluon theory is not going to accept it. And Parmenides gives us no reason to do so. There appears to be no defence of the Principle in Greek philosophy before Aristotle's badly flawed defence of it in *Metaphysics* Γ[7]—or in subsequent Western philosophy.

---

[4] The reconstructed poem is from Barnes (1987), pp. 132ff.

[5] See, further, White (1993), pp. xxiiff., and Kahn (2003), pp. vii–xl.

[6] Or at least an instance of it. That depends on how one interprets the verb 'to be', which is multiply ambiguous in Ancient Greek. (See Section 9.5.) I suspect that most Greek philosophers were oblivious to the distinctions, at least until Plato. It is he who starts to untangle matters in the *Sophist*, as we shall see in Chapter 9.

[7] On which, see Priest (2006), ch. 1.

After enunciating the principle, Parmenides then proceeds to tell us how *what is* is, as follows:

> Only one story, one road, now
> is left: that it is. And on this there are signs
> in plenty that, being, it is ungenerated and indestructible,
> whole, of one kind and unwavering, and complete.
> Nor was it, nor will it be, since now it is, all together,
> one, continuous.

He states nine properties of *what is*. Let me enumerate them. *What is* is: [1] ungenerated; [2] indestructible; [3] whole; [4] of one kind; [5] unwavering (changeless); [6] complete; [7] not in the past; [8] not in the future; [9] continuous.

The next lines of the poem argue for [1] and [2], as follows:

> For what generation will you seek for it?
> How, whence, did it grow? That it came from what is not,
>   I shall not allow
> you to say or think—for it is not sayable or thinkable
> that it is not. And what need would have impelled it,
> later or earlier, to grow—if it began from nothing?
> Thus, it must altogether be or not be.
> Nor from what is will the strength of trust permit it
> to come to be anything apart from itself. For that reason
> Justice has not relaxed her fetters and let it come into being
>   or perish
> but she holds it. Decision in these matters lies in this:
> it is or it is not. But it has been decided, as is necessary
> to leave that road unthought and unnamed (for it is not a true
> road), and to take the other as being and being genuine.
> How might what is then perish? How might it come into being?
> For if it came into being it is not, nor is it if it is ever going to be.
> Thus generation is quenched and perishing unheard of.

The main argument here would appear to be the following. Suppose that *what is* had come to be. Then before it was, there was only *what is not*. But if there was *what is not*, this would have to be, which it does not, by the Principle of Non-Contradiction. Symmetrically, if *what is* ceased to be, then after this there would again be only *what is not*, which is contradictory for the same reason.

Now, the argument is, in fact, fallacious. If there was, indeed, a time before *what is* came into being, then before that time there was **nothing**. And **nothing**, as we noted in Section 4.5, both is (something) and is not (something). Parmenides was right about this, then: if there was a state of affairs before *what is* came into being, it was a contradictory one. The Principle of Non-Contradiction notwithstanding, that is exactly what it should be.[8]

6.4 The Partlessness of Being

Next in the poem, we have a brief argument for [3], that *what is* is a whole; that is, that it has no parts. Let us come back to the argument in a second. I note, first, that all the subsequent properties enumerated are really corollaries of this. For if *what is* were constituted by different kinds of things it would have distinguishable parts [4]. If it wavered, it would change over time, and hence have different temporal parts [5]. If it were not complete, it would be missing a part, and so have parts [6]. If it was or will be, then it is extended over time, and so, again, has temporal parts [7], [8]. And if it had discontinuities, it would obviously have parts either side of the discontinuity [9]. So the rest of the argument can just mop up:

> Hence it is all continuous; for what is approaches what is.
> And unmoving in the limits of great chains it is beginningless
> and ceaseless, since generation and destruction
> have wandered far away, and true trust has thrust them off.
> The same and remaining in the same state, it lies by itself,
> and thus remains fixed there. For powerful necessity
> holds it enchained in a limit which hems it round,
> because it is right that what is should be not incomplete.
> For it is not lacking—if it were it would lack everything.

There are some more lines, but nothing new that need concern us here, except a striking phrase that Parmenides uses to describe *what is*, and which I note for future reference.

> And since there is a last limit, it is completed
> on all sides, like the bulk of a well-rounded ball,
> equal in every way from the middle.

If it is indeed like a ball, then it has parts, since it is extended is space. But no doubt Parmenides would say that this is just a metaphor (for homogeneity?), and claim poetic licence at this point.

---

[8] There is also a subsidiary argument in the text. Suppose that there was a time when there was just **nothing**. Nothing comes from **nothing**. So, what is could never have come into existence. The principle that nothing comes from **nothing** is a plausible one, though moot in the light of the fact that things can come into existence spontaneously in a quantum vacuum.

So let us go back to the crucial argument that *what is* has no parts. This goes as follows:

> Nor is it divided, since it all alike is—
> neither more here (which would prevent it from cohering)
> nor less; but it is all full of what is.

The argument is opaque; the best I can make of it is the following. Suppose that *what is* had parts, say p_1 and p_2. Then since they are distinct parts, p_1 would be something that p_2 is not (at the very least, p_1). But then, p_2 is not, which is impossible, by the Principle of Non-Contradiction, since p_2 is. Once we have distinguished between being (*Sein*) and being something (*Sosein*), the argument—whatever one thinks about the Principle of Non-Contradiction—appears invalid. The fact that p_2 is not something does not entail that it is not, *simpliciter*; that is, that it does not exist.

If there is a more plausible interpretation of Parmenides' argument, I do not know it.[9]

6.5 Plato on Parmenides

Plato, of course, rejected Parmenidean monism. Indeed, in the *Sophist*, 244d–245e, he mounts an explicit attack on the view. We will meet the *Sophist* properly in Chapter 9. For the moment, let us just look at the attack on Parmenides. We pick up the discussion just after Parmenides' view has been tabled. There is just one real thing: a partless whole, *what is*. The attack on the view is undertaken by an Eleatic stranger (E); the foil is Theaetetus (T).

Plato has a bit of fun with the thought that if there is only one thing, it can have only one name, and, in fact, it must be its own name. We then get to the argument relevant to our present concerns. The argument is a tangled one. I will do my best to make sense of it. I provide in footnotes an alternative translation by White

---

[9] Bradley's arguments for his monism are quite different. The claim that no object has parts is taken to follow from the "Bradley regress". The regress is supposed to demonstrate that a bunch of parts can never constitute a unity. Given gluon theory, this argument fails, since the regress is broken. Why, however, does he suppose that there cannot be a plurality of partless wholes? Because, if there were, there would have to be relations between them (such as difference). And all relations are, for Bradley, unreal. The arguments against the reality of relations are developed in chapters 2 and 3 of *Appearance and Reality*. (For a review of the matter, see Candlish (2009), section 6.) At root, the argument is this. It is the nature of relations to relate. But R cannot relate a to b, say, unless there is something that relates R to a, and so on, and we are off on a (vicious) regress. Nothing ultimately relates, and so there are no relations. This argument is not successful either. If aRb, there is certainly a relationship between a and R, and so on. But this is not a vicious regress, any more than the instantiation regress is. (See Section 3.6.) Bradley's argument gets its force by an illicit assimilation of relating to unifying. But a relation between two objects does not need to unify them in any way. Sydney is north of Melbourne. But if Sydney and Melbourne are joined by anything, it is the road between them, not this relation.

(1993) of some of the crucial speeches, for comparison. The following diagram may help to keep track of the overall analysis, where Ω is *what is*. E presents us with a series of options, all of which turn out to be unacceptable. So we have a three-pronged *reductio ad contradictionem*. The letters correspond to Cornford's annotations in the text:

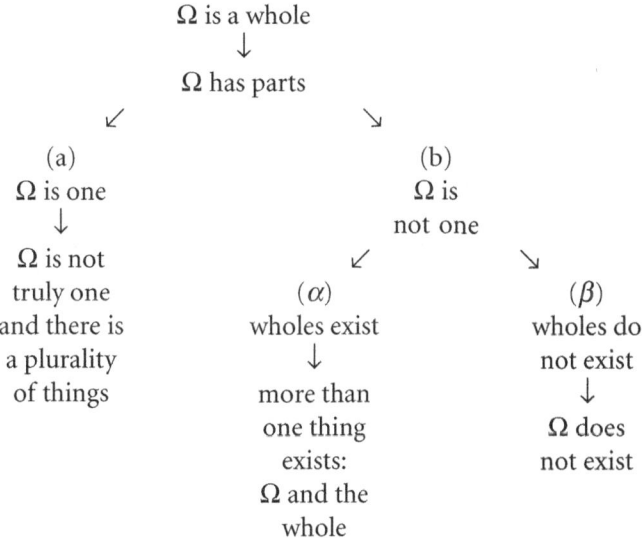

To the text. E starts by asking whether what is, is a whole:

E: And what of 'this whole'? Will they [Parmenideans] say that this is other than their 'one real thing' or the same?
T: Certainly that it is the same. In fact they do say so.

Indeed they do. This was property [3] of Parmenides' poem. So what, exactly, of this whole?

E: Then if it is a whole—as indeed Parmenides says, 'Every way like the mass of a well-rounded sphere, evenly balanced from the midst in every direction, for there must not be something more nor something less here then there'—if the real is like that, it has a middle and extremities, and consequently must have parts.
T: It must.

This is unfair to Parmenides. *What is* is a whole for him precisely in the sense that it does *not* have parts. True, he uses the metaphor of the ball; but, as we have already observed, he may just claim poetic licence for this. In fact, then, the argument collapses here; what follows is beside the point for Parmenides. But for reasons that will become clear, let us try to disentangle the rest of the argument.

E now draws a crucial distinction between two senses of being one, and claims that a whole can be one in only one of these senses:

> E: Well, if a thing is divided into parts, there is nothing against it having the property of unity as applied to the aggregate of all the parts and being in that way one, as being a sum or whole.[10]
> T: Of course.
> E: On the other hand, the thing which has these properties cannot be just unity itself, can it?[11]
> T: Why not?
> E: Surely, unity in the true sense and rightly defined must be altogether without parts.
> T: Yes, it must.
> E: Whereas a thing such as we described, consisting of several parts, will not answer that definition.
> T: I see.

A whole with parts can be one thing, in the sense that it is the sum of all its parts. But it cannot be a true unity. 'Unity itself' and 'the one' are often code in Plato for the form of unity. But it hardly seems apt to bring the theory of forms into this discussion. 'True unity' seems to make better sense of the argument.

Having established this, E now presents T with a dilemma. Is *what is* one in this sense (a true unity) or not? (This is not quite how the second alternative is phrased, but it is what the logic of the argument requires, and it is how it is glossed in the part of the argument concerning this alternative. Literally, what is said would contradict the agreed fact that *what is* is a whole.[12])

> E: Then, (a) is the real one and a whole in the sense that it has the property of unity, or (b) are we to say that the real is not a whole at all?[13]
> T: That is a hard choice.

So it is. Both possibilities lead to problems. In the first case, in the only sense in which it can be a unity, since it is not a true unity, there is still a plurality of things.

---

[10] But if a thing has parts then nothing keeps it from having the characteristic of being one in all its parts, and in that way it is all *being* and it is also *one whole*.

[11] But something with that characteristic cannot be just *the one* itself, can it?

[12] Harte (2002), p. 103, takes this as a sign that the monist has now reneged on the original agreement that what is is a whole. However, if that is right then the argument of option (β) fails, since this uses exactly this premise.

[13] Now, if *that which is* has the characteristic of *the one* in this way, will it be one and a whole? Or shall we simply deny that it is a whole at all?

E: Quite true. For if (a) the real has the property of being in a sense one, it will evidently not be the same thing as a unity, and so all things will be more than one.[14]

T: Yes.

In the second case, *what is* is not a unity in any sense. This case itself then divides, according to whether wholes are real or are not. In the first of these cases, *what is* is just one part of the whole, so it will not exhaust everything, some of the whole will not exist, and in any case, there will be at least two things: *what is*, and the whole.

E: And again (b) if the real is not a whole by virtue of having the property of unity, while (a) at the same time wholeness itself is real, it follows that the real falls short of itself.[15]

T: Certainly.

E: So, on this line of argument too, the real will be deprived of reality and will not be a thing that is.[16]

T: Yes.

E: And further, once more all things will be more than one, since reality on the one side and wholeness on the other have now each a distinct nature.[17]

And if, on the other hand, wholes do not exist, then *what is* does not exist, since *what is* is the whole (nor could it even come to exist).

T: Yes.

E: But if, (β) on the one hand, there is no such thing as wholeness at all, not only are the same things true of the real, but also that, besides not being a thing that really is, it could never even become such.[18]

T: Why not?

E: Whenever a thing comes into being, at that moment it has come to be as a whole; accordingly, if you do not reckon unity or wholeness among the real things, you have no right to speak of either being or coming-into-being as having any existence.

---

[14] You are right. If it has the characteristic of somehow being one, it will not appear to be the same as *the one*. Moreover, everything will be more than one.

[15] Further, if *that which is* is not a whole by possessing that as a characteristic, but rather just is the whole itself, *that which is* will turn out to be less than itself.

[16] And because it is deprived of itself, *that which is* will be *not being*, according to this account.

[17] And everything will be more than one, since *that which is* and *the whole* will each have its own separate nature.

[18] But if the whole is not at all, then the very same things are true of *that which is*, and in addition to not being, it would not even become a being.

88 IN PLATO'S TRAJECTORY

T: That seems perfectly true.

All the possibilities have ended in a refutation of Parmenides' monism. One might certainly jib at some of the steps in the three limbs of the refutation, though we need not go into this here; the failure at the first step is enough.

6.6 Refocusing the Argument

The argument, then, fails. But, one might wonder, what happens if one applies the argument not to Parmenides' *what is*, but to any one thing. Most one things do have parts, so we are immediately over the initial hurdle at which the attack on Parmenides fails. Go back to the diagram of the argument, and let Ω be any unity with parts. What follows? The one thing is certainly one. So we may disregard the right-hand side of the diagram (option (b)). The left-hand side (option (a)) is a different matter. Part of its conclusion is that there is a plurality of things. That was what was meant to target Parmenides, but it is not a problem for us. The other part, however, concludes that Ω is not a true unity. That cannot be right. Any one object is as much one as any object can be. The crucial step in the argument is, in fact, where Plato makes his distinction between two senses of being one. The distinction itself obviously presupposes (without argument) one between an object and the sum of its parts. But does this distinction, in fact, hold water?[19]

We must investigate the relationship between an object and the mereological sum of its parts. Before we do that, let us look at the two notions involved more closely: parthood and mereological sums.

6.7 Parthood

Many things have parts. Cars have wheels and engine blocks; people have hands and feet; countries have states or counties. Mereology is the investigation of the part/whole relation. In normal parlance, we would not normally think of the

---

[19] It is not just Plato who takes an object to be different from the mereological sum of its parts. So do the Neo-Aristotelians Fine (1999) and Koslicki (2008). Fine's major argument (which is also taken over by Koslicki (IV.2) as her main argument) is that a ham sandwich cannot be the mereological sum of its parts (even if one takes one of these to be the universal *sandwich*) simply because the mereological sum exists before the sandwich does. The most obvious reply is that the relationship between the sandwich and the sum is the same as the relationship, discussed in Section 5.5, between the lump of clay and the statue. Let h be the ham sandwich, and σ be the mereological sum. Before the construction of the sandwich, σ exists and h does not; hence, $h \neq \sigma$. After, $h = \sigma$. (And any part of σ is a part of h only when h exists.) Alternatively, one might hold that before the parts came into the appropriate configuration, the mereological sum did not, in fact, exist. It was simply an object of thought. It became an existent object at the same time as the sandwich (and its gluon) did.

whole as a part of itself. But it does not harm to think of it as so—as a limiting case. Parts in the usual sense are *proper* parts. Let us write '*x* is a proper part of *y*' as $x < y$. We can define $x \leq y$, '*x* is a part (proper or improper) of *y*', naturally, as: $x < y \vee x = y$.

Even when gluons are not in the picture, the properties of the parthood relation are somewhat contentious.[20] However, it is standardly assumed that $<$ is at least anti-symmetric and transitive. That is:

- if $x < y$ then it is not the case that $y < x$
- if $x < y$ and $y < z$ then $x < z$

Transitivity is not obvious, even in a normal case. Suppose that I am a part of the band, and that my spleen is part of me. It is not clear that one would want to say that my spleen is part of the band. One may think of the parts of an object as falling under some sortal kind—such as *person*—(which is quite compatible with gluon theory), in which case the sortal may change for different cases of $<$. There is always a way to turn a relation, R, into a transitive relation, however: merely take its transitive closure, R^c. So, xR^cy iff for some set $\{z_1, \ldots z_n\}$, possibly empty, $xRz_1Rz_2 \ldots Rz_nRy$. $<^c$ is transitive, and clearly expresses something which might plausibly be called parthood. We may suppose that it is the notion of parthood with which mereology concerns itself. (Whether it is the notion of parthood with which gluon theory concerns itself is another matter; but my policy in the book is to be as neutral as possible on that question.)

Anti-symmetry has to be given up on gluon theory, however. Take some object, *y*, with parts and a prime gluon, *g*. Suppose, as may well be the case, that *g* is a part of *x* which is itself a part of *y*. (For example, *x* might be the mereological sum of *g* and some other independent part of *x*.) Then we have the following:

(*) $g < x < y$

Since *g* is prime, *g* has every property that every part of *y* has. But $g < x$ and *x* is a part of *y*; so $g < g$.

Odd though it may sound at first that $g < g$, one should remember some analogies. In set theory, a proper subset of a set can be as big as the set itself. Closer to home, there is the possibility of non-well-founded sets.[21] For such sets, one can have a set, *x*, of the form, say, $\{x, \emptyset\}$. Given that the parts of a set include its members (as I shall suggest in Section 9.2), we have exactly a proper part which is identical with the whole.

---

[20] For a survey of matters mereological, see Varzi (2009).
[21] As demonstrated, for example, in Aczel (1988).

90 IN PLATO'S TRAJECTORY

At any rate, what we see is that a mereology appropriate for gluon theory will be one where parthood is non-well-founded. In particular, it must allow for cycles (so that < is only a preorder).[22] This is certainly non-standard, but we do not need to work out the details for present purposes.[23]

6.8 Mereological Sums

Let us now turn to mereological summation, or *fusion*. Given two objects, a and b, we may consider their mereological sum, or fusion, $a \oplus b$. Thus, if a is the Western half of the Australian land mass, and b is its Eastern half, then $a \oplus b$ is the whole Australian land mass. More generally, if we have a set of objects, Σ, then we can consider the sum of all its members, $\oplus\Sigma$. Thus, if $\Sigma = \{WA, SA, NSW, VIC, QLD, TAS\}$ (the land masses of the six states of Australia), then the mereological sum of Σ, $\oplus\Sigma$, is again the whole Australian land mass—well, not quite, it is missing the Northern Territory and the Australian Capital Territory, but near enough.

The formal definition of fusion employs the notion of *overlap*. Two things overlap if they have a part in common. Writing ∘ for overlap, we may define $x \circ y$ as: $\mathfrak{S}z(z \leq x \wedge z \leq y)$. Clearly, every object overlaps itself and all of its proper parts. The fusion of a set of objects, Σ, can be characterized as an object which is such that something overlaps it iff it overlaps one of the members of Σ.

The *Principle of Composition* then tells us that for appropriate Σ, the members of Σ have a fusion:

(1) $\mathfrak{S}y\mathfrak{A}x(x \circ y \leftrightarrow \mathfrak{S}z \in \Sigma\ x \circ z)$

If we define $\oplus\Sigma$ as $\varepsilon y\mathfrak{A}x(x \circ y \leftrightarrow \mathfrak{S}z \in \Sigma\ x \circ z)$, then by the properties of descriptions, we have:

(2) $\mathfrak{A}x(x \circ \oplus\Sigma \leftrightarrow \mathfrak{S}z \in \Sigma\ x \circ z)$

Mereological identity conditions can be given in various ways. A simple approach in the present context is as follows. If two objects are distinct, it is natural to assume that some object overlaps at least one of them but not the other. In other words, two objects are the same if everything that overlaps one, overlaps the

---

[22] There are models of classical mereology that are "gunky"; that is, in which all parts have parts; but < is still a partial order, so it has no cycles.
[23] See Cotnoir and Bacon (2012) for a discussion of the shape of a non-well-founded mereology which may have cycles, together with rationales for such a theory which have nothing to do with gluons.

other: $\mathfrak{A}x((x \circ y \leftrightarrow x \circ z) \to y = z)$. From this it follows immediately that the mereological sum of any set with one is unique.

I said that every appropriate set has a fusion. But what does 'appropriate' mean here? For a start, there is near-univeral consensus that Σ must be non-empty. For parts to fuse, there must be some of them. I have already suggested (in Section 4.5) that we may take **nothing** to be the fusion of the empty set. **Nothing** will play an important role in the third part of the book, and so I want to put this idea on a firm footing. However, to do so right here would take us off at something of a tangent to the main discussion. Hence I defer it to an an interlude between this chapter and the next, Section 6.13. For the nonce, I will go with orthodoxy, and set the fusion of the empty set aside.

Beyond that general consensus about the empty set, there is a debate in standard mereology between those who think that any non-empty collection of objects has a sum (unrestricted, or general, composition), and those who think that not all do (restricted, or special, composition).[24] There must be some kind of coherence between objects for them to fuse. If $\Delta = $ {the Buddha's left ear-lobe, the rings of Saturn, the Empire State Building}, then Δ hardly seems to fuse into a coherent whole.

Who is right? From a noneist perspective, both sides can be right!—in a way. Like all noun phrases, '$\oplus \Sigma$' ('the whole constituted by fusing exactly the members of Σ') refers to something—at least if the set Σ is definable (that is, specifiable with a noun phrase). After all, we can think about it, consider whether or not it exists, and so on. In other words, for any non-empty set, Σ, $\mathfrak{S}z\, z = \oplus \Sigma$. There is no guarantee that it does what one might think it does, though: that it has exactly the parts in Σ: $\mathfrak{A}x(x \circ \oplus \Sigma \leftrightarrow \mathfrak{S}z \in \Sigma\ x \circ z)$. For that we need the truth of (1), and there is no guarantee that this holds. When Σ is Δ, this seems somewhat implausible.

It is frequently objected to noneism that it has a "bloated ontology". In more prosaic (and less inflammatory) terms, it requires us to accept more objects to exist, or subsist, than is required by necessity. One issue here is what, exactly, necessity requires, and in particular whether there is a workable account of intentionality without non-existent objects. However, the objection is not a very good one anyway. Objects that do not exist, do not exist; they are not; they are not part of one's ontology. (Recall the Greek meaning of the root: *ontos* = being.) They have, as Meinong put it, *Nichtsein*, non-being. I suspect that the objection gets its pull from confusing Meinong (and noneism), with the pre-'On Denoting' views of

---

[24] Lewis (1991) is a general compositionalist. Van Inwagen (1981) is a special compositionalist. An extreme example of the special compositionalist is the mereological nihilist, such as Unger (1979), who holds that no sets fuse.

Russell, who did give all objects some kind of being: subsistence, if not existence. Be that as it may, it is frequently objected to general compositionalists that they, too, have a "bloated ontology" of strange objects such as $\oplus \Delta$. The reply is the same. Such objects are purely objects of thought. They have no being, and so are not part of an ontology.

In sum then, for any non-empty (definable) set, Σ, there is an object $\oplus \Sigma$. This has exactly the parts which are members of Σ, but maybe not at the actual world. It has them at some worlds—maybe impossible worlds. For these to include the actual world, (1) has to hold there. This does not answer the question as to which Σs it does hold for. The natural idea is that it will hold if the members of Σ are not a disparate collection, that is, it does not have some members which fail to "cohere" with others. How to flesh out this idea is not at all obvious. However, we do not need to settle the matter here.[25] An intuitive understanding will, for the most part, suffice.

6.9 An Object and the Sum of its Parts

We can come at last to Plato's distinction. Let s be an object with proper parts, and let $\Sigma = \{x : x < s\}$. Suppose that $\oplus \Sigma$ does behave in the expected way (that is, it satisfies its characterization). What is one to say of the relationship between $\oplus \Sigma$ and s? Are they two objects, or just one? The natural answer, contra Plato, is that they are one. Certainly, Ockam's razor provides this counsel *ceteris paribus*: $s = \oplus \{x : x < s\}$.

Why might one think to distinguish between s and the fusion? There are two obvious reasons. The first is that different objects can be the same mereological sum of parts; the second is that one and the same object can be different mereological sums of parts. Let us consider these matters in turn.

First reason. Suppose, to illustrate the objection, I have a bunch of Lego bricks. I assemble them into a (model of a) house, h. I then disassemble them and reassemble them into a (model of a) boat, b. The totality of parts (including the gluon), and hence the mereological sum, σ, has not changed; but h and b are distinct objects. If an object were the sum of its parts, we would have $h = b$, since $h = \sigma = b$. (This is an instance of SI, but a quite legitimate one if σ is an ordinary consistent object. See Section 2.5.)[26]

Given that time is involved, there is an obvious reply. Let the time at which the house exists be t_1, and the time at which the boat exists be t_2. Then at t_1, $\sigma = h$;

---

[25] Some interesting possibilities are discussed in Hudson (2006).
[26] There is a modal analogue of the example, where the parts are built into h at one world, and b at another. What one may say about this is analogous.

and at t_2, $\sigma = b$. We can no longer infer, at either time, that $h = b$. Thus, σ exists at both times; it simply changes it properties between the times.

There are, however, similar cases where time is not involved. Thus, two different words may have exactly the same letters (types in both cases), and so parts (for example, 'god', and 'dog'). In this case, the natural thing to say is that there are more parts to each word than the letters: the universal that is their arrangement is also a part.[27] One can, of course, make the same move in the tensed case as well.

Second reason. An object can survive the addition or removal of parts. Thus, a car is the same, even if a hub cap falls off. And you are the same person, even if you put on a kilo or two. A mereological whole is a different whole if parts are added or subtracted.[28] One might insist that the car is literally a different (though very similar) object at the two times.[29] I think there is a better way to go. Let the car be c. Let t_1 be the time before the hub cap falls off, and let σ_1 be the mereological whole of the parts at t_1. Let t_2 be the time after the hub cap falls off, and let σ_2 be the mereological whole of the parts at t_2. Then at t_1, $c = \sigma_1$; and at t_2, $c = \sigma_2$. We cannot infer that $\sigma_1 = \sigma_2$ at either time.

As with the first objection, there are similar examples where time is not involved, however. It is not uncommon for operatic composers to rewrite an opera, by adding or deleting an aria. So it would appear to be the case that one and the same opera (*qua* abstract object), can have different parts. I think that in such cases, the correct thing to say is exactly that there really are two operas (the abstract objects), which are just very similar in important ways.

What we see, then, is that the most obvious objections to the claim that a partite object is the sum of its parts fail. Possibly there are others, but I know of no such things. And absent these, we should assume that such an object is this mereological sum.

Since the issue of an object changing parts has arisen in the course of our discussion, let me finish with one final matter. When an objects changes its parts, what happens to its gluon? Does it remain the same gluon, or is the later gluon a different object? Perhaps the most natural answer is that the gluon remains the same object; it just changes its properties. After all, all objects can change their properties over time. Why not gluons? It would be odd, at the very least, to suppose that what unified something were different things at different times. In some sense, this would appear to void any diachronic unity.[30] Suppose, then,

---

[27] We will employ this strategy to handle the case of propositions in Section 9.2.

[28] And again there is an analogous modal example, and replies.

[29] Abelard takes this line. See Arlig (2007). This view is consistent with gluon theory, though I rejected it in the case of people in Section 5.5. I will return to the general matter, *en passant*, in Section 11.8.

[30] I reserve a fuller discussion of diachronic unity for Chapter 11.

that we have an object, c, with gluon g, and different parts, Σ_1 and Σ_2, at times t_1 and t_2. At t_1, g is every member of Σ_1, and at t_2, g is every member of Σ_2. (Note, then, that given the account of universals in Section 3.5, a universal is numerically identical across worlds/times.)

6.10 Plural Reference

We are not quite done yet. There is another way in which one might hear Plato's crucial distinction: not between an object and the aggregate of its parts, but between an object (singular) and its parts (plural). If an object—or Ω—is its parts, then it would certainly seem not to be a unity: it is a plurality. In fact, it is sometimes thought that a contradiction follows whether or not an object is its parts. This may be worked into an argument to the much more damaging conclusion that there are no wholes at all. Jones states the argument as follows:[31]

Suppose, for *reductio ad absurdum*, that wholes are real. Then a whole is either numerically identical to or else numerically distinct from its collection of parts. Since numerically identical entities share all of their properties, and since a whole has the property of being a unity, whereas the collection of parts has the property of being a multiplicity, a whole is not identical to its collection of parts. But neither is the whole numerically distinct from this collection. For a whole and its collection of parts occupy the same space at the same time, and numerically distinct entities cannot do this: This is the *Problem of the One over the Many*. Hence, since a whole is neither identical to nor different from its collection of parts, wholes are not real.

What is one to say about this argument and its parts? To address this, we need to get some facts about reference straight.

The machinery of reference allows us to refer to objects by name, *Melbourne*, by descriptions and demonstratives, *that car, the oldest car*, to quantify over them, *some car is such that*, and say things of them, *is in Australia, is an antique*. But language allows us to refer to more than one object—pluralities—by name, *Joan and Mary*, by descriptions and demonstratives, *those cars, the oldest cars*, to quantify over them, *some cars are such that*, and say things of them, *are married to each other, were made at the same time*. Sometimes what is said with plural reference can be said equivalently with singular references. Thus, *his knife and fork were made of plastic* clearly means much the same as *his knife was made of plastic and*

---

[31] Jones (2010), p. 215. (Note, though, that he does not endorse the conclusion.) He takes the argument from Buddhist philosophy, where it is sometimes called 'the argument of neither one nor many'. See Siderits (2007), 6.1. Śāntarakṣita, in particular, makes heavy use of it. See Blumenthal (2008).

his fork was made of plastic. But sometimes this is not the case. *Joan and Mary got married* does not mean the same as *Joan got married and Mary got married*.

Grammar is a good guide to plural reference, but it is by no means infallible. *Trousers* is grammatically plural (*his trousers are too big*), but refers to a single item of clothing, just as much as *jacket* (*his jacket is too big*).[32] And sometimes it is of no help at all. One can say both *the cabinet has already made its decision* and *the cabinet have already made their decision*. How many things does *cabinet* refer to? What phrases are numerically ambiguous. *He took out what was in the cupboard. This was a statue of the Buddha./These were statues of the Buddha.* And of course, some languages (like Japanese) have no lexical mark for singular and plural. So in the end, we have to use our (metaphysical) judgement about whether reference is being made to one object or a plurality of objects.

Note also, that in many cases the same predicate can be applied equally to a singular thing and to plural things. Merely consider the pairs:

- The author of *Hamlet* lived in England
- The authors of *Principia Mathematica* lived in England
- That car is very old
- Those cars are very old
- I hit the old man
- I hit the old men

Prima facie, it would appear that plurals can occur as the objects of intentional verbs, thus: *I am thinking of the authors of PM*. This is odd, since intentionality is normally defined as a mental state that is focused on *an* object. Maybe it can be focused on more than one object? (In this case, Russell and Whitehead.) This seems implausible, though. Consider: *I am thinking of the even numbers*. Surely one cannot have an infinite number of mental foci?

Better, it seems to me, is to suppose that when we have a plural noun in such a context, it refers to one *object*, which is the (unique) focus of the intentional state. We may take this to be the mereological sum of the apparent plurality. So if I am thinking of the authors of *PM*, I am thinking of the sum ⊕{Russell, Whitehead}. It might be thought that this cannot be right for the following reason. Consider: *I am thinking of the authors of PM. They lived in England*. The 'they' in the second sentence appears to refer to a plurality. This, however, could just be a "pronoun of laziness". (*I am thinking of the authors of PM. The authors of PM lived in England.*) But quantifiers give rise to more problems. One can say: *I am thinking of the*

---

[32] See Cotnoir (2010). What follows is at odds with his position, but owes much to his discussion of the matter.

authors of PM. *So I am thinking of something* (sing.) But one can also say: *I am thinking about some people who live in England* (pl.). If I am right, one cannot have:[33]

- $\mathfrak{S}xx(xx$ lived in England, and I am thinking of $xx)$.

We have to have instead:

- $\mathfrak{S}xx(xx$ lived in England, and $\mathfrak{S}y(y = \oplus\{x : x$ is one of the $xx\}$, and I am thinking of $y))$.

We may take it, then, that intentional states are, indeed, directed at a single object.

6.11 An Object and its Parts

In the light of these observations, what is to be made of the two halves of Jones' *reductio*? Take the second first. Let a be some partite physical object, and suppose that a occupies some volume of space(time), V. Let bb be the parts of a. bb also occupy V. Does it follow that there are distinct objects occupying V? No. a is one object, but bb are not an object (unity) at all. So if R is the relationship between a and bb, we have:

- $\mathfrak{S}x\mathfrak{S}yy(xRyy \wedge x$ occupies $V \wedge yy$ occupy $V)$.

(Can one have a relationship between an object and a plurality of objects? Of course; merely consider: The priest married Joan and Mary.) Jones' *reductio* is already broken at this point.

But what is this relationship, R? This takes us to the first argument. Take a and bb again. a is a unity, and bb are a plurality. Does this show that a is not bb? Not necessarily. This depends on how one formulates the Substitutivity of Identicals (SI). Identity between objects is relatively unproblematic, and SI tells us that, for appropriate contexts, A, if $a = b$ then $A_x(a)$ iff $A_x(b)$.[34] The identity relation between pluralities is also relatively unproblematic: $aa = bb$ iff $\mathfrak{A}x(x$ is one of aa iff x is one off bb). And SI for pluralities tells us that, for appropriate contexts, if $aa = bb$ then $A_{xx}(aa)$ iff $A_{xx}(bb)$. Given these forms, one cannot infer that a is a plurality, or that aa is a unity.[35] Again, Jones *reductio* is broken, as is the

---

[33] Here and in what follows the notation for plural reference is that of Linnebo (2008). A double variable, xx, is a plural variable, 'xs'; a double constant, aa, is a plural constant, 'as'.

[34] Setting aside issues of consistency and intensionality, which are not relevant here.

[35] A number of the problematic consequences of endorsing the mixed version of SI (if $a = bb$ then anything is true of a iff it is true of bb) are spelled out in Sider (1993a).

argument we derived from Plato to the effect that Ω—and other objects—are not unities.

Notwithstanding any of this, one does not have to take R to be identity, and it seems to me to be better to say that 'a is bb' is what it appears to be: some sort of category mistake—of the same kind as saying that the number 3 is the colour blue. The categories just do not match up. Both arguments are again, then, broken. This does not mean that a sentence of the form $a = bb$ is meaningless or truth-valueless. $a = bb$ can just be plain false. This still does not give us, note, two things occupying the same place at the same time. We have neither of:

- $\mathfrak{S}x\mathfrak{S}y(x \neq y \wedge x$ occupies $V \wedge y$ occupies $V)$.
- $\mathfrak{S}xx\mathfrak{S}yy(xx \neq yy \wedge xx$ occupies $V \wedge yy$ occupies $V)$.

In this case, what is the relation between an object a, and its parts, bb? Simply that when you put bb together you get a. That is, $a = \oplus\{b: b$ is one of $bb\}$. Call this *constitution* if you wish.[36]

Whatever option one takes, then, both the argument which Jones describes and the Plato-derived argument fail.

6.12 The Bell for the End of Round One

Our considerations have taken us a long way away from the Plato passage with which we started. Let us, finally, return to this. In the passage from the *Sophist* with which we were concerned, Plato takes it that we must distinguish between an object and the mereological sum of its parts, which is not a true unity. As we have seen, Plato was wrong. An appropriate sum can have a unity in the same way that any object can: indeed, it can be the object which is the sum of its parts.

So much for Round One of Plato vs. Parmenides. This is only a warm-up.

6.13 Interlude on Nothing

6.13.1 *The empty fusion*

Because **nothing** will play an important role in the next part of the book, I want, in this interlude, to spell out a very precise understanding of it: as the fusion of the empty set, $\oplus\emptyset$.[37] The motivating idea is a very simple and natural one. **Nothing**

---

[36] Or maybe one might say that it is identity in 'the loose and popular sense'. See Baxter (1988).
[37] This material comes from Priest (2014b).

is what you get when you fuse no things. There is nothing in the empty set, so **nothing** is absolute absence: the absence of all objects, as one would expect.

As an object, $\oplus \emptyset$ is just as as good as $\oplus \Sigma$ for any other Σ. To ensure that it really does satisfy its defining condition, we have to take the empty set to be one of those for which we can apply the schema (1) of Section 6.8. But this does not seem problematic. The members of the empty set are not a disparate collection; it has no members which fail to cohere with others—whatever that means. The members are all as intimately connected as one might wish!

But how best to formulate mereology with the empty fusion? Let us write **n** for $\oplus \emptyset$. As in set-theory, each object now has two improper parts: itself and **n**. $x < y$ still means that x is a proper part of y. We require that:

- $\neg \mathbf{n} < x$
- $\neg x < \mathbf{n}$

Nothing is not a proper part of anything, and itself has no proper parts.

$x \leq y$ is defined exactly as before. It follows that $\mathbf{n} \leq \mathbf{n}$. '$x$ is a part of y (in the most general sense)', $x \leq_n y$, can be defined in the obvious way, as: $x = \mathbf{n} \vee x \leq y$. So for any y, $\mathbf{n} \leq_n y$. The empty fusion, then, is a part of everything.

Overlap is also defined exactly as before: $x \circ y$ is $\mathfrak{S}z(z \leq x \wedge z \leq y)$. It follows that $\mathbf{n} \circ \mathbf{n}$ (since $\mathbf{n} \leq \mathbf{n}$). Note that it would not be appropriate to replace '$\leq$' with '$\leq_n$', since it would then follow that all thing overlap with each other. (In the same way, one does not say that two sets overlap just because the empty set is a subset of each.) Fusion, too, is defined as before: $\mathfrak{A}x(x \circ \oplus \Sigma \leftrightarrow \mathfrak{S}y(y \in \Sigma \wedge x \circ y))$. Note that the definition of $\oplus$ does not involve **n**, so our definition of **n** is not circular.

Now for some fireworks. Since $\neg \mathfrak{S}y\, y \in \emptyset$, it follows from the definition of n that that $\mathfrak{A}x \neg x \circ \mathbf{n}$. Hence, $\neg \mathbf{n} \circ \mathbf{n}$. By definition of $\circ$, $\mathfrak{A}z \neg z \leq \mathbf{n}$, so $\neg \mathbf{n} \leq \mathbf{n}$. By now, it is clear that the theory is inconsistent, but let us continue. Since $\neg \mathbf{n} \leq \mathbf{n}$ it follows that $\neg \mathbf{n} < \mathbf{n} \wedge \mathbf{n} \neq \mathbf{n}$. So $\mathbf{n} \neq \mathbf{n}$. By Fact 2 of 2.8, it follows that $x \neq \mathbf{n}$. Hence $\neg \mathfrak{S}x\, x = \mathbf{n}$. But of course, $\mathfrak{S}x\, x = \mathbf{n}$. (That is a logical truth.) To be an object is to be something. So **nothing** both is and is not an object, as we noted in Section 4.5.

Of course, some will take the fact that we have ended up with contradictions as a sign that the formalization is incorrect.[38] Personally, I do not see it that way. The inconsistency of the theory of **nothing** is exactly what one should expect, given its nature. The approach I have laid out is simple and natural. Its coherence can be

---

[38] And there are certainly consistent formulations of mereology with the empty fusion; for example, that of Bunt (1985). Contradiction is avoided by defining overlap differently. $x \circ y$ is $\mathfrak{S}z(x \neq \mathbf{n} \wedge z \leq_n x \wedge z \leq_n y)$. It then no longer follows that $\mathbf{n} \circ \mathbf{n}$ or that $\neg \mathbf{n} \leq \mathbf{n}$.

demonstrated by a simple model, which I spell out in the next subsection, which can be omitted without prejudice.

6.13.2 A formal model

The model is the four-valued Boolean algebra:

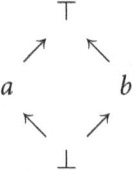

where everything is classical, except that the bottom element is both self-identical and non-self-identical. (It is not hard to see that the construction extends to an arbitrary Boolean algebra.)

I set this up as a first-order interpretation for the paraconsistent logic *LP*. The domain of the interpretation is $\{\top, a, b, \bot\}$. I will use the elements as their own names; and if I say that an open sentence is true in the interpretation, this means that it is true for all values of the variables.

The constant **n** denotes $\bot$. The interpretations of the two predicates are as follows. (+ indicates membership of the extension; −, membership of the anti-extension; and ±, both.)

<	$\top$	a	b	$\bot$
$\top$	−	−	−	−
a	+	−	−	−
b	+	−	−	−
$\bot$	−	−	−	−

=	$\top$	a	b	$\bot$
$\top$	+	−	−	−
a	−	+	−	−
b	−	−	+	−
$\bot$	−	−	−	±

Clearly, $\neg \bot < x$ and $\neg x < \bot$ are both true, and so is $\bot = \bot \land \neg \bot = \bot$.

Computing the extensions of $\leq$ and $\circ$, we obtain the following:

$\leq$	$\top$	a	b	$\bot$
$\top$	+	−	−	−
a	+	+	−	−
b	+	−	+	−
$\bot$	−	−	−	±

$\circ$	$\top$	a	b	$\bot$
$\top$	+	+	+	−
a	+	+	−	−
b	+	−	+	−
$\bot$	−	−	−	±

We can see that $\bot \leq \bot \land \neg \bot \leq \bot$ and $\bot \circ \bot \land \neg \bot \circ \bot$.

The denotations of the fusion terms are specified as follows.

- If $\Sigma \neq \emptyset$ and $\bot \notin \Sigma$, $\oplus\Sigma$ is $Lub(\Sigma)$ (the least upper bound of Σ). [Case 1]
- If $\Sigma \neq \emptyset$ and $\bot \in \Sigma$:

- if $\Sigma = \{\bot\}$, then $\oplus\Sigma$ is $\bot$ [Case 2a]
- otherwise, $\oplus\Sigma$ is arbitrary [Case 2b]
• If $\Sigma = \emptyset$, $\oplus\Sigma$ is $\bot$ (of course) [Case 3]

Since there is no conditional in the language, we cannot verify (2) of Section 6.8 exactly, but we can show that the two sides of the biconditional have exactly the same truth values—which would suffice for the truth of the universally quantified biconditional if one were in the language. There is one exception. There is no value for $\oplus\Sigma$ which can do this in the Case 2b. This is not, then, a model of general composition.

Let us prove these facts. We are concerned with the biconditional: $x \circ \oplus\Sigma \leftrightarrow \mathfrak{S}z \in \Sigma\ x \circ z$.

Consider an instance of Case 1, that where Σ is $\{\top, a\}$. The biconditional comes to this: $x \circ \top \leftrightarrow (x \circ \top \vee x \circ a)$. If x is $\bot$, both sides are just false. Otherwise, both sides are just true. The other instances of this case are the same.

In Case 2a, the biconditional reduces to: $x \circ \bot \leftrightarrow x \circ \bot$. The result in this case is trivial.

Now consider an instance of Case 2b, that where Σ is $\{\bot, a\}$. The biconditional reduces to this: $x \circ s \leftrightarrow (x \circ \bot \vee x \circ a)$. Since $\bot \circ \bot$, and $a \circ a$, $\bot \circ s$ and $a \circ s$. There is no s for which this is true. The other instances of this case are similar.

Finally, and crucially, Case 3. Take the standard definition of the empty set: $\emptyset = \{x : x \neq x\}$. Then the biconditional reduces to: $x \circ \bot \leftrightarrow \mathfrak{S}z(z \neq z \wedge x \circ z)$. If x has any value other than $\bot$, the left-hand side is just false, as is the right-hand side. For the only z that could make the first conjunct true is $\bot$, and this does not make the second conjunct true. If, on the other hand, x is $\bot$, the left-hand side is true and false. The right-hand side is true (take $\bot$ for z). But it is also false; that is, its negation is true, since this is equivalent to $\mathfrak{A}z(z = z \vee \neg x \circ z)$, which is a logical truth.

There is a variation on the model which is worth noting. We change the entry for $\langle \bot, \top \rangle$ for $<$ from $-$ to $\pm$, so that $\bot$ both is and is not a proper part of $\top$. This does the same to the corresponding entries in the tables for $\leq$ and $\circ$. Since the connectives are monotonic, everything true/false before remains so. The arguments that the fusions have the appropriate properties also go through, except in the instance in Case 1 where $\Sigma = \{a, b\}$. ($\bot$ overlaps $\top$, but neither of a and b.) But now, in Case 2b if $\top \in \Sigma$, we can define $\oplus\Sigma$ as $\top$, and the argument goes through. For example, if Σ is $\{\bot, a, \top\}$, the biconditional is $x \circ \top \leftrightarrow (x \circ \bot \vee x \circ a \vee x \circ \top)$. If x is a, b, or $\top$, both sides are true only. If x is $\bot$, both sides are both true and false, as is easily checked. Since, in the present context, $\{\bot, a, b, \top\}$ is the universal set, we can take its fusion to be **everything**.

7

Problems with the Forms—and their Solutions

7.1 The *Parmenides*

The most substantial encounter between Plato and Parmenides is staged by Plato in the dialogue he named after Parmenides. In this chapter and the next we will look at this. The *Parmenides* falls into two clearly distinguishable parts. The first raises a number of problems for the theory of forms. The second is a long and strange series of deductions, of obscure purpose. In this chapter we will look at the first half of the dialogue, and continue the discussion of universals started in Chapter 3. We will see how the gluon theory of universals resolves the problems raised in the dialogue. We will turn to the second part of the dialogue in the next chapter.

A major upshot of these two chapters is a novel interpretation of the *Parmenides*, based on the theory of universals and participation of Chapter 3. As I indicated at the end of Chapter 2, something which speaks firmly in favour of gluon theory is the fact that it can be applied to solve a number of different problems. Some of these we have looked at in previous chapters. How to interpret the *Parmenides* is one of the most outstanding puzzles in Plato scholarship. This is another problem that gluon theory solves. True, it is a problem in the history of philosophy, not in metaphysics as such. But the fact that a theory can solve problems in quite different areas is a well-noted methodological virtue.

7.2 Background

The *Parmenides* is, as nearly all commentators agree, the most difficult and puzzling of all of Plato's dialogues—as well as one of the most influential. Gill, for example, says: 'The *Parmenides* is one of Plato's most important dialogues and without doubt his most enigmatic'.[1]

Many things make it puzzling. For a start, there is the odd fact that although Socrates—Plato's usual mouthpiece—is in the dialogue, he is on the back foot most of the time he is involved, the driver of the dialogue being Parmenides. Next, in the first half of the dialogue, Plato, in the voice of Parmenides, launches an attack on his own theory of forms. It is clear that he regards the objections as serious; but he nowhere answers them explicitly—in the *Parmenides* or elsewhere. Nor does he recant on the theory of forms in any (later) dialogue.[2] For another, the second half of the dialogue is a relentless sequence of arguments quite unlike anything else in the Platonic corpus. The arguments appear to establish that the one (whatever that is) has a variety of contradictory properties. Indeed the dialogue ends abruptly with the simple endorsement of a contradiction (166c):[3]

> "Let us say..., as it seems, whether one is or is not, it and the others both are and are not, and both appear and do not appear all things in all ways, both in relation to themselves and in relation to others."—"Very true."

So much is agreed by all commentators, but, as Rickless puts it:[4]

> Beyond this, there is precious little scholarly consensus. Commentators disagree about the proper way to reconstruct Parmenides' challenges, about the overall logical structure of the Deductions, about the main subject of the Deductions, about the function of the Deductions in relation to the challenges, and about the final philosophical moral of the dialogue as a whole.

The central idea of the interpretation of the *Parmenides* to be offered in this chapter and the next is to take the final conclusion at face value. Plato is indeed suggesting that the one has contradictory properties, and that this is a key to answering Parmenides' arguments.

Such a possibility has never been countenanced before.[5] This is presumably for two reasons. The first is that dialetheism itself is taken to be manifestly untenable. But dialetheism, whatever one thinks about its truth, is a coherent view with many

---

[1] Gill (1996), p. 1; the sentiment is echoed by Miller (1986), p. 1, Scolnicov (2003), p. 1, and Rickless at the beginning of (2007).

[2] For example, it is employed in the *Timaeus*, which most scholars now date later than the *Parmenides*. See, for example, Cherniss (1957).

[3] Translations from the *Parmenides* in this chapter and the next are taken from Gill and Ryan (1996).

[4] In the introduction to Rickless (2007).

[5] With the notable exception of Hegel (and, according to him, some of the Neo-Platonists—notably Proclus). That the one and the many had contradictory properties was all grist to his dialectical mill. See Haldane and Simson (1995), pp. 59ff.

interesting applications.⁶ The second is that it is implausible to attribute to Plato the possibility of countenancing dialetheism. If this is not just an appeal to the first point, together with the claim that Plato was a sensible fellow, the basis for it is, presumably, the fact that Plato himself appears to endorse a version of the Principle of Non-Contradiction (PNC) in the *Republic* (436b):⁷

> It is obvious that the same thing will never do or suffer opposites in the same respect in relation to the same thing and at the same time.

But little weight can be placed on this, since the *Republic* is earlier (according to standard chronologies), and Plato, it appears, is being forced to rethink his views in the light of the problems with the theory of forms which he has discovered.⁸ So even if we take it that Plato endorsed the PNC in the *Republic*,⁹ he may well be arguing against his previous self in the *Parmenides*. Indeed, on standard chronologies, the *Parmenides* marks something of a turning point in Plato's dialectical method. After the *Parmenides*, the earlier method of finding a definition by hypothesis/counter-example/improved hypothesis/counter-example/ and so on, is replaced in the *Sophist* and the *Statesman* with the method of finding a definition by iterated subdivision of categories. It should be remembered, also, that Plato is writing before Aristotle's attack on dialetheism in the *Metaphysics*, the attack which firmly locked the PNC into Western philosophical orthodoxy.

Next on preliminary matters, an important word on the methodology adopted here. Beyond the prophylactic comments of the last paragraph, I shall have little to say about the relationship of the *Parmenides* to the other texts in the Platonic corpus. The *Parmenides*, it seems to me, has a certain integrity; and my aim is to let the text speak for itself.¹⁰

Of course, the relationship between the text and the rest of the Platonic corpus *is* an important scholarly question. Crucially, one may ask, how does the *Parmenides*, on my account, relate to the works generally taken to be later? Does the

---

⁶ See Priest (1987), (1997), (2006).

⁷ There is certainly room to dispute that this is a statement of the PNC, however. (See Robinson (1971), pp. 38–40.) And in any case, it should be noted that, a little later (437a), he calls the Principle an hypothesis, and countenances the possibility that it might turn out to be untenable.

⁸ Quite generally, and for the same reason, the method of citing quotations from earlier dialogues in support of some interpretation of the *Parmenides* is one that must be used with caution. Whilst it can provide some evidence for the sort of thing that Plato may have been sympathetic to, it cannot be definitive.

⁹ One of the problems of the dialogue form is the provisionality of what is said: a view expressed by a character, even Plato's presumed mouthpiece, cannot necessarily be taken to represent his *considered* opinion.

¹⁰ Plato, it would seem, loves to play with ideas. He clearly runs incompatible lines in different dialogues—to take an obvious example: in the *Phaedo* it is crucial that the soul is simple; in the *Republic*, it is crucial that it is not. Arguably, one should understand the integrity of each text before worrying about how they do or do not fit together.

view which I shall attribute to Plato inform these, or was it just something that he tried out, and quietly gave up?[11] I am content to leave such questions to scholars who are much better placed to address them than I.

A few final comments to help orient the reader to what is to come. I shall proceed by giving a commentary on the text. Not until the end of the next chapter will I stand back and look at the whole. The commentary I shall give is not intended to be a scholarly one. I am not qualified for such an undertaking.[12] The point of the commentary is to show how many puzzling features of the text make sense from the perspective of gluon theory—though I make no claim to explain every one of its puzzling features.[13] Indeed, that so many such features fall into place is the fact that speaks most strongly in favour of the interpretation I shall offer. However, I shall make no serious attempt to describe other possible interpretations of the text, nor to argue that the interpretation I suggest is preferable. That would require an inordinately longer and more scholarly work than this.[14]

7.3 The Reply to Zeno (126a–130a)

To the text, then.

After a brief stage-setting, the dialogue starts just after Zeno has finished reading his book. It is established that the content of the book is a defence of Parmenides' view that *what is* is not a multitude. Many had objected to Parmenides' view that it had contradictory consequences. Zeno's tract attempts to 'pay them back in kind' (128d), by showing that the view that there is a multitude of things entails contradictions, such as that these things are like and unlike, one and many, and so on.[15]

Socrates then responds with a crucial speech, which I quote in its entirety (129a–130a):

"But tell me this: don't you acknowledge that there is a form, itself by itself, of likeness, and another form, opposite to this, which is what unlike is. Don't you and I and the other

---

[11] There are also important questions about the interpretation and texts outside the Platonic corpus. If Plato at least played with the idea of contradictory forms, why did not Aristotle mention Plato in his attack on dialetheism in the *Metaphysics*? Was he, perhaps, just as puzzled by the *Parmenides* as the rest of us are?

[12] There are many such commentaries. Gill (1996) is one dependable one.

[13] I wonder whether Plato himself could have done this. Creators of literary works are not always able to explain, themselves, exactly why they put particular features into them.

[14] Rickless (2007) provides an admirable account of various interpretations of the text which have so far been offered, with some attempts to adjudicate.

[15] According to Proclus, Zeno's book contained forty arguments, each one deriving some contradiction from the hypothesis that there is a multitude of things. The only argument that we have left is reported by Simplicius, and is to the effect that if there are many things, each is both limited and unlimited. See Gill (1996), p. 11.

things we call 'many' get a share of those two entities? And don't things that get a share of likeness come to be like in that way and to the extent that they get a share, whereas things that get a share of unlikeness come to be unlike, and that things that get a share of both come to be both? And even if all things get a share of both, though they are opposites, and by partaking of them are both like and unlike themselves, what's astonishing about that?

If someone showed that the likes themselves come to be unlike or the unlikes like—that, I think, would be a marvel; but if he shows that things that partake of both of these have both properties, then there seems to me to be nothing strange about that, Zeno—not even if someone shows that all things are one by partaking of oneness, and these same things are many by partaking also of multitude. But if he should demonstrate this thing itself, what one is, to be many, or conversely, that many to be one—at this I'll be astonished.

And it's the same with all the others: if he could show that the kinds and forms themselves have in themselves opposite properties, that would call for astonishment. But if someone should demonstrate that I am one thing and many, what's astonishing about that? He will say, when he wants to show that I am many, that my right side is different from my left, and likewise with my upper and lower parts—since I take it I do partake of multitude. But when he wants to show that I'm one, he will say that I'm one person among seven of us, because I also partake of oneness. Thus he shows that both are true.

So if—in the case of sticks and stones and such things—someone tries to show that the same thing is many and one, we'll say that he is demonstrating *something* to be many and one, not the one to be many or the many to one—and we'll say that he is saying nothing astonishing, but just what all of us would agree to. But if someone first distinguishes as separate the forms, themselves by themselves, of the things I was talking about a moment ago—for example, likeness and unlikeness, multitude and oneness, rest and motion, and everything of that sort—and then shows that in themselves they can mix together and separate, I for my part," he said, "would be utterly amazed, Zeno. I think these issues have been handled with great vigour in your book; but I would, as I say, be much more impressed if someone were able to display this same difficulty, which you and Parmenides went through in the case of visible things, also similarly entwined in multifarious ways in the forms themselves—in things that are grasped by reason."

Three things are clear about this speech. The first is that the theory of forms is tabled. There are forms, separate from physical objects, and something is F just to the extent that (iff) it partakes in ('gets a share of') the form of F-ness. The second is that Socrates says that it is not at all puzzling that physical objects can partake of contradictory forms. The third we will come to in a moment.

Two reasons—not clearly separated—are given as to why it is unsurprising that physical objects may be F and not-F. One (in the third paragraph), which does not involve the theory of forms, is to the effect that the object may be F in one respect, and not-F in another: I am a multitude of *bodily parts*, but one *person*; or I am *like my mother* but *unlike my father*, and so on. In other words, the property F is under-specified, and once one makes a complete specification, the contradiction disappears. This cannot be all there is to the matter, however. If it were, there would be no need for the theory of forms to be mentioned here at all; nor would there be anything surprising in the fact that the forms themselves could appear to be contradictory in exactly the same way that physical objects are. Presumably, then, Plato must think that there are cases in which the *F* in question is taken to be completely specified. It may be, for example, that an object is one object *of a certain kind*, and many objects *of the same kind*. Or it may be that an object is both at rest and in motion, where these are absolute, not relative to anything. (Of course, we are now used to thinking that motion is relative—to a frame of reference; but this is with two millennia of science after Plato.)

The second reason why it is not surprising that physical objects have contradictory properties (first paragraph) does involve the theory of forms, and is something, I take it, like this. If Px is some predicate, let us write $\overline{P}x$ for its contradictory (opposite). Let us write $\pi x Px$ for the form of *P*-ness, and $\rightarrow$ for 'participates in'. Then, the apparent contradiction:

(0) $Py \wedge \overline{P}y$

is really of the form:

(1) $y \rightarrow \pi x Px \wedge y \rightarrow \pi x \overline{P}x$

which is 'not surprising'—presumably, since this is not a contradiction.

This reason, though, is not a very good one. Plato is committed to the view that what makes something *P* is precisely its participation in the form of *P*-ness:

(2) Py iff $y \rightarrow \pi x Px$

For future reference, call (2) the *Grounding Principle* (since participation in the forms grounds the truth of the predication). Given this, (1) is not a replacement for the contradiction; it is equivalent to it. What we have here is an explanation for the contradiction, not a defusing of it.[16]

If the forms themselves turned out to be contradictory, could a similar explanation be attempted? Perhaps, if forms can themselves partake of forms. But Plato is quite clear that the forms are not contradictory. This is, indeed, the third thing that is clear from the speech: Socrates is adamant that the forms are not contradictory in the same way that physical objects may be. If f is a form, there can be no predicate, Px, completely specifying a property, such that $Pf \wedge \overline{P}f$.

Note that (in the second and fourth paragraphs) Socrates shows special interest in whether or not a form can have its opposite property, whether the like can be unlike, or unity can be many—whether, that is, it can be the case that:

(3) $\overline{P}\pi x Px$

---

[16] Indeed, (0), (2), and contraposition, immediately give that $(y \rightarrow \pi x Px) \wedge \neg(y \rightarrow \pi x Px)$.

Since he clearly takes this to be a contradiction, it must be because he is assuming that the form must have its own property: the like is like, the one is one:

(4) $P\pi xPx$

For future reference, let us call (4) *Self-Predication*. To establish that $\overline{P\pi xPx}$ would, then, be the most direct way of establishing that a form could have contradictory properties. Thus, Socrates appears to be committed to the thought that we always have (4), and never (3).

At any rate, the upshot of all this is that Socrates has laid down a challenge: to show that the forms are contradictory in exactly the way that physical objects are—and it is exactly this which is admitted to have been shown at the end of the dialogue. The forms are indeed contradictory.

7.4 Parmenides' Attack, 1 (130a–131e)

At this point, Parmenides enters the debate. Parmenides gets Socrates to confirm his picture of the forms (130b). Then, after some banter about exactly what forms there are, he launches into an attack on the theory.

The first objection starts as follows (130e–131b):

"But tell me this: is it your view that, as you say, there are certain forms from which these other things, by getting a share of them, derive their names—as, for instance, they come to be like by getting a share of likeness, large by getting a share of largeness, and just and beautiful by getting a share of justice and beauty?"

"It certainly is," Socrates replied.

"So does each thing that gets a share get as its share the form as a whole or part of it? Or could there be some other means of getting a share apart from these two?"

"How could there be?" he said.

"Do you think, then, that the form as a whole—one thing—is in each of the many? Or what do you think?

"What's to prevent it from being one, Parmenides?" said Socrates.

"So, being one and the same, it will be at the same time, as a whole, in things that are many and separate; and thus it would be separate from itself."

Parmenides has offered Socrates a choice: does something that is *F* partake in the whole of *F*-ness or just a part of it? Socrates tentatively accepts the first possibility, and Parmenides then points out that the whole form would then be 'in things that are many and separate'. Socrates objects (131b–131c):

"No it wouldn't," Socrates said. "Not if it's like one and the same day. That is in many places at the same time and is none the less not separate from itself. If it's like that, each of the forms might be, at the same time, one and the same in all."

"Socrates," he said, "how neatly you make one and the same thing be in many places at the same time! It's as if you were to cover many people with a sail, and then say that one thing as a whole is over many. Or isn't that the sort of thing you mean to say?"

"Perhaps," he replied.

"In that case, would the sail be, as a whole, over each person, or would part of it be over one person and another part over another?

"A part."

"So the forms themselves are divisible, Socrates," he said, "and things that partake of them would partake of a part; no longer would a whole form, but only a part of it, be in each thing."

"It does appear in that way."

Socrates has offered a way in which the whole of something might be in different places. Parmenides argues that it is only part of the thing in each place, and so we really have the second of the alternatives that Socrates was offered. Parmenides then goes on to attack this (131c–131e), pointing out a number of supposedly absurd consequences of the possibility that something is F by partaking of part of F-ness; and Socrates is floored. The details of this part of the text need not concern us here.

There is much that could be said about the argument—and much that has been said. One could balk at virtually every one of Parmenides' arguments. But for present purposes, we do not need to dissect the dialectic in detail. The point is to see how, armed with the theory of forms delivered by gluon theory, we may deal with Parmenides' objections.

To address this, let us start by asking what, exactly, a part of a form is. The only natural answer is that the parts of F-ness are a's F-ness, b's F-ness, and so on, where $a, b, \ldots$ are the F-objects. But this is not correct. F-ness itself is, according to our account, the prime gluon of the whole comprising these pins. Given this, it is not at all clear in what sense F-ness might have proper parts, or, therefore, in what sense something can get a share of one. In this case, we are left with the other alternative: an F-object participates in a form by sharing all of it, or just it itself. In a similar way, when we say that 0 is a member of the set $\{0, 1, 2\}$, we are saying that 0 is a member of the whole set. It may be a member of a part ($0 \in \{0, 1\}$), or it may not ($0 \notin \{1, 2\}$). These are different matters.

The problem we face is, then, the one posed by the first horn of Parmenides' dilemma. This was how the form, as a whole, is in 'things that are many and separate' and thus 'separate from itself'. The objection could be interpreted in a number of ways, but the most obvious is simply as an objection to the effect that something cannot be (completely) in more than one place at the same time; that were a contradiction.[17] So be it: the form is a contradictory object.

Note, however, that this is by no means the *ad hoc* acceptance of a contradiction. The contradiction in question is exactly one that the theory of forms at hand delivers. According to this theory, the form of *F*-ness, that gluon, has all the properties possessed by the *F*-ness of any object which is *F*. That is, indeed, how it manages to be identical with it. Now, suppose that I am red. My redness is located where I am; it moves with me; it is not located anywhere else. (Similarly for my shape, my beauty (harumph), and so on: these things are located where I am, and nowhere else.) But suppose that you are red too; then your redness is located where you are, and nowhere else. So redness itself is located where I am, and nowhere else, and where you are, and nowhere else. It is wholly present at both places.

7.5 Parmenides' Attack, 2 (132a–133a)

Parmenides' next argument is a regress argument, later to be dubbed the "Third Man Argument" by Aristotle (for example, *Metaphysics* 990^b17–1079^a13). Parmenides begins as follows (132a–132b):

"I suppose that you think that each form is one on the following ground: whenever some number of things seem to you to be large, perhaps there seems to be some one character, the same as you look at all of them, and from that you conclude that the large is one."

"That's true," he said.

"What about the large itself, and the other large things? If you look at them all in the same way with the mind's eye, again won't some one thing appear large, by which all these appear large?"

"It seems so."

"So another form of largeness will make its appearance, which has emerged alongside largeness itself and the other things that partake of it, and in turn another over all these, by which all of them will be large. Each of your forms will no longer be one, but unlimited in number."

Parmenides argues that there is not a unique form by virtue of participation in which things are large, contradicting the Grounding Principle. Largeness of course, is just an example. It could be any other form. Socrates replies (132b–132c):

[17] One might suggest that the absurdity involved is that if the form can be completely in different objects, then it has parts, and so is not a unity. But it seems clear that a unity can have parts. It is a simplex that cannot have parts. The thought that a form is a simplex has not been tabled at this stage of the dialogue.

"But, Parmenides, maybe each of these forms is a thought," Socrates said, "and properly occurs in minds. In that way each of them might be one and no longer face the difficulties mentioned just now."

"What do you mean?" he asked. "Is each of the thoughts one, but a thought of nothing?"

"No, that's impossible," he said.

"Of something, rather?"

"Yes."

"Of something that is, or of something that is not?"

"Of something that is."

"Isn't it of some one thing, which that thought thinks is over all the instances, being some one character?"

"Yes."

"Then won't this thing that is thought to be one, being the same over all instances, be a form?"

"That, too, appears necessary."

"And what about this?" said Parmenides. "Given your claim that other things partake of these forms, won't you necessarily think either that each thing is composed of thoughts and all things think, or that, although they are thoughts, they are unthinking?"

Socrates' reply appears to miss the point. Parmenides' argument is not affected by whether the form is within the mind or without it.[18] The argument makes no assumptions on this score. But Parmenides ignores this, and attacks the claim that forms are in the mind. Parmenides' reply is itself confused. For a start, Socrates has said that the form is a thought, but Parmenides takes him to be talking of a thought of form. And the final *coup de grâce* is a complete *non-sequitur*.[19] Still, it is enough to force Socrates to recant. Socrates then goes on to proffer the idea that participation in a form is resemblance to it. Parmenides merely has to point out that the regress strikes anyway (132c–133a). The argument makes no substantive assumptions about the nature of instantiation.[20]

Perhaps even more has been written about this argument than about the previous one; and one might, again, question many of the assumptions packed into it. But the crucial question here is whether one can solve the regress problem which Parmenides raises on the model of forms and participation on the agenda here, and if so how.

---

[18] Maybe the idea is that if forms are in the mind then Self-Predication is false (and we are not required to hold that largeness itself is large), since thoughts apply only to things outside the mind. But if this is the idea, it will not get very far. Clearly, thoughts can be of thoughts; and 'the thoughts I have had today' applies to that very thought.

[19] For some way of making sense of the whole passage, see Gill (1996), pp. 38–42.

[20] Some commentators take this part of the text to establish a regress specifically about the form of likeness. This strikes me as an unnatural interpretation.

Consider a bunch of large things, say a, b, and c. According to the theory of forms, each is large by participating in largeness. So we have:

$$a \to \pi x L x \leftarrow c$$
$$\uparrow$$
$$b$$

If the form of largeness could participate in itself, we would have:

$$\curvearrowright$$
$$a \to \pi x L x \leftarrow c$$
$$\uparrow$$
$$b$$

The regress argument assumes, without explicit argument, that this cannot happen, that the arrow of participation cannot be reflexive. So largeness itself (and the other large things) must participate in a different form, and we are off on the regress. If it stopped at some stage, then there would be a "highest" form that all large things participated in. But it does not.

But why does Socrates agree to the irreflexivity assumption? For the answer, look to Parmenides' summary of the theory of forms, to which Socrates agrees, at the start of the first argument (130b):

"Tell me. Have you yourself distinguished as separate, in the way you mention, certain forms themselves, and also as separate the things that partake of them? And do you think that likeness itself is something, separate from the likeness we have? And one and many and all the things you heard Zeno read about a while ago?'

"I do indeed," Socrates answered.

Socrates takes the forms to be *separate* from the things that instantiate them. A form, then, cannot be identical to any of its instances.

On the theory of forms at hand, however, largeness itself may be distinct from all its instances, and so itself; but that does not rule out largeness itself being identical with itself as well, and so identical to one of its own instances! And if largeness is, indeed, one of its own instances, as Self-Predication plus the Grounding Principle tell us, the regress is broken.[21]

Indeed, that the form is both identical to and different from itself is exactly a consequence of the theory of forms at hand. Everything is identical with itself, $x = x$: that is a logical truth—$\mathfrak{A}Z(Zx \equiv Zx)$. But the properties of largeness itself

---

[21] Note that if a form instantiates itself, there are no empty universals. On the present account what does it mean for the form, F, to instantiate itself? It is for it to have a pin, the F-ness of F, which is identical to F. What is the F-ness of F? The most obvious suggestion is F itself, which is certainly identical to F.

are the properties of the largeness of *a*, the largeness of *b*, and so on. Now the largeness of *a* is distinct from the largeness of *b*. Hence largeness itself is distinct from the largeness of *b*; and so again, largeness itself is distinct from largeness itself.[22]

7.6 Parmenides' Attack, 3 (133b–135b)

Parmenides' third attack is, it seems to me, the hardest to understand. It has two parts. In the first, Parmenides argues that the forms cannot be known (by us) (133b–134b):

" . . . I think that you, Socrates, and anyone else who posits that there is for each thing some being, itself by itself, would agree, to begin with, that none of those beings is in us."

"Yes—how could it still be itself by itself?" replied Socrates.

"Very good," said Parmenides. "And so all the characters that are what they are in relation to each other have their being in relation to themselves but not in relation to things that belong to us. And whether one posits these as likenesses or in some other way, it is by partaking of them that we come to be called by their various names.[23] These things that belong to us, although they could have the same names as the forms, are in their turn what they are in relation to themselves but not in relation to the forms; and all the things named in this way are *of* themselves but not *of* the forms."

"What do you mean?" Socrates asked.

What indeed?! Parmenides goes on to explain. The explanation is opaque, so I refrain from attempting to summarize.

"Take an example," said Parmenides. "If one of us is somebody's master or somebody's slave, he is surely not a slave of master itself—of what master is—nor is the master a master of slave itself—of what slave is. On the contrary, being a human being, he is a master or a slave of a human being. Master itself, on the other hand, is what it is of slavery itself. Things in us do not have their power in relation to forms, nor do they have theirs in relation to us; but, I repeat, forms are what they are *of* themselves and in relation to themselves, and things that belong to us are, in the same way, what they are in relation to themselves. You do understand what I mean?"

"Certainly," said Socrates, "I understand."

"So too," he said, "knowledge itself, what knowledge is, would be knowledge of the truth itself, which is what truth is?"

---

[22] See the argument of Section 2.8, *Fact* 1.

[23] Cornford translates these two sentences, somewhat more intelligibly, as 'And further, those forms which are what they are with reference to one another have their beings in such references among themselves, not with reference to those likenesses, or whatever we are to call them, in our world, which we possess and so come to be called by their several names' (Hamilton and Cairns (1961)).

"Certainly."

"Furthermore, each particular knowledge, what it is, would be knowledge of some particular thing, of what that thing is. Isn't that so?"

"Yes."

"But wouldn't knowledge that belongs to us be of the truth that belongs to our world? And wouldn't it follow that each particular knowledge that belongs to us is in turn knowledge of some particular thing in our world?"

"Necessarily."

"But, as you agree, we neither have these forms themselves nor can they belong to us."

"Yes, you are quite right."

"And surely the kinds themselves, what each of them is, are known by the form of knowledge itself."

"Yes."

"The very thing we don't have."

"No, we don't."

"So none of the forms is known by us, because we don't partake of knowledge itself."

"It seems not."

"Then the beautiful itself, what it is, cannot be known by us, nor can the good, nor, indeed, can any of the things we take to be characters in themselves."

"It looks that way."

In the second part of his argument (134b–134e), Parmenides suggests that, for similar reasons, the gods cannot know of us and our affairs. We do not need to worry about the details here, though.

Parmenides' overall point is the following. There are, it has been agreed, two kinds of things, the visibles and the intelligibles; and if a relation holds between two things, both the relation and the relata must be of the same kind.[24] Thus, if we know something, the knowledge must be of a mundane kind, as must the object of our knowledge. And if something knows the forms, both the knower and the relationship must be of the same kind, the relationship being knowledge itself, and the knower being (a) god. There can be no cross-kind relations. Hence we cannot have any kind of knowledge-relation to the forms (and god cannot bear any kind of knowledge-relation to us).

The main problem with this argument is to see why Socrates finds it to be a problem. The claim that there cannot be cross–kind relations seems to be based entirely on generalizing the master/slave example. Of course, the relation between

---

[24] It might be suggested that it is only definitional relations which require this. But that cannot be the argument. For it is applied to our knowledge of the forms, and the gods' knowledge of us. These are not definitional matters.

a master and a slave is between things of the same kind. But it is hardly the case that all relations are like this. Participation relations, such as that between red things and the form of redness clearly seem quite different; and a knowledge-relation between us and the forms is of the same kind.

The key here, perhaps, is the way that Parmenides actually introduces the argument–a paragraph I omitted (133b):

"There are many reasons [why it is difficult to maintain the theory of forms]," Parmenides said, "but the main one is this: suppose someone were to say that if the forms are such as we claim they must be, they cannot even be known. If anyone should raise this objection, you wouldn't be able to show that he is wrong, unless the objector happened to be widely experienced and not ungifted, and consented to pay attention while in your effort to show him you dealt with many distant considerations. Otherwise, the person who insists that they are necessarily unknowable would remain unconvinced."

Parmenides does not claim to show that the forms are unknowable. What he claims is that if someone were to say that the forms were unknowable, it would be very hard to show otherwise. Perhaps, then, the point of Parmenides' arguments is to throw down a challenge as to how one should understand cross-kind relations, participation being a paradigm of these. Socrates is at a loss to answer.

But the theory of forms at hand does address this issue. As explained in Section 3.6, for a to participate in the form of F-ness is precisely for a's F-ness to be identical with F-ness itself. The F-ness of a is part of the visible world, but F-ness itself has all the properties of the F-ness of a, and so is part of the visible world. This does not stop it from being part of the intelligible world as well: it is both. This is a contradiction, but such is the nature of the beast. The form crosses the boundary between the two worlds in a contradictory fashion. (This is a case in which a prime gluon can have properties that none of its parts has.)

Applying this to knowledge: when a knows f, then a participates in the form $\pi x(x \text{ knows } f)$. So a's knowledge of f is identical with $\pi x(x \text{ knows } f)$. a's knowledge of f is part of this world, so $\pi x(x \text{ knows } f)$ has the property of being part in this world, even though it is not. Our theory of forms meets Parmenides' challenge about knowledge.

7.7 Transition to Part Two (135c–137c)

So much for Parmenides' arguments against the theory of forms. In the light of these, one might expect him, at this point, to reject it; but, in the turning point of the dialogue, he says, in effect, that one cannot do this (135b–135c):

"[I]f someone, having an eye on all the difficulties we have just brought up and others of the same sort, won't allow that there are forms for things and won't mark off a form for each one, he won't have anywhere to turn his thought, since he doesn't allow that for each thing there is a character that is always the same. In this way he will destroy the power of dialectic entirely."

It is not entirely clear what Parmenides takes the problem of giving up the theory of forms to be.[25] But presumably this is just Plato saying that he is not going to give up the theory. The question must then be how one is to answer Parmenides' objections. Parmenides himself makes a suggestion. To answer the objections one needs a 'proper training' (135d): 'you must not only hypothesize, if each thing is, and examine the consequences of that hypothesis; you must also hypothesize, if that same thing is not' (135e–136a). He explains (136a–136c):

"If you like," said Parmenides, "take as an example this hypothesis that Zeno entertained: if many are, what must the consequences be for the many themselves in relation to themselves and in relation to the one, and for the one itself in relation to itself and in relation to the many? And, in turn, on the hypothesis, if many are not, you must again examine what the consequences will be both for the one and for the many themselves in relation to themselves and in relation to each other. And again, in turn, if you hypothesize if likeness is or is not, you must examine what the consequences will be of each hypothesis, both for the things hypothesized themselves and for the others, both in relation to themselves and in relation to each other. And the same method applies to unlike, to motion, to rest, to generation, to destruction, and to being itself and not-being. And, in a word, concerning whatever you might hypothesize as being or as not being or as having any other property, you must examine the consequences for the things you hypothesize in relation to itself and in relation to each of the others, whichever you select, and in relation to several of them and to all of them in the same way; and, in turn, you must examine the others, both in relation to themselves and in relation to whatever other thing you select on each occasion, whether what you hypothesize you hypothesize as being or as not being. All this you must do if, after completing your training, you are to achieve a full view of the truth."

Socrates, not unreasonably, asks for an example. After some hesitation, because of how demanding the task is, Parmenides agrees (137b):

"Well then, at what point shall we start? What shall we hypothesize first? I know: since we have in fact decided to play this strenuous game, is it all right with you if I begin with my own hypothesis? Shall I hypothesize about the one itself and consider what the consequences must be, if it is one or it is not one?"[26]

It is agreed, and the deductions begin, with Aristotle as respondent (not *the* Aristotle, another; if, as is said early in the dialogue, Zeno is about 40, *the* Aristotle would not be born for about another 65 years).

[25] 'Dialectic' is a translation of 'dialegesthai' which could be translated equally as 'discourse' or 'conversation' (Gill and Ryan (1996), p. 138).
[26] In the context, what one would expect for the last clause is 'if one is, or one is not'. Gill (1996), p. 67, notes that the text can be read this way if it is emended as endorsed by a number of scholars, such as Cornford in Hamilton and Cairns (1961).

The deduction has four main parts. There is also a somewhat anomalous intrusion: an appendix to the first part. Each main part is a pair of arguments ending in contradictory conclusions. (Shades of Kant's Antinomies in the first *Critique*!) The first two main parts depend on the assumption that the one is. The second two depend on the assumption that it is not. The first and third are about the one. The second and fourth are about the others. Let us write *u* (*unum*) for the one, and *a* (*alia*) for the others, then the main deductions have the following form:

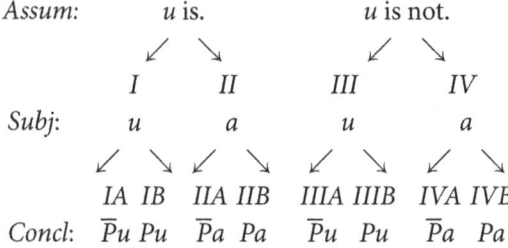

The *P*s are various. Each *Px* is to the effect that *x* has some property, and, generally speaking, is twinned with its negation in a corresponding conclusion of the pair. It should be noted though, that the *P*s themselves are often contradictory (or at least contrary) properties, of the form $Qx \wedge \overline{Q}x$. Thus, for example, *IB* concludes that the one is both at rest and in motion; whilst *IA* concludes that it is neither at rest nor in motion.

The most obvious issue to be faced at this point is what, exactly, the one is; and, correlatively, what the others are. First, the one. Parmenides calls this 'his own hypothesis', and so we might expect it to be the *what is* of his poem, whose properties Zeno defended in his book. But in the context, this is implausible. We are in the middle of an argument about the forms; bringing in Parmenides' one at this point would be changing the subject. More plausibly, this is just a literary device on Plato's part, and the one, whatever it is, is a form. Which one? One might suppose that it is any form, but it is more plausible here to suppose that it is one particular form: the form of unity. This makes more sense of the deductions, if only because the first claim in *IA* is that the one is one. If the one is the form of unity, this holds because of Self-Predication. But the step is not to be taken for granted in the case of other forms. To claim that the many is one, for example, is problematic precisely because of Self-Predication. (Of course, Parmenides has said that we have to undertake the same sort of process with all the things one hypothesizes: the one, the many, likeness, unlikeness, motion, rest, generation, destruction, being, non-being. So there is reason to suppose that Plato is taking the form of unity to be a typical example in some sense.)

If the one is the form of unity, what are the others? There are several possibilities. One is the opposite form, plurality. After all, in Parmenides' first example, the object in question is the many, and this is contrasted with the one. But this seems to be ruled out by the fact that when explaining the general case, Plato uses the plural: *others*. Another possible answer is that the others are all the instances of the form of unity, all single things. But this cannot be right, just because in Plato's first example the other is a single form, and not those things that instantiate plurality. The most plausible candidates for the others would seem to be other forms. Which ones? One of them, several of them, all of them. You can pursue the method with any of these things it would seem (136b–136c: 'you must examine the consequences for the things you hypothesize in relation to itself and in relation to each of the others, whichever you select, and in relation to several of them and to all of them in the same way'). In the case of the deductions given, Plato seems to have no specific others in mind; so the most natural assumption is that the others are all the other forms.

7.8 From Part One to Part Two

In this chapter we have seen how the gluon theory of forms solves all the problems about forms which Parmenides raises. We have also laid the groundwork for the daunting task of looking at the second part of the dialogue. We turn to this in the next chapter.

8

The One—and the Others

8.1 The Unity of the *Parmenides*

In this chapter we turn to the second part of the *Parmenides*. How to interpret this is, it seems to me, *the* key point concerning the interpretation of the *Parmenides*. At first glance, it might appear that the two halves of the dialogue have been spliced together accidentally by some compiler. Since this is, it would seem, not the case, one cannot but believe that Plato takes something about the deductions to hold the key to the solution to Parmenides' objections in the first half of the dialogue—but what this is, is, to put it mildly, opaque. We have here, then, another problem of unity. What is it that constitutes the conceptual unity of the dialogue? It is a gluon, no doubt; but why is there such a thing?

8.2 Approaches to the Second Part of the *Parmenides*

Before we return to the commentary on the text, let us look, briefly, at how some of the more notable commentators have interpreted it. What follows is not intended to be a systematic discussion of the literature. It is just meant to give a feel for the size of the problem at hand.

The traditional Neo-Platonist interpretation of the deductions was to take the first three deductions, 1A, 1B, and 2A, as being about different things. They took the subjects of the first three deductions to be the three Hypostases: the One, the Intellect, and the Soul.[1] The most obvious failing of this approach is that it completely ignores the other five deductions! But there are other problems. Most notably, the text clearly states that deductions 1A and 1B are about the same thing. Worse, the conclusions of deduction 1B are themselves contradictory. So this is no way of obtaining consistency. Finally, and crucially, it is not at all clear how this strategy is meant to address the question of how to solve the problems of part one.

[1] See Dodds (1928).

Allen ((1983), pp. vii–viii) says that the function of the deductions is simply to induce puzzlement. This seems most implausible. Why would Plato foist on the reader page after page of apparent argument-salad just to induce perplexity? We were already perplexed by the problems about the forms in the first part of the dialogue anyway! No, we are meant to learn something from the pages—and something, presumably, which tells us how to address the issues raised in the first part.

Some commentators, for example Pemberton (1984), have taken Plato at his apparent word, and endorsed the thought that the second part of the dialogue is indeed a training in dialectics, in preparation for solving these problems. It is most unclear just how following through a bunch of deductions could prepare one to solve the problems. If a training in dialectics were a training in how to analyse and critique arguments, this could be a good preparation; but that is not what we have here.[2] In the second part of the *Parmenides* there are not just the arguments, of course. Maybe learning the eight-fold method is supposed to be an essential part of the training. Beyond the rather anodyne advice 'you should look at both sides of the issue', it is difficult to see how this would really help, though. It is hard to hear Plato's words about a training in dialectics as anything but a literary device on his part. (Though maybe what we need a training in is in rejecting the PNC itself!)

A much more plausible interpretation of part two is to the effect that the deductions are, in effect, a *reductio ad absurdum* of some of their premises, and that rejecting these premises will resolve the problems of the first part. This is the response of, for example, Gill (1996) and Rickless (1998).[3] The problem here is to see which assumptions are to be rejected, and how rejecting them is to solve the problems of part one. Gill ((1996), pp. 104–109) suggest that it is the assumption that the one cannot be many which is to be rejected. We have to suppose that the one can be both one and many—in some presumably consistent way. How to do this, and how, exactly, this will solve the problems of part one, Gill leaves as a challenge for the reader! Rickless suggests more extensive rejections than Gill. He would give up not only what Gill would give up, but also two further claims: (i) that the form of F-ness is unique, and (ii) that if something is F it cannot make anything have a property contrary to F. What is worth having of the theory of forms if one rejects (i) is a moot point. But a challenge for Rickless, as it is for Gill, is to explain consistently how an object can have contrary properties. And

---

[2] Cornford (1939), pp. 244–5, tries to turn it into one, but not in a very helpful way: 'It is a challenge for the student to discover for himself the ambiguities of the Hypotheses and any fallacies there may be in the form of the deductions'.

[3] Miller (1986) runs a similar line.

even then, as he points out, his approach leaves unanswered the question of how to address Parmenides' third attack: it is a 'challenge for future work'![4]

Ryle (1939) urges us to take the deductions in the second part of the *Parmenides* to show that the assumptions from which they start are not just false but "category mistakes". The trouble with this is that if we take them to be so, then pretty much the whole theory of forms turns out to be in the same boat. This is less of a defence of the theory of forms than a trashing of it. Ryle appears to accept this conclusion without blinking (p. 314), on the ground that Plato was a great philosopher who was entitled to change his mind. So be it. But then why stitch these deductions together with the more mundane objections of the first part, then declare that it was not possible to give up the theory of forms, and that going through the motion of the deductions would help to resolve the problems?

Another plausible interpretation of the second part of the dialogue is the tried and tested method of *distinguo*: when in trouble, draw a distinction. The deductions force us to diagnose some ambiguities; this resolves the contradictory conclusions, and the disambiguations also solve the problems of part one. The most notable advocate of the approach is Meinwald (1991).[5] The idea here is to distinguish between having a property 'for itself' (or *pros heauto*) and having it 'for another' (or *pros ta alla*). For each pair in the A and B deductions, one is true in one sense, the other in the other. Some of the arguments here turn on nice points of Greek grammar, but the crucial question is how, exactly, drawing the distinction resolves the problems of part one. Diagnosing an ambiguity does not, generally speaking, make matters better: it makes them worse. For the original arguments now fragment into multiples: one for each possible disambiguation. One must explain why every uniformly disambiguated argument fails to deliver a contradiction. And it would appear that there are versions of at least Parmenides' second attack that go through after disambiguation.[6] Worse, drawing the distinction and applying it in the way suggested does not resolve all contradictions. A number of the conclusions of arguments *IB* and *IIA*, for example, even if these are "for itself" or "for another" are themselves contradictory.[7]

And when all is said and done, if the lesson of the second part of the Parmenides is that we should reject some premise, or diagnose some ambiguity in the arguments of the first half of the dialogue, it is difficult to see why we need the lengthy

---

[4] The last sentence of Rickless (2007).   [5] Scolnicov (2003) has a similar approach.

[6] See Frances (1996).

[7] If one tries to resolve these contradictions by applying the *pros heuto/pros ta alla* distinction as well, then the contradictions between the conclusions of the A and the B deductions are not resolved. Thus, take conclusion 13 of deduction *IB*. This says that the one is both equal and unequal to itself. If one disambiguates this, then one of these conjuncts will contradict conclusion 10 of argument *IA*, whichever disambiguation of that one takes.

and extended deductions that Plato provides. Parmenides' attacks in the first part of the dialogue *already* provide sufficient ground for making such a move. We do not need more—especially the more of the extraordinary kind we find in the second part of the dialogue. If Plato had had such a move in mind, he could simply have had Socrates point it out in the first half of the dialogue. So this is not what Plato intends us to take away from part two.

What he intends us to take away is exactly what the dialogue says: the possibility that the forms are contradictory. Let us see how, by analysing the four deductions.

8.3 Deduction IA (137c–142a)

Deduction I is by far the longest textually. The first of its parts, *IA*, starts with an instance of Self-Predication, the one is one, and then concludes that the one can neither have parts nor be a whole, as follows (137c–137d):

"If it is one, the one would not be many, would it?"—"No, how could it?"—"Then there cannot be a part of it nor can it be a whole."—"Why?"—"A part is surely a part of a whole."—"Yes."—"But what is the whole? Wouldn't that from which no part is missing be a whole?"—"Certainly."—"In both cases, then, the one would be composed of parts, both if it is a whole and if it has parts."—"Necessarily."—"So in both cases the one would be many rather than one."—"True."—"Yet is must be not many but one."—"It must."—"Therefore if the one is to be one, it will neither be a whole nor have parts."—"No, it won't."

There then follow about five Stephanus pages of tightly reasoned argument. There is no point in hammering through the details of this deduction—or any of the others—here. The steps are many, and there are many places at which one might balk. The point at issue is not whether the arguments are, in fact, cogent, but whether Plato takes them to be plausible. There is no indication that he does not—Aristotle never balks seriously.[8]

The various conclusions reached are all to the effect that the one does not have various properties, which are listed in the following table.[9] I put the conclusions of *IB* on the same table for comparison.[10] The numbers in the columns represent the order in which the conclusions are reached. It is worth noting that the conclusions

---

[8] One might argue about the exact logical form of each argument, but it is clear that many of the arguments are by contraposition. This is valid in most paraconsistent logics: $A \to B \vdash \neg B \to \neg A$. Even forms of *reductio* are valid in paraconsistent logics with Excluded Middle and De Morgan. For then $A \to (B \wedge \neg B) \vdash \neg(B \wedge \neg B) \to \neg A \vdash (\neg B \vee \neg\neg B) \to \neg A$, and Excluded Middle does the rest.

[9] Of course, how one pulls out the vertebral conclusions is, to a certain extent, a matter of judgment. The tables that follow are taken with minor amendments from Gill (1996), pp. 117–123. The numbering is hers.

[10] Except 2, which is not about the one. I will comment on this later.

of *IA* are, for the most part, those about *what is*, which the historical Parmenides argued for in his poem. Naturally, this can hardly be a coincidence.

Deduction IA	Deduction IB
1. Is not many.	
2. Is not a whole and does not have parts.	3. Is a whole and has parts.
3. Does not have a beginning, middle or end.	6. Has a beginning, middle, and end.
	4. Is unlimited in multitude.
4. Is unlimited.	5. Is limited.
5. Is without shape.	7. Has a shape.
6. Is not in itself or another.	8. Is in itself and others.
7. Is not in motion or at rest.	9. Is in motion and at rest.
8. Is not the same as or different from another or itself.	10. Is the same as and different from itself and others.
9. Is not like or unlike another or itself.	11. Is like and unlike the others and itself.
	12. Touches and does not touch the others or itself.
10. Is not equal to or unequal to itself or another.	13. Is equal and unequal to the other and itself.
11. Is not younger than, older than, or the same age as itself or another.	15. Is and comes to be older and younger than itself and the others and neither comes to be older or younger than itself and the others.
12. Is not in time.	14. Is in time.
	16. Partakes of past, present, future.
13. Is not.	1. Partakes of being.
14. Is not one.	
15. Is not named or spoken of, or the object of opinion, knowledge or perception.	17. Is named and spoken of, and is the object of opinion, knowledge, and perception.

In fact, there is a single argument that underlies all the conclusions of *IA*. It is invoked explicitly at conclusion 9 (139e–140a, my italics):

"Furthermore, it will be neither like nor unlike anything, either itself or another."—"Why?"—"Because whatever has a property the same is surely like."—"Yes."—"But it was shown that the same is separate in nature from the one."—"Yes it was."—"*But if the one has any property apart from being one, it would be more than one; and that is impossible.*"—"Yes."—"Therefore the one can in no way have a property the same as another or itself."—"Apparently not."—"So it cannot be like another or itself either."—"It seems not."

If the one had any properties other than being the one, it would be a many—it would have parts: its *P*-ness, its *Q*-ness, and so on—which is what it is not, as was said right at the beginning.

It should be noted that conclusion 13 is anomalous in a certain sense. All the conclusions up to this point are, at least *prima facie*, consistent; but conclusion 13 denies the assumption of the whole deduction. In a similar way, conclusion 14 denies the initial application of Self-Predication in the argument. (Conclusion 15 is not inconsistent in the same way, though it is self-referentially inconsistent.) I will return to this later. For the moment, just note that the conclusions of *IA* are sufficient, in themselves, to establish that the one has certain contradictory properties. But you ain't seen nothin' yet.

8.4 Deduction IB (142a–155e)

IA concludes as follows (142c):

"Is it possible that these things are so for the one?"—"I certainly don't think so."

So one might expect Parmenides or Aristotle to go back on something. (And some commentators do take this as a hint that we need to go back on something.) But this is not what we find. What we find is this (142b–142c):

"Do you want to return to the hypothesis from the beginning, in the hope that another kind of result may come to light as we go back over it?"—"I do indeed."—"If one is, we are saying, aren't we, that we must agree on the consequences for it, whatever they happen to be?"—"Yes."—"Consider from the beginning: if one is, can it *be*, but not partake of being?"—"It cannot."—"So there would also be the being of the one, and that is not the same thing as the one. For if it were, it couldn't be the being of the one, nor could the one partake of it. On the contrary, saying that one is would be like saying that one is one. But this time that is not the hypothesis, namely, what the consequences must be, if one is one, but if one is.¹¹ Isn't that so?"—"Of course."—"Is this because 'is' signifies something other than 'one'?"—"Necessarily."—"So whenever someone, being brief, says 'one is', would this simply mean that the one partakes of being?"—"Certainly".

No taking back. We get *more*: all of *IB*. This deduction amounts to 13 Stephanus pages—more than all the other deductions put together; but its germ is already in the passage just quoted. The one is, so it is one and has being. Being is different from oneness. (Gill lists this as the first conclusion in *IB*, but it is not about the one, and I think it better to take it to be an intermediate step.) So the one has at least two distinct properties. It therefore has parts, and so off we go. What we find,

---

¹¹ Cornford translates this, a bit more intelligibly, as "But in fact, the supposition whose consequences we are to consider is not 'if one [is] *one*', but 'if one *is*.'" (Hamilton and Cairns (1961).)

generally speaking, in *IB* is a mate which is the negation of each conclusion in *IA*. The one, then, is established to have a whole bunch of contradictory properties. The order in which these properties are established is not exactly the same as in *IA*, but it is obviously reasonable to allow Plato some slack here.

There are a few exceptions to this general picture. 14 of *IA* has no mate, though it contradicts the initial application of Self-Predication, as we have already observed. Neither does 1, that the one is not a many. But Plato fills that gap *en passant* in *IB*—twice in fact. The one has parts, and 'for this reason the one that is was shown to be many' (143a). And again: the one has many parts, and each of these is one, so 'not only is it that the one being is many, but also that the one itself, completely distributed by being, must be many' (144e). So all the conclusions of *IA* are contradicted somewhere.

The aberrations are more anomalous in *IB*. 16 of *IB* appears to be little more than a stylistic variation of 14, perhaps repeated for exegetical reasons. At any rate, it mates explicitly with 141d–142e of *IA*, where it is spelled out that the one is not past, present, or future.

For 4 of *IB*, Plato gives two recursive-style arguments to the effect that the one has not just two parts but an infinite number, and so is unlimited (142d–144e). This conclusion has no explicit mate in *IA*. But, oddly, it itself already occurs at 4 in *IA*—though the argument used to establish it there is quite different—and so contradicts the mate of 4: 5, in *IB*.

12 of *IB* appears to correspond to nothing in *IA*. Its conclusion is to the effect that the one both touches and does not touch itself and the others. However, this conclusion is self-contradictory, and its negative parts could have appeared under *IA*, because of the general argument that the one cannot have any positive properties other than being one. 15 of *IB* is a mate of 11 in *IA*, but also goes on to repeat its negative claims.

So, anomalies notwithstanding, each claim of *IA* and *IB* is actually contradicted somewhere in the ledger. This is, in fact, exactly what one should expect on the model of the forms at hand. Oneness will have each property that the oneness of each one thing has. Given the plausible assumption that the *F*-ness of x is located where x is, this is going to ensure many contradictory properties. Some one things are in motion (and so not at rest), so oneness is in motion (and not at rest). Some one things are at rest (and so not in motion), so oneness will be at rest (and not in motion). Everything is touched by some one thing, so everything is touched by oneness. But everything is not touched by something, so everything will not be touched by oneness. The oneness of anything is identical to itself. So oneness is identical with itself. The oneness of Socrates is distinct from the oneness of Plato. So oneness is distinct from the oneness of Plato; and so oneness is distinct from itself. And so on. The construction may not, perhaps, generate *all* the contradictory pairs on the list. (I will return to this matter in due course.) But the general point is clear: given the theory of forms at hand, one should expect the form of unity to have exactly the sort of contradictory properties that Deduction *I* establishes.

Perhaps more importantly, what drives the deductions *IA* and *IB* is one fundamental contradiction. For *IA*, the one is one—and so not many. For *IB*, the one is many—and so not one. This is what the gluon model of the forms delivers. As before, let u be unity (the one), and let u_S, u_P, u_A ... be the unity of Socrates, the unity of Plato, the unity of Aristotle, etc. Then $u = u$: one is one; but $u_S \neq u_P$, so $u_S \neq u$, and similarly, $u_P \neq u$, and so on; so the one is not many. But by the properties of prime gluons, $u = u_S$, $u = u_P, \ldots$, and since these are all distinct, u is a many; finally, since $u_P \neq u_S$, $u \neq u$: the one is not one.[12] In Plato's actual argument, the multitude are not the concrete instances of the form; the various properties of the form are taken to deliver its multitude: unity's oneness, unity's being, and so on. But we can think of Socrates' unity, Plato's unity, and so on, equally well, as unity's Platoness, unity's Socratesness, and so on; so we are not so far away.

8.5 Deduction II (157b–160b)

There is, as observed previously, an apparently anomalous appendix to Deduction *I*. Let us return to this later, and pass on to Deduction *II*. Deduction *II* retains the assumption that the one is, and considers the properties of the others—the other forms (159b–159c):

"Must we not examine what would be proper for the others to undergo, if one is?"—"We must."—"Are we to say, then, what properties things other than the one must have, if one is?"—"Let's do."—"Well then, since they are other than the one, the things are not the one. For if they were, they would not be other than the one."—"That's right."

The nerve of the deduction concerns wholeness and parthood. Even though the others are not one, they partake of the one in some sense (157c–158a):

"And yet the others are not absolutely deprived of the one, but somehow partake of it."—"In what way?"—"In that things other than the one are surely other because they have parts; for if they didn't have parts, they would be altogether one."—"That's right."—"And parts, we say, are parts of that which is a whole?"—"Yes, we do."—"Yet the whole of which the parts are to be parts must be one thing composed of many, because each of the parts must be part, not of many, but of a whole." ... "So the part would not be part of many

---

[12] See the Prime Gluon Corollary of Section 2.10.4.

things or all, but of some one character and of some one thing, which we call a 'whole', since it has come to be one complete thing composed of all. This is what the part would be part of."—"Absolutely."—"So if the others have parts, they would also partake of some one whole."—"Certainly."—"So things other than the one must be one complete whole with parts."

The whole is one thing, and so the parts which comprise it partake of the one in some sense. And, Parmenides goes on to note, each part is also severally one. Having established these things, the deduction proceeds. It is much shorter than the two previous ones, but that is partly because Plato truncates it abruptly (159a–159b):

"And indeed we will have no further trouble in finding that things other than the one are both the same and different from each other, both in motion and in rest, and have all the opposite properties, since in fact they were shown to have those we mentioned."—"You're right."

How one is to do this, is—it must be said—not immediately obvious. The following table lists the conclusions about the others in *IIA*—and in *IIB* for comparison.

Deduction IIA	Deduction IIB
	1. Are separate from the one.
1. Are not the one.	
2. Somehow partake of the one.	2. Are in no way one.
3. Are many.	3. Are not many.
4. Are unlimited and partake of a limit.	
5. Are like and unlike themselves and others.	4. Are not like or unlike the one.
6. Have all the other properties.	5. Have no other properties.

Deduction *IIB* now goes back to the start again (159b):

"Well then, suppose we now concede those results as evident and examine again, if one is: Are things other than the one also not so, or only so?"—"Of course."—"Let's say from the beginning, what properties things other than the one have, if one is."—"Yes, let's do."

The nerve of this deduction is again the relationship between parts and wholes (159c–e):

"Furthermore, we say that what is really one doesn't have parts."—"Obviously not."—"So the one could not be in the others as a whole, nor could parts of it be in them, if it is separate from the others and doesn't have parts."—"Obviously not."—"So the others could in no way partake of the one, if they partake neither by getting some part of it nor by getting it as a whole. "It seems not."—"In no way, then, are the others one, nor do they have any oneness in them."—"Yes, you're quite right."

"So the others aren't many either; for each of them would be one part of a whole, if they were many . . . Therefore, the others are not themselves two or three, nor are two or three in them, if they are entirely deprived of the one."—"Just so."

Having established that the others are neither a one nor a many, the rest of the deduction is relatively terse, concluding, this time, with a general argument for most of the properties at issue (160a–160b):

"So they are neither the same nor different, neither in motion nor at rest, neither coming to be nor ceasing to be, neither greater nor less nor equal. Nor do they have any such properties. For if the others submit to having any such property, they will partake of one and two and three and odd and even, of which it was shown that they could not partake, since they are in every way deprived of the one."—"Very true."

If the others have any of the properties in question, they can be numbered, which, it has been established, they cannot be.

The final conclusion of the deduction appears somewhat anomalous, since it summarizes the result of just Deduction *I* (160b):[13]

"Thus, if one is, the one is all things, and not even one, both in relation to itself and, likewise, in relation to the others."—"Exactly."

Be that as it may, as consulting the table shows, deduction *II* has established that the others have a bunch of properties—many of them themselves contradictory— and do not have them. The first conclusions in each of *IIA* and *IIB*, are, interestingly enough, much the same, and set up the subsequent trains of deduction. After that, the conclusions pair off, one for one, with the exception of 4 of *IIA*, which is appealed to in establishing 5, and may therefore be taken to be merely an intermediate conclusion.

So now we have inferred that all the forms, not just the form of unity, have contradictory properties—as they should have on the gluon theory of forms. For just as the one has all the properties of the oneness of Socrates, the oneness of Plato, and so on, so for any other form F, if $x, y, \ldots$ are the things that are F, F-ness has the properties of the F-ness of x, the F-ness of y, and so on.

---

[13] Gill (1996), p. 391, notes that with an emendation of the text, as endorsed by some commentators (for example, Meinwald (1991), pp. 142–4), this can be rectified, so that the translation is: "Thus, if one is, the one is all things and not even one, both in relation to itself and in relation to others, and likewise for the others".

8.6 Deduction III (160b–164b)

At this stage, then, the deductions have established that oneness and all the other forms have contradictory properties. The deductions do not finish here, however. Parmenides reminds us that we now need to look at the other side of the picture and consider what is the case if the one is not (160b–160d). The topic in Deduction *III* is back to the one (160d):

"Then we must start from the beginning as follows [*sic*] what must be the case, if one is not. First, this must be so for it, that there is knowledge of it; otherwise we don't even know what is meant when someone says, 'if one is not.'"—"True." . . .

The conclusions of *IIIA* concerning the one are given in the following table, with *IIIB* for comparison.[14]

Deduction IIIA	Deduction IIIB
	10. Is in no state at all.
1. Is knowable.	9. Knowledge, and so on, are not applicable to it.
	8. Past, present, and future are not applicable.
2. Is different from the others.	7.′ It is neither like nor different from itself or others.
3. Partakes of *that*, *something*, *this*, and so on.	7. *This*, *that*, *something*, and so on, are not applicable to it.
4. Is unlike the others, and like itself.	6a. The others are neither like it nor unlike it.
5. Is not equal to the others.	6b. The others are neither the same as nor different from it.
5.′ Has a share of equality, largeness and smallness.	5.′ Largeness, smallness and equality do not belong to it.
	5. Nothing that is belongs to it.
6. Somehow partakes of being.	1. In no way partakes of being.
7. Has being and not being.	
8. Is in motion and at rest.	4. Is neither in motion nor at rest.
9. Is both altered and not altered.	3. Is not altered.
10. Comes and ceases to be, and neither comes nor ceases to be.	2. Neither comes nor ceases to be.

---

[14] The numbering is again Gill's, except that the primes account for my slight restructuring.

THE ONE—AND THE OTHERS 129

The pivots of the deduction in *IIIA* are two. First, for 3, Parmenides points out that if the one is not, or anything else is true of it, it must be possible to predicate things of it, and so to describe it (160e–161a):

"Furthermore, the one that is not partakes of *that* and of *something, this, to this, these*, and so on; for the one could not be mentioned, nor could things be different from the one, nor could anything belong to it or be of it, nor could it be said to be anything, unless it had a share of *something* and the rest."—"That's right."—"The one can't *be*, if in fact it is not, but nothing prevents it from partaking of many things. Indeed, it's even necessary, if in fact it's that one and not another that is not. If, however, neither the one nor *that* is not to be, but the account is about something else, we shouldn't even utter a sound. But if that one and not another is not to be, it must have a share of *that* and of many other things."—"Quite certainly."

Parmenides seems on pretty safe ground here.

The other pivot is the Parmenidean claim that anything one can speak about has being, which, again, is acceptable provided that 'being' is understood appropriately (see Section 6.3). As he puts it (161e–162b):

"Furthermore, it must also somehow partake of being."—"How is that?"—"It must be in the state we describe; for if it is not so, we wouldn't speak truly when we say that the one is not. But if we speak truly, it is clear that we say things that are. Isn't that so?"—"It is indeed so."—"And since we claim to speak truly, we must claim also to speak of things that are."—"Necessarily." . . . "Then the one, if it is not, appears also to have being."—"Apparently."—"And of course not-being, if in fact it is not."—"Doubtless."

Thus, we have conclusion 6 of *IIIA*; and so, as Parmenides points out at the end of that quotation, by our assumption that one is not, the contradictory 7. We need not pause over the details concerning the extraction of the other conclusions.

Now to *IIIB*. The deductions in *IIIB* start thus (163b–163d):

"Let's go back again to the beginning to see whether things will appear the same to us as they do now, or different."—"Indeed, we must."—"Aren't we saying, if one is not, what the consequences must be for it?"—"Yes."—"When we say 'is not', the words don't signify anything other than the absence of being for whatever we say is not, do they?'—"Nothing other."—"When we say that something is not, are we saying that in a way it is not, but in a way it is? Or does this 'is not' signify without qualification that what is not is in no way at all and does not in any way partake of being?"—"Absolutely without qualification."—"Therefore what is not could neither be nor partake of being in any other way at all."—"No it couldn't."

And finish thus (164a–164b):

"What about this? Can the others be related to it, if necessarily, nothing belongs to it?"—"They can't."—So the others are neither like nor unlike it, and they are neither the same as nor different from it."—"No, they aren't."—"And again: will *of that, to that, something, this, of this, of another, to another,* or time past, hereafter, or now, or knowledge, opinion, perception, and account, a name, or anything else that is be applicable to what is not?"—"It will not."—"Thus one, since it is not, is not in any state at all."—"At any rate, it certainly seems to be in no state at all."

In fact, the whole deduction turns round the contrapositive of the second pivot of *IIIA*. What is not can have no properties. This is stated at 5 of *IIIB* (164a): "But in fact, nothing that is belongs to it; for then, by partaking of that, it would partake of being."—"Clearly." And of course, anything one can talk about is. Every other conclusion of *IIIB* follows.

A striking fact about Deduction *III* is that Plato chooses to establish the corresponding consequences of its two parts in inverse orders. However, as I have just observed, he could have established 5 first, and then everything else would be a corollary; so he could have ordered the conclusions of *IIIB* in essentially the same order as those of *IIIA*. Why he chose not to do this, I have no idea.

Another slight oddity of *IIIA* and *IIIB* is that some conclusions in one deduction have no mates in the other. The negative half of 7 in *IIIA* could equally be in the *IIIB* column. 10 in *IIIB* is really just a summary of what precedes it. This leaves 5 and 8 of *IIIB* opposite genuine blanks. It would have been easy enough for Plato to fill them in. If one is not, then non-being belongs to it, and non-being, like all things, is. This gives 5 a mate. And Parmenides has already claimed that if something is, it is in time, and so partakes of past, present, and future (151e–152a). This gives 8 a mate. Why he did not fill in the blanks, again I have no idea.

At any rate, these aberrations aside, by the end of *IIIB*, we have established that if one is not, it has contradictory properties. We now come to the crucial question of why Plato is going through this exercise. The reason, I take it, is as follows: Plato thinks that the one is. Deduction *I* has established that it has contradictory properties. If I am right, he takes these conclusions seriously. He expects people to object. (To the matter of whom, exactly, Plato takes his opponents in the dialogue to be, I will return at the end of the chapter.) The function of Deduction *III* is to show that you are stuck with contradictions even if you suppose that the one is not. So you might as well get used to it! This, of course, was the strategy articulated by Zeno at the very start of the dialogue.

8.7 Deduction IV (164b–165d)

And so we come to the final deduction, *IV*. It is still supposed that the one is not, but now we establish the properties of the others on this assumption. Parmenides commences Deduction *IVA* as follows (164b), and starts by establishing that the others are a plurality:

"Let's go on and say what properties the others must have, if one is not."—"Yes, let's do."—"They must surely be other; for if they weren't even other, we wouldn't be talking about the others."—"Just so."—"But if the argument is about the others, the others are different. Or don't you apply the names 'other' and 'different' to the same thing?"—"I do."—"And surely we say that the different is different from a different thing, and the other is other than another thing?"—"Yes."—"So the others, too, if they are to be other, have something they will be other than?"—"Necessarily."—"What would it be then? For they won't be other than the one, if it is indeed not."—"No, they won't."—"So they are other than each other, since that alternative remains for them, or else to be other than nothing."—"That's right."

"So they each are other than each other as multitudes; for they couldn't be so as ones, if one is not. But each mass of them, is unlimited in multitude..."

And concludes (165d–165e):

"Accordingly, if one is not and many are, the many must appear both the same as and different from each other, both in contact and separate from themselves, both moving with every motion and in every way at rest, both coming to be and ceasing to be and neither, and surely everything of that sort, which would now be easy enough for us to go through."—"Very true indeed."

Whether it is very true is a moot point. The arguments are getting terser and terser, and it is not clear how one would fill in all the details. The conclusions of *IVA* and *IVB* about the others are listed in the following table.[15]

Deduction IVA	Deduction IVB
	1. Are neither one nor many.
1. Are other than the others.	
2. Are each a mass unlimited in multitude.	
3. Appear one, but are not so.	2. Do not appear to be one or many.
4. Appear to be numbered, but are not.	
5. Appear equal and unequal.	
6. Appear limited and unlimited.	
7. Appear to be both like and unlike themselves and each other.	$2'(a)$. Are neither like nor unlike.
$7'$. Appear to be the same and different, in contact and separate, and so on.	$2'(b)$. Are neither the same nor different, in contact or separate, and so on.
8. Appear to have all the usual opposites.	3. Neither are nor appear to have any of the usual opposites.
	4. Nothing is.

[15] Again, the primes indicate a variation from Gill.

The most striking thing about the chain of deductions in *IVA* is the appearance of the notion of appearance. After the first few moves, each conclusion is of one of the forms:

  (i) appears to be so, but is not
  (ii) appears to be both so and not so

Why does Plato bring in the notion of appearances at this stage? This would certainly seem to be a nod in the direction of the historical Parmenides. The *Parmenides'* deductions start, effectively, with a recapitulation of the first part of the historical Parmenides' poem; this is about what is. The next part of his poem was about the world of appearances. So it is at least appropriate for Plato to finish his deduction with the world of appearances as well. Let us come back to this in a moment.

Deduction *IVB* begins (165e):

"Let's go back to the beginning once more and say what must be the case, if the one is not, but things other than the one are."—"Yes, let's do."—"Well, the others won't be one."—"Obviously not."—"And surely they won't be many either, since oneness would also be present in things that are many. For if none of them is one, they are all nothing—so they couldn't be many."—"True."—"If oneness isn't present in the others, the others are neither many nor one."—"No, they aren't."

And concludes (175b–175c):

"So they aren't like or unlike either."—"No, they aren't."—"And indeed, they are neither the same nor different, neither in contact nor separate, neither anything else that they appeared to be in the argument we went through before. The others neither are nor appear to be any of those things, if one is not."—"True."—"Then if we were to say, to sum up, 'if one is not, nothing is,' wouldn't we be speaking correctly?"—"Absolutely."

The deduction is by far the shortest, well under one Stephanus page. Parmenides—or Plato—is clearly running out of steam, and the tight correspondence between the *A* conclusions and the *B* conclusions has disappeared. For the most part, the main form of the conclusion of the *B* deduction is:

  neither appears to be (so or not so), nor is (so or not so)

The first conjunct contradicts the generic form (ii) of the *A* conclusions, and the second conjunct grounds the final nihilistic conclusion: nothing is.

We may again ask what Plato is up to here. The answer is essentially as in the case for deductions *I* and *III*. Deduction *II* has shown that if the one is, which of course Plato takes it to be so, the other forms have contradictory properties. Deduction *IV* has shown that even if the one is not, the other forms have contradictory properties of the form: *appear to be so and not so and do not appear to be so or not so*. So we may as well accept the contradictory nature of the forms anyway. As Parmenides puts it in the very last statement of the dialogue (166c):

"Let us say . . . , as it seems, whether one is or is not, it and the others both are and are not, and both appear and do not appear all things in all ways, both in relation to themselves and in relation to others."—"Very true."

—though this is a bit of an overstatement. No conclusions about how the one appears were drawn. And the "all things in all ways" is presumably all the things and ways of the kind discussed, not literally *all* things: no attempt was made, for example, to establish that the one is a frog. (Natural-language quantifiers are usually bounded—the bound being determined by the context. See Section 9.4.)

There is a stronger point here as well. Assuming that the one is not, we now have not just contradictory conclusions, but the nihilist conclusion that nothing is (*IVB*, conclusion 4) as well. This seems even more absurd. Some things are, after all, more absurd than some contradictions: that you are a frog is more absurd than that the liar sentence is both true and false. So the final nihilistic conclusion can be seen as making the point that the consequences of the one not being are not just as bad as those of its being; they are worse.

There is an apparent problem with this line of thought, though. In deduction *IA*, Plato himself has argued that if the one is, then it is not—conclusion 13. It would therefore seem that he himself is committed to the consequences of this, and so to this nihilism. What is one to say about this?[16]

Perhaps Plato just did not notice the matter. After all, as we all know, it is easy to miss what is obvious in retrospect. Moreover, there is an obvious thing he could say once he does notice the matter. Deduction *IA* infers conclusion 13 from conclusion 12: the one is not in time, and so is not. He could just reject this conclusion, and truncate *IA* at this point. Given his view of forms, he should have done this anyway.[17] Moreover, and notably, the gluon model itself tells us that there is no reason to suppose that the one is not. The one, being a prime gluon, must have all the properties of the oneness of Socrates, the oneness of Plato, and so on. All of these are, so the one is. But none of these is not, so we have no reason to suppose that the one is not. Plato need not, therefore, be committed to the claim that the one is not.[18]

---

[16] I am not the first person to note this oddity. For discussion and references, see Petersen (1996).

[17] Indeed, as we will see in a moment, in deduction *IC* Plato argues that there are instants of change which are not in time.

[18] Nor, as far as this argument goes, to the things that follow from it, conclusions 14 and 15. However, we have already noted in connection with deduction *IB* that the gluon model delivers at

However, there is another, and more intriguing, possibility. The conclusions of deduction *III* are essentially just a reprise of things that have gone before in deductions *I* and *II*. The conclusions of deduction *IV* are quite different. As we observed, appearances enter the plot for the first time. Deduction *IVA* starts by establishing that the others are a plurality. Given Parmenides' own view, pluralities are not real; they are all appearances. And given that one is not, there are no unities either. So everything is just appearances. The rest of *IVA* merely spells out the consequences. Deduction *IVB* takes up the theme. If there are no unities, there are only pluralities; and these do not exist either. It is all appearances again. And if it is all appearances, then one can say nothing true of the form 'that something is so and so *is* the case'—not even something of the form 'that something appears to be so and so is the case'. And so we end up with the final spectacular nihilism: *nothing* is (the case).

Against Parmenides and the other Eleatics, this is a pretty good argument. Plato does not have to subscribe to the conclusion, however. Even if the others form a multitude, it does not follow that all is appearance. *Plato* is not committed to the view that multitudes are inherently unreal. Even if the one is not, there can still be a many; and a group of things can instantiate the form of being a manifold. The fact that something is a plurality means that it is not one. That is quite consistent with nothing *else* being a one either. The elements of a multitude, then, are multitudes. It is multitudes all the way down.[19]

I suggest, then, that Plato's real opponents in the dialogue are the Eleatics. Deduction *IV* employs the premise that pluralities are unreal enthymematically. It is not a premise that he subscribes to, but it makes for a powerful *ad hominem* argument.

8.8 Deduction IC (155e–157b)

We have not quite finished with the deductions yet. It remains to consider the apparently anomalous appendix to Deduction *I*, *IC*. What is it doing there? In a way, this is the most puzzling feature of the deductions.

least *one* understanding of conclusion 14. And Plato might well have been happy to get away from the obvious self-refutation delivered by 15.

[19] There is an argument we noted in Deduction *IIB* which might appear to gainsay this interpretation (159d): ' "In no way, then, are the others one, nor do they have any oneness in them."—"Yes, you're quite right." "So the others aren't many either; for each of them would be one part of a whole, if they were many . . . " ' Each of a multitude of parts is one part of a whole, and so one. But this assumes that there are wholes (ones). This is perfectly acceptable in deduction *IIB*, which is carried out under the assumption that one is. The reasoning cannot be carried out in Deduction *IV*, which is based on the negation of this assumption.

IC is still about the one, and starts as follows (155e–156a):

"Let's speak of it a third time. If one is as we have described it—being both one and many and neither one nor many, and partaking of time—must it not, because it is one, sometimes partake of being, and in turn because it is not, sometimes not partake of being?"—"Necessarily."—"When it partakes, can it at that time not partake, or partake when it doesn't?"—"It cannot."—"So it partakes at one time, and doesn't partake at another; for only in this way could it partake and not partake of the same thing."—"That's right."—"Isn't there, then, a definite time when it gets a share of being and when it parts from it? Or how can it at one time have and at another time not have the same thing, if it never gets and releases it?"—"In no way."

Parmenides says that he is speaking about the one 'for a third time', but unlike the second, he does not go back to the beginning, but, as is clear, *assumes* the results of the first two deductions. The point is that if the one both is and is not, there is no time at which both are the case. At some times it is one, at some times it is the other. The next paragraph applies the same thoughts to some other categories: one and many, like and unlike, greater and lesser, equal and unequal, rest and motion.

Many commentators[20] have seen this as a way of resolving the contradictions established in *IA* and *IB*. But whatever it is, it is not that. We are taking over the results of *IA* and *IB*. Indeed, it is conclusion 14 of *IB* that the one is in time. But conclusion 12 of *IA* establishes that the one is *not* in time. We still have this contradiction. If we tried to resolve it in the same way, we would get: there is a time when the one is in time, and a time when it is not in time—the second conjunction of which is just as contradictory. In any case, if this were the point of the deduction, it could finish here; but it continues. The conclusions of the deduction are as follows:

Deduction IC

1. The one partakes of being at one time, but does not partake at another.
2. There is a definite time where one gets a share of being, and when it leaves it.
3. The one comes to be and ceases to be when it gets and releases being.
4. If an object moves at one time and is at rest at another, it must change from one state to the other.
5. At this time, it is neither in motion nor at rest.
6. There is no time at which an object is neither in motion nor at rest.
7. The change occurs at an instant which is not in time.
8. At the instant of change, the one is neither in motion nor at rest.
9. At the instant of change, the one neither is nor is not, and neither comes to be nor ceases to be.
10. Similarly with other states and processes.

---

[20] For example, Gill (1996), pp. 85–6.

When the deduction continues, it argues that if an object is in different states at different times, there must be an instant of change, which is itself outside time (156c):

"And whenever, being in motion, it comes to rest and whenever, being at rest, it changes to moving, it must itself, presumably, be in no time at all."—"How's that?"—"It won't be able to undergo being previously at rest and later in motion or being previously in motion and later at rest without changing."—"Obviously not."—"Yet there is no time in which something can, simultaneously, be neither in motion nor at rest."—"Yes, you're quite right."—"Yet surely it doesn't change without changing."—"Hardly."—"So when does it change? For it does not change while it is at rest or in motion, or while it is in time."—"Yes, you're quite right."

Moreover, at the instant outside time, the one is neither at rest nor in motion (156d–156e):

"Is there, then, this queer thing in which it might be, just when it changes?"—"What queer thing?"—"The instant. The instant seems to signify something such that changing occurs from it to each of the two states. For a thing doesn't change from rest while rest continues, or from motion while motion continues. Rather, this queer creature, the instant, lurks between motion and rest—being in no time at all—and to it and from it the moving thing changes to resting and the resting thing changes to moving."—"It looks that way."—"And the one, if in fact it both rests and moves, could change to each state—for only in that way could it do both. But in changing, it changes at an instant, and when it changes, it would be in no time at all, and just then would be neither in motion nor at rest."—"No, it wouldn't."

The next paragraph claims that the same is true of other pairs of states, being and not being, many and one, like and unlike, equal and unequal, and so on. The subject is then abruptly dropped, and Deduction *IIA* commences.

What to make of this? The point, it is clear, is to establish something about an instant of change, outside time; and *prima facie* this something is that at this instant, neither of the pairs of states, prior and posterior, is realized. But wait a minute. Were not these states contradictories: to be in rest is not to be an motion, and *vice versa*? So to be in neither of them is itself a contradiction. The instant, then, is a contradictory creature. Plato is careful to say that it is only at the same *time* that something cannot, for example, both be and not be (155e, my italics): "When it partakes, can it *at that time* not partake, or partake when it doesn't?"—"It cannot." The instant is outside time.

It might be suggested that rest and motion, for example, are not contradictories, but contraries. The trouble with this suggestion is that the opposing pairs are not always specified independently (rest/motion, same/different), but are frequently specified using negation. Thus, we have in Deduction *I*: is [is not] a whole (*IA*, 2; *IB*, 3), has [has not] a beginning (*IA*, 3; *IB*, 6), is [is not] in itself (*IA*, 6; *IB*, 8), is [is not] in time (*IA*, 12; *IB*, 14). And negation is a contradictory-forming operator. To say that something has neither of a pair of contradictory properties is itself contradictory.

Plato is blunt about the matter concerning one such pair: is [is not]. Just after the last passage quoted, Parmenides says (157a, my italics):

"Is it so with the other changes too? Whenever the one changes from being to ceasing-to-be, or from not-being to coming-to-be, isn't it then between states of motion and rest? And then *it neither is nor is not*, and neither comes nor ceases to be."

Look at the italicized claim. It says that the one is not, and it is not the case that it is not. Even without the law of double negation (which would convert this into 'the one is not and is'), this is a flat contradiction.

There is a general point here: to say that neither $\neg A$ nor A is to say $\neg(\neg A \vee A)$, and by De Morgan's law (and double negation),[21] this is equivalent to $A \wedge \neg A$. To be in a state of *neither* is to be in a state of *both*.

So what is going on here? *IA* and *IB* have established that the one has contradictory properties. Plato expects objections. *IC* starts with a natural one: the one is not really contradictory, since the contradictions may be defused by an appeal to time. The rest of the deduction then shows that, even if one appeals to time, one still ends up with a contradictory object: the instant.

And now, crucially: Plato puts in an appendix to Deduction *I*, but not to the others; why not? He has no reason to. If I am right, the deduction is not an attempt to establish further properties of something, an exercise that could be repeated in ensuing cases. It is a reply to an objection to the effect that contradictions can be avoided by appealing to time. He does not have to reply to this objection more than once.

8.9 The Big Picture

We have, in this chapter and the last, looked at the details of both parts of the dialogue. Let us now step back and put the whole thing into perspective.

According to the interpretation of the *Parmenides* I am offering, things look like this. At some stage after Plato had formulated his theory of forms, he came to see that there were problems with it, and especially with the notion of participation. Maybe these occurred to him, himself; more likely, I would guess, they were put to him by others. The fact that he has Parmenides put the arguments suggests it was by Eleatics. This is the dialogue he wrote about the problems.

---

[21] Both of which are valid in most paraconsistent logics. There is nothing about dialetheism that renders them invalid.

In the first part of the dialogue, the problems are expounded. Plato is not sure of the exact solution, though he wants to see if they can be answered. The key to a solution, it occurs to him, could be in the contradictory nature of the forms. A satisfactory solution can not just, of course, simply accept the theory and the contradictory conclusions posed by the objections. That would be *ad hoc* and entirely unsatisfactory.[22] There has to be a principled and unified account of participation that solves the worries. Still, he knows that the possibility of contradictory forms is likely to meet opposition. This is what the second part of the dialogue is about.

He sets things up at the beginning of the dialogue by getting the young (and naive) Socrates to contrast the world of the forms and the world of appearances, and claim that even if the latter are contradictory, the forms are not. This is what gets knocked down in the second part of the dialogue.

Deductions *IA* and *IB* establish that the form of unity is contradictory. The conclusion is liable to force a substantial balk in members of Plato's audience; the arguments of Deduction *I* are therefore the most extensive and detailed. And it does not matter if not all the arguments to contradiction work, as long as some of the arguments of the barrage do. At the end of Deduction *I*, Plato imagines an opponent objecting by suggesting that the contradictions may be resolved by appealing to time. *IC* shows that this objection will not work.

For the solution to work, there must be nothing special about the contradictory nature of the form of unity. So Deduction *II* establishes that the other forms have contradictory properties too.

He knows that proponents of the PNC will still want to object; they may do so by denying the assumption of deductions *I* and *II*: that Plato's one is. So we have *III* and *IV*. These show that the consequences of its not being (with contradictory properties) are just as bad—or even worse. This was the method reputed to have been used by Zeno in defence of Parmenides. So Plato brings Zeno into the dialogue, and has him spell out the method right at the start (128d):

"[M]y book speaks against those who assert the many and pays them back in kind with something for good measure, since it aims to make clear that their hypothesis, if one is many, would, if someone examined the matter thoroughly, suffer consequences even more absurd than those suffered by the hypothesis of its being one."

By the end of the dialogue, the contradictory nature of the forms is defended, and the dialogue ends.

What was left for Plato to do to finish this defence of the theory of forms—the dialogue obviously ends in mid air—was to use the possibility that the forms are contradictory to articulate a principled account of the notion of participation

---

[22] See Priest (1998), Objections 3 and 4, and more generally, Priest (2006), chs. 7, 8.

which answered the objections to the theory of forms he had found. There are clearly thoughts that might feed into the project at places in the deductions; but he never succeeded in doing this—at least to judge by his extant dialogues. Maybe, like a particularly elusive form, he perceived it dimly, but was never able to get it into exact focus. As he has Parmenides say (135a–135b):

"Only a very gifted man can come to know that for each thing there is some kind, a being by itself; but only a prodigy more remarkable still will discover that and be able to teach someone else who has sifted through all these difficulties thoroughly and critically for himself."

At any rate, more than two millennia later, when the Aristotle-inspired *horror contradictionis* is finally beginning to fade, Plato's project can now be brought to fruition.

Let me end by returning to the very first oddity of the dialogue that I noted in Section 7.1. Why does Plato make Parmenides the driver of the dialogue? One of the things centrally under attack in the dialogue, as I have interpreted it, is the PNC. As we noted in Section 6.3, Parmenides was the first person to formulate and advocate the Principle. Indeed, as we also noted there, the PNC is the cornerstone of his view. Ostensibly, the *Parmenides* is a critique of Plato (in the form of Socrates) by Parmenides. But in reality, the tables are actually turned, and the dialogue is a critique of Parmenides by Plato, since it attacks this cornerstone of his view—indeed if deduction *IV* is *ad hominem*, the Eleatics are his real opponents in the dialogue.[23] Moreover, in this critique, Plato not only commandeers Parmenides' argument as part of his own (in *IA*), but mischievously puts the whole argument in Parmenides' own mouth—an act of chutzpah perhaps unrivalled in Western philosophy!

---

[23] For what it is worth, after Socrates' death, Plato studied with the Parmenidean Hermogenes, according to Diogenes Laertius, *Lives of Eminent Philosophers*, III, 6.

9

In Search of Falsity

9.1 From the *Parmenides* to the *Sophist*

In this chapter we will be concerned with another appearance of questions of the relationship between parts and wholes in the *Sophist*. These concern meaning, truth, and falsity. The discussion will take us back to the question of the unity of the proposition, with which the book started, as well as confronting an issue about paraconsistent semantics in general.

In the *Sophist*, a stranger from Elea has just arrived in town. The arrival occasions a discussion between the stranger (E), who drives it, and Theaetetus (T), his foil. The topic of the discussion is sophistry. The first part of the dialogue looks for a definition of the sophist. It transpires that it is one who traffics in falsehoods. This exposes the real concern of the dialogue: the nature of falsity (non-being). E exposes some Parmenidean tangles with the notion. He then points out that the notion of truth (being) is just as problematic. (The passage we looked at in Section 6.5, where E attacks Parmenides' *what is*, comes from this section.) He decides to get this sorted out first. This involves a discussion of how the form of being relates to a number of the other important forms (rest, motion, sameness, and difference). This then leads in to a formulation of how falsity is possible—which just leaves a couple of pages to mop up the definition of the sophist himself. (Yes, it is a man.)

One might expect the content of the *Sophist* to bear on the tangle in the *Parmenides* in some way—if only because it is written just after the *Parmenides* (at least according to usual chronologies), it discusses the forms and their properties, and it is driven by another Eleatic. Indeed, many people *have* taken it to bear on the problems of the *Parmenides*. It is really not clear how it is supposed to do this, however.[1]

---

[1] Thus, McPherran (1986) finds in the dialogue an answer to Parmenides' third argument against the forms in the *Parmenides*; Gerson (1986), too, takes the *Sophist* to cast light on the way that the forms can be both transcendent and immanent; Nehamas (1982) takes the dialogue to speak to the problem about self-predication exposed in the *Parmenides*; Pelletier (1990) finds an answer

Some things related to the *Parmenides* are clear. First, E exposes some new problems for the theory of forms (248 ff). According to Plato, the things of the phenomenal world are becoming, but do not have being; only the forms have this. E argues against this (249): both sorts of things have being.[2] Next, Plato has E launch a new attack on Parmenides (241d):

> We shall find it necessary in self-defence to put to the question the pronouncement of father Parmenides, and establish by main force that what is not, in some respect has being, and conversely that what is, in a way is not.

Next, there is an explicit endorsement of the thought that some forms can (but need not) instantiate some (other) forms (251dff). Indeed, being (like change and rest) is (and so instantiates being); and being is not, in the sense that it is different from the other forms, and so is not them (256d–e).[3]

It is in the last of these, perhaps, that one might sense the best hope of finding a key which unlocks the *Parmenides*. Maybe it is the disambiguation of the is/is-not contradiction in this way which explains how the endorsement of a contradiction at the end of the dialogue is to be understood? Unfortunately, not—if for no other reason than that many of the contradictions which arise in the Deductions are not of this form: rest/motion, same/different, older/younger. And in any case, it is difficult to see how diagnosing this ambiguity would help to resolve the problems that Parmenides raises for the forms, since none of these arguments turns explicitly on the is/is-not pair.

At any rate, let us now set the *Parmenides* behind us, and turn to the core problem of the *Sophist*. How is falsity possible?

9.2 The Unity of the Proposition Again

Let us pick up the dialogue where E starts to explain his solution to the problem of falsity. To understand how false predication is possible, we have to understand the prior question of how predication itself is possible. Hence, Plato has to deal with that first. As we saw in Section 3.2, for Aristotle, how to understand predication was a special case of the more general issue of how parts fit together. So it was for Plato. The discussion commences as follows (261d–e):

---

to Parmenides' claim that without the forms discourse would be impossible; and Anscombe (1966) claims to discover a whole new theory of forms in the dialogue.

[2] Note that the claim that objects that instantiate the forms do not have being is no part of the gluon theory of forms.

[3] As a general account of non-being, this is incorrect, as we will see in due course.

E: Now, remembering what we said about forms and letters,[4] let us consider words in the same way. The solution of our present problem promises to lie in that quarter.
T: What are you going to ask me about words?
E: Whether they fit together, or none of them, or some will and some will not.
T: That is plain enough. Some will, some will not.
E: You mean perhaps something like this. Words which, when spoken in succession, signify something, do fit together, while those which mean nothing when they are strung together do not.

E goes on to illustrate. To make a sentence, you need a noun and a verb. 'Theaetetus flies' is a grammatical sentence. 'Theatetus Socrates' and 'sits flies' are not. The point is clear enough. Since Plato is interested in the matter at hand only *en route* to a discussion of truth and falsity, he does not ask why. We should.

The obvious answer is that certain sequences of words express some meaning—some proposition—and some do not. But this just succeeds in relocating the problem. We want to know how it is that some combinations of meanings work together to form a whole. We are back with the problem of the unity of the proposition.[5] Let us apply gluon theory.

Consider, first of all, atomic sentences, those with a verb-phrase, P, and an appropriate number of noun-phrases, $a_1 \ldots a_n$. In the syntax of modern logic: $Pa_1 \ldots a_n$. To keep the account as general as possible, I will make no assumption about what, exactly, the meanings of lexical items are (except that they are not ordered n-tuples). If x is any lexical item, I will write $\mu(x)$ for its meaning (and for ease of reading, I will often drop quotation marks, thus, for example, writing $\mu(P)$ instead of the more cumbersome $\mu('P')$.

The meaning of a sentence is a function of the meanings of its parts, and the way that they are put together. We can cash out this thought by taking $\mu(Pa_1 \ldots a_n)$ to have the parts $\mu(P)$ and $\langle n, \mu(a_1), \ldots, \mu(a_n) \rangle$, where the angle brackets denote, as usual, ordered sets.[6] The first member of the ordered $n+1$-tuple is necessary to determine how many arguments P has, since, for example, the three-tuple $\langle a_1, a_2, a_3 \rangle$ is itself a two-tuple, $\langle a_1, \langle a_2, a_3 \rangle \rangle$. Further, if the sentence is monadic,

---

[4] 252e–253a.

[5] Plato's anticipation of Frege and the problem of the unity of the proposition is noted by Ryle (1960).

[6] One may, of course, ask what sets are. They are themselves unities, and so have their own gluon. Take, for example, a set whose members are x_1, x_2, and x_3. It is natural to take these to be the parts of the set. But some way must be found of showing that these are combined set-wise. We may achieve this by taking the universal of sethood, σ, to be an additional part. If we wish to consider sets which have σ itself as a member, we will need to use a surrogate for this, for example, $\langle 0, \sigma \rangle$. Alternatively, we could follow David Lewis (1991), and take $\{x_1, x_2, x_3\}$ to be the mereological whole of the singletons of its three members, where singletons are simples.

Pa_1, and $\mu(a_1)$ is the kind of thing that can itself be predicative, it serves to code which is the subject of the sentence. (Compare: 'Virtue is rare' and 'Rarity is a virtue'.[7]) And since this is a single thing, there is a gluon, g, which ties them together. The unity is produced because g is identical with the other two parts (and, of course, itself). This is the solution to Frege's problem of the unity of the proposition. Unity does, indeed, require a contradictory entity. Think of the gluon, if you like, as predication (the copula).[8]

This account of the unity of atomic propositions (the meanings of atomic sentences) tells us why and how atomic propositions have a unity, when they do. It also tells us why some collections of meanings have no unity. Thus for example, the two objects, μ(Theaetetus) and μ(Socrates) are a simple congeries. There is no unity with those parts joined by a gluon.

Why, however, is this so? This is not a question to be answered by gluon theory. We look to other theories to tell us what objects there are in the world.[9] For example, we look to physics to tell us what subatomic particles there are; in Chapter 3, metaphysical unities of a certain kind were postulated to provide an account of universals; and in the next chapter we will have a metaphysical theory concerning certain objects which arise in connection with intentionality. In the present case, it is the science of linguistics which will tell us when there are objects (unities) and when there are not. Consider, in this regard, Frege's account of the unity of the proposition. μ(flies) combines with μ(Theaetetus) because the former "has a gap in it", which the latter fills. μ(Socrates), by contrast, does not, and so μ(Socrates) and μ(Theaetetus) do not combine. Fine, but why does μ(Socrates) not have a gap in it? That is its nature. How do we know that it has that nature? Because 'Socrates Theaetetus' does not express a proposition. And how do we know that? Because of our knowledge of linguistics. The situation is no different on the present account.[10]

9.3 Extending the Account

The account of the unity of the proposition may be extended from propositions expressed by atomic sentences to those expressed by compound sentences. This

---

[7] So does the proposition expressed by 'virtue is rare' have the same parts as that expressed by '$\langle 1, \mu(\text{virtue})\rangle$ is rare'? No. The latter has parts μ(rare), and $\langle 1, \mu \langle 1, \mu(\text{virtue})\rangle\rangle$.

[8] See the discussion of Heidegger in Section 4.5.

[9] Or since things of the form 'the so and so' always refer to an object, it might be better to say that we look to other theories to tell us when something characterized as 'the so and so' really is so and so.

[10] There is a related question which *is* a question appropriate for gluon theory: what to make of the mereological whole whose parts are μ(Socrates), μ(Theaetetus), if there is one. That matter was addressed in Section 6.8.

proceeds by recursion, and what recursive clauses there are, will depend on what means are present for generating complex sentences.

Consider, first, a sentence, B, of the form $*(A_1,\ldots,A_n)$, where $*$ is an n-place propositional operator, like negation (1-place) or conjunction (2-place). We may take $\mu(B)$ to be the unity whose parts are $\mu(*)$, $\langle n, \mu(A_1),\ldots,\mu(A_n)\rangle$, and the appropriate gluon.

Quantifiers are a bit more complicated. Take first-order quantification. (Second-order quantification is similar.) First, the account needs to be extended to atomic sentences with free variables, $v_0, v_1, \ldots$. It is natural to think of the variables, in this context, as pronouns: it_0, it_1, and so on. It is clear that pronouns have meanings (unlike letter-salads) and that sentences containing pronouns express some kind of unity. Thus 'it is an elephant' expresses a single thing in a way that 'it it' does not. The meanings of sentences with free variables are not propositions, but they are proposition-like things. I will call them, for want of a better phrase, schematic propositions. The unity which is the meaning of a sentence can be a proposition or a schematic proposition.

For atomic sentences, we now have the following. If A is an atomic sentence, $Pt_1\ldots t_n$, where the ts are either names or pronouns, $\mu(A)$ is the unity of $\mu(P)$, $\langle n, \mu(t_1),\ldots,\mu(t_n)\rangle$, and the appropriate gluon. The change has no effect on the clause for propositional connectives. And now we can formulate the clauses for the quantifiers in a natural way. If Q is a quantifier ($\mathfrak{S}$ or $\mathfrak{A}$) and B is the sentence Qv_nA, then $\mu(B)$ is the entity which is the unity of $\mu(Q)$ and $\langle n, \mu(A)\rangle$, with the appropriate gluon.

So much for the unity of the proposition. Let us now return to the *Sophist*.

9.4 Truth

The point of the discussion of the structure of sentences in the passage we looked at in Section 9.2 was to understand a certain notion of fitting together (blending). This was to help us get to grips with the notions of truth and falsity. To this, E now turns (262e–263b):

> E: Whenever there is a statement it must be about something; it cannot be about nothing.
> T: That is so.
> E: And must it not have a certain character?
> T: Of course.
> E: Now let us fix our attention on ourselves.
> T: We will.

E: I will make a statement to you, then, putting together a thing with an action by means of a name and a verb. You are to tell me what the statement is about.
T: I will do my best.
E: 'Theaetetus sits'—not a lengthy statement is it?
T: No, of very modest length.
E: Now it is for you to say what it is about—to whom it belongs.
T: Clearly about me. It belongs to me.
E: Now take another.
T: Namely?
E: 'Theaetetus, whom I am talking to at the moment, flies.'
T: That too can only be described as belonging to me and about me.
E: And moreover we agree that any statement must have a certain character.
T: Yes.
E: Then what sort of character can we assign to each of these?
T: One is false, the other true.
E: And the true one states about you the things that are [or the facts] as they are.
T: Certainly.

E has given us an account of truth. The true is what says of an object something that is. How is one to understand this? Given the machinery at hand, as follows.

Let us look at a simple case first: that where we have an atomic sentence without pronouns. The idea is straightforward. True predication simply mirrors instantiation. Thus, 'P' is truly predicable of 'a' iff the object referred to by 'a' instantiates the universal referred to by 'P'. In more detail, we suppose that $\mu(P)$ serves to pick out a universal, $\delta(P)$, and $\mu(a)$ serves to pick out an object, $\delta(a)$.[11] (One can think of δ as 'the denotation of'.) Then to say that $\mu(Pa_1 \ldots a_n)$ is true is to say that $\langle \delta(a_1), \ldots, \delta(a_n) \rangle$ instantiates $\delta(P)$.[12]

To generalize this to complex sentences, we need first to be able to handle sentences with pronouns. These are not true or false, but true or false only with respect to some fixing of the denotations of the pronouns. This is normally provided by some context, c. So if t is a name, let $\delta_c(t)$ simply be $\delta(t)$, and if it is a pronoun, let $\delta_c(t)$ be the object assigned to t by the context, c. We now have:

- $\mu(Pt_1 \ldots t_n)$ is true in context c iff $\langle \delta_c(a_1), \ldots, \delta_c(a_n) \rangle$ instantiates $\delta(P)$.

[11] For all we have said, μ could even be δ.
[12] If we do not make the assumption that all predicates denote universals, we have to operate with sets instead. Thus, we take $\delta(P)$ to be a set of (n-tuples of) objects, and we then have:

- $\mu(Pt_1 \ldots t_n)$ is true iff $\langle \delta(a_1), \ldots, \delta(a_n) \rangle \in \delta(P)$.

This variation may be carried through in what follows.

Truth in a context can now be extended to complex propositions in a familiar recursive fashion. I illustrate with respect to the particular quantifier, conjunction, and negation—which, for the nonce, we will take to be classical.

- $\mu(\neg A)$ is true in context c iff $\mu(A)$ is not true in context c
- $\mu(A \wedge B)$ is true in context c iff $\mu(A)$ and $\mu(B)$ are true in context c

The truth of quantified sentences adds a new aspect of contextual dependence. Though a quantifier can range over absolutely everything, normally it ranges over a domain of objects contextually determined. (Thus, if I were to say 'Everyone is dismayed by the dismal state of higher education in Australia' I would not be talking about Australian politicians, let alone Buddhist monks in Japan. I would be talking about those who currently work in the Australian university system.) So let c determine the domain of objects D_c. Then:

- $\mu(\mathfrak{S}v_n B)$ is true in context c iff for some $d \in D_c$, $\mu(B)$ is true in context $c_n(d)$

where $c_n(d)$ is a context that is exactly the same as c, except that it assigns the object d to v_n.

Note that on this account, because of the behaviour of the quantifiers, not only schematic propositions, but also propositions can change their truth values from context to context. One can, if one wishes, obtain quantified propositions whose truth values are not context-dependent simply by taking D_c to be the same in all cases: the context-independent domain of all objects.

The account extends to second-order quantifiers in the obvious way. For modal operators, we must suppose that a context, c, determines not only denotations for the pronouns and a domain of quantification, but also a possible world, w_c. (Normally, of course, we are interested in truth in contexts where the world in question is the actual world.) The pins of an object are now world-relative, as, then, is the instantiation relation. The truth conditions for atomic sentences then become:

- $\mu(Pt_1 \ldots t_n)$ is true in context c iff $\langle \delta_c(a_1), \ldots, \delta_c(a_n) \rangle$ instantiates $\delta(P)$ at w_c

and the truth conditions for a modal $\square$ is:

- $\mu(\square A)$ is true in context c iff for every possible world, w, $\mu(B)$ is true in context $c(w)$

where $c(w)$ is the same as c, except that its world is w.

9.5 Falsity: the Problem

Finally, we come to the nature of falsity. Let us pick up the dialogue where we left off (263b–d):

> E: Whereas the false statement states about you things that are *different* from the things that are.
> T: Yes.
> E: And accordingly states *things that are not* as being.
> T: No doubt.
> E: Yes, but things that *exist*, different from things that exist in your case. For we said that in the case of everything there are many things that are and also many that are not.
> T: Quite so.
> E: So the second statement I made about you, in the first place, according to our definition of the nature of a statement, must itself necessarily be one of the shortest possible.
> T: So we agreed just now.
> E: And secondly it must be about something.
> T: Yes.
> E: And if it is not about you, it is not about anything else.
> T: Certainly.
> E: And if it were about nothing, it would not be a statement at all, for we pointed out that there could not be a statement that was a statement about nothing.
> T: Quite true.
> E: So what is stated about you, but so that what is different is stated as the same or what is not as what is—a combination of verbs and names answering to that description finally seems to be really and truly a false statement.
> T: Perfectly true.

To say something false, is, as E puts it in his first speech in the last quotation, to say something 'different from things that are'. But what does that mean? To approach this, let us look at the problem about falsity that Plato thought he had to solve. He explains this earlier in the dialogue as follows (236e–237a):

> E: The truth is, my friend, that we are faced with an extremely difficult question. The 'appearing' or 'seeming' without really 'being', and the saying of something which is yet not true—all these expressions have always been and still are deeply involved in perplexity. It is extremely hard, Theaetetus, to find correct terms in which one may say or think that falsehoods have a real existence, without being caught in a contradiction by the mere utterance of such words.
> T: Why?
> E: The audacity of the statement lies in its implication that 'what is not' has being, for in no other way could a falsehood come to have being. But, my young friend, when we were of your age the great Parmenides from beginning to end testified

> against this, constantly telling us what he also says in his poem, 'Never shall this be proved—that things that are not are, but do thou, in thy inquiry, hold back thy thought from this way.'

How to understand the problem about falsehood is not completely clear here either. One might take it to be something that is an artifact of the Greek language. The natural way to express that something is false in Greek is to say that it is not, as in: Theaetetus' flying is not. But Ancient Greek has no word to express existence other than the copula, 'is'.[13] Hence, to say something false is to talk of the non-existent. Perhaps Frede is making the point when he says:[14]

> There is a problem about the very possibility of false statements. For a statement, in order to be a statement at all, has to manage to say something, that is, there has to be something that gets said by it. But both in ordinary Greek and in the language of the Greek philosophers a false statement is one that says what is not (or: what is not being). Yet what is not being does not seem to be something that is there to be said. Hence it would seem that there is nothing that gets said by a false statement. But in this case it fails to be a statement. So it seems that there can be no false statements.

If the problem is this, it does not seem too hard a matter to untangle. There is a conceptual distinction between 'exists' and 'is true'; and correspondingly, between 'does not exist', and 'is not true'. In particular, the inference from '*a* is not true' to '*a* does not exist', like Theaetetus, will not fly.

But I think there is a better way to understand the problem. This comes over more clearly in a passage in the *Theaetetus* itself (a dialogue we will meet in more detail in the next chapter). At one point in this, the nature of falsity rears its ugly head. The relevant passage is as follows. The driver of the dialogue is Socrates (S); his foil is again Theaetetus (T). I quote the whole passage (188d–189b):

> s: May it not simply be that one who thinks *what is not* about anything cannot but be thinking of what is false, whatever his state of mind may be in other respects?
> t: There is some likelihood in that, Socrates.
> s: Then what shall we say, Theaetetus, if we are asked, 'But is what you describe possible for anyone? Can any man think what is not, either about something that is or absolutely? I suppose we must answer to that, 'Yes, when he believes something and what he believes is not true.' Or what are we to say?
> t: We must say that.
> s: Then is the same sort of thing possible in any other case?
> t: What sort of thing?
> s: That a man should see something, and yet what he sees should be nothing.
> t: No. How could that be?

---

[13] On these things, see Kahn (2003), pp. vii–xl.
[14] Frede (1992), p. 397. Though he might also be making the next point to be taken up.

s: Yet surely, if what he sees is something, it must be a thing that is. Or do you suppose that 'something' can be reckoned among the things that have no being at all?
t: No, I don't.
s: Then, if he sees something, he sees a thing that is?
t: Evidently.
s: And if he hears a thing, he hears something, and hears a thing that is?
t: Yes.
s: And if he touches a thing, he touches something, and if something, then a thing that is.
t: That is also true.
s: And if he thinks, he thinks something, doesn't he?
t: Necessarily.
s: And when he thinks something, he thinks a thing that is?
t: I agree.
s: So to think what is not is to think nothing.
t: Clearly.
s: But surely to think nothing is the same as not to think at all.
t: That seems plain.
s: If so, it is impossible to think what is not, either about anything that is or absolutely.
t: Evidently.
s: Then thinking falsely must be something different from thinking what is not.
t: So it seems.
s: False judgement, then, is no more possible for us on these lines than on those we were following just now.
t: No, it certainly is not.

The problem here appears to be this. When one utters a sentence (has a thought), this has a content. The content is some state of affairs (as, perhaps in the *Tractatus*). But if the sentence (thought) is false, the state of affairs does not exist. That is, the sentence (thought) has no content. It is therefore impossible to utter a false sentence (have a false thought).

There is no obvious dependence on the Greek language in this argument, but it still may be contested on a number of grounds. First, one might hold that the content of a sentence is not a state of affairs. It is a proposition. The proposition, in turn, may be given its content by its truth conditions (in the way we saw in Section 9.4). And even if one does take the content of a statement to be a state of affairs, one does not have to agree that the state must exist: it may be a non-existent object, as noneists would have it. (In general, there is no reason to suppose that the object of an intentional state, like thinking, is an existent object.)

Plato's problem, then, is solved. But this solution was not his. So what was it? With the problem clarified, let us now return to that question.

9.6 Falsity: the Solution

For Plato, to give an account of falsity (of simple predications), he has to explain what thing it is that a false statement is about, and what it is that is said about it. Both of these should exist. Plato's solution is as follows. 'Theaetetus flies' is about Theaetetus, who certainly exists. So far so good. When something false is said about him, what is said is something 'different from the things that are'. But what, exactly, does that mean? The most obvious interpretation is that to say something false (that is not) about Theaetetus is to predicate something of him different from anything which is true.

Unfortunately, this cannot be right as an account of falsity, since I can say something false without predicating anything at all. You ask me if Theaetetus sits. I say 'no'. What I have said is (we may suppose) false. Yet my utterance contains no predication at all. Perhaps this is uncharitable. One might plausibly suggest that my utterance is really short for 'Theaetetus is not sitting' which does contain a predication, 'not sitting'. And indeed, 'not sitting' is different from anything truly predicable of Theaetetus.

But now we have just moved the problem. Essentially, to say something false of Theaetetus is to say of him something that is not true. Clearly, this presupposes an account of negation. Negation and falsity are so intimately connected that matters cannot end here. We need an account of negation. E in fact, provides this earlier in the dialogue. (This is just after he explains in what sense being is not. Indeed, it is really just a version of the same idea.) To say that a is not b is to say that a is c, where b is different from c (257a–c):

> E: Now let us mark this.
> T: Yes?
> E: When we speak of 'that which is not,' it seems that we do not mean something contrary to what exists, but only something that is different.
> T: How?
> E: In the same way that when, for example, we speak of something as 'not tall,' we may just as well say by that phrase 'what is equal' as 'what is short,' mayn't we?
> T: Certainly.
> E: So, when it is asserted that a negative signifies a contrary, we shall not agree, but admit no more than this—that the prefix 'not' indicates something different from the words that follow, or rather from the things designated by the words pronounced after the negative.
> T: Exactly.

The trouble with this answer is that it is just plain wrong. To say that Socrates is not short is not to say that he is white, even though *short* and *white* are different from each other. For both may be true together.[15]

For the idea to work, what is needed is not just something different from being short, but something *incompatible* with it, such as being tall. So let us try: to say that *a* is not *b* is to say that *a* is *c*, where *c* is incompatible with *b*. The trouble with this answer, as was pointed out by Russell in his lectures on Logical Atomism,[16] is that to say that something is incompatible with something else is to say that they are *not* compatible, that one can*not* have both together. We have not eliminated negation—just smuggled it in.

From a contemporary perspective, Plato would just seem to be trying to do the impossible. You might define falsity in terms of negation, or *vice versa*; but ultimately something of this kind has to be taken as a "primitive notion".[17] Some things, after all, cannot be defined in terms of more basic things. Plato, then, may just have to settle for something like: x is false (in context c) iff x is not true (in context c), and have done with it.

9.7 Negative Properties

This account of negation is, of course, exactly the one that is given in classical logic, and the one we employed in Section 6.4. It is not, however, how negation standardly works in a paraconsistent logic. As we noted in Section P.5 (and in more detail in Section 2.10.1), in the semantics of *LP* and similar paraconsistent logics, falsity is not the simple complement of truth: the two can overlap. Truth and falsity are therefore (at least partially) independent. Hence, the account of truth in Section 9.4 has to be revised in the light of this.

How to do so for atomic sentences, we have, in fact, already seen in Section 3.6. Let me put what was said there in a slightly different way. We take it that every property has an "opposite"; so, corresponding to redness, there is non-redness, corresponding to being an adult, there is being a non-adult, and so on. Let us write these property pairs with a '+' and a '−'. So if *r* is some property, we write r^+ (for example, redness) and r^- (for example, non-redness). In standard cases, objects

---

[15] Similar comments apply to a theory according to which *not to be* is simply to be different from being. If something is red, it is something different from being. But it may *be* as well.
[16] Pears (1972), p. 69f.
[17] See Priest (1987), 4.7. One might think to avoid the problem by defining $\neg A$ as $A \rightarrow \bot$, where, for any B, $\bot \rightarrow B$. But this gives the wrong definition of negation in most paraconsistent logics. See Priest (2006), 4.7.

will instantiate one or other of r^+ and r^-, but sometimes they may instantiate both.[18]

We can use the pairs of opposites to define truth and falsity for atomic sentences, as follows:

- $\mu(Pt_1 \ldots t_n)$ is true in context c iff $\langle \delta_c(a_1), \ldots, \delta_c(a_n) \rangle$ instantiates $\delta(P)$; that is, it has a pin identical with $\delta^+(P)$
- $\mu(Pt_1 \ldots t_n)$ is false in context c iff $\langle \delta_c(a_1), \ldots, \delta_c(a_n) \rangle$ does not instantiate $\delta(P)$; that is, it has a pin identical with $\delta^-(P)$

The truth and falsity conditions for negation now become:

- $\mu(\neg A)$ is false in context c iff $\mu(A)$ is true in context c
- $\mu(\neg A)$ is true in context c iff $\mu(A)$ is false in context c

We also have to add falsity conditions to the truth conditions of the other connectives and the quantifiers. Given the semantics of *LP*, these are pretty obvious. Thus, for example:

- $\mu(A \wedge B)$ is false in context c iff $\mu(A)$ or $\mu(B)$ is false in context c
- $\mu(\mathsf{S}v_n B)$ is false in context c iff for all $d \in D_c$, $\mu(B)$ is false in context $c_n(d)$
- $\mu(\Box A)$ is false in context c iff for some possible world, w, $\mu(B)$ is false in context $c(w)$

The account, it is true, makes use of the polarity of properties, at the root of the recursion. But something of this sort must be taken as basic, as I have already noted. Compare, in this regard, the theory of Wittgenstein's *Tractatus*. In this, atomic sentences are true if they correspond to a fact. Their negations are true if there is no such fact. But, in natural language, it is not clear, given a pair of contradictory propositions, which one is really the negated one. '*a*' is translucent' and '*a* is opaque' are equally good candidates for "positive" sentences. Each can be taken as the negation of the other. Wittgenstein's assymmetry does not appear.[19]

One might be suspicious of "negative properties". Traditionally, many philosophers have been suspicious of negative entities in general. Everything that is, it might be felt, is positively; over and above that, there is nothing. But negative properties are, in exactly the same way that positive properties are—whatever that is. They just ground the truth of the negative—negative sentences. (Or better—since, as I have just noted, the question of which sentences are negative is not really well defined—the polar opposite facts ground the truth of the polar

---

[18] And if we want to allow for truth value gaps, neither.
[19] See Molnar (2000).

opposite sentences.) Moreover, we are all accustomed to the idea that physical reality comes with polarities (positive and negative charge, spin-up and spin-down, and so on). Why should metaphysical reality not have similar polarities?

One argument sometimes given against negative entities is that one cannot see them. In the days of modern physics, few, I guess, would still take seriously the thought that something must be perceivable to be real. But in any case, we can see negative pins. Suppose that a piece of glass, *a*, alternates between the polar opposites of being transparent and being opaque. As we look at the glass we can see both its transparency and its opaqueness. The opposite pins are both visible. "Negative" properties are, then, no more problematic than "positive" ones.[20]

9.8 From Plato to Paraconsistency

In this chapter, with the help of Plato, we have addressed the problem of falsity—tying up some loose ends left over from Part I of the book as well; notably, the unity of the proposition. Few now, I think, would have the same sort of concerns about falsity as Plato had; but paraconsistency raises its own questions about falsity. Falsity is not simply the *absence* of truth; in some sense, it is a positive. Or perhaps better, reality contains certain "negative" elements. Perhaps worries about such matters are in the same ballpark as Plato's worries; perhaps not. At any rate, they can be assuaged, as we have seen—and in a way much more satisfactory than Plato's own attempt to untangle the problem of falsity.

But we are not finished yet. The account of truth and falsity I have in this chapter given makes use of the notion of denotation. What is it for a word to denote an object? More generally, how is it that any representation represents that which it represents? We turn to this question in the next chapter.

[20] For a related discussion of negative facts and perceiving negative states of affairs, see Priest (2006), 2.7 and ch. 3.

10

Perception, Intentionality, and Representation

10.1 To Represent and be Represented

The last chapter made use of the notion of denotation. This is a species of the genus *representation*. This chapter is about that.

Many things represent—words, maps, thoughts, scores; and many things are represented—places, animals, music, numbers. But how is this representation achieved? Naively, one might think that representation is achieved by some form of similarity. In such a way does a photograph of a person represent them. But similarity is neither necessary nor sufficient. A piece of music may be represented by a configuration of dots on a page, which is the score, or a series of binary numbers coding an electronic file. Neither of these is similar to, say, the music of *Madame Butterfly* in any normal sense of the word.[1] Conversely, if a chance configuration of clouds formed for five minutes, which looked exactly like the Taj Mahal, then (absent some fairly elaborate story about the context) this would not represent the Taj itself. So what is representation?

We will approach an answer to the question via an analysis of intentionality. The nature of intentionality is itself a highly vexed question. How is it that a mental state can be *of* something. Wherein resides aboutness? An answer to this question will provide yet another application for gluon theory.

10.2 From the *Sophist* to the *Theaetetus*

We will approach the intentionality, in the first instance, by looking at a special case of it, perception; and we will do this with the help of a passage from Plato's *Theaetetus*. The *Theaetetus* is a discussion set the day before the *Sophist*[2] with an

---

[1] Though one could perhaps invent some technical sense of similarity, according to which these things are similar, as does Wittgenstein in the *Tractatus*.
[2] *Theaetetus*, 210d; *Sophist*, 216a.

overlapping cast of characters. In the *Sophist*, it is an Eleatic stranger who takes his turn to grill Theaetetus. In the *Theaetetus*, it is Socrates (S), the driver of the dialogue, who wracks the hapless Theaetetus (T).

The concern of the *Theaetetus* is the nature of knowledge. Three main answers are tabled. The first is that knowledge is perception; the second that knowledge is true belief; the third that knowledge is true belief plus an "account" (*logos*). All three are rejected, the dialogue moving through discussions of many related matters. (The passage we looked at concerning falsity in the last chapter (Section 9.5) occurs in connection with the notion of truth, invoked in the second answer.)

The passage we will be concerned with in this chapter arises in connection with the first suggestion: that knowledge is perception. More accurately: if something appears to someone in a certain way, then the content of the appearance is knowledge. (There is no suggestion that the appearance has to be a sensory appearance.) The view is attributed to Protagoras. In the process of discussing this, Socrates tables a certain theory of perception. The theory appears somewhat bizarre, and there is no suggestion that Socrates himself subscribes to it, but let us take a look at it. There is more going for it than might at first have been thought.

10.3 Socrates' Story of Perception

The theory is set out at 155d–157c:[3]

s: ... [The] first principle, on which all that we have said just now depends, is that the universe really is motion and nothing else. And there are two kinds of motion. Of each kind there are any number of instances, but they differ in that the one kind has the power of acting, and the other of being acted upon. From the intercourse and friction of these with one another arise offspring, endless in number, but in pairs of twins. One of each pair is something perceived, the other a perception, whose birth always coincides with that of the thing perceived. Now, for the perceptions we have names like 'seeing', 'hearing', 'smelling', 'feeling cold', 'feeling hot', and again pleasures and pains and desires and fears, as they are called, and so on. There are any number that are nameless, though names have been found for a whole multitude. On the other side, the brood of things perceived always comes to birth at the same moment with one or another of these—with instances of seeing, colours of corresponding variety, with instances of hearing, sounds in the same way, and with all the other perceptions, the other things that are perceived that are akin to them. Now, what light does this story throw on what has gone before, Theaetetus? Do you see?

Theaetetus clearly has a troubled look on his face. Socrates continues.

[3] It is again summarized at 182a–b.

s: Well, consider whether we can round it [the account] off. The point is that all these things are, as we were saying, in motion, but there is a quickness or slowness in their motion. The slow sort has its motion without change of place and with respect to what comes within range of it, and that is how it generates offspring, but the offspring generated are quicker, in as much as they move from place to place and their motion consists of change of place. As soon, then, as an eye and something else whose structure is adjusted to the eye come within range and give birth to the whiteness together with its cognate perception—things that would never have come into existence if either of the two had approached anything else—then it is that as the vision comes from the eyes and the whiteness from the thing that joins in giving birth to the colour pass in the space between, the eye becomes filled with vision and now sees, and becomes, not a vision, but a seeing eye, while the other parent of the colour is saturated with whiteness and becomes, on its side, not whiteness, but a white thing, be it stick[4] or stone or whatever else may change to be coloured.

And so, too, we must think in the same way as the rest—'hard', 'hot', and all of them—that no one of them has any being just by itself, as indeed was said before, but that it is in their intercourse with one another that all arise in their variety as a result of their motion, since it is impossible to have any 'firm notion', as they say, of either what is active or what is passive in them, in any single case, as having any being. For there is no such thing as an agent until it meets with a patient, nor any patient until it meets with its agent...

Does all this please you, Theaetetus? Will you accept it as palatable to your taste?

Theaetetus still doubts, and wonders what game Socrates is playing. Socrates then makes his common (and disingenuous) reply, that he is merely helping his interlocutor to figure out what he himself thinks.

Never mind. According to the theory of perception proffered, in an act of perception, two things come into existence, a perception and a thing perceived. Although they are two, since they are coordinate, we may think of them as a single thing with two poles, a subject pole, s, and an object pole, o. Being a single thing, it will have a gluon, g. More of this anon.

Let us call the single thing, for reasons that will become clear later, an *i-couple*. The nature of the subject pole of the couple is reasonably straightforward. We may naturally understand it as a certain mental state. (Though the nature of mental states is itself moot, no harm is done in the present context, if one takes them to be appropriate brain states, though this is not necessary.) The nature of the object pole of the couple is less clear. Socrates gives whiteness as an example, and so one might think of this view as some form of the doctrine of secondary properties. But this is wrong, since many of the things one can perceive, such as shape, are not secondary properties.

---

[4] The text has 'stock', but this is obviously a misprint.

A much more natural way to think of the matter is in phenomenological terms. For Husserl, the subject pole of the *i*-couple is the *noesis*, the act of cognition, and its object pole is its content, its *noema*. In *Ideas*, Husserl explains the notion as follows:[5]

> Corresponding at all points to the manifold data of the real noetic content, there is a variety of data displayable in really pure intuition, and in a correlative "*noematic content*", or briefly "*noema*"—terms which we shall henceforth be continually using.
>
> Perception, for instance, has its noema, and at the base of this its perceptual meaning, that is, the *perceived as such*. Similarly, recollection, when it occurs, has as its own *remembered as such* precisely as it is "meant" and "consciously known" in it; so again judging has its own *judged as such*, pleasure the *pleasure as such*, and so forth. We must everywhere take the noematic correlate, which (in the very extended meaning of the term) is here referred to as "meaning" (*Sinn*) precisely as it lies "immanent" in the experience of perception, of judgement, of liking, and so forth, that is, *if we question in pure form this experience itself*, as we find it there presented to us.

We should think of the object-pole, then, as a noema.

10.4 Noema and Object

What, exactly, however, is a noema? In particular, if I look at a tree, for example, and so form a mental representation, how does its content relate to the tree itself? Husserl, himself, stepped back from this question. Given the attitude of *epoche*, the structure of the noema was to be investigated in its own right, bracketing off its relationship to any object outside consciousness.[6]

However, there are good reasons to be less guarded. Suppose that I look at the Taj Mahal. *Prima facie*, this is a relationship between two things: me and the Taj. It is such a relation *seconda facie*, as well. Suppose that I see the Taj Mahal, and that it is white. Then it would appear to follow that $\mathfrak{S}x(I$ see x and x is white). My perceptual representation is, then, of the Taj itself. This is its content. Taking the noema to be the external object is precisely the move that Heidegger makes when he takes over Husserl's phenomenological methodology, but dispenses with the bracketing.[7]

Understood in this way, then, the subject pole of a perceptual couple is a mental state, and the object pole is the object of which it is a representation. This, of course, goes back on Socrates' idea that the object pole itself comes into existence with the *i*-couple. However, my aim here is not to defend the view Socrates describes, but to develop it into a workable theory.

---

[5] Husserl (1931), p. 258.   [6] For example, *Ideas*, §31.
[7] See the discussion of the phenomenological method in *Being and Time*, § 7.

A problem with this understanding of the object pole immediately arises. In fact, just after the passage from the *Theaetetus* quoted in the last section, Socrates goes on to raise it (157d–158a):

s: Once more, then, tell me whether you like this notion that nothing is, but is always becoming, good, or beautiful or any other of the other things we mentioned?
t: Well, when I hear you explaining it as you have, it strikes me as extraordinarily reasonable, and to be accepted as you have stated it.
s: Then let us not leave it incomplete. There remains the question of dreams and disorders, especially madness and all the mistakes that madness is said to make in seeing or hearing or otherwise misperceiving. You know, of course, that in all these cases the theory we have just stated is supposed to be admittedly disproved, on the ground that in these conditions we certainly have false perceptions and that so far from its being true that what appears to any man also is, on the contrary none of these appearances is real.
t: That is quite true, Socrates.
s: What argument, then, is left for us who maintain that each perception is knowledge, and what appears to each man 'is' for him to whom it appears?
t: I hesitate to say that I have no reply, Socrates...

The problem is that there are hallucinations and the like—perceptual experiences where there is no object that corresponds to the perceptual content. Hence, the content of a mental state cannot be the object itself—at least in such cases. Or, to put it the other way around: if perception really does relate the agent to the object itself, such non-veridical perception would be impossible.

Theaetetus may be stuck for an answer to the problem; and we can leave Protagoras to look after himself.[8] But, for a noneist, there is an obvious answer to the question of how non-veridical perceptions are possible. The object pole of an *i*-couple is indeed an object; in a non-veridical perceptual experience, it is just that the object is a non-existent one.[9] Some people prefer to use 'see' veridically, so that one cannot see something that does not exist. The veridical sense of seeing can be defined very simply from the more general sense. It is just a seeing, in this sense, where the object pole exits. Veridical and non-veridical perceptual states will, of course, have different etiologies.[10]

---

[8] Socrates suggests (158a–160e) that Protagoras would say that the object of perception must exist *for the perceiver*, so tying the view to Protagorean relativism.
[9] There is a sense of mis-perceiving according to which I perceive an actual object, but do not see it accurately. Thus, I may look at a typo and see the word that is supposed to be there instead. In this case, there is indeed an object of perception, but the mental representation of it is just inaccurate.
[10] It is interesting, in this context, to compare the view with that of Thomas Reid, who held a direct realist account of perception, and a noneism to go with it. See the discussion in Yaffe and Nichols (2009). A noneist account of perception is defended in Routley (1980), 8.10.

10.5 Intentionality

With this material in place, we now have a straightforward analysis of the perceptual relation. Simply:

(*) agent a perceives o iff there is some perceptual state of a, s, such that there is an i-couple s-o

This will not quite do, though. The problem is that an object of perception can itself be a perceptual mental state, s'. (One can have a mental representation of a mental representation.) And if s' is such a state of a, then, according to this definition, if a perceives s then a also perceives s'. Clearly, this may not be the case. The problem is that since an i-couple is intrinsically symmetric, we have no way of telling which is the subject pole and which is the object pole. A solution is to code that information into the i-couple itself.

This can be done in (at least) two ways. The first (and simplest) is to take the object pole of the i-couple to be o', where $o' = \langle s, o \rangle$. Alternatively, and perhaps more naturally, whenever I see something, I see it under some aspect, a (front on, from above, and so on). One may take the object pole to be $o' = \langle a, o \rangle$. Since no mental state is an ordered pair, each of these constructions determines the subject pole uniquely. If we replace s-o in (*) with s-o', we may accept the restatement.

There is nothing peculiar to perception about this analysis; it may apply equally to any intentional relation. Indeed, Socrates and Husserl (and Heidegger) are clear on this matter. So let R be any intentional relation (perceives, admires, fears, dreams...). Then aRo iff there is some R-mental state of a, s, such there is an i-couple a, s-o'. (Of course, a can bear more than one intentional relation to the same object.)

We may now come, at last, to the nature of intentionality. Intentionality is a feature of a mental state whereby it is *of* some object. Differently put, a mental state can represent some object. How are we to understand this? An intentional mental state is simply one that is the subject pole of an appropriate i-couple. And crucially, since an i-couple is an object, it has a gluon, g.[11] So $s = g = o'$. We may take this relation between s and o to constitute intentionality, representation. Many people have found intentionality deeply puzzling.[12] A mental state is simply what it is. It can causally interact with other things; but how can it "capture" an object? What, then, constitutes intentionality of a mental state, s? Simply the fact that it is glued to its object o, via o'. Gluons are literally the glue of intentionality. And why, it might be asked, do we think of the intentionality as a property of the

---

[11] Assuming that the gluon is prime, the gluon of an i-couple always exists, because its subject pole does.

[12] See, for example, the discussion in Jacob (2010).

mental state and not its object? Because the mental state cannot exist without its object, whereas the object does not depend on the mental state. In other words, the relation '*s* intends *o*' is an internal relation in its first place, but not its second.

Perhaps a critic may be less than satisfied with this explanation. Of course intentionality involves a connection—some sort of joining—between the mental state and the object intended. What has been done but simply give this a name? Much. Intentionality has been explained in terms of there being a certain object, an *i*-couple. And the intentional bond is the gluon of that unity. This is a substantial explanation of intentionality. Of course, it does not tell us when the relation of intentionality obtains. As I have already stressed (Section 9.2), we look to other theories to tell us what objects exist and when. In the present case, this is in the provenance of cognitive science.[13]

10.6 Representation

The intentionality of mental states is one kind of representation. It is not the only kind. As I observed at the start of the chapter, many things are said to represent, and most of these are not mental states; for example, maps, words, and so on. However, the representation of mental states is, arguably, the most fundamental kind. If there were no cognitive agents who represented the world to themselves in various ways, nothing else would represent. Thus, the idea of a language with words that represent, when there are no cognitive agents who can use the language, would seem mere whimsy.

This suggests that we may be able to account for all other forms of representation in terms of the intentionality of mental states. One way to do so is as follows. Let us take words as examples—and here we may think of the relation as being one of denotation. Other forms of representation, such as maps, scores, and so on, may be taken to work in essentially the same way.

Words are not mental states. (They are abstract objects (types), air waves (spoken tokens), and so on.) But when a word is in the repertoire of a speaker, it is presumably coordinated with a kind of mental representation in their cognitive architecture. (I do not assume that this is anything as crude as a mental image.) If this represents (intends) the object *o*, then we may say that the word represents *o* for that speaker. If the word is used in a language spoken by a group of speakers,

---

[13] In this chapter I have discussed only intentional verbs where the complement is a noun-phrase. What of those where the complement is a verb phrase, as in 'I believe (that) the sun is shining'. Our account can be extended to these quite straightforwardly by taking such verbs to express a relation between the agent and a proposition. These are glued into an *i*-couple.

then, as a first cut, we can say that the word represents *o* (*simpliciter*) if for every member, *m*, of the group it represents *o* for *m*.

The account has to be fine-tuned in various ways. Universality is, in general, too much to hope for. In any linguistic community there will be outliers. Provided that they are a small minority, they will not disrupt matters. Hence, it is necessary only that, for *most* speakers in the group, the word represents *o*. (And yes, since 'most' is vague, this means that a claim to the effect that a word represents an object is vague too.)

More importantly, word-representation is, to a certain extent, a matter of public record. Hence, it is hard to maintain that a word represents an object, *o*, *simpliciter*, if it represents *o* for most of the speakers, but none of them realizes that it represents *o* for the others. The fact that the word represents *o* for most of the speakers has therefore to be something like common knowledge. How, exactly, to cash out the notion of common knowledge required is a nice point; but a naive understanding will suffice here.[14] How we achieve such knowledge is also an interesting question, though one that, again, does not need to be discussed here. It suffices that we do have it. It is common knowledge, for example, amongst English-speakers that 'London' represents London for most English-speakers.

Doubtless, there may be more fine-tuning to be done, but this can safely be left to those with a penchant for chisholming;[15] the basic pieces of the account of representation are in place.

10.7 From Part II to Part III

In this second part of the book we have been untangling various problems bequeathed to philosophy by Plato. These concerned mereological wholes, universals, meaning, falsity, perception, and intentionality. We have also found a new interpretation of the *Parmenides*, that troubling dialogue. These are some of the interesting applications of gluon theory.

In the next part of the book we will change focus. A major concern for us so far has been the *relation* of identity: what it is, and how it functions. A major concern in the next part of the book will be a different sense of identity: the identity *of* something. And just as we have learned something from Plato in this part of the book, we will learn something from Buddhist philosophy in the next.

---

[14] For a general discussion of common knowledge, see Vanderschraaf and Sillari (2007).
[15] As the *Philosophical Lexicon* has it. Dennett and Steglich-Petersen (2008).

PART III
Buddhist Themes

Society does not consist of individuals but expresses the sum of interrelations, the relations within which the individual stand.

Marx, *Grundrisse* [Nicholaus (1973), p. 265]

11

Absence of Self, and the Net of Indra

11.1 Identity Again

In this part of the book we change tack somewhat. Gluons, in particular, will take a back seat for a while. We start with a new question. I am a person. What makes me the thing that I am? What makes me that particular person? There are a number of ways one might phrase this question. One natural way to put it would be to ask what it is that gives me my identity. This notion of identity is quite different from the notion of identity that has so far concerned us in the book. Identity in the sense that we have been dealing with so far is the identity relation, $=$. The notion of identity at issue now will be the identity *of* something. When we ask for the identity of something, we are asking for information which will, as it were, allow us to pick the thing out from the myriad things. 'Identity of' is not a relation; it is a functional expression. To avoid any confusion, I will eschew talking of identity for what is now at issue.[1]

Another way of asking the question is this. I have a certain being. What is that: what is it to have my being? The word 'being' also has many senses, and I have already used it to mean 'being something'. So it is wise to avoid putting the matter in this way as well. A better terminology is this. What we are after is the what-it-is to be the person in question. I will call this the *quiddity* of the object.[2] This terminology is not entirely danger-free either. The term is used in Medieval Western philosophy in a not unrelated way. However, to forestall any misunderstandings immediately, I disassociate my use of the term from its Medieval connotations. In particular, it has nothing whatever to do with Aristotelian essences.

---

[1] One might initially think that one could define one notion of identity in terms of the other. This is not the case. Thus, one might try: $x = y$ iff the identity of x = the identity of y. This is clearly circular. In the other direction, one might try: the identity of x is the (a) y such that $y = x$. This just delivers the wrong kind of thing.

[2] From the Latin 'quid' = *what*.

So far, I have talked of people. But the question concerning quiddity can, of course, be asked about anything. Take the Earth, for example; what gives it the quiddity it has?—or what gives Australia the quiddity it has? There is no *a priori* reason why there should be a uniform answer to this kind of question. Maybe different kinds of things have their quiddities constituted in different ways. However, in this chapter I will provide an account of what it is that constitutes the quiddity of an object, and the account is uniform: it works for any kind of object. It is essentially that of the Buddhist Madhyamaka philosophers. The Chinese Huayan tradition will also get in on the act towards the end of the chapter.

11.2 Look for Your Self

Let us start with a particular case: that of a person. This is a singularly tough case, and if we can sort this out, getting other things to fall into place will be relatively easy. So take a particular person—say you. What makes you the person you are? What gives you your quiddity? A standard answer is that you have a *self*, a part of you which exists as the selfsame thing at all the times that you do, and which defines you as you. But is this, indeed, the case?

Consider a car. A car is simply a bunch of parts: the carburettor, engine block, exhaust pipe, and so on. These come together when caused to do so, interact; sometimes particular parts wear out and are replaced; and eventually, the whole thing wears out and ceases to exist. There is no one thing which needs to be constant through the entire history of the car which makes it that very car.[3] A fortiori, no self for the car. Surely, you are just the same as this?[4]

If one is a physicalist, the car analogy seems very apt. People are just collections of biological parts, which come and go, or at least change their composition, during a person's life. Some of these parts are neurons, which are responsible for a person's mental states. But these are, in principle, no different from any of the others. The whole bunch of things is constantly changing, the elements being held together by various kinds of causal connections. To employ an analogy used by Wittgenstein in a different context,[5] people are like a long rope

---

[3] What about its gluon? This is just another part of the car. True, it may remain numerically the same gluon over the life of the car. (See Section 6.10.) But of course, the object itself remains numerically the same over time too. And just as the object changes over time, so does the gluon. A self is something that is intrinsically changeless.

[4] That people are like this is an orthodox view in Buddhist philosophy. (See, for example, Siderits (2007), ch. 3.) Persons, to the extent that they exist at all, are just collections of parts. Standardly they are taken to be parts pertaining to: the body, evaluative sentiments, perceptions, beliefs, and consciousness (the *skandhas*). They come into existence in virtue of the appropriate causes, interact with each other, change, and finally go out of existence in virtue of the appropriate causes.

[5] *Philosophical Investigations*, Section 67. The context is a discussion of family resemblance.

made up of many strands. Each strand goes part way through the rope, but only part way.

If one is not a physicalist about the mind, things are less straightforward. It is not an implausible thought that what identifies a person as that very person is some core mental state, maybe consciousness.[6] Kant, for example, suggests that there is such a thing. In the *Critique of Pure Reason* he argues (B131–132) that any thought I have is accompanied by a special thought, an 'I think'. This is, indeed, what determines the unity of my consciousness, and makes the thought *mine*.

Even if he is right about the existence of such a companion to thought, there is an evident problem about taking the identity of a person to be defined by its presence. Such a thing is present only when one is conscious. It is not there when one is asleep and not thinking, or knocked out and in oblivion. But you are still you at these times. So it cannot be the presence of this which identifies you as you.

Even if one were to solve this problem is some way, another, perhaps more fundamental, strikes. The claim that there is such a constant companion to thoughts does not bear scrutiny, as explained by David Hume, some forty years before Kant wrote. As he puts it in the *Treatise of Human Nature* (I, IV, 6):[7]

There are some philosophers who imagine that we are every moment intimately conscious of what we call our SELF; that we feel its existence and its continuance in existence; and are certain, beyond the evidence of a demonstration, both of its perfect identity and simplicity. The strongest sensation, the most violent passion, say they, instead of distracting us from this view, only fix it the more intensely, and make us consider their influence on *self* either by their pain or pleasure...

For my part, when I enter most intimately into what I call *myself*, I always stumble on some particular perception or other, of heat or cold, light or shade, love or hatred, pain or pleasure. I never can catch *myself* at any time without a perception, and never can observe anything but the perception... If anyone, upon serious and unprejudiced reflection, thinks he has a different notion of *himself*, I must confess, I can reason no longer with him. All I can allow him is, that he may be in the right as well as I, and that we are essentially different in this particular. He may, perhaps, perceive something simple and continued, which he calls *himself*; though I am certain there is no such principle in me.

But setting aside some metaphysician of this kind, I may venture to affirm of the rest of mankind, that they are nothing but a bundle or collection of different perceptions which succeed each other with an inconceivable rapidity and are in perpetual flux and movement...

---

[6] Buddhists, note, have not traditionally been physicalists about the mind. The *skandhas* are both physical and mental. One of the *skandhas* is consciousness; but this is itself composed of parts which are just as transient and evanescent as any other.

[7] Selby-Bigge (1978), pp. 251–2.

Introspection, then, reveals no such "master-thought"—merely fleeting and disparate fragments.[8] Whether one looks for a self in physical parts or mental parts, then, the result is the same: we find nothing but a bunch of parts, which come, interact, and go.

11.3 The Illusion of Self

Hume's point is reinforced by modern developments in cognitive science. It would appear, by analogy with a standard well-written computer program, that one's cognitive functioning has a number of distinct parts, or, as it is more normal to call them in this context, modules: a speech module, a vision module, and so on (each of which may have its own sub-modules). The modules perform their proper functions, and in so doing, interact with each other, providing the appropriate inputs and outputs.[9] In one model of the modular architecture, there is a control module, which keeps command of the whole system, and coordinates all the other modules. But there is a different model of modular architecture in which the whole system is more like anarchy—or at least, syndicalism. There is no central controlling unit, and things proceed as a result simply of the interaction. (The difference is rather like that between a command economy and a totally free-market economy.) Moreover, there seems to be much evidence suggesting that human cognitive architecture is of the latter kind. Dennett describes the situation as follows:[10]

> There is no single, definitive "stream of consciousness", because there is no central Headquarters, no Cartesian Theater where "it all comes together" for the perusal of a Central Meaner. Instead of such a single stream (however wide), there are multiple channels in which specialized circuits try, in parallel pandemoniums, to do their various things, creating Multiple Drafts [GP: of a narrative of the self] as they go. Most of these fragmentary drafts of "narrative" play short-lived roles in the modulation of current activity but some get promoted to further functional roles, in swift succession, by the activity of a virtual machine in the brain. The seriality of this machine (its "von Neumannesque" character) is not a "hard-wired" design feature, but rather the upshot of a coalition of these specialists.

It may be acknowledged that normally it does *appear* to us that we have a conscious self of a kind the existence of which Dennett denies. But things are

---

[8] Hume's sentiments are confirmed in the Buddhist practice of Vipaśyanā meditation, where the fragmentary nature of consciousness is exposed. See Keown (2003), p. 332. For a contemporary attack on the existence of a self from a Humean direction, see Parfit (1984), chs. 10–12.

[9] For one account of this, see Minsky (1986).

[10] Dennett (1993), pp. 253–4. The book reviews the evidence and mounts the case for this model of the architecture. See, especially, Part II of the book.

not always as they appear. And on this account, such a self is an illusion.[11] Indeed, we can find an explanation for the illusion. Illusions can be helpful. The illusion provided by a mirror, for example, can be helpful in allowing us to see what is behind us. Closer to home, someone may have an illusory belief that they are loved and cherished by their friends and colleagues. This may well help them to live a happy life, and not collapse into a miserable depression. There is, presumably, an evolutionary explanation of the usefulness of the illusion of the self. It is not implausible that a creature with an illusion of a self will be more likely to survive and pass on its genes than a similar one without it. It can be an important motivating factor in survival, reproduction, and so on. In short, it is conducive to producing behaviour of a kind that gives its possessor an edge in evolutionary competition.

Of course, the fact that the self does not exist does not mean that it is not an object: we can think about it, believe in it, and so on. The self is a fictional object of a certain sort: a perfectly good non-existent object.[12] On a noneist picture, this means that it has its defining properties (constancy, identifying a person), though not at this world. It has its properties at those worlds which realize the way things are taken to be when we take the self to exist. But as in all illusions, we are caused, as it were, to mistake which world we are in.

11.4 Relational Quiddity

So, if a person is not the person they are in virtue of the possesion of a self, what makes them the person they are?

My being the person I am is constituted by being born in London in 1948, being the child of George and Laura, having the DNA that I do, going to the schools I went to, having the friends I have had, residing most of my adult life in Australia, being the father of Marcus and Annika, dying in ?, and so on. Anything that related to those things—or maybe just some of them—in those ways would be me; there is no *ding an sich*, Graham Priest. In other words, I am the very person I am, not because of some intrinsic nature or self; my quiddity is essentially constituted by my place in that web of relationships. It is, to use the useful medieval tag, *secundum quid*.

So for persons. And the same is true of any object in the causal stream. Our friend the car, for example, is what it is in exactly the same way: by having appro-

---

[11] And a very important one from a Buddhist perspective. It is a cause of the unhealthy attitude of attachment. Much more of this in later chapters.

[12] That the self is a fictional object is also argued for by Dennett (1992), and (1993), ch. 13—though Dennett does not endorse a noneist account of fictional objects.

priate relationships: to its parts at any time, the circumstances of its construction, its registration number, and so on. It is what it is in virtue of those relationships.

But what of things not in the causal flux? Obviously the matter is not exactly the same there. Not exactly the same; but effectively the same. The relations in the nature-constituting nexus need not just be causal. Take, for example, an abstract object, such as the number 3. This is what it is because of its place in (relation to) the natural number sequence, being the successor of 2, the predecessor of 4, and so on. Any object which related to those things in those ways would *ipso facto* be the number 3.[13]

We may, in fact, frame a quite general argument for relational quiddity.[14] Any object is what it is in virtue of the properties it bears. Thus, for example space has various properties: being infinite in all directions, being inhabited by physical objects, and so on. (Every object has properties: if an object had no properties, it would have the property of having no properties!) Now, to be space just is to be the bearer of those properties. Any entity which bore those properties would *be* space. In other words, the quiddity of space is constituted by relations that include the instantiation relation. And so for any object.

Quite generally, then, the quiddity of an object is constituted by its locus in a network of relations.[15] A natural question at this point is 'which relations'? Set theoretically, a relation is just a set of ordered pairs. It can be gerrymandered at will. We are not talking about this sort of relation. Just as for properties (see Section 2.6), we may distinguish between sparse relations and abundant ones. The sparse relations are the ones that have metaphysical grunt. We are talking about these. We may take these to include, note, trans-temporal relations, such as my relation to my birth—and maybe death.[16]

But are all (sparse) relations relevant? Yes. Take me again, for example. All of my relations combine to make me what I am. Of course, some are more important than others. Arguably, the behaviour of my parents towards me in my infant years is more important in making me what I am than, say, the behaviour of my

---

[13] This view is a familiar one from mathematical structuralism. See, for example, Resnik (1997), Shapiro (2000), Hellman (2001). I will return to the matter of mathematical structuralism in 12.6.

[14] The argument is one Nāgārjuna himself uses in connection with space, in ch. 5 of the *Mūlamadhyamakakārikā*. See Garfield (1995), pp. 14–15 and 149–52.

[15] What about the object **everything**? It might be thought that the analysis cannot apply to this, for there is nothing else for it to relate to. But there is. It can relate to each of its parts. **Everything** could not be what it is unless it had every other object as its part. Perhaps the most important one of these is **nothing**. **Everything** is, by definition, the complement of **nothing**. Each is what it is, in virtue of the other. More of **nothing** later.

[16] These are B-series relations, not A series relations. Thus, my being in Melbourne now is not a sparse relation, though being in Melbourne on 14 January 2013 is. One might note that the fact that aRb is a sparse relation between a and b is no guarantee that the property $\lambda x.xRb$ is a sparse property of a.

first girlfriend. But all these things have some role in the making. The matter is rather like that in classical gravitational theory. Every object exerts a gravitational influence on every other, however far apart. Thus, the nett gravitational force on me is partly determined by a rock on a planet in another galaxy. Of course, since gravitational attraction falls off rapidly with distance, this will be very small, but it is there none the less. So it is with the relations which constitute my quiddity; and the same for other objects. This is quite compatible, note, with the thought that some of the relations of an object are essential to it, and some are not. The relations into which an object enters will change from world to world. If some of these obtain at all possible worlds (or all possible worlds where it exists), they will be essential.

11.5 Emptiness

The view that some things have an essentially relational quiddity is not unknown in the history of Western philosophy.

Consider the disagreement between Newton and Leibniz on the nature of locations in space and time. This can be illustrated by a simple thought-experiment. Suppose that everything were picked up and moved uniformly a kilometre in a particular direction. Alternatively, suppose that all the events in the universe were just as they are, except that they all started one hour later. Do these suppositions make sense?

Newton said 'yes': spatio-temporal location would have changed. He was an absolutist about spatial and temporal places. He held that:[17]

absolute, true, and mathematical time, of itself, and from its own nature, flows equably without relation to anything external, and by another name is called duration.

and that:

absolute space, in its own nature, without relation to anything else, remains always similar and immovable.

In other words, spatial and temporal locations exist in and of themselves, and would be what they are even if there were no physical things that occupied space and time.

Leibniz said 'no': nothing would have changed. So the situation described is incoherent. He was a relationalist about spatio-temporal locations. He held:[18]

---

[17] From the Scholium to the Definitions, *Principia Mathematica*. See Smart (1964), p. 81.
[18] From Leibniz's third letter to Clarke. See Smart (1964), p. 89.

space to be merely relative, as time is; that... it... be an order of coexistences, as time is an order of successions.

In other words, spatial and temporal locations have no intrinsic nature. Physical events bear temporal relations (befores and afters) to each other, and there is nothing more to occurring at a particular time than having certain of those relationships to other things. Similarly, physical objects have spatial relations to each other (norths and souths), and there is nothing more to being in a particular place than having certain of those relations to other things. So, to be 1066 is to be after Caesar's invasion of Britain, in the same year as the Battle of Hastings, before the British colonization of Australia, and so on.[19]

Thus, for Newton, spatial and temporal locations are what they are in and of themselves: they have self-nature. By contrast, for Leibniz, they do not. To be a spatial/temporal position just is to be a locus in a field of spatial/temporal relations. That is, it has only a relational quiddity.

There are other examples from Western philosophy of things taken to have only relational quiddity. Mathematical structuralism, we have already noted. Let me give just one more.[20] Words and sentences have meanings. What is the status of meanings? Many philosophers have held that there are meanings which exist over and above words and sentences, and have a nature independently of these things. A notable person who held this view was, of course, Frege. For him, the senses of words and sentences exist in just this way. By contrast, structuralist linguists, beginning with Saussure, have held that meanings do not have this kind self-nature. Words and sentences enter into various kinds of relationships with other words and sentences. For example, 'blue' contrasts with 'red' in a way that 'scarlet' does not. To have a certain meaning is simply to be related to other words/sentences in certain ways. That is, meanings have no intrinsic nature, merely a relational one.

Though the thought that some objects have a merely relational quiddity is, then, well known in Western philosophy, what we have arrived at is a much stronger view: that *all* things have a merely relational quiddity. They are what they are in relation to other things.[21] This view is largely unknown in the history of Western philosophy.[22] It is, however, well known in Buddhist philosophy. The

---

[19] Does this mean that 1066 does not exist? In a sense, yes—the sense that Newton had in mind. In a sense, no: Leibniz is certainly not going to deny that there was a year 1066.

[20] There are certainly others. One is Marx's view of the commodity. A commodity is not a thing in itself, but just something that occupies a relational role (notably between producer and consumer) in certain capitalist practices. (See *Capital* Vol. 1, ch. 1, sec. 4.)

[21] And maybe themselves as well, as we will see in a moment.

[22] Perhaps some structuralists have come close to it. For example, 'that the world is made up of relationships rather than things, constitutes the first principle of the way of thinking that can properly

early Abhidharma schools of Buddhism held that there are things with their own self-nature (*svabhāva*); namely, the ultimate parts into which all things may be decomposed. A signature of the Madhyamaka school is a rejection of this: there is nothing that has self-nature. All things are what they are only in relation to other things. That is, they are empty of self-nature—or just *empty* (*śūnya*).[23] We have seen that everything is empty.

11.6 Structural Trees

Let me spell out the implications of emptiness further.[24] The quiddity of any object is determined by its location in a network of relations. Thus, given any object, a, there will be a bunch of objects b_j ($j \in J$), and relations, R_i ($i \in I$), such that the quiddity of a is determined by a bunch of relations of the form aR_ib_j and b_jR_ia. In fact, we can take it that a is always in the left-hand place of the relation in question.[25] Every relation, R, has a converse, $\check{R}$, such that xRy iff $y\check{R}x$. Thus, the converse of *loving* is *being loved by*. xRy and $y\check{R}x$ amount to the same thing, and we can choose whichever of these has a on the left-hand side. Thus, the nature of a is produced by a bunch of relations of the form aR_ib_j. We can depict this in the form of a graph. Suppose, for the sake of illustration, that there are three objects and two relations, as follows: aR_1b, aR_1c, an aR_2d. We have:

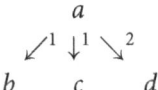

Arrows denote the relations (arrows rather than lines, since relationships are inherently directional); superscripts to the arrows indicate which of the relations

---

be called "structuralist" '. Hawkes (1977), pp. 17–18. The Ontic Structural Realism of Ladyman, Ross, Spurrett, and Collier (2007) also seems to be in the same ballpark, as, maybe, does Buchler's metaphysics of complexes (1990). As I read the views of these writers, however, they take structure itself to be self-standing. This is obviously not compatible with emptiness. I will return to this matter in the next chapter.

[23] See Garfield (1995), Priest (2009b), and Westerhoff (2009), ch. 3.

[24] Much of the following comes from Priest (2015a).

[25] This is not necessary. The restriction can be dropped. The resulting structures are then graphs, instead of trees; but essentially the same points can be made. I choose the form of representation I do, because the points I wish to make are more salient this way. An interesting, but different, graph-theoretic account of the nature of reality is given by Dipert (1997). He moots the idea (which we will effectively end up endorsing) that the world is a single connected graph. For him, however, the graph has a single symmetric binary relation (the meaning of which is not entirely clear), and each object of the world is not a locus in the graph, but a certain kind of sub-graph.

is in question.[26] To be *a* is exactly to occupy the spot which is the root of the tree. So all there is to being *a* is this slot. Let us mark it with a bullet, •:

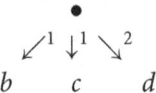

Of course, exactly the same is true of *b*. Suppose, for example, that bR_2e and bR_3f. Similarly for *c* and *d*. When we "expand" *b*, *c*, and *d* in this way we get:

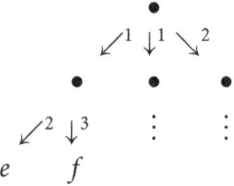

The quiddity of *a* is now determined by its locus in this larger tree. Of course, *e*, *f*, and all the other bottom nodes have to be "expanded" in the same way; and the process continues indefinitely. If something has its nature only by relating to other things, then anything that relates to nothing has no nature; but everything is a thing, so it must be the thing it is in virtue of *something*; that is, it must have some nature. So every point must relate to some things.

When all points have been expanded, we have a tree, every branch of which is infinite:

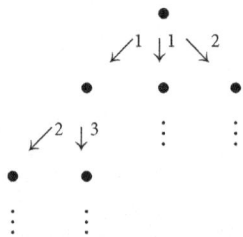

The quiddity of *a* is, then, ultimately determined by its location at the root (topmost node) of this tree. Under ultimate analysis, all content has disappeared. What is left is pure form (structure). Or maybe better, content *is* pure form. Indeed, what the tree gives is exactly the ontological structure of *a*. Let us call the tree for an object its *structural tree*.[27]

---

[26] To represent the fact that some of these relations are more important than others, one would need to add to the picture a weighting for each arrow. But this extra complexity is unnecessary for present purposes.

[27] I have assumed that all relations are binary. If $n > 1$, an $n + 1$-ary relation is just a binary relation between objects and ordered *n*-tuples of objects.

Does it follow that all objects are the same kind of thing? Yes and no. All have the same kind of ontological structure—that determined by being the root of a tree. It does not follow that cats are the same kind of thing as dogs, since each of them will enter into different relations (for example, with respect to DNA). Similarly, abstract objects and concrete objects are different kinds of things, since they enter into different kinds of relations. The latter, in particular, enter into causal relations (at least at some possible worlds).

11.7 Trans-Temporal "Identity"

Quiddities can be taken to provide a criterion of trans-temporal (and trans-world) identity. The question of trans-temporal identity may be stated very simply: what is it that makes an object the same object over time? What, for example, makes me in 1960 the same as me in 2013? The problem is how to understand this question in a sensible way. Me in 1960 is, after all, just me; as is me in 2013. So it looks as though the question is asking what makes me me. To the extent that this is a sensible question at all, it is not the one that people who ask about diachronic identity are targetting.

To appreciate what this is, one needs to see it in the context of the possibility of change. (No one has ever raised the question about the identity of abstract objects over time—though 3 is certainly the same object in 1960 and 2013.) If an object changes, then something changes and something remains the same. The properties change. What remains the same? Emptiness provides an answer. The relational network determining something's quiddity remains the same. (As we noted in Section 11.4, this contains trans-temporal relations.)

What, though, are the identity conditions of such networks? In standard mathematical fashion, we may take two trees to be identical if they are isomorphic. It might be thought that this criterion would make identity itself transitive, since isomorphism is transitive. Thus, let $\sigma(x)$ be the structural tree for x, and let $\cong$ denote isomorphism. Suppose that $x = y$ and $y = z$; then $\sigma(x) \cong \sigma(y)$ and $\sigma(y) \cong \sigma(z)$. Hence, $\sigma(x) \cong \sigma(z)$, and so $x = z$. The argument fails for two reasons. First, if $x = y$, it does not follow that $\sigma(x) = \sigma(y)$. Thus if we have some object with part p, and gluon g, then $p = g$. But in general, g will have more properties; hence p and g will have different structural trees.[28] Secondly, identity is significantly tensed, and the fact that $p = g$ at a certain time does not entail that $p = g$ at other times: p and g may therefore have different structural trees.

---

[28] The transitivity of isomorphism might also fail, depending on how the details of the set theory employed are cashed out.

What of the so called problem of "trans-world identity". Much the same comments apply to that (except that the variation in an object from world to world is merely difference, not change); and much the same solution is available. The relations on the tree may be taken to be trans-world (though not indexical), whatever, in the end one supposes such relations to be.

11.8 Interpenetration

Let us now look at another relationship between structural trees—indeed, a singularly important one. Consider a magnet, and, in particular, its north pole, *n*. This is what it is only in virtue of a relationship which it bears to the south pole, *s*. (It could not be a north pole unless there were a corresponding south pole.) Hence if we consider the structural tree for *n*, we get the following:

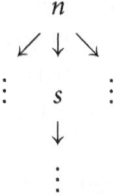

Here, I label the nodes to keep track of which tree is which, but omit the details of the arrows in the cause of perspicuity. What we see is that the tree for *n* contains the tree for *s* as a proper sub-tree. Metaphysically speaking, then, the ontological structure of *n* contains that of *s*.

But of course, *s* depends on *n* in exactly the same way. So if we fill out the tree for *s* a little, we will have the following:

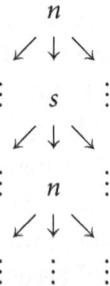

The tree for *n* is a subtree of the tree for *s* as well.[29] The ontological structure of each contains the other as a part. (Note that this is possible only because the trees

---

[29] Well, to be precise, the tree for *n* has a subtree which is isomorphic to the tree for *s*. But we may simply identify isomorphic trees.

are infinite.) The two mutually encode each other. Metaphysically, they are like two mirrors, each facing the other, each reflecting the other and its contents to infinity.

Let us say that two objects *interpenetrate* if the structural tree for each is a subtree of the tree for the other. Interpenetration is obviously a symmetric and transitive relation. It does no harm to think of every tree as a subtree of itself. Every object then interpenetrates with itself, and interpenetration is an equivalence relation.

11.9 The Net of Indra

I take the word 'interpenetrate' from the Chinese Buddhist Huayan tradition.[30] The Huayan tradition on emptiness takes it "to the limit". It is not just the case that some things interpenetrate with some other things. All things interpenetrate with all things. This is illustrated in what is one of the most beautiful metaphors in the Buddhist traditions: the Net of Indra. This is described by one modern commentator as follows:

Far away in the heavenly abode of the great god Indra, there is a wonderful net which has been hung by some cunning artificer in such a manner that it stretches out indefinitely in all directions. In accordance with the extravagant tastes of deities, the artificer has hung a single glittering jewel at the net's every node, and since the net itself is infinite in all dimensions, the jewels are infinite in number. There hang the jewels, glittering like stars of the first magnitude, a wonderful sight to behold. If we now arbitrarily select one of the jewels for inspection and look closely at it, we will discover that in its polished surface there are reflected all the other jewels in the net, infinite in number. Not only that, but each of the jewels reflected in this one jewel is also reflecting all the other jewels, so that the process of reflection is infinite.[31]

---

[30] The Chinese word is *ji* (Jap: *soku*), which is sometimes also translated as 'is'. But this needs to be clearly distinguished from the *is* of numerical identity (Chin: *t'ung*; Jap: *dou*).

[31] Cook (1977), p. 2. Fazang himself, puts it like this: 'It is like the net of Indra which is entirely made up of jewels. Due to their brightness and transparence, they reflect each other. In each of the jewels, the images of all other jewels are [completely] reflected. This is the case with any one of the jewels, and will remain forever so. Now, if we take a jewel in the southwestern direction and examine it, [we can see] that this one jewel can reflect simultaneously the images of all other jewels at once. It is so with the one jewel, and is also so with each of all the others. Since each of the jewels simultaneously reflects the images of all other jewels at once, it follows that this jewel in the southwestern direction also reflects all the images of the jewels in each of the other jewels [at once]. It is so with this jewel, and is also so with all the others. Thus, the images multiply infinitely, and all these multiple infinite images are bright and clear inside this single jewel. The rest of the jewels can be understood in the same manner.' (Quoted in Liu (1982), p. 65.) In his short story, 'The Aleph' (in Borges (2000)), Borges describes a point in space, the aleph, where all things are present (including the Earth, which itself contains the aleph). Each jewel is such an aleph.

All the jewels in the net encode each other. Each one, as it were, contains the whole.[32]

The Huayan were right. Consider any object, a. This relates to **nothing** (that gluon) in a very particular way. As we noted in Section 4.5, $\neg \mathfrak{S}xx = 無$, and so $\mathfrak{A}xx \neq 無$; thus, in particular, for any object, a, $a \neq 無$. But the relationship between a and **nothing** is tighter than mere difference. Part of the quiddity of a is to be an object. (It could not be a unless it were at least an object.) And it could not be this, unless it stood out, as it were, against **nothing**. Its not being nothing makes it possible to be (an object). Heidegger puts it in his own distinctive terms, thus:[33]

> The nothing is neither an object nor any being at all. The nothing comes forward neither for itself nor next to beings, to which it would, as it were, adhere. For human existence the nothing makes possible the openedness of beings as such. The nothing does not merely serve as the counterconcept of beings; rather it originally belongs to their essential unfolding as such.[34]

Conversely, **nothing** is what it is in virtue of being the ontological backdrop of every object, and so a.[35]

Any object and **nothing** are, then, like the magnetic n and s. That is, they interpenetrate. Writing $\rightleftharpoons$ for interpenetration, and letting a an b be any two objects, we have: $a \rightleftharpoons 無 \rightleftharpoons b$. And since interpenetration is a transitive relation, we have the interpenetration of a and b:

$$a \rightleftharpoons b$$

Every thing interpenetrates with every thing, as the Huayan had it.

Commenting on the interpenetration of all things, Chengguan (the fourth patriarch of Huayan) noted that:[36]

> Because they have no Selfhood, the large and the small can mutually contain each other ... Since the very small is very large Mount Sumeru is contained in a mustard seed; and since the very large is the very small, the ocean is included in a hair.

---

[32] Of course, this is a metaphor, and has its limitations. One would normally take the jewels to be self-standing (but interacting) entities. It is precisely this view which emptiness undercuts.

[33] Heidegger (1977), p. 106.

[34] The paragraph concludes: 'In the Being of beings the nihilation of the nothing occurs.' The last sentence is one of Heidegger's darker sayings. I take it to mean that beings are produced when **nothing** negates itself. Not nothing is, after all, something. (See Priest (1995a), 2nd ed., 15.5.) I do not wish to follow Heidegger down the path of attributing agency to **nothing**.

[35] I will return to the matter of the relationship between **nothing** and (other) objects in Section 13.11.

[36] Quoted in Chang (1972), p. 165.

'Selfhood' here translates 'self-nature' (*svabhāva*). As we have seen, it is the fact that things are empty of self-nature which allows their natures to be represented by a tree, all branches of which are infinite. The infinitude allows for interpenetration. And the fact that all things interpenetrate with **nothing** means that the tree for something very large interpenetrates with the tree for something very small.[37] The mustard seed can, then, metaphysically contain Mount Sumeru.

Note the consequences of this. Take any two objects—say me and a flower in the desert; and consider a (sparse) relation that contributes to making the flower what it is.[38] By transitivity, this also contributes, in the great scheme of things, to making we what I am. Of course, as I observed in Section 11.4, not all relations are of equal weight; and one would expect the relations inherited by me from the flower to be pretty negligible. One can express this thought in terms of the Net of Indra: the image of one jewel in another will be larger/brighter the closer it is.

A final comment. The Huayan held not only that each object interpenetrates with each other object, but also that each object interpenetrates with the totality of all objects. They were right about this too. **Everything** and **nothing** are like north and south. Each could not be what it is unless the other was what it is. **Everything** and **nothing** then interpenetrate. And since any thing interpenetrates with **nothing**, it interpenetrates with **everything**: for any a, $a \rightleftharpoons \mathbf{e}$.[39]

So much for an analysis of emptiness (and its Huayan articulation). We can now go on to look at some of its implications. But before we do this, we need to pause and address a couple of important objections to the very coherence of the notion of emptiness. In the next chapter, we turn to this.

---

[37] In Huayan thought, it is not **nothing** which links all things together; it is ultimate reality (principle, *li*). But in this respect, **nothing** is behaving very much like a Buddhist ultimate reality. We will meet some other important ways in which this is the case in a later chapter.

[38] Not all relations between me and the flower are sparse, however. Thus, the fact that I am drinking tea when the flower is blossoming is, presumably, not.

[39] In the Huayan tradition it is held that any object (not just **everything**) interpenetrates with each of its parts. So the identity of an object depends on the identity of its parts, and *vice versa*. This is a harder position to sustain. For a start, it seems natural to suppose that an object can remain the very object it is if one part is changed. Thus, if I change a tyre on my bike, it is still the same bike. Moreover, and again, it is natural to suppose that a part can remain exactly the same part, independently of the rest of the object. The new tyre was the tyre it was even if it was made before the bike was. Against the first objection, the Huayan argued that when the tyre is replaced, the old bike literally does go out of existence. What comes into existence is an object which is very similar, and functionally equivalent. (One could also argue, as I did in Section 6.9, that *at any time* an object is the sum of its parts, but the parts can change while the object remains the same.) Against the second, they argued that the new tyre is not really a tyre at all, let alone *that* tyre, until it is put on the bike. Till then, it is just a tyre-in-waiting. (Aristotle runs this line for animal parts. See *Parts of Animals*, 1.1, esp. $640^b 34$–$641^a 10$.) For a defence of the Huayan view, see Jones (2009) and (201+).

12

Embracing the Groundlessness of Things

12.1 Problems of Emptiness

In the previous chapter I argued that everything is empty. Things have no self-nature: everything is what it is in relation to, and only in relation to, other things. In this chapter I will discuss two important (and interacting) objections to the view.

The first objection is to the effect that the view collapses into nihilism. It generates a vicious regress, voiding all things of being. The second objection is to the effect that the view is self-refuting. If anything is empty, this can only be because some things (such as the relations between things) are not.

In the first part of this chapter, I will take up the first objection; in the second, we will turn to the second.

12.2 The Regress of Quiddities

If an object is empty, its nature (quiddity) depends on its relation to other objects. In particular, it is what it is, at least in part, because they are what they are. This obviously generates a regress. Indeed, as we saw in Section 11.4, every branch of the structural tree for an object is infinite downwards. And one might think—indeed, many people have thought—that such a regress is vicious. a_0 depends for its nature on a_{-1}, which depends for its nature a_{-2}, which depends for its nature on.... If this regress never bottoms out then there is nothing, ultimately, to determine the quiddity of anything. So nothing has a quiddity.

Why would this be a problem?—Maybe things are inherently natureless. But anything that is an object has a quiddity—if only that of being an object. So if there are no quiddities, there are no objects. Nothing would be (an object). The whole position therefore collapses into nihilism. If there were no ultimate ground of being then, as Schaffer puts it, 'being would be infinitely deferred, never achieved'.[1]

The argument taps into a certain intuition.[2] There is an old story about Bertrand Russell giving a public lecture on Ancient cosmology in the early years of the twentieth century. He said that the Ancients wondered why the Earth did not fall down through space. It must rest on something. What? An elephant. After a while it occurred to them to wonder why the elephant did not fall down. It must rest on something. What? A turtle. After a while it occurred to them to wonder why the turtle did not fall down. At this point they decided... to change the subject, as did Russell in the lecture. At the end of the lecture, a little old lady, waving an umbrella, rushed up to Russell. 'Mr Russell, Mr Russell,' she said, 'I've got it. I've got it. It's turtles, turtles, all the way down.'

We find the story amusing because, if one turtle will not do the job, a whole infinite descent of turtles will not do the job. They would all fall down together. This is the intuition.

As we will see, however, the regress generated by emptiness is not a vicious one. When it comes to objects and their quiddities, it really is turtles all the way down. We will start by looking at the history of the regress argument. We will then see that it is not only question-begging, but unsound.

12.3 The History of this Kind of Objection

In Western philosophy, a major location for arguments of this kind is where the reality of a whole is taken to depend on the reality of its parts. It occurs in this way in Kant, for example. In the Second Antinomy of the *Critique of Pure Reason*, Kant gives an argument that reality cannot be infinitely divisible, which goes as follows (A434=B462):[3]

Let us assume that composite substances are not made up of simple parts. If all composition then be removed in thought, no composite part, and (since we admit no simple parts) also no simple parts, that is to say, nothing at all, will remain, and accordingly, no substance will be given.

---

[1] Schaffer (2010a), 2.4. Bird (2007) defends the view that all properties are dispositional against a version of exactly this sort of argument. Interestingly, he also appeals to the same sort of graph-theoretic considerations to which I appeal in the last chapter and this.

[2] Cameron (2008) discusses the intuition, concluding that he can find no real grounds for it, but says that we should accept it anyway because it is an *intuition*. As we will see below, the intuition is flawed.

[3] Translation taken from Kemp Smith (1933). A similar argument is used by Aristotle, *On Generation and Corruption*, $316^a 15$–34.

In other words, consider any substance: suppose that it is a composition of smaller parts, and each such part is a composition of smaller parts, and so on *ad infinitum*. Then upon complete decomposition, there would be nothing left. Thus, there could have been no substance there in the first place.

Kant does not spell out the regress explicitly. About a century before, Leibniz had already done so. In a letter to Arnauld, he writes:[4]

> Were there only beings by aggregation [composite objects], there are no real beings. For every being by aggregation presupposes beings endowed with real unity [simples], because every being derives its reality only from the reality of those beings of which it is composed, so that it will not have any reality at all if each being of which it is composed is itself a being by aggregation, a being for which we must still seek a further ground for its reality, grounds which can never be found in this way, if we must always continue to seek for them.

Nor is the situation unique to Western philosophy. In his *Mūlamadhyamakākārikā*, Nāgārjuna is clearly concerned to reject the idea that everything's being empty entails nihilism. He does not identify those who claim so, nor their arguments.[5] But regress arguments of this kind were certainly used by the Hindu Vaiśeṣika philosophers for the existence of atomic substances,[6] and Nāgārjuna would presumably have been aware of this.

12.4 Cosmological Arguments

Neither Kant's nor Leibniz' version of the argument gets beyond a fairly bald and dogmatic (and so question-begging) assertion that if there were no ground to a reality-dependence regress, there would be no reality; that is, that the regress would be vicious. That is exactly the question at issue. One person who does give an argument that such a regress is vicious is Aquinas. In one of his cosmological arguments for the existence of God in the *Summa Theologia*, he argues as follows:[7]

> In the world of sensible things we find that there is an order of efficient causes. There is no case known (neither is it, indeed, possible) in which a thing is found to be an efficient cause of itself; for if so it would be prior to itself, which is impossible. Now in efficient causes it is

---

[4] Ariew and Garber (1989), p. 85.

[5] Though such a thought might come naturally to any Buddhist working in the older Abhidharma tradition. That tradition insists on a fundamental distinction between primary existents (*dravyasat*) and secondary existents (*prañaptisat*), with the latter being conceptually constructed out of the former. For an Abhidharmika the Madhyamaka doctrine of universal emptiness would appear to imply the apparent absurdity that everything is conceptually constructed, though there is nothing, in the end, out of which to construct it.

[6] Koller (2002), p. 74. Ch. 14 also claims that Sarvāstivāda Buddhists used regress arguments of this kind.

[7] Hick (1964), pp. 83–4.

not possible to go on to infinity, because in all efficient causes following in order, the first is the cause of the intermediate cause, and the intermediate is the cause of the ultimate cause, whether the intermediate cause be several, or one only. Now to take away the cause is to take away the effect. Therefore if there be no first cause amongst efficient causes, there would be no ultimate, nor any intermediate cause. But if in efficient causes it is possible to go on to infinity, there will be no first efficient cause, neither will there be an ultimate effect, nor any intermediate efficient causes; all of which is plainly false. Therefore it is necessary to admit a first efficient cause, to which everyone gives the name God.

The final sentence seems a complete *non sequitur*, but that is not our concern here, which is whether the rest of the argument works.

It may not be clear that the regress involved is of the kind we are concerned with here. It might be thought to be about a sequence of causes going backwards in time—what the medievals called causes *per accidens*. Thus, for example: Annie was engendered by Bettie, who was engendered by Cathie, who... and so on. It is not. Aquinas does hold that one cannot, in fact, go back indefinitely in causes of this kind; but there is, he thinks, nothing *logically* impossible about such a regress. One can know that it terminates only by revelation.[8] The notion of efficient causation he has in mind in the argument is what the medievals called causation *per se*. The mark of this kind of causation is that the effect of a *per se* cause cannot exist unless the cause exists at the same time. One might call this a *sustaining* cause.[9] A standard example is as follows. Consider a moving train with ten coaches. Coach 10 moves because it is pulled by coach 9, which moves because it is pulled ... which moves because it is pulled by coach 1, which moves because it is pulled by the engine. The motion of each coach is a cause *per se* of the motion of the next coach towards the end. In such cases, the cause is effectively the ontological ground of the effect. The reality of the motion of coach 10 depends on the reality of the motion of coach 9, and so on. So when Aquinas talks about something being prior to itself, it is not temporal priority that is at issue, but ontological dependence—in the train example, of the state of motion. This is precisely the kind of dependence that we are concerned with here, where the what-it-is of an object (being in motion) ontologically depends on the what-it-is of something else.

So what are we to say about the cogency of Aquinas' argument? First, it is fallacious. Aquinas notes that (i) if there is a first cause then, (ii) if this were "taken away" no subsequent effects would occur; that, *if there were no first cause nothing would happen*. He then points out that if there were an infinite regress there would be no first cause, and then applies the italicized conditional to conclude that

---

[8] See Hick (1970), p. 41 for discussion and references.
[9] See, for example, Copleston (1961), pp. 117ff., Hick (1970), pp. 41ff., Kenny (1969) pp. 41f.

there would be no effect. But this is illicit, for the italicized conditional (ii) was established on the assumption that there was a first cause (i). As an argument for a first cause, it therefore begs the question.

Not only is the argument fallacious, but an infinite regress of causes *per se* is quite possible. To see this, consider the following example.[10] We have an infinite sequence of objects, $a_0, a_{-1}, a_{-2}, \ldots$. Each of these is in one of two states, *active* or *passive*. For each $n \leqslant 0$, if a_{n-1} is passive, it does nothing. If it is active, it (instantaneously) renders a_n active. Thus, if $\rightarrow$ represents the dependence, we have the following situation:

$$\ldots \rightarrow a_{-2} \rightarrow a_{-1} \rightarrow a_0$$

We may suppose that if a_0 is in an active state it goes red; if it is in a passive state it goes blue. Now, there are only two states of the system: a_0 red (all states active), and a_0 blue (all states passive). Consider the first of these. For each $n < 0$, a_n is active and affects a_{n+1}, but it can do this only if it, in turn, is affected by a_{n-1} because it, itself, is in an active state. That is, the sequence is an infinite regress of red *per se* causes, as is the *all blue* possibility.

12.5 Viciousness

We see, then, that an infinite regress of quiddities need not be at all vicious; it may be quite coherent. To understand further, return to the question of what constitutes a *vicious* regress. As we saw in Section 2.1, a regress is vicious if, after every step, what is to be accounted for is the very same thing as was to be accounted for before. Thus, if we try to explain how to join two links of a chain by saying that we insert an intervening link, we have exactly the same problem of how to join two links. And if we want to explain how a bunch of objects form a unity we cannot do so just by invoking another object, since we have exactly the same problem (Bradley's regress).[11]

In the example of the last section, that a_0 is red is determined by a_{-1}'s being active. This is a *different* state of affairs. Similarly, a_{-1}'s being active is determined by a_{-2}'s being active—again, something different. And to return to an example from the previous chapter, suppose that my quiddity is determined by my DNA

---

[10] See Priest (1995), 2.7.

[11] And what really bothered the Ancients in Russell's turtle story was why an unsupported object does not fall. (That it was the Earth which was in question, really had nothing to do with it.) If one posits another unsupported object, the problem is *exactly the same*. If their problem was why *the Earth* does not fall, this would have been quite happily answered by the claim that it rests on something. Strictly, then, it is not regresses themselves which are vicious or non-vicious, but regresses with respect to some explanatory project.

and my upbringing. We may, of course, ask what determines the quiddity of my DNA (and upbringing), but this is a quite different question; so asking it is not vicious.

Of course, what an infinite regress will not explain is why the whole regress is as it is. Thus, in the example of the previous section, the state of each a_n is determined by the state of a_{n-1}, but there is nothing in this story to explain why the whole system is in the *all active* state, as opposed to the *all passive* state. If there is such an explanation, it must come from elsewhere. In the same way, if our aim is to explain why there is a whole network of things with natures, this will not be explained by saying that the quiddity of each element is determined by the quiddities of the things on which it depends. As far as that goes, the whole may or may not depend on something else. (Since everything is empty, it does.) But all this is quite consistent with each object having its being (quiddity) in virtue of its dependence on something else. And of course, to insist that the regress must bottom out in fundamental things, will itself leave something unexplained: the quiddity of the fundamental things.

There is an extra wrinkle that needs to be considered. As we saw in Section 11.6, the structural tree of any object will not just be infinite, it will interpenetrate with the tree for **nothing**, and so with itself. Going down any branch of the tree, we will therefore find a repetition of things that have gone before. It might be thought that *this* makes the situation vicious.[12] As Aquinas puts it, it is not possible for something to be 'prior to itself'. But it is. In the example of the last section, it would have made no difference if the regress had bent back round on itself, a_0 determining the state of a_{-7} thus:

$$
\begin{array}{ccc}
a_{-1} \rightarrow & a_0 \rightarrow & a_{-7} \\
\uparrow & & \downarrow \\
a_{-2} & & a_{-6} \\
\uparrow & & \downarrow \\
a_{-3} \leftarrow & a_{-4} \leftarrow & a_{-5}
\end{array}
$$

There are still two states of the system: *all active*, and *all passive*, and the state of each object is still determined by the state of its predecessor. (Though this does not tell us why the whole system is in whichever of the two possible states it is in.)[13]

---

[12] In (2010), Kit Fine notes some things which he calls paradoxes of dependence, and their connection with paradoxes of self-reference. He just *assumes*, however, that dependence loops are unacceptably vicious. Without this assumption, there is no paradox. We will see other connections between grounding and the paradoxes of self-reference in ch. 13.

[13] The situation is similar to that in certain "paradoxical" time travel stories, where someone discovers a note telling them how to build a time machine. They build it, and then travel back in time (leaving the note behind), where they write the note and leave it where it will be found.

12.6 The Regress of Relations

Let us turn to the second objection. This was to the effect that if anything is empty, some things cannot be empty. The most obvious candidates are the relations in virtue of which things are related. Note, in particular, that in the ("expanded") structural trees of Section 11.4, the relations (arrows) of the tree are not analysed away in the same way in which the nodes are: they stay unanalysed. That some things are empty therefore presupposes that others are not.

There is a simple answer to this, however. The relations involved are just as empty as anything else. They too have their quiddity by relating to other things. They are therefore at the roots of their own trees. Indeed, there was nothing in the arboreal discussion to suggest that the object at the root of our original tree could not have been a relation. (Relations are objects too.)[14] Of course, this will raise a question about the relations involved in those trees. But the response is exactly the same. Those relations are empty, and have their own trees. Obviously we have a regress. But there is no more reason to think this regress vicious than to think our original regress so.[15]

This raises another worry, though. Understanding the quiddity of objects and relations as I have done shows that they are not "free-standing". But the understanding suggests another candidate for something which *is*—not the objects and relations themselves, but the very structure in which they are all embedded. Here is one way to see the worry. The account I have given is obviously some kind of structuralism. As we have already noted, structuralism is also a view held by some people in the philosophy of mathematics. Numbers are not platonic (freestanding) objects, but simply places in structures. Thus, the number 0 is just the marker for the first place in any ω-sequence. But what is a structure? One view is that these structures themselves are "ante rem". That is, they are platonic structures that lie behind things like numbers.[16] In such a view, then, we still have free-standing things: the structures. In the same way, I have analysed the quiddities of relations and (other) objects in terms of certain structure. But do we not, then, have to understand this structure as free-standing? After all, it is the very provider of loci, not itself a locus.

To assuage this worry, we will need to look more closely at something I have so far taken very much for granted: the notion of a locus. A suitable analysis will show that structure is as empty as anything else. The analysis I will give is somewhat

---

[14] There may even be relations in a tree of which they, themselves, are nodes. The mathematical representation of this requires non-well-founded sets. More of this anon.

[15] In reply to Bird (2007), Barker (2009) notes one regress of this kind, and simply claims that it is vicious. It is not.

[16] See, for example, Shapiro (2000).

technical. There may be better, or simpler, ways of achieving the same end, but I do not know them. Those with no taste for matters technical can take my word that such an analysis exists, and skip the rest of this chapter. Nothing in subsequent chapters presupposes it.[17]

12.7 Analysing Loci

So what exactly is a locus? Suppose that we have a structure $\langle X_0, \rho_0 \rangle$ where X_0 is a set of objects, and ρ_0 is a set of relations between them $\{R_i : i \in I\}$. Let me illustrate with respect to the simple example of Section 11.6. Suppose that $X_0 = \{a, b, c, d\}$ and $\rho_0 = \{R_1, R_2\}$, where the graph of the relations between the objects is as follows:

$$\begin{array}{c} a \\ \swarrow^1 \downarrow^1 \searrow^2 \\ b \quad c \quad d \end{array}$$

Understood in the usual way, the loci are determined by a bunch of free-standing objects—the members of X_0. Clearly we want to avoid this.

Suppose that one has just the relations. Each, R_i, has a collection of instances (pins), $\langle R_i \rangle$. The standard way to think of these is as sets of ordered pairs—or actually, ordered triples, the third member indexing the relation. Thus, in the above example, the members of $\langle R_1 \rangle$ would be $\langle a, b, 1 \rangle$ and $\langle a, c, 1 \rangle$; and those of $\langle R_2 \rangle$ would be just $\langle a, d, 2 \rangle$. This, of course, is still to take the members of X_0 as free-standing. Since we do not wish to make this assumption, we will not adopt this reductive analysis of instances, but think of them, instead, as *sui generis*. However, bearing in mind the reduction will provide a useful heuristic in what follows.

We may now consider a certain relation, T, that holds between relation-instances. Intuitively, the relation holds between those instances that come from the same object. Thus, if one again thinks of instances as ordered sets, $\langle x, y, i \rangle T \langle z, w, j \rangle$ iff x is z; but if one is to jettison this idea, T must be understood as a primitive relation; and, as the heuristic indicates, it is natural to take this to be an equivalence relation.

One can now identify loci in a very simple manner. A locus is given by a non-empty bunch of instances that bear the T relation to each other. One can, if one likes, think of this as a set. If α is any relation-instance, then $\{\beta : \alpha T \beta\}$ is

---

[17] The following material comes, essentially, from Priest (2009b).

a locus. The loci are simply equivalence classes of instances.[18] In particular, and again thinking of objects as independently existing for a moment, we can map X_0 into the set of loci by the function that maps x to $\hat{x} = \{a:$ for some $y \in X_0$ and $i \in I$, $a = \langle x, y, i \rangle\}$. (Alternatively, and in standard fashion, we may take $\hat{x}$ to be some particular member of this set.) Given that everything relates to some other things—as I noted in Section 11.6—none of these classes is empty. This is a one-to-one correspondence. Moreover, any relation, R, on the domain of objects induces a corresponding relation, $R^\uparrow$, on the loci. Namely, $\hat{x} R^\uparrow \hat{y}$ iff xRy. The map $\widehat{}$ is then an isomorphism.[19]

I note that we may treat not just the objects, but also the relations between them, as themselves sets of instances of a certain kind. R_i may be identified with $\widehat{R_i} = \{a:$ for some $x \in X_0, y \in X_0, a = \langle x, y, i \rangle\}$.[20] If we do this, then the relations on loci may be defined in terms of the relations between the instances, plus set-membership. Thus, let P be the permutation relation on instances, such that, intuitively, $\langle x, y, i \rangle P \langle y, x, i \rangle$. Then, as is not difficult to check: $\hat{x} R^\uparrow \hat{y}$ iff xRy iff for some $\alpha \in \hat{x}$ and $\beta \in \hat{y}$ ($\alpha \in \widehat{R}$ and $\alpha P \beta$).

Given our original structure with free-standing objects (and relations), we have now seen how we may dispense with this, and operate equivalently in terms of loci and the relationships between them. In particular, the loci are just sets of relation instances.[21] Thus we have a structure of the form $\langle X_1, \rho_1 \rangle$ where X_1 is the power set of the power set of relation instances, and ρ_1 is the appropriate set of relations on these. We have seen that $\langle X_0, \rho_0 \rangle$ is isomorphic to a substructure of this.

So far so good. But the analysis still takes sets of relation instances to be free-standing objects. So we have still not eliminated the need for such things. The structure we now have, though, has exactly the same form as the one with which we started: a bunch of objects, with a bunch of relations between them. We can simply, therefore, apply the same analysis as before. This will give us a set, X_2, of

---

[18] Keränen (2001) poses a problem for certain kinds of mathematical structuralism, concerning how to give the identity condition for the loci of structures. The identity of loci given here is of neither of the kinds Keränen considers, and so avoids the objection. Identity is defined in terms of relation-instances, and the relations between them. It is true that, at the moment, these are taken to be free-standing entities, so the account has something in common with Keränen's haecceity account. As we shall see in a moment, however, this is only a temporary measure.

[19] *Proof:* A locus is a set of the form $\{a : \exists y \in X_0, i \in I, a = \langle x, y, i \rangle\}$. Since every object in X_0 is the domain of some relation, every locus is non-empty; and since $\widehat{}$ maps x to this set, the function is onto. If $\{a : \exists y \in X_0, i \in I, a = \langle x, y, i \rangle\} = \{a : \exists y \in X_0, i \in I, a = \langle z, y, i \rangle\}$, then $x = z$, so the function is one to one. Finally, the definition of $\uparrow$ makes $\widehat{}$ structure-preserving, by definition.

[20] As noted, the relation instances are just pins (tropes), and this construction is of a fairly standard kind in trope theory. See, for example, Bacon (1995). Trope theory is not unknown in classical India. For example, the metaphysical theory of the fifth century Buddhist logician Dignāga can be seen as a trope theory. See Ganeri (2001), esp. ch. 4.

[21] Or just relation instances themselves, if we choose a representative member of each equivalence class.

objects with a bunch of relations, ρ_2, between them. These can be analysed in the same way; and so on. We repeat the analysis ω times. In the limit, everything will have been analysed. We are left with nothing "free-standing"!

12.8 Nihilism Again

This might be thought to raise the spectre of nihilism again. If everything disappears under analysis, does not this show that ultimately there is nothing? No. As we have just seen, each X_i can be embedded in (that is, is isomorphic to a part of) X_{i+1}. If we identify the isomorphic objects, we obtain a chain of sets $X_0 \subseteq X_1 \subseteq X_2 \subseteq \ldots$. At each stage, what we obtain, therefore, is a richer structure. The result at the limit is $\bigcup_{i<\omega} X_i = X_\omega$. This is how things turn out, in fact, to be when we apply the analysis relentlessly; and X_ω is not the empty set. So this is not nihilism.[22]

An even more interesting perspective emerges if we interpret loci as sets of relation-instances, but now subject, not the sets, but the relation-instances themselves to the same kind of recursive analysis. This takes the relation-instances to be sets of relation-instances (of a higher order). We then iterate the procedure. To see what happens when we do this, take an object, a, in X_0, as an example. This is a class of instances. Let us suppose, for the sake of illustration, that there are only three instances, b_0, b_1, and b_2. Thus, $a = \{b_0, b_1, b_2\}$. Each of the bs in turn is a class. Suppose, again for the sake of simplicity, that each b_i is $\{c_{i_1}, c_{i_2}, c_{i_3}\}$. Then $a = \{\{c_{0_0}, c_{0_1}, c_{0_2}\}, \{c_{1_0}, c_{1_1}, c_{1_2}\}, \{c_{2_0}, c_{2_1}, c_{2_2}\}\}$. And so on. If we pursue this to the limit we obtain a non-well-founded set that can be depicted in the following way (the arrows now depict the membership relation):

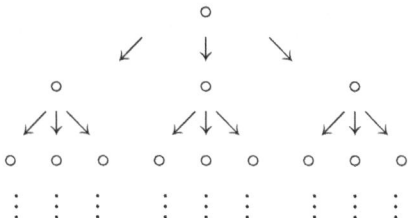

In orthodox set theory (ZF with the Axiom of Foundation) there are no non-well-founded sets of this kind. But there are perfectly respectable set theories where

---

[22] Since isomorphic elements may not be literally identical with each other, perhaps a better way of looking at the matter is as follows. At each stage of the proceedings an ontology is thrown away, and replaced by another with a richer structure. When all the ontologies have been thrown away, all that is left is the structure of the limit itself, X_ω, which is not ∅. So emptiness does not deliver the empty set.

there are such sets.[23] In such a set theory, membership regresses *may* bottom out to give a perfectly well-founded set. Thus, consider the well-founded set $a = \{\alpha, \{\beta, \gamma\}, \{\delta, \varepsilon, \eta\}\}$, where the Greek letters represent non-sets (or the empty set). This is represented by the diagram:

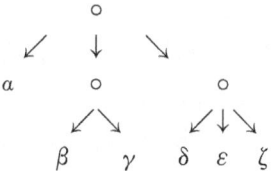

Alternatively, some chains may bottom out, whilst others do not. Such a situation might be the following:

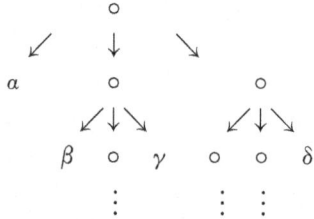

Alternatively again, no branch may ever bottom out. Let us call sets where this is the case *purely non-well-founded sets*.[24] When the analysis of relational existence is pursued to its limit, this is the sort of set to which it gives rise. Non-well-foundedness appears in a new guise. This time in the form of sets.

And what is to be said about the collapse into nihilism on this perspective? Whatever we take as X_0, the result, after iterating the construction to its limit, is a set, X_ϖ of purely non-well-founded sets—which is itself a purely non-well-founded set. Again, we see that the result is not the empty set (which is a well-founded set).

It might be suggested that the failure to collapse into nihilism obtains only because we are still left with things that have not been analysed, and so which have non-relational being: the members of set X_ω in the first case, or the members of the set X_ϖ in the second. So it is still not the case that everything is empty. In reply to this, one might suggest that the analysis simply be repeated again, applied to X_ω or X_ϖ. But in fact, this is unnecessary. As far as the analysis went, the initial set

---

[23] See Aczel (1988).

[24] One might wonder how to account for the identity and difference of such non-well-founded sets. There are various possible answers. Each proceeds by taking some equivalence relation on trees, and taking members of the same equivalence class to define the same set. Perhaps the most plausible account in this context is what Aczel calls SAFA. See Aczel (1988), pp. 49ff.

of objects, X_0, could have been anything. We may take X_ω or X_ϖ to be subsets of X_0. Indeed, we may just take X_0 to be the universal set, V, which contains everything.[25] In this case, the members of X_ω and X_ϖ have already been analysed.

And now, finally, to return to the problem with which we started this part of the investigation: the worry was that the structure which provides loci is itself a free-standing object. We now see that we do not need to assume this. The overall structure is X_ω or X_ϖ (depending how you look at it); and this has turned out to be as empty as anything else. Indeed, we may suppose that the whole Net of Indra is a node in its own network. The whole network is one jewel amongst many.[26]

12.9 Happy Anachronism

In this chapter we have looked at two objections to emptiness. The first was that it gives rise to a vicious regress. The second was that even to say that something is empty presupposes that some things are not thus. Both charges are, as we have seen, without foundation. The legitimacy of non-well-founded structures, including non-well-founded sets, has played an important role in this discussion. Buddhist philosophers who have taken the Madhyamaka and Huayan insight to heart have always insisted on the ontological groundlessness of things. They did not have the resources of contemporary non-well-founded mathematics to employ in their theorisation, of course. However, I have no doubt that they would have been absolutely delighted to learn of such a possibility!

So much for the coherence of emptiness. In the next few chapters, we will look at some of its implications, starting, in the next one, with implications concerning language and its limits.

---

[25] There is no universal set in standard non-well-founded set theory—or contradiction would arise. However, naive (paraconsistent) set theory has a universal set, V, as well as non-well-founded sets; indeed, the universal set is one of them, since $V \in V$. (See Priest (1987), chs. 10 and 18.) V is the totality of all (empty) objects. In Madhyamaka terms, one might think of this as emptiness (ultimate reality) itself. And since $V \in V$, emptiness is itself empty, as Madhyamaka has it.

[26] In non-well-founded set theory, we can construct a tree which is its own root, as follows. Take a tree, t (which is a set of ordered pairs) with root, r. The set, x, which is a solution to the equation $x = \{\langle x, r \rangle\} \cup t$, is a tree which is its own root. (See, for example, Barwise and Etchemendy (1987), ch. 3, or Aczel (1988), ch. 1.)

13
The World, Language, and their Limits

13.1 Concepts and the World

This chapter concerns matters of seminal importance to philosophy, concerning relationships between thought and the world. By 'thought', I mean the concepts which structure our thinking, or the language in which these can be expressed. Perhaps there are some important distinctions between these two things. However, there appear to be none that are germane to present matters, and I shall use the two terminologies indifferently. By 'the world' I will mean whatever it is that our language talks about—whatever it is, about which, concepts structure our thinking. Of course, one thing we think/talk about is our language/conceptual structure. In a sense, then, these are part of the world, too. But the relationship that will concern us is largely that between our concepts and the rest of the world.

Three main topics, in particular, will be at issue. The first is the perennial one of realism *vs* idealism: whether our concepts answer to the world, or *vice versa*. In the previous two chapters I argued that everything is empty (of self-being), and defended the idea against some natural objections. We will see that the view has important consequences for the matter, driving, as it were, between the two horns of the two options.

The second topic which will concern us is whether there are things which, as a matter of principle, transcend our ability to think/talk about them: the ineffable. It will then be time for gluon theory to reappear significantly in the discussion. We will see that the theory has distinctive consequences for this matter, engaging us in contradictions at the limits of thought. The metaphysics of emptiness will also be embroiled in this discussion. Indeed, we will discover a singular convergence between gluons and emptiness.

Finally, we will return to the topic of **nothing**. We will see that it has an intimate connection with the issue of what can be represented in language, with paradoxical implications of its own.

13.2 Idealism and Realism

To the first of these: the debate between realism and idealism. Realisms and idealisms come in many varieties. The kind of realism I have in mind here is that according to which there is a world which is, and is what it is, independently of any conceptual grasp to be had of the matter. The idealism we will be concerned with is the antithesis of this. There is no such world: reality is inherently conceptual. *Esse est concipi.*

Both of these positions are attractive in their different ways. Realism appeals to our common-sense and scientific thinking. The cosmos existed a long time before there was sentient life anywhere in it. Its history was driven by the laws of physics, and concerned quantum waves, subatomic particles, or whatever the current physics tells us to be our best understanding of the matter. These do not depend in any way on sentience. Indeed, sentience might never have evolved, and all this might have gone on, as it were, behind everyone's backs. But sentience did evolve, and a necessary condition for sentient beings to survive in the cosmos was that they have a certain grasp of their environment. This required a conceptual understanding of matters; and if this was to be effective then the concepts had to be adequate, at least in a gross way, to the reality they were trying to grasp. A badly flawed understanding of one's environment leads to failure in action. In the human species, many of the concepts involved were generated in the process of pre-linguistic evolution, inadequate concepts delivering the literal extinction of their bearers. More sophisticated concepts started to become available when the production of concepts itself came under conceptual control. But even then, their adequacy had, again, to be filtered though practical success and failure.

Idealism appeals to a different way of looking at matters. We have no grasp of the world outwith our conceptual apparatus. To think of a world as it is, independently of deploying any concepts, is to reduce it to the realm of *dinge an sich*. If there are such things, we can know nothing of them. The reality we inhabit is thoroughly conceptually saturated. This is not to say that there was no world temporally prior to sentience; but only that any such world, like anything else is (and was) what it is (and was) only in virtue of our conceptualizing it in a certain way. The world, then, answers to our conceptualization.

13.3 Realism, East and West

There have been many realists, both East and West: the Abhidharma Buddhists, Aristotle, the Hindu Nyāya school, Marx, Wittgenstein (of the *Tractatus*).[1] And each of them has articulated the realist picture in their own distinctive terms. On the other side, there have been many idealists, East and West: the Yogācāra Buddhists, Kant, Bradley, Kuhn, Foucault. And each of these, too, has articulated the idealist picture in their own distinctive terms.

This is no place to survey the various positions. Let us look briefly at a couple, starting with realists. One view of realism is spelled out by twentieth-century scientific realists, such as Jack Smart.[2] According to this, the world is a collection of entities interacting in accordance with the laws of nature, all of which are objective and mind-independent. What these objects and laws are—or at least our current best estimate thereof—is given to us by the laws of fundamental physics. And our physical theory is no mere instrumentalism, but is a shot at an accurate description of said reality. Of course, there are things like tables, people, nations, in some sense. But these are composed, in the ultimate analysis, of the fundamental physical particles, and their behaviour supervenes on the behaviour of these.

On the Eastern side, let us take the Abhidharma Buddhists.[3] According to them, the world is ultimately composed of basic building blocks, the *dharmas*. The precise nature of these was debated, but they were certainly metaphysical atoms of some kind; one standard view was that they were pins (tropes). The objects of day-to-day common sense were not real in the same way, but were conceptual constructions out of the dharmas. These objects were obviously not, therefore, conceptually independent. But in this way, they contrasted with the dharmas, which were not conceptual constructions.[4]

So much for our two examples. As is clear, a realist does not have to claim that *everything* we think/talk about is conceptually independent. But the crucial realist stand is that, somewhere down the line, there are building blocks of the world, and that these are what they are independently of our conceptualization. Our concepts, to be adequate, must answer to these. Note the asymmetry. The objects are primary; our concepts must respond.

---

[1] There are, notoriously, suggestions of solipsism in the final pages of the *Tractatus*. It is not at all clear how this relates to the correspondence theory of truth articulated in the main body of the work—or even that it is compatible with it.

[2] For example, Smart (1963).

[3] See Siderits (2007), ch. 6, and Koller (2002), ch. 14.

[4] Certainly, some of the dharmas were of mental states, and so obviously mind-dependent in that sense, though not the one at issue here.

13.4 Idealism, East and West

Turning to the idealist side of things: on the West, it is hard to go past Kant's transcendental idealism.[5] According to him, the human mind has a bunch of *a priori* concepts, such as the forms of intuition (perception), space and time, and the categories of the understanding delivered by (largely Aristotelian) logical form. These structure our cognitions. We naively take it that the forms (such as space), and categories (such as causality), are "out there" in the world. But this is a mistake. The structure that these provide is imposed on our raw sensations. So the objects of empirical experience are constructed conceptually. Kant did not deny that there were things beyond the objects of empirical experience; but these *dinge an sich* were forever beyond our ken. The world, our world, the only world we can know, is through and through conceptual.

On the Eastern side, Buddhists of the Yogācāra school, such as Vasubandhu, were idealists (or at least, this is the most natural interpretation of many of their texts).[6] For the older Abidharma philosophers, the dharmas were ultimately real. Everything else was a conceptual construction. The Yogācārins took *everything* to be a conceptual construction.[7] Take *any* object—say a tree. One might take the tree to be an object out there in mind-independent reality. But there is no such thing. There is simply the mental representation of a tree. The representation is constructed by the application of concepts, such as *leafyness*, *rootedness*, and so on. One can ask what is left if one "peels off" these concepts. The answer is not a nothing. It is an underlying "thusness", *tathātā*.[8] One may have a direct perceptual acquaintance with this (if one works hard at it), but one can say nothing of it; for nothing is available to be said when all the concepts have been stripped off.

So much for our two examples. As is clear, an idealist can be open to the claim that there is some sort of ultimate reality, though only of a kind that is closed off to us in a certain way. The crucial idealist stand is that our ordinary reality, our *lebenswelt*, is thoroughly conceptually saturated. Our concepts are primary; the objects of the world respond to these. The asymmetry is the exact opposite of the realist asymmetry.

---

[5] The *locus classicus* is, of course, the *Critique of Pure Reason*; but the *Prolegomenon to any Future Metaphysics* is often easier to get one's head around.

[6] See Siderits (2007), ch. 8, and Garfield (2002), chs. 7 and 9.

[7] There are nice points of exegesis here. Yogācāra takes there to be a deep level of consciousness, the *ālaya vijñāna*. To what extent this had self-being (and so was not a conceptual construction) was a point of contention between Yogācāra philosophers and Madhyamaka philosophers. In the end, as far as I can see, the mere fact that one can conceptualize it (talk about it) requires it to be a conceptual construction.

[8] Keown (2003), p. 296.

13.5 Between the Horns

Now let us come to emptiness: the view that all things are what they are in relation to other things. In the Huayan version, this relatedness spreads everywhere. All things are what they are, in the last instance, only because each other thing is what it is. This delivers a sort of holism—though this does not mean that all relations are of equal importance (as I noted in Section 11.4).

Now, both concepts and things in the world are empty.[9] And the important relations involved, in both cases, are to things in the world *and* to concepts. Take concepts first. Concepts are what they are, in important part, because they relate to each other in certain ways. Thus, for example, the concept *stray dog* is what it is in relation to other concepts; for example, the concept *dog*. But concepts do not float in some ethereal space. Concepts can be what they are only because they relate to things in the world in certain ways. Thus, the concept *dog* is what it is, in part, because it relates to dogs—the (generally four-legged) canine creatures in the world. If it related in the same way to cats instead, it would not mean what it does.

Conversely, things in the world are what they are, in important part, because they relate to other things in the world. Thus, I am what I am because of my parents, my DNA, and so on. But the objects of the world are no sub-conceptual *dinge an sich*. I am what I am, in part, because of how others think of me, conceptualize me, carve me out from the rest of the world. I am an Australian. But this is possible only because people think of me in certain ways. In particular, the Australian Government regards me in a certain fashion. If they ceased to do so, even though nothing else in my life changed, I would cease to be Australian. A more radical example: Am I the same person I was when I was one day old? Convention says 'yes'; but in truth, I now have virtually nothing in common with the neonate. Convention could equally have had it that I came into existence at puberty, in the same way that a caterpillar turns into butterfly at a crucial point of a certain causal trajectory.

The view that everything is empty—objects in the world and concepts—is neither, therefore, a realism nor an idealism. It goes between the horns of the two positions.[10] Realists were right in seeing that concepts depend for their nature on the world. Idealists were right in seeing that objects in the world depend for their nature on concepts. Both were wrong in seeing the dependence as one-way. Each,

---

[9] Indeed, the considerations marshalled in Chapter 11 apply to all objects; and concepts are just one kind of object.

[10] The present point is developed in a more historical way in Priest (2013a). 'Madhyamaka' means, in fact, 'middle way'. The view goes between the horns of a number of polarities. This is just one of them. Another such polarity is that of intrinsic existence and intrinsic non-existence.

as it were, saw only half of the picture. The interdependence is symmetric, not asymmetric, as each of the two "isms" has it. Sometimes, perhaps, it is conceptual dependence which is the more important of the two; sometimes, it is dependence on the world. The point, however, is that there is no uniform asymmetry.

13.6 The *Tractatus*, Same and Different

Let us turn to our second topic: the limits of language. In the *Tractatus* Wittgenstein gave an analysis of the structure of the world and the propositions which describe it. Facts are composed of objects, and propositions are composed of names which refer to them. Both facts and propositions have form. Indeed, when a proposition is true of the world, it shares its form with the corresponding fact. But form is not an object. It is the way that objects or their names are put together. Form *cannot* be just another object. For if it were, it and the objects or names that it enforms would simply be a congeries, and we would have no explanation of the unity of a proposition or a fact. Since form is not an object, there are no facts about it; neither are there any propositions true of it. Form can be shown but not said. The rub is that the *Tractatus* is full of claims about form, what it is, and what it does. The problem is just the intellectual descendent of Frege's problem about the concept *horse*, which we met in Section 1.2.[11] It triggered the final stunning few propositions of the *Tractatus*. Wittgenstein gritted his teeth (albeit with evident pleasure), and pronounced much of the book meaningless.

The cure for the illness is, however, fatal. Not only *do* we understand the propositions of the *Tractatus*; but if they were not true, we would have no reason to suppose that propositions about form and such things *are* meaningless. The move therefore saws through the very branch on which Wittgenstein was sitting.

In many ways, gluon theory appears to be in the same situation. Gluons are not forms in Wittgenstein's sense, but they are what account for the unity of propositions and other objects, as we have seen in prior parts of the book. Moreover, gluons are not themselves objects—or, rather, proper gluons are not. (I will take this qualification as read in what follows.) And since any claim we make is about objects, we can say nothing of them. They are ineffable. Clearly, though, this book is itself full of claims about them.

We are not, however, forced down Wittgenstein's self-destructive path. This is for two reasons. First, it is clear that if we can make a claim about something, it is an object. (In any world, anything in its domain of quantification is an object.) What is required for the contradiction, though, is the contrapositive: if something

---

[11] See Priest (1995a), p. 192.

is not an object, one cannot make a claim about it. Can we contrapose, even if something both is and is not an object? In a paraconsistent context, contraposition is never to be taken for granted. We could deny it here, on the ground that it spreads contradictions beyond necessity.[12] This move is not one available to Wittgenstein—or Heidegger—of course.

The second, and more straightforward, reason that we are not forced into Wittgenstein's predicament is that we can simply accept the contradiction. Gluons are, after all, objects as well, and so we can make claims about them. We can speak of the ineffable. That is a contradiction. But the thought that gluons are contradictory objects is hardly a new one at this point of the book. (Indeed, speaking of the ineffable played a central role in the discussion of being in 4.3.) On this approach, then, there are no true statements about gluons—and that is one of them! Call this *Gluon Paradox #1*.

As we noted in Section P.6, all the standard paradoxes of self-reference are inclosure paradoxes; and some of these are paradoxes of expressibility, such as König's (and Berry's) paradox.[13] Gluon Paradox #1 is obviously a paradox of expressibility—and it fits the Inclosure Schema. To see this, take the components of the Schema to be as follows:

- $\varphi(y)$ is 'y is a true statement'
- $\psi(x)$ is 'x is definable'
- $\delta(x)$ is 'there is no statement in $\dot{x}$ about gluons'

In the definition of δ, $\dot{x}$ is a name that refers to x. There is such a thing if x is definable. So, $\delta(x)$ is defined when $\psi(x)$ holds. Ω is the totality of all true statements. Checking the inclosure conditions: $\psi(\Omega)$ holds, since Ω is defined by the term: $\{y : y$ is a true statement$\}$. Now suppose that $x \subseteq \Omega$ and $\psi(x)$. Since gluons are not objects, there are no statements about gluons, and *a fortiori* no statements about gluons in x. That is, $\delta(x)$ is true. (Closure.) And since it is true, and is itself a statement about gluons, $\delta(x) \notin x$. (Transcendence.) The contradiction is that $\delta(\Omega) \in \Omega$ and $\delta(\Omega) \notin \Omega$. That is, 'there are no true statements about gluons' is both true and not true. There are no true statements about gluons—and that is one of them.

Now, a moment's thought shows that Gluon Paradox #1 is generated by a more fundamental one not involving expressibility at all: that proper gluons both are and are not objects. This itself produces an inclosure paradox. To see this, take the components of the Inclosure Schema to be as follows:

---

[12] See Priest (1987), 4.9. Conditionals are naturally understood as preserving truth forwards. Whether a conditional preserves falsity backwards, is always a separate issue.

[13] Priest (1995a), part 3, esp. 9.4.

- $\varphi(y)$ is 'y is an object'
- $\psi(x)$ is 'for some particular object, z, x contains the objects which are parts of z'
- $\delta(x)$ is the gluon of the z in question

$\delta(x)$ is clearly well defined when $\psi(x)$ holds. Ω is the totality of all objects. Checking the inclosure conditions: $\psi(\Omega)$, since the objects contained in Ω are exactly the parts of **everything**. Suppose that $x \subseteq \Omega$ and $\psi(x)$. Then $\delta(x)$ is an object. (Closure) But it is not an object, so it is not a member of Ω, and *a fortiori*, it is not a member of x. The limit contradiction is that the gluon of Ω, the totality of all objects, both is and is not an object. Let us call this *Gluon Paradox #2*. There is more to be said about this, but to see what it is, we need to look at the connection between emptiness and gluon theory.

13.7 Emptiness and Gluon Theory

As we saw in Chapter 11, all things are empty. But emptiness is no ordinary property. Things are not empty by accident. *To be just is to be empty.*[14] This means two things.

First, objects are not just empty at this world, they are empty at all worlds. To see this, note simply that, as we saw in Section 11.7, the quiddity of an object is world-invariant. Emptiness is not world-dependent.

Secondly, being empty is a self-nature. For take any object, a, and consider a world where there is nothing other than a. (It does not have to be a *possible* world.) In this world, a is still empty. This is so for (at least) two reasons. (i) In this world, a, *it*, is still one thing. So it has at least the property of being one. Hence, it is what it is in relation to these properties. (ii) a is an object; and it can be this only because it relates to **nothing** in a certain way (as I argued in Section 11.8).[15] Hence, for both reasons, a has relational being at this world; that is, it is empty in that world. Since the property of being empty survives the demise of all else, it is a self-nature.

---

[14] As Candrakīrti put it in *Prasannapadā* (XIII, 83b-84a), quoting the *Ratnakūta Sūtra*:

> Things are empty not because of emptiness; to be a thing is to be empty. Things are not without defining characteristics through characteristicalessness; to be a thing is to be without a defining characteristic...

The translation is by Garfield, and is taken from Priest and Garfield (2003), sec. 7. The situation in Buddhist philosophy is discussed at greater length there.

[15] How can this be, when there is only one thing in the world, a? **Nothing** can be in the world, because it is not an object, so there is still only one object in the world. Of course, nothing is an object, too. So there are two things in the world (as well). As I noted, this does not have to be a possible world.

In fact, these two things are equivalent. For if an object is empty at every world, then it is empty even at worlds where there is nothing else. So this is a self-nature. And if emptiness is a self-nature, an object is empty in and of itself; hence, it is thus, whatever the rest of the world is like. That is, it is empty in every world.

Now, consider the consequences of this. To be is to be empty. But we have already seen (Section 4.2) that to be is to be one object. That is, to be empty is to be one. Hence, what it is that makes something one—namely, its gluon—is what it is that makes it empty, that is, its relatedness to all things.

In one direction, this is, perhaps, unsurprising. For a thing to be empty is for it to be what it is by relating to other things; and this obviously requires it to be one thing. But now we see the converse as well. For something to be one thing is for it to have its being by relating to other things: something could not be a one thing unless is was located in a field of relations.

It might have seemed that emptiness and gluon theory were quite independent subjects. We now see that there is a profound connection.

13.8 Nāgārjuna's Paradox

We may now return to Gluon Paradox #2. Empty things (that is, all things) have, by definition, no self-nature. But as we have just seen, to be empty is a self-nature. And so we have a paradox. As the *Aṣṭasāhasrikā Prajñāpāramitā Sūtra* puts it:[16]

By their nature, the things are not a determinate entity. Their nature is a non-nature; it is their non-nature that is their nature. For they have only one nature; that is, no nature . . .

And as Candrakīrti, the influential seventh century commentator on Nāgārjuna, puts it in his commentary on *Mūlamadhyamakakārikā*, XV: 2:[17]

Whatever is called the dharma-ness of dharmas, just that is the own-form of that. But what is the dharma-ness of dharmas? It is the intrinsic nature of dharmas. What is this intrinsic nature? Essence? And what is that essence? Emptiness. And what is this emptiness? Being devoid of intrinsic nature.

That is, all things have no nature; that is their nature. We may dub this *Nāgārjuna's Paradox*: the nature of everything (emptiness) is a non-nature (empty).

Nāgārjuna's Paradox is itself an inclosure paradox. To see this, take the components of the Inclosure Schema to be as follows:

---

[16] Quotation and translation from Bhattacharya, Johnston, and Kunst (1978), pp. 23f.
[17] La Vallée Poussin (1970), pp. 264–5. Note that 'essence' here translates *svabhāva*.

- $\varphi(y)$ is 'y is empty'
- $\psi(x)$ is 'for some particular object, z, x contains the objects which are the parts of z'
- $\delta(x)$ is the nature of the z in question

$\delta(x)$ is obviously well defined when $\psi(x)$ holds. Ω is the set of empty things, that is, of everything. Checking the inclosure conditions: $\psi(\Omega)$ holds, since the object in question is **everything**: all objects are parts of this. Suppose that $x \subseteq \Omega$ and $\psi(x)$. Then $\delta(x)$ is empty. (Closure.) But that is a self-nature, so $\delta(x)$ is not in Ω. A fortiori, it is not in x. So $\delta(x) \notin x$. (Transcendence.) The contradiction is that the nature of **everything**—that is, emptiness—both is and is not empty.[18]

Indeed, as is not difficult to see, the Gluon Paradox #2 and Nāgārjuna's Paradox are just versions of the same thing.[19] In the Gluon Paradox $\varphi(y)$ is 'y is empty'; in Nāgārjuna's Paradox, it is 'y is an object'. But to be an object, that is, to be, is to be empty. And in the Gluon Paradox $\delta(x)$ is the gluon of the object whose parts are in x; in Nāgārjuna's Paradox it is the nature of the object whose parts are in x. But the gluon of an object is its unity; that is its being; that is, its being empty; that is, its (self-)nature.

13.9 *Tathātā*

We can now turn to the third topic of the chapter—one very particular gluon: **nothing**. First, though, in this section, and for the sake of comparison, a brief digression on an aspect of ineffability that arises in connection with certain Buddhist views. As we saw in Section 13.4, the Yogācāra idealists took our *lebenswelt*, our conventional reality, to be a conceptual construction. What is left when all concepts are stripped away, what there is ultimately, is an ineffable *tathātā*. Despite this, they had quite a lot to say about it. In particular, just as Wittgenstein in the *Tractatus* explains *why* one cannot talk about form, in so doing talking about it, the Yogācārins explain why one cannot talk about ultimate reality—in essentially the way that I did—and, in so doing, talk about it.[20]

---

[18] The naming of the paradox, and showing that it is an inclosure paradox are taken from Garfield and Priest (2003), sec. 8. In the formulation of the inclosure conditions given there, $\psi(x)$ is slightly different. There, $\psi(x)$ is 'x is a set of things with some common nature'. But there is no significant difference between being a set of things with some common nature and being the parts of some particular object. If x is a part of y then it is one of the members of the set of things with the nature 'part of y'. Conversely, if x is a set of things with a common nature, x is a part of the whole which is the sum of those parts.

[19] And the relation between the two gluon paradoxes is essentially the same as that between Nāgārjuna's two paradoxes of emptiness, on which see Priest and Garfield (2003), sec. 7.

[20] This is not a feature of just these two theories. There are many philosophical theories, East and West, which claim that there is something ineffable, and then explain why it *is* ineffable. See Priest (2005b).

There are various ways one may react to the contradiction. One is to go in for the sort of kicking away of the ladder that Wittgenstein does in the *Tractatus*: language is, in the end, merely a skillful means (*upāya*).[21] It is just a helpful device to be thrown away when it has done its work. But a quite different reaction is simply to endorse the paradox: one can speak of the ineffable.[22]

There are certainly texts that suggest this. The *Vimilakīrti Sūtra* is a text that was very influential, especially in Chinese Buddhism. At one point in this, a goddess appears in the room. When Śāriputra tries to brush off the flower petals she scatters around, a dialogue ensues. This turns to the question of how long Śāriputra has been enlightened (emancipated). Śāriputra refuses to answer, on the ground that since to be enlightened is to grasp the ineffable, one can say nothing of it. Śāriputra then receives a sharp rebuke:[23]

> The goddess said, "Words, writing, all are marks of emancipation. Why? Because emancipation is not internal, not external, and not in between. And words, likewise, are not internal, not external, and not in between. Therefore, Shariputra, you can speak of emancipation without putting words aside. Why? Because all things that exist are marks of emancipation."

The goddess is not denying that things are ineffable (as becomes clear later in the sūtra). She is explaining why one can speak of the ineffable. Words themselves are empty (as we saw in Section 13.5). So words are not something over and above emptiness; they are in it.

Notwithstanding any of this, conceptual constructivism of the Yogācāra kind cannot be sustained, not because the view generates contradiction: because of a more intractable problem. For such an idealism, the structure of the world is due to the imposition of the structure of language (concepts) on a substratum. All well and good, but where does the structure of language come from? As I observed in Section 13.1, language itself is part of the world. Hence, its structure is determined by... the structure of language imposed on the substratum. But that cannot be. The structure of language was what was to be accounted for. We have a vicious circle.[24]

Compare the situation with that in Kantian idealism. For Kant, the structure of the world is due to the imposition of the structure of the mind. What accounts for the structure of the mind? According to Kant, the mind is a noumenal entity outside of the world, and its structure is *sui generis*. Whatever one is to make of

---

[21] See Keown (2003), p. 318.

[22] For a general discussion of accepting contradictions in Buddhist philosophy, see Deguchi, Garfield, and Priest (2008). For a discussion of speaking of the ineffable, in particular, see Priest (2014).

[23] Translation from Watson (1997b), p. 87.   [24] See Priest (1997).

this answer, the fact that the mind is outside of the world means that the circularity does not arise. This position is not available to the conceptual constructivist we are dealing with here. Language and thought are firmly part of the *lebenswelt*—that which it is whose structure is to be explained.

13.10 The Preconditions of Representation

Though the conceptual constructivism of Yogācāra cannot be sustained, a paradoxical situation of a very similar kind arises in connection with the gluon **nothing**. As we have already seen (Section 11.8), in some ways **nothing** behaves as does ultimate reality (*li*) in the Huayan account. It also behaves very much like ultimate reality (*tathātā*) does in the Yogācāra account.

To see why, we need, first, to consider some general facts about systems of representations. What we will see is that for any system of representations there are preconditions of it functioning as such a system, and these cannot be expressed in the system itself, though they may be expressible in a "metasystem".

Let me illustrate the point with a couple of familiar examples. Consider ordinary maps, which are certainly systems of representation. Given a map, it may represent various information; for example, that there is a church north of a crossroads. All well and good, but for the map to be applied, one must know various facts about how the map relates to reality: for example, which symbol on the map represents some particular geographical place, which direction on the map corresponds to which direction on the ground. And this information is not contained on the map itself. The map depicts spatial relations between geographical objects, but not the relationships between the map and the objects themselves. There is therefore clearly determinate information that transcends expression in this form of representation; namely, that which allows the map to function as a map.[25] This information is hardly ineffable in an absolute sense, though: one can explain all of this in a discourse about the map and its relation to the ground; but in the representation the map provides, this cannot be expressed.

A second illustration: coördinate systems. Consider one of these—say, of a kind used in physics. Given such a system, there are many facts that it can be used to express. We can say, for example, that a particle with a certain velocity is located at a certain place (coördinate location); or that a particle with a certain

---

[25] Some maps are, literally, nailed to a spot; and carry a little arrow saying 'you are here'. Such maps do carry certain information of the required kind. But there is then other information that is not in them, for example, the information that the map is, indeed, nailed to the right place.

trajectory will pass through a certain location. But what we cannot express is the relationship of the coördinate system to the reality it coördinates. All places are expressible relative to the coördinate system: the coördinate system cannot locate itself: that must be done by some other information. For example, that the origin is located at a certain spot in physical space. There must be such information; for, just as with the map, it is necessary to know it to apply the information provided in terms of the coördinate system in practice. Without it, manipulating the information would just be a game, like chess. The inexpressible information is therefore information that is crucial to the very possibility that the coördinate system provide a system of representations at all. Once again, this information is hardly ineffable in an absolute sense: it can be expressed in a discourse about the coördinate system and its relation to the world; but in the representation simply provided by the coördinate system, it cannot be expressed.

Though I have illustrated the matter with a couple of examples, the point is, in fact, quite general. It was made by Wittgenstein; not the Wittgenstein of the *Tractatus,* but the Wittgenstein of the *Investigations*. At Section 139 of this, Wittgenstein gets us to consider a mental image (representation) of a cube, and asks what it is that makes it an image of a *cube*. The interlocutor says that the image simply 'fits' a cube but not, for example, a triangular prism. Wittgenstein continues:[26]

139... But doesn't it fit? I have purposely so chosen the example that it is quite easy to imagine a *method of projection* according to which the picture does fit after all.

140... What was the effect of my argument? It called our attention to (reminded us of) the fact that there are other processes, besides the one we originally thought of, which we should sometimes be prepared to call 'applying a picture of a cube'.

141... Suppose, however, that not merely the picture of the cube, but also the method of projection comes before the mind?—How am I to imagine this?—Perhaps I see before me a schema shewing the method of projection: say a picture of two cubes connected by lines of projection.—But does this really get me any further? Can't I now imagine different applications of that schema too?

The point that Wittgenstein is making is that a representation is one thing, and how it is to be applied, another. Moreover, how it is applied is not part of the representation; it is presupposed by it. This information may be expressible in a meta-representation; but this does not finesse this fact, since the same situation then arises with respect to *that* representation.

[26] Wittgenstein (1953), p. 139f.

What we see, then, is that for any system of representations there will be preconditions of it functioning *as* a system of representations which are not expressible in the system itself.

13.11 The Paradox of Nothingness

We are now in a position to establish our paradox. Given any family of systems of representations, we can form what we might call the *union* of all the members of the family. This is itself a system of representations. Something is an element of the union if it is an element of some member of the family; and it means something in the union if it means that in the member of the family from which it comes. (This may make elements of the union ambiguous. But no matter: ambiguity is rife in many systems of representation.) Now consider the union of *all* systems of representation, $\mathfrak{R}$.[27] Since this is itself a system of representations, it follows by the considerations of the previous section that there will be things about how it can function as a system of representations that cannot be expressed in it. Since we are dealing with the totality of all representations, these must be absolutely ineffable.

In truth, there is already a paradox here. There is something that is absolutely ineffable. This is something that makes it possible for $\mathfrak{R}$ to act as a system of representations. But this is to describe it in a certain way. Hence it is not ineffable.[28]

But what is this contradictory object? One candidate naturally suggests itself: **nothing**. For a start, one can talk about **nothing**: I am doing so now. But one cannot talk about **nothing** for the following reason (whatever one says about the ineffability of gluons in general). **Nothing** is the *absence* of all things. So there is literally nothing there to talk about! To pin a predicate on it is like trying to grasp thin air. Heidegger was here before us:[29]

> What is the nothing? Our very first approach to the question has something unusual about it. In our asking, we posit the nothing in advance as something that 'is' such and such; we posit it as a being. But that is exactly what it is distinguished from. Interrogating the nothing—asking what, and how, the nothing is—turns what is interrogated into its opposite. The question deprives itself of its own object.
>
> Accordingly, every answer to the question is also impossible from the start. For it necessarily assumes the form: the nothing 'is' this or that. With regard to the nothing, question and answer alike are inherently absurd.

---

[27] It might be suggested that there is no such totality, since it is indefinitely extensible. This does not follow at all. See Priest (2013b).
[28] See Priest (1995b), p. 223. The argument given there is piecemeal. The argument here is the general argument which I did not know how to give there. See also Priest (1997).
[29] Heidegger (1977), p. 98f.

But what has **nothing** to do with the possibility of the applicability of the system $\mathfrak{R}$? $\mathfrak{R}$ is the most general system of representation possible. Hence, the paradoxical thing we seek will be something which concerns the very possibility of representation in general. Now, all forms of representation represent things, objects. Hence, a natural candidate for the thing in question is something to do with the very possibility of objects.

Let us now revisit the discussion of **nothing** in 11.8. We saw there that to be an object is to be dependent on **nothing**. Something could not be an object if it were not so related. To be an object is to stand out against nothingness, as it were. Again, Heidegger, has been here before us:[30]

> In the clear night of the nothing... the original openness of beings as such arises: they are beings—and not nothing. But this 'and not nothing' we add in our talk is not some kind of appended clarification. Rather, it makes possible in advance the revelation of beings in general.

To put the matter in Kantian transcendental terms: **nothing** is a precondition of the possibility of anything at all being an object; that is, **nothing** is a precondition for the possibility of objects.

To use an analogy that Wittgenstein deploys in an entirely different context (*Tractatus* 5.633): what makes visual representation possible, the eye, is not represented in the visual field itself. Similarly, what makes systems of representation possible *as* systems of representation, the possibility of objecthood, is not representable in those systems. And this is **nothing**.

We are faced, then, with exactly the paradoxical situation which Yogācāra faces with respect to its notion of ultimate reality. **Nothing** is a contradictory object about which one can not talk, even though one obviously can. Call this the *Paradox of Nothingness*.

The Paradox of Nothingness is another paradox of expressibility—and it fits the Inclosure Schema. To see this, take the components of the Schema to be as follows:

- $\varphi(y)$ is 'y is a statement expressible in some system of representations'
- $\psi(x)$ is 'for some system of representations z, x is a set of statements of z'
- $\delta(x)$ is a statement about the preconditions of the z in question being a system of representation. In particular, when $x = \Omega$, let this be the statement that **nothing** makes objects possible.

By construction, $\delta(x)$ is always defined when $\psi(x)$ holds. Ω is the totality of all things that can be expressed in $\mathfrak{R}$. Checking the inclosure conditions: $\psi(\Omega)$ holds,

---

[30] Heidegger (1977), p. 105.

since the members of Ω can be expressed in it. Now suppose that $x \subseteq \Omega$ and $\psi(x)$. Then $\delta(x) \notin x$, by construction. But $\delta(x)$ is expressible, even when $x = \Omega$. (If the z in question is not Ω, $\delta(x)$ is expressible in its metasystem; if z is Ω, it is evidently expressible.) So $\delta(x) \in \Omega$. At the limit, a certain statement about **nothing** both can and cannot be expressed. The Paradox of Nothingness is, then, an inclosure paradox.

We have seen that **nothing**, 無, is a paradoxical notion. It resides at the very limits of language—something we can talk about which makes language possible, and so goes beyond it. 無 is well known in Buddhist contexts, notably for its role in a famous kōan: as an answer to the question of whether a dog has Buddha nature (a kind of ultimate reality).[31] We have just seen it to be involved in a kōan of its own: does 無 have expressibility-nature?

13.12 From Metaphysics to Ethics

So much for various connections between language, emptiness, and gluon theory. In the previous three chapters we grappled with a number of metaphysical issues. In the process, we have seen that there is much to be learned from Buddhist metaphysics. In the next two chapters we will see what is to be learned from Buddhist ethics.

---

[31] Yamada (2004), Kōan 2.

14

Peace of Mind

14.1 Appeals to Authority

In this chapter we move from metaphysics to ethics. Buddhist ideas will be of central importance here too—though, as ever, if they are acceptable, it is not because they are Buddhist; it is because they stand up to independent scrutiny. Indeed, there is an element of Buddhism according to which one not should accept something merely because an authority of some kind endorses it. As the Buddha himself is reported as saying in the *Kālāma Sutra*:[1]

Do not go upon what has been acquired by repeated hearing; nor upon tradition; nor upon rumour; nor upon what is in a scripture; nor upon surmise; nor upon an axiom; nor upon specious reasoning; nor upon a bias towards a notion that has been pondered over; nor upon another's seeming ability; nor upon the consideration, 'The monk is our teacher.'... [W]hen you yourselves know: 'These things are good; these things are not blameable; these things are praised by the wise; undertaken and observed, these things lead to benefit and happiness,' enter on and abide in them.

It may well be that the ethical view I will defend would not be accepted as Buddhist by some who regard themselves as Buddhists—and I will certainly reject some aspects of some Buddhist thought. But whether or not the ethics I describe should properly be called 'Buddhist' is, in fact, of little interest to me. All that concerns me is its truth.[2]

In the first half of this chapter I will articulate the central ideas of the ethics I will endorse. In the second, I will consider some natural objections.

---

[1] Translation from Thera (2010).
[2] For what it is worth, I find disputes about whether something is *really* Buddhism unenlightening. There are many forms of Buddhism, and no doubt we have not yet seen the last of them. When ideas morph from one culture to another, they change—dropping things which were brought to it by the old culture, and adding things present in the new one. The movement of Buddhism from India to China provides a striking case-study in the matter. Buddhism is now moving into "Western" cultures, and I have no doubt that it will morph again in the process.

14.2 The Four Noble Truths

The fundamental ideas that will concern us in this chapter are found in what are usually called the Four Noble Truths.[3] (These were the first teachings of the historical Buddha.) Let us start by looking at these.

The First Noble Truth is that life is *duḥkha*. This is a Sanskrit word that is hard to translate. The most frequent translation is 'suffering'. This captures something of what is at issue, but is not adequate. The word's connotations standardly include: suffering, pain, discontent, unsatisfactoriness, unhappiness, sorrow, affliction, anxiety, dissatisfaction, discomfort, anguish, stress, misery, and frustration. In what follows, I will just say *being disquieted*. The thought, whatever word one uses, is that all people get ill, suffer pain, age (if they are lucky to live long enough to do so), lose limbs, loved ones, jobs, treasured possessions—all of which gives rise to unhappiness, insecurity, mental dis-ease, and so on. This is not to say that there are not also times of happiness and joy. But like everything else in life, these are transient, and so prone to occasion the unhappiness of loss. For a mark of things in life is their impermanence: nothing lasts for ever.

I must confess that the First Noble Truth strikes me as pretty ungainsayable: events of the kind I have mentioned are parts of anyone's life. And all things will pass, destroyed by the heat death of the universe, or the machinations of the third law of thermodynamics—if not much more mundane things. There is not much to argue about here.

The Second Noble Truth says that there is a cause of duḥkha. This is *tṛṣṇā* (pronounced: *trishna*)—another word difficult to translate. The common translation is 'craving', which suggests the feeling one has for water when one has had no fluid for four days. (Literally, 'tṛṣṇā' means *thirst*.) This really does give the wrong impression. Better, is something like 'attachment and aversion': mental attitudes connected with wanting something good to go on, or wanting something bad to go away. The thought is that when we experience duḥkha, it is caused by this attitude which we bring to affairs, the result of which is unpleasant—sometimes very unpleasant.

The truth of the Second Noble Truth is, I think, less obvious than that of the First. But if one reflects on the times when one has been disquieted, I, at least, find it hard to think of one when this kind of attitude did not play a role. This is not, of course, to say that the attitude is the only cause of disquietude. Many causes have to conspire to bring about an effect. No doubt, unhappiness of this kind can

---

[3] See, for example, Harvey (2000), ch. 1, and Siderits (2007), ch. 2. In this context, 'noble' just means something like 'worthy of respect'.

be brought about by cars crashing, stock markets collapsing, earthquakes, tidal waves, and so on. But of all the causes that conspire, our mental attitude is the only one that is significantly under our control. It makes sense, therefore, to single that out.

The Third Noble Truth is but a corollary of the Second. If you can get rid of the attitude of tṛṣṇā, you can get rid of the duḥkha.

The Fourth Noble Truth is a series of suggestions as to how to get rid of the attitude: the Eightfold Noble Path. The eight kinds of action of the path fall into three categories. *Wisdom*: right view, right intention. *Action*: right speech, right action, right livelihood. *Mental state*: right effort, right mindfulness, right concentration.

When these suggestions are implemented in the appropriate way, they constitute what Foucault calls a technology of the self[4]—though given Buddhists' views concerning the self (which we noted in Sections 11.2 and 11.3), this is not a happy way of putting it. We might better say 'personal technology': these are practices which bring about dispositional changes in a person. Only the middle group would be thought of as ethical in traditional Western terms. But on the present picture, there is no real distinction. They all provide advice for attaining the same end. And, for the most part, when suitably spelled out, these strike me as pretty good advice; though I am sure that there is much other good advice out there as well. Further details are not germane to the present inquiry, however.

The important point to take away from the preceding discussion is that the Noble Truths—especially the First and the Second—serve to ground our ethics. When in doubt, it is reference back to these that will provide guidance.

14.3 Rebirth

At this point, a natural objection will strike many people. If the point of it all is to get rid of duḥkha, there is a very easy way to do so: kill yourself. That will certainly end it. Or if one is concerned with the duḥkha of other sentient creatures as well, nuke the planet. (Unlike committing suicide, this option is not practically available to most of us; but the thought-experiment is still good.) Surely, that cannot be right.

A standard reply will come immediately to most Buddhists (at least most Buddhists in the Indo-Tibetan tradition). Death will not work, because one is going to have to come back and do it all again: rebirth. One is locked into as many rebirths as it takes to get it right.

---

[4] Foucault (1988).

Now, in all religions, there are cultural accretions—things inessential to the religion, which are simply taken over from the ambient culture, and taken for granted. Buddhism is no exception. Abortion, for example, is deeply frowned upon in most Indo-Tibetan Buddhisms, but not generally in Japanese Buddhisms.[5] The reason for the attitude in Indo-Tibetan Buddhisms is that in Ayurvedic medical theory, as in the medieval Christian teaching, life begins at conception. Sino-Japanese medicine is different in this regard, and I take it that this is the reason for the difference in attitude. Similarly, Buddhism, like all major world religions, is patriarchal. It has its share of misogynistic texts. There has never been a female Dalai Lama; virtually all temple-heads in Japan have been men, and so on. But there is nothing essentially patriarchal about Buddhism—quite the contrary: gender is of no theoretical importance whatever. So why the patriarchy? Simply because Buddhism evolved in times and places (India and China between about 500 BC and 1000 AD) which were deeply patriarchal societies. The religion simply reflected this fact.

Rebirth might be thought to be a cultural accretion of this kind too, just taken for granted given the general culture of India circa 500 BC. Certainly, there are no significant *arguments* for this in the canon.[6] But the suicide objection suggests that this is wrong. Rebirth, though it may never have been argued for, is, in fact, integral to making the whole perspective coherent—though doubt may be cast on this by the fact that rebirth plays virtually no role in some Buddhisms: notably Zen, for example. (Zen Buddhists never explicitly repudiated rebirth, to my knowledge; it just becomes strangely irrelevant to where the action is: the present moment.)

Whatever one makes of this matter, however, I, at least, find it impossible to accept the doctrine of rebirth. There are, of course, problems about how even to conceptualize rebirth when there is no self to be reborn. (Here, Hindus, who believe in a self (*ātman*), have a much easier time.) I think that one probably can, in fact, make sense of the notion in an appropriate way. The problem is not this. It is simply one of lack of evidence. An old woman dies in downtown Melbourne in 2010. In the next year or two, hundreds of thousands of children are born all over the world. If rebirth is to mean anything, there must be something that makes one of them *her*. And there could be evidence for this. For example, if a child born in Osaka seems to remember Melbourne, and especially some of the things that no one but the old woman knew, but which can be independently verified (say, that

---

[5] Keown (2005), ch. 6.
[6] Indeed, a common claim is that the doctrine of rebirth is *atyantaparokṣa*: it can be known only be revelation (not divine, but by an omniscient Buddha)—a convenient view when you do not have any evidence!

before her death she hid a box in a certain location), then we would have such evidence—especially if this sort of occurrence were common.

But we do not have such evidence. There is no more evidence for rebirth, of a kind that would stand up to scientific scrutiny, than, I take it, for the existence of miracles in Christian traditions.[7] This does not, of course, show that rebirth is false. But the wise person, as Hume put it, proportions their beliefs according to the evidence.[8] Accordingly, one should not believe it. In particular, one most certainly should not base a system of ethics on such unsupported views.

Let me add that a rejection of rebirth does not mean a rejection of *karma* (action). Karma is the view that one's actions have effects, both good and bad, both for oneself and for others. In Indo-Tibetan Buddhism especially, the karma of one's actions plays an important role in how fortunate a human rebirth one has—indeed whether one has a *human* rebirth at all.[9] Clearly, if one does not endorse rebirth, one will not endorse this. But the doctrine of karma makes perfectly good sense within one life. For example: If you go around being friendly to others, others are more likely to be friendly to you; if you go around being mean to others, others are more likely to be mean to you. And if you are constantly friendly, it will make you into a person with a friendly disposition; whereas if you go around being mean, it will make you into a person with a mean disposition. As Aristotle noted, we train ourselves into virtues and vices.[10] All this seems to me little more than plain naturalistic (common sense) psychology.

14.4 Inner Peace

Given, then, that one can not appeal to rebirth, the suicide objection strikes me as a knock-down argument—as much as anything can be in philosophy. What it knocks down is the thought that an adequate ethics is simply about the elimination of the negative. It has to be about accentuating a positive. There must something positive to promote. But what?

The natural candidate is the antithesis of duḥkha: equanimity, inner peace, or peace of mind. Most of us experience this sometimes, and we know when it happens that it is good. Of course, most of us lose it when things go wrong. That is when the unhappiness kicks in, and we know it to be bad.

---

[7] As in the case of Christian miracles, there are, of course, people who claim to find evidence, such as Stevenson (1997). Such evidence is subject to standard debunkings, as in Edwards (1996).
[8] *Enquiry Concerning Human Understanding*, Section 10, Part 1. Selby-Bigge (1902), p. 110.
[9] See, for example, Keown (1996), ch. 3.
[10] *Nichomachean Ethics*, Book 2, ch. 1.

The idea that ethics is about the promotion of peace of mind is not unique to Buddhist thought. It is a common thought in Hellenistic philosophy.[11] The Greeks tended to call it *ataraxia*; the Romans *tranquillitas*. Buddhism itself has a name for it: *upekṣa*. Maybe these are not all exactly the same thing, but they are certainly in the same ball-park: a tranquil state of mind, not disturbed by unpleasant thoughts or emotions typically generated by the buffeting and turbulence of events, the slings and arrows of (sometimes not so) outrageous fortune.

It would be a mistake to think of inner peace as emotional flat-lining. It is quite compatible with joy of a certain kind, for example. Clearly, though, there are certain emotions that are incompatible with it. The obvious example is hatred. Hatred destroys inner peace. Between these two extremes, however, there is a range of emotions where matters are not so clear. It might be thought, for example, that sadness is not compatible with inner peace. But there would seem to be a certain kind of sadness that is compatible with it. There is much beautiful Japanese Zen poetry, especially on the theme of the transience of things, that undeniably has an air of sadness about it. The Japanese term for this is '*aware*', which is a sort of bittersweet sadness (or wistfulness) at the transience of things. This appears to be quite compatible with inner peace.

It would also be wrong to think of inner peace as a simple sensation. It is a state of mind; it certainly has affective elements; but in human beings at least, it is hard to see how these cannot but presuppose cognitive elements as well: at the very least, a certain kind of understanding of oneself, the greater order of things, and one's place in it.[12]

There is more to be said about the nature of inner peace; but that will do for the moment. I suggest that the aim of an adequate ethics is the promotion of this inner peace. (The Eightfold Noble Path can be thought of as steps in this direction.) Of course, it needs to be said that one should not be *attached* to the goal of inner peace. That would be self-defeating.

14.5 Other Goods

So much for the ethics—or at least the first part of it. As for any ethics, there are obvious objections. For a start: what we have so far concerns solely how each person should act with respect to themself; it says nothing about how they should act with respect to others. Surely, this cannot be all there is to the matter?—ethics concerns essentially our relation to others. Indeed so. This matter is so important

---

[11] It is also close to the unperturbed state advocated in the *Zhuangzi*. See Fraser (2011).
[12] In the case of sentient creatures of lesser degrees of mentality it may suffice that they do not have cognitive attitudes that generate an incorrect understanding.

that I devote the whole of the next chapter to it. But even setting this aside for the nonce, there are other obvious objections on the horizon. In the rest of the chapter I will consider some of these.[13]

First, according to these ethics, the good to be promoted is inner peace. This is surely a good, but there are many goods. Should these not be promoted too? Why single out just this one?

There are, indeed, goods other than inner peace which are worth having. A Verdi opera, a bottle of wine with friends, an interesting philosophical discussion. These are quite compatible with inner peace. But these goods are quite subjective. I love all the things just mentioned, but some people do not enjoy opera, wine, or philosophical discussion. And things that some others enjoy I most certainly do not: rap music, contemporary visual art, sodas. It seems to me that each individual can be safely left to choose their own goods of this kind. Such things are simply matters of ethical "free choice".[14] It needs to be remembered, though, that attachment to any of these goods will destroy inner peace.

However, inner peace is quite different. Its value is not subjective in the same way. Almost by definition, being disquieted is a negatively valued state. One may, perhaps, be prepared to put up with it if other things one values require it. (More of this in a moment.) But that does not mean that it is not valuable in and of itself.

Moreover, there is some sense in which all the other goods presuppose inner peace. Suppose that you are listening to an opera or chatting with friends, but at the back of your mind there is a niggling worry about what the pain you have been experiencing means, what your kids are up to, or losing your job. The experiences of the moment will be marred. To enjoy them properly, and experience these goods to the full, one needs to have inner peace.

14.6 Goods Incompatible with Inner Peace

The next objection concerns the thought that there are not just goods other than inner peace, but goods that are incompatible with it. There are goods such as love and the success of an ambition achieved. These are incompatible with inner peace. Yet it is necessary to have them for a full life. Life without such things would be bland and boring. Inner peace would ruin a full life.

One might pin something like this view on Nietzsche. Interpreting Nietzsche is always a fraught task, but one may see him as painting a picture of life as a

---

[13] Some of these objections are discussed in similar terms, with respect to Zhuangzi, in Fraser (2011).
[14] But should an ethics not recommend the encouragement of a multitude of these to enhance the richness of life? No. If one wishes to become a monk and live a quiet, withdrawn, life, this is a perfectly legitimate ethical choice.

struggle. What gives it meaning is constantly facing challenges and overcoming them—and sometimes failing. So, he tells us:[15]

> To the rabble, wisdom seems like a kind of escape, a device or trick for pulling yourself out of the game when things get rough. But the real philosopher . . . lives "unphilosophically", "unwisely", in a manner which is above all *not clever*, and feels the weight and duty of a hundred experiments and temptations of life:—he constantly puts *himself* at risk, he plays *the* rough game . . .

I think that this is, perhaps, one of the hardest objections to be faced. In replying, let me start by re-emphasizing that inner peace is not emotional flat-lining. It is not life after a lobotomy, or on constant valium. It is quite compatible with joy, for example; just not with attachment to the joy. This is hardly even the start of a reply, though. Let us look more closely at a couple of notable examples: love and aiming at a goal. These I think are typical. Are they really incompatible with inner peace?

Love is, at least for most people, a good in life. The joy of loving and being loved, whether it be of a child or of a partner, certainly enriches most people's lives (which is not to say that one cannot live a perfectly rich life without them). But as anyone who has loved knows, love normally comes with suffering: jealously, being rejected, the death of a child, and so on. Of course, we all hope that our particular loves will not result in such things. But I have never yet known a love relation—mine or others'—which did not occasion some sufferings.

Must it do so? Arguably, the suffering is not caused by the love, but by the state of attachment that normally goes with it. We suffer because we cling when our lover leaves, or our child dies. We want the other person to be something, do something—often, perhaps very often, in a self-centred way. But one can have the joy of the relationship without the clinging attachment. Indeed, arguably, a non-clinging love is better not only for oneself, but also for the beloved, and for the thriving of the relationship itself.

I have heard it argued that this is impossible, that the experience of attachment is *phenomenologically constitutive* of love—at least the love of a partner. It is not really love if one does not want to posses and be possessed. I doubt this claim, though I certainly do not want to deny that love is often accompanied by this kind of possessiveness. But if it is constitutive in this way, what I am inclined to say is that there is something very much like love: the caring, the sharing, the giving, the receiving, which is not accompanied by possessiveness. Call this love*, if you like. And we are better off without love, but with love* instead.

---

[15] *Beyond Good and Evil*, sec. 205. The translation is from Nietzsche (2002), p. 96. See Tanner (1994), ch. 4, and Spinks (2003), ch. 1.

A word about passion in this connection. 'Passion' is a weasel word, covering a multitude of things. At one end of the spectrum is when we say that someone has a passion for philosophy (or stamp collecting, or travel). This just means that they enjoy doing it, and spend much time doing so. There is nothing incompatible with peace of mind here. At the other end of the spectrum are crimes of passion (such as a murder), where someone loses emotional control. Clearly, this is incompatible with peace of mind, though there is nothing valuable about it either. Somewhere in the middle, there is a feeling that "wells up in one's breast", usually in connection with a loved one: an intense emotion with typical phenomenology, and various manifestations. If this occasions a loss of control (obsession, and other derailing things), so pushing towards the bad end of the spectrum, this is clearly problematic. However, I see nothing problematic about the emotion as such, any more than I see with a deep joy for life, or an intense experience of the sublime. The question is simply one of attachment.

What, to change the topic, about achieving goals? Let us take sport as an example. Most people who play sport do so with the aim of winning, sometimes at very high levels of performance. When they succeed, this brings them great joy. But in the process they fail often (in fact, the joy is often greater if winning has meant overcoming many failures). And in most sports, training involves painful activities of physical endurance to build up strength, stamina, and so on.

But again, the question is whether these things must entail disquietude. For a start, physical pain does not, necessarily, entail suffering. Most athletes take on the pain of training gladly. It is certainly compatible with inner peace. Suffering is something to do with the mental attitude which we bring to bear on our pain (though one which, when it accompanies illness, is very hard to shake). And failure brings suffering only if one does not accept it with equanimity. If one fails, one should just accept it, pick oneself up, and carry on. On the other side, if one does succeed, one should accept this also with equanimity, enjoying the moment without clinging to something which is sure to pass.

Before we leave the subject of goods incompatible with inner peace, there is another kind of example that might occur to one in this context. It is frequently claimed that there would be no great art—which is certainly a good for many of us—if there were no suffering, both in the process of creation and (sometimes) in that which is the subject of the art. As far as the latter goes, the First Noble Truth tells us that we are unlikely to run out of that very soon. If the thought is that one has to struggle to produce great art, which is no doubt true, the matter has already been addressed. There remains the claim that the artist must live in a garret, starve, go deaf, cut an ear off, to produce great art. I see no real evidence of this. Bach,

Picasso, Shakespeare, did not lead tragic lives. They were very successful people. This is not to deny that suffering can result in great works of art sometimes: many things occasion great art.

14.7 The Unrealistic Nature of the Ethics

The final two objections concern the thought that an ethics based on inner peace is unrealistic.

First objection: it is *psychologically* unrealistic. How can one, for example, love a child, without mourning their death (or struggle to win without an attachment to the project).

Suppose that one loves a child, who is killed suddenly and tragically in a motor accident. If one did not grieve, would this not be the sign of some mental pathology? Indeed, yes, it normally would be. But if the person has learned non-attachment, why should it be? No mental state can bring the child back, or reverse the tragic events. The child themself does not benefit from the grief—and neither does the person who grieves. None of this means that the person could not have loved the child, cared for it, sought the best for it, enjoyed times together. But all things must pass, one way or another, sooner or later. One should not cling.[16]

No one said that pursuing an ethical path is easy. The practice of this one may take much discipline. Perfection may even be unobtainable. But that does not mean that one should not work towards it. Ethical ideals may well not be fully realisable in practice.

Second objection: the ethics is *theoretically* impossible. Standard belief/desire psychology tells us that one needs beliefs and desires to act at all. Relinquishing all desires would result in no action at all.

Belief/desire psychology[17] gives us the following picture. I am thirsty and desire to alleviate the thirst. I believe that drinking a glass of water will do so. So I drink a glass of water. Without both the belief and the desire I would have done nothing. Without the desire, I would have had no reason to drink the water; and without the belief that this would be efficacious, I would not have known what to do. According to this account of action, desire is necessary for action because it provides the motor for action (and belief is necessary since it provides the method).

---

[16] This does not mean, though, that one's immediate reaction should be to shrug one's shoulders when it happens. Why should one not cry? One can do this whilst accepting what has happened, and not cling to the past—or to one's tears.

[17] As found, for example, in Davidson (1963).

A couple of things need to be said about this. First, though desire may provide one kind of motive to act, it is not clear that it is the only thing that can do this. Arguably, a belief that I *ought* to act in a certain way could itself motivate an act.[18]

Next, the ethics I have described is not about the elimination of desire in one sense. There is nothing wrong with aiming to develop inner peace (or act compassionately—we will come to this in the next chapter). What is wrong is being attached to this aiming. This is the state of being mentally disquieted until the aim has been fulfilled, or after one has failed to fulfil it—desire in a different sense. Though the two senses may normally go together, the ethics teaches divorcing them.[19]

14.8 Freedom for Life

I have argued that the aim of ethics should be the development and maintenance of peace of mind, of inner peace. I have stressed that this does not mean emotional flat-lining. Let me forestall another possible misconception. It may be thought that inner peace requires a withdrawal from the world, a monk-like existence, eschewing an engagement with its hurly-burly. Nothing could be further from the truth. Inner peace does not free you *from* the world, it frees you *for* the world.[20] It allows people to immerse themselves in life, engaging in other things they find of value (provided that these do not involve hate and similar things which destroy inner peace), confident that they can cope with the uncertainties and brickbats which life brings.

Indeed, it *requires* engagement of a certain kind. I turn to this matter in the next chapter.

---

[18] See, further, Humberstone (1987).
[19] The state is one of detachment-in-engagement, in the helpful phrase of Nivison (2000), p. 200.
[20] As Garfield and Priest (2009), p. 76, put it.

15

Compassion

15.1 Others

In the previous chapter we saw how the aim of ethics should be the development of inner peace. If we were to leave the matter there, however, it would be most one-sided and misleading. It might be thought to follow that inner peace entails a total indifference to others. It does not. One should be concerned with the inner peace of others, just as much as of oneself: compassion.

I should say immediately that 'compassion' may not be the best word for what I have in mind, due to its connotations. (I use the word since it is the usual—though perhaps not the best—translation of the Sanskrit *karuṇā*.) So let me cancel some of these immediately. First of all, the very etymology of the word suggests passivity, simply suffering with another. What I have in mind, as will become clear, is a very active state, involving actions aimed at the peace of mind of others. Secondly, the word may suggest that one has to suffer oneself to be compassionate: one has to *feel* the suffering of another. Now, to exercise compassion one certainly has to have a sympathetic understanding of the suffering of another; but one does not have to feel the same way. That, indeed, would probably be counterproductive. To give an obvious example: you cannot help a depressed person if you, yourself, get depressed. Maybe 'beneficence' or 'care' would be a better word to use (and translation);[1] but I will stick with 'compassion'.

That one should be compassionate (beneficent, caring) does not follow simply from the ethical principles we looked at in the previous chapter. More is needed—the more being some metaphysical input. It is common—maybe even inevitable—for ethical theories to have metaphysical underpinnings. Thus, Aristotle's virtue ethics presupposed his teleological account of nature; and a Hobbesean ethics presupposed a metaphysics of autonomous, independent, agents. In our case, the metaphysical underpinning comes from the emptiness of things, which we looked at in Chapter 11.

[1] As suggested to me by Jay Garfield and Amber Carpenter.

In this chapter we will start by seeing why the emptiness of things generalizes the concern with inner peace from oneself to others. In the next part of the chapter we will look at some ramifications of the view, and at some natural objections to it. In the final part of the chapter we will look briefly at some of the socio-political consequences of the ethics at hand.

15.2 Interconnectedness

First, why is emptiness the ground of compassion? Start by coming back to a Hobbesean ethics. This makes sense because (and only because) one thinks of individuals as atomic existences, which are what they are independently of others—providing the autonomy for each to enter into a compact with others of the same kind. In other words, one has to think of each individual as possessing svabhāva. This grounds the picture in which each looks after their own interests, and their own interests only—indeed, of their having independent interests in the first place. From the point of view of emptiness, this is precisely not the case—much as it might sometimes appear that my being is atomic and autonomous in this way. My nature (quiddity) is not self-standing, but depends for what it is on other things; and perhaps the most important of these are the individuals with whom I interact causally. *Their* natures, in turn, are determined in exactly the same way. By the very order of things, then, there is an interconnectedness and interdependence between things, and between people in particular. Thus, I am what I am, most importantly, because of my causal interactions with others: my parents, my friends, the people I read (about), and so on. Similarly for all people. Let us call this their inter-being.[2] This inter-being is what makes the Hobbesean picture illusory. It is also this which grounds compassion.

Some have held that the mere interdependence of people is sufficient to establish the claim that we should have regard for the interests of others, and so be compassionate;[3] but this certainly does not seem to follow. The slave and the slave-owner are mutually dependent. The owner depends on the slave to labour for him and make him rich. Reciprocally, the slaves depend on their owner to give them food, shelter, and any other means of life they see fit to provide. It does not follow *from this* that the owner should have any moral compunction to look after the slaves' interests at all. Without further consideration, it could equally be the case that they are permitted to exploit them ruthlessly till they die—especially if they can buy new slaves cheaply.

---

[2] I take the term from the Vietnamese Zen monk Thich Nhat Hanh; for example, Hanh (1993).
[3] See, for example, King (2005), esp. p. 160.

15.3 From the Net of Indra to Compassion

Mere interconectedness does not, therefore, provide the moral conclusion. There is one to be obtained, however.

To see how, come back to the metaphor of the Net of Indra. Suppose that a mental state of being disquieted (*duḥkha*) manifests itself as a red fleck in a jewel in the net. Then any red fleck in a jewel will cause a red fleck in any other jewel. So disquiet in any jewel will be coded in any other. Of course, this is true of all jewels, those that represent normal adults and those that represent, for example, rocks, cows, or infants. So this encoding does not imply that the fleck is *experienced* as disquiet. That requires (the agent represented by) the jewel to have certain cognitive abilities and attainments. In particular, a certain kind of awareness is necessary—and rocks, cows, and infants do not have it.[4]

All this is a metaphor, of course. But what it indicates is that disquiet in others occasions disquiet in other sentient creatures of sufficient awareness, such as me. In one way, we are all very familiar with this phenomenon. Negative emotions of others, even of those we simply pass in the street, tend to be communicated to us. We naturally respond to fear, hostility, anger, in a like manner. Fear in others can trigger a wave of fear in us; the hostility of another triggers a hostile response; and so on.

Of course, matters are not altogether as simple as that. We do not always seem to be troubled by others we know to be suffering. I know, for example, that poverty is rife in certain countries (and certain parts of even affluent countries); but sometimes I do not seem to be moved by this at all. However, all kinds of things can affect us unknowingly. For example, as doctors often note, one can be stressed, but quite unaware of this until the stress manifests as headaches, other bodily pains, and even serious illness. I take it that disquiet in others *does* affect us, even if we are not conscious of this. Deep in the unconscious, it plants the seeds of unease—if only because we know that things of the kind that have happened to others to disquiet them can equally happen to us—much as we might want to repress this thought with an act of bad faith.[5]

Is this simply special pleading? No. There is evidence from experimental psychology that this is, indeed, the case. One recent study says:[6]

---

[4] Maybe even certain psychopaths do not have it. Then they are no more *moral* agents than infants.
[5] Returning to our metaphor, the further away the source of the red fleck is, the weaker the effect. Similarly, the further I am from the sufferer (cognitively), the weaker the effect. It may not be surprising, then, that much of the effect of the suffering of others falls below my conscious cognitive horizon.
[6] Singer, *et al.* (2004), p. 1158.

The key suggestion is that observation or imagination of another person in a particular emotional state automatically activates a representation of that state in the observer, with its associated autonomic and somatic responses...

These results suggest that regions associated with feelings of emotion can be activated by seeing the facial expression of the same emotion, a phenomenon described as emotional contagion.

Another says:[7]

... results showed that those participants who have viewed negative news items reported significantly greater increase in anxiety and negative affect along with greater decrease in positive affect than those participants who viewed the combined positive and negative news items.

This study... demonstrates that anxiety and momentary mood disturbance do not dissipate with a distraction activity.

And yet a third says:[8]

The study... adds to a small but growing, number of studies indicating that television coverage of traumatic events may have significant [negative] secondary impacts on on public mental health.

Disquiet in others does, then, disquiet us—even if we are unaware of it.

Sometimes, of course, a response to suffering can be more negative than mere indifference. We can actually enjoy the suffering of others. Thus, for example, most of us know what it is like to experience pleasure when something bad happens to someone we dislike, such as someone against whom we bear a grudge. In such cases, something is blocking or undercutting the natural "resonance". But as the example makes clear, we enjoy the suffering because we have a negative attitude to the other in the first place—such as dislike, envy, or hatred. In other words, such a thing is possible only because we are already in a state of disquiet.[9] (The jewel, as it were, is clouded by such attitudes.) If that disquiet goes, so will the pleasure in the other's disquiet.

In sum, if all this is right, it follows that the disquiet of others is very much my concern. It may be suggested that it follows only that I should be concerned with the well-being of those with whom I come into contact: I do not need to have any concern for anyone else. This is short-sighted, however. It may be true that the immediate effects on me are from those with whom I interact personally. But

---

[7] Szabo and Hopkins, (2007), pp. 58, 61.
[8] Putnam (2002), p. 310.
[9] And if someone *is* truly indifferent to the disquiet of others, this, itself, is likely a sign of a troubled person; indeed, in extreme cases, it is the sign of some sort of disturbed psychopathology. See, further, Garfield (2011).

they, in their turn, are affected by others, who are affected by others, and so on. And the chain of encoding in the Net of Indra is transitive. Disquiet will knock on down the line.

Indeed, many of the effects on a person are ultimately from sources entirely beyond their ken. And one does not have to have a profound understanding of the world to see that duḥkha—in the form of poverty, oppression, greed, distrust, hate, desire for power—generates much suffering in the world: from simple violence and theft, to war and genocide. Even when the events are at a distant location in space, their effects ricochet through international relations, concerning the use of the military, international aid, refugees, and so on. These events and their consequences ultimately involve us all. As John Donne expressed it in his poem of 1624:[10]

No man is an iland, intire of it selfe; every man is a peece of the Continent, a part of the maine; if a clod bee washed away by the Sea, Europe is the lesse, as well as if a Promontorie were, as well as if a Mannor of thy friends or of thine owne were; any mans death diminishes me, because I am involved in Mankinde; And therefore never send to know for whom the bell tolls; It tolls for thee.

And if it be suggested (unrealistically) that I should just, then, take myself off to a desert island so that I do not have to interact with others, one should remember that putting people in solitary confinement is a form of punishment. The inability to interact with others is wont to generate profound disquiet of its own.

15.4 The Import of Metaphysics

Let us be clear about the nature of the project I am engaged in here. This is to read off facts about moral psychology from a metaphysical picture of the world. It might be thought that there is something fundamentally misguided about such a project: inferring facts of cognitive psychology, such as disquiet, from facts about the metaphysical nature of people. I think not. Facts concerning the physical nature of people can obviously have consequences in cognitive psychology; and facts of metaphysical nature are even more fundamental. Recall, also, that the understanding of the Net of Indra which I have articulated is based on the structural trees of objects (see Section 11.6), and that the relations involved in such trees include causal relations.

Nor am I the first person to engage in this kind of project. A moment ago I mentioned bad faith—the pushing to the back of the mind unpalatable thoughts. As hardly needs to be said, the notion is Sartre's. And Sartre is a master of trying

[10] *Devotions Upon Emergent Occasions and Severall Steps in my Sickness—Meditation XVII.*

to read off facts of human cognitive psychology from the metaphysical nature of people (*être pour soi*)—both in his philosophical writings, such as *L'Etre et le Néant*, and in his novels, such as *La Nausée*. Sartre's metaphysics of essencelessness, and its consequences of radical freedom, are not, of course, the metaphysics of emptiness.[11] But the move from metaphysics to moral psychology which Sartre makes is of the same kind.

So once more back to the Net of Indra. Change the metaphor slightly. Let us suppose that the interaction between the jewels is not one of reflection; suppose instead that the interaction is one of resonance—in the way that vibrations of an object can cause similar vibrations in closely located free-standing objects. Interpret the vibrations as the "vibes" of a tranquil mind or of a disquieted mind which we all show to others. When we are surrounded by people who are agitated, angry, aggressive, it is much harder to be peaceful; and conversely, disquiet will normally be mitigated if we are surrounded by compassionate, peaceful, people—and so on, transitively. The effect, of course, is reciprocal. There can, then, be no radical disjuncture of being between myself and others.[12]

What I have been arguing is that inter-being grounds an important solidarity in people. In the end, my inner peace cannot be divorced from that of others. Compassion is the order of inter-being.

15.5 Two Observations

Let me make a couple of further comments on the ethics of compassion that has now emerged.

First, the account I have given provides a framework within which particular ethical decisions are to be made. It does not of itself, though, determine any particular ethical decision. Such decisions will depend on contingent facts concerning the outcomes of any particular action in its context, and on laws of human

---

[11] Though there certainly are similarities which it would be worth exploring. For example, his slogan that *hell (suffering) is other people* (from the play *Huis Clos*) could be thought of as simply the downside of the slogan that heaven (peace of mind) can be other people. As the Zen story goes: 'A Soldier named Nobushige came to Hakuin, and asked: "Is there a paradise and a hell?" "Who are you?" inquired Hakuin. "I am a samurai," the warrior replied. "You are a soldier!" exclaimed Hakuin. "What kind of ruler would have you as a guard? Your face looks like that of a beggar." Nobushige became so angry that he began to draw his sword, but Hakuin continued: "So you have a sword! Your weapon is probably much too dull to cut off my head." As Nobushige drew his sword Hakuin remarked: "Here are the gates of hell!" At these words the samurai, perceiving the master's discipline, sheathed his sword and bowed. "Here open the gates of paradise," said Hakuin.' (Reps and Senzaki (1971), p. 80.)

[12] To change the metaphor yet again: Jay Garfield once commented to me that Buddhist ethics is like plumbing. You have a problem with your draining and sewage system? Okay, let me show you how to fix it. I would add: and if the people in the next apartment have a problem with their drainage and sewage system, it quickly becomes yours. You should help them fix it too.

(or better, sentient) psychology. In other words, this ethics is not some *a priori* deduction of the good: it is very much situated in the actual world we have, and the facts about cognitive agents in that world.

Neither may making particular judgements be expected to be easy much of the time. Just because of the Net of Indra, situations are always complex. Any action is likely to have both good consequences and bad consequences. The determination of the best course of action will therefore require an act of judgement, or *phronesis* (practical wisdom) as Aristotle put it.[13] This does not, of course, mean that all situations are unclear. In many situations the most important effects of a possible action will obviously be on a certain individual and those close to them. We should act in such a way as to promote their inner peace. Thus, it is quite clear that if, next time I am in pub, I pull out a gun, and shoot one of those enjoying a quiet drink, this is not going to do this.

But life often presents hard moral choices. If I am a doctor, should I respect the wish of a parent for their child not to be given a blood transfusion, even though I know that without it the child is very likely to die? Buddhist ethics provides no magic bullet in hard cases. Phronesis is required.

Secondly, it might be thought to follow from what I have said that compassion does not need to concern itself with the physical suffering of others: it is a waste of time to try to feed people who are hungry, cure those who are ill. If the cause of duḥkha is a mental attitude, one should just teach them to meditate, or whatever. Nothing could be further from the truth. For first, you cannot acquire inner peace by simply turning on a switch. Tṛṣṇā is a hard, ingrained, and thoroughly insistent mental attitude. Perhaps it is deeply inscribed into our psyche for evolutionary reasons. To rid oneself of it requires much practice and self-discipline. It is utopian to suppose that one could take the steps to rid oneself of the attitude when one is starving, in great pain due to illness, the subject of war and violence, and so on. Alleviating such things (that is, generating outer peace) is therefore a necessary condition of getting much further. Secondly, as I noted in Section 14.2, tṛṣṇā is but one cause of suffering. If it be a singularly important one, there are also others. And if getting rid of suffering is a good thing to do, getting rid of other of its causes is good too.

15.6 Interlude on Buddhism

Before we pass on to look at some objections, let us have a brief interlude on Buddhism. Two points in particular.[14]

[13] *Nichomachean Ethics*, Book 6, chs. 5, 7.
[14] The Buddhist connections of this chapter are discussed in much greater detail in Priest (2015b).

The insistence on compassion does not take us away from Buddhism. Even early Buddhism stresses compassion (*karuṇā*). However, it becomes the central virtue only of later (Mahāyāna) Buddhism. Moreover, it is standard to hold that inner peace requires compassion. Here, for example, is a quotation from the contemporary Theravadin Bikkhu Bodhi. Recall that the Sanskrit for inner peace is *upekṣā* (Pali: *upekkhā*):[15]

> The real meaning of upekkha is equanimity, not indifference in the sense of unconcern for others. As a spiritual virtue, upekkha means equanimity in the face of the fluctuations of worldly fortune. It is evenness of mind, unshakeable freedom of mind, a state of inner equipoise that cannot be upset by gain and loss, honor and dishonour, praise and blame, pleasure and pain. Upekkha is freedom from all points of self-reference; it is indifference only to the demands of the ego-self with its craving for pleasure and position, not to the well-being of one's fellow human beings. True equanimity is the pinnacle of the four social attitudes that the Buddhist texts call the 'divine abodes': boundless loving-kindness, compassion, altruistic joy, and equanimity. The last does not override and negate the preceding three, but perfects and consummates them.

Naturally, one may ask: why did Buddhists take a compassionate attitude to be important? (As far as I know, the answer I have given is not to be found in the Buddhist literature.) A simple and important answer is that compassion is an important piece of personal technology (see Section 14.2), conducive to helping a person get rid of attachment to the (non-existent) self. A theoretical (not simply pragmatic) reason can be given, assuming Abhidharma metaphysics. The ultimately real things are dharmas: everything else is a conceptual construction out of these. (See Section 13.2.) There are abroad, then, lots of psycho-biological states of being disquieted. There is no sense, however, in which some of these belong to *my* self, and some belong to *other* selves: there are no selves in the relevant sense. Nor does it make any sense to suppose that the dharmas of disquiet belong to any particular person. Persons have no real existence. The badness of these states, then, does not depend on *whose* they are. They are all equally bad. We should therefore be concerned to eliminate *all* mental states of disquietude.

Essentially this argument was given by Śāntideva in his *Bodhicaryavatāra* (VIII: 99–103).[16] This is somewhat ironical because the argument appeals to the Abhidharma view of persons; and Śāntideva is not an Abhidharmika, but a Mādhyamika. Whilst the Mādhyamika endorsed the Abhidharma view that there is no self, they did not accept the reductionist view of what it is to be a person.

---

[15] Bodhi (1998)—'Bikkhu' (Skrt: Bikṣu) is the Pali name for a monk.

[16] Thus, at sec. 102 he says: 'Since there is no independent possessor of suffering,/ There is no real difference between my own and others' suffering./ Thus, we should dispel all suffering simply because it is painful—/ Why cling to false distinctions with such certainty?' (Translation from Gyatso (2002), p. 130.)

For them, a person is just as real or unreal as the parts out of which they are made. All have exactly the same existential status: empty. In particular, then, there is a person—albeit a conventionally real one. And this person experiences their own mental states of disquiet, in a way that they do not experience those of other people. The states *are*, then, located in an existent being. (Nor does it help to point out that the person has no *ultimate* reality; for neither do the mental states of disquiet.)[17]

Second topic: in virtue of what I have said about the need for phronesis in making judgements about concrete situations, those familiar with standard discussions of Buddhist ethics will be tempted to ask: what of the Precepts? In Buddhism there is a standard set of moral guidelines: do not kill, do not lie, and so on.[18] These look like pretty universal edicts. Violating them can certainly get one kicked out of the Saṃgha (the monastic community). Especially in the Mahāyāna traditions, it is recognized that it might be right to violate the Precepts sometimes. There are stories, for example, of the Buddha in an earlier rebirth killing someone because it was the best thing to do in the context. But none the less, the edicts are enforced pretty rigidly. Do not expect to get away with breaking one if you are a much lesser mortal!

As is clear from what I have said, however, rules of any kind can be at best rules of thumb, and they should never be promoted to thoughtless demands. This does not mean that the Precepts are not generally good guidelines. Mostly they are. But the effects of an action will always be context-dependent, and this must be taken into account. In particular, it must be remembered that the Precepts were formulated at particular times and places, and might well be heavily dependent on the socio-historical contexts in question. And rules of thumb that were pretty good at one time, may not work at another. This should be borne in mind when thinking what is of value in historical formulations of Buddhist ethical codes. For example, historically, much traditional Buddhism has been down on gays and lesbians (and being patriarchal, particularly down on male homosexuality).[19] Now it may well have been the case that being gay at various times in Indian and Chinese history was not a great strategy for leading a happy life. But in enlightened contemporary societies—or at least those parts of them that are enlightened—where sexual preference is not an issue, gay sexuality is no more (or less) problematic than straight sexuality.

---

[17] The point is made and discussed in Williams (2000), ch. 5, and Wetelsen (2002). This interpretation of the Śāntideva passage is, however, contentious. See Garfield, Jenkins, and Priest (201+).

[18] See Harvey (2000), ch. 2, and Keown (2005), ch. 1.

[19] See Harvey (2010), ch. 10, and Keown (2005), ch. 4.

15.7 Making Others Suffer

Let me now turn to a couple of objections to what I have said about compassion and the virtues thereof.

For the first of these, let us return to Nietzsche. Nietzsche seems to hold the view that suffering is not only justified by the goods which it makes possible—but that the mere surviving of suffering is itself good. As he said, notoriously: anything that does not kill me makes me stronger.[20] More than this, he often suggests that making others suffer is good. Thus we have:[21]

> Let us be clear as to the logic of this form of compensation: it is strange enough. An equivalence is provided by the creditor receiving, in place of literal compensation for an injury (thus in the place of money, land, possessions of any kind), a recompense in the form of a kind of pleasure—the pleasure of being allowed to vent his power freely upon one who is powerless, the voluptuous pleasure "*de faire le mal pour le plaisir de le faire*", the enjoyment of violation. This enjoyment will be greater the lower the creditor stands in the social order, and can easily appear to him as a most delicious morsel, indeed as a foretaste of higher rank. In "punishing" the debtor, the creditor participates in the *right of the masters*: at last, he, too, may experience for once the exalted sensation of being allowed to despise and mistreat someone as "beneath him" . . .

and:[22]

> [T]he essential feature of a good, healthy aristocracy is that it does *not* feel that it is a function (whether of the kingdom or of the community) but instead feels itself to be the *meaning* of highest justification (of the kingdom or the community),—and, consequently, that it accepts in good conscience the sacrifice of countless people who have to be pushed down and shrunk into incomplete human beings, into slaves, into tools, all *for the sake of the aristocracy*.

Why does Nietzsche make these somewhat extraordinary claims? As best I can understand it, it is because the surviving of suffering, and its infliction on others, is an exercise of the "will to power", which characterizes the "superior person" (*übermensch*).

Now, it is true that one who survives a tragic experience, such as a Nazi concentration camp, may well have had to develop an admirable strength of character; but it would have been better had it not had to be done in this tragic way. The self-discipline required to develop a robust inner peace is much to be preferred. And, it must be said: for all that some people develop the strength to survive a tragic experience, such circumstances will just as often, if not more often, damage

---

[20] *Twilight of the Idols* 1, Maxim 8. A good rhetorical line, but one which is obviously false. (Ask the inmates of Guantanamo Bay.)
[21] *On the Genealogy of Morals*, second essay, sec. 5. Translation from Nietzsche (1969), pp. 64–5.
[22] *Beyond Good and Evil*, sec. 258; Nietzsche (2002), p. 152.

and crush people in the process—as the example of the Nazi concentration camps reminds us too clearly.

As for the need to valorize oneself by making others suffer, I can but regard this as a sign of a deeply troubled person, a symptom of deep tṛṣṇā. (Nietzsche, indeed, is not known for his untroubled psyche.) Why would one feel any need to do this unless one felt some deep sense of inadequacy and the duḥkha that goes along with it? There are better ways of dealing with this.

Nietzsche was contemptuous for those who had the mentality of sheep, who followed the herd, and submitted passively. Whether or not he was right in this matter (he was not), it should now be obvious that inner peace does not entail such passivity. Compassionate action is often not easy—it often means *not* going along with the herd—and neither is non-violent resistance of the kind sometimes undertaken by Buddhists.[23] Indeed, compassion often requires as much strength of character as surviving suffering; and others do not come off worse as a result of it.

15.8 Those who Cause Suffering

The first objection quickly brings a second in its wake. How should we respond to those who make others suffer? I have said that the inner peace of all sentient creatures is important;[24] but surely one should not work for the inner peace of those things that cause others harm, such as colonies of malaria-bearing mosquitoes in Africa?

For a start, the only sorts of creatures that can have or fail to have inner peace are sentient creatures. How far down the evolutionary scale sentience goes is debatable. But mosquitoes are too far down. Of course one should eradicate mosquitoes that cause much human suffering, and if that means draining the swampy environments in which they flourish, so be it. In human history, improvement of living conditions, health, and well-being owes much to our ability to manipulate inhospitable environments and hostile species (such as those of certain parasites), with engineering, drugs, and other technological devices.

I should note that some have suggested that Buddhist ethics are naturally an environmental ethics, concerned with the flourishing of all environments/species.[25] This is certainly not the case with the present view. It is

[23] See, for example, Keown (2005), ch. 7.
[24] Which is certainly not to say that all sentient creatures are *equally* important. If there is a hard choice between the suffering of a person and the suffering of a cat then, *ceteris paribus*, phronesis would dictate attending to the well-being of the person.
[25] See, for example, Keown (2005), ch. 3. For further references, and a critique of ways in which this is often done, see Ives (2009).

sentience-centric. This is not to say, or course, that we may treat the environment and other species in a cavalier fashion. Many species other than humans are sentient. Compassion requires a regard for their well-being. And many of the things we are now doing to the environment are likely to cause significant suffering to future generations. Compassion requires us to stop these, and find better ways to bring about any beneficial ends these activities are supposed to deliver.

That is not an end to the matter concerning the agents of suffering, however. For there obviously are sentient beings—people, in particular—who cause others to suffer, and destroy their inner peace. How should one treat them? The exact answer in any particular case will depend on the context; but, whatever it is, it should be determined by considerations of compassion—both to those who are suffering, and to those who are causing the suffering. Violence is never good in itself, and should be avoided if possible. But sometimes it may be necessary to avoid greater suffering. Perhaps, if it had been possible to kill Hitler in 1933, this would have been the best thing to do in the context.

It should be remembered that those who make others suffer are almost certainly suffering themselves. Plausibly, this is the source of their desire to hurt others. At the very least, I find it very hard to see how someone at peace with themself could want to perpetrate suffering on others. Ideally, one should stop the infliction of suffering, whilst helping the person causing it to develop inner peace.

15.9 Why be Moral?

Before we turn to socio-political matters, let us look at one other topic. There is a standard conundrum about morality: why should one be moral? If, for example, one were given the Ring of Gyges, which makes its wearer invisible, why should one not behave entirely out of self-interest? There are various standard answers to the question. I will just point out here that the above account of ethics provides a very simple answer to the question.

For a start, why should a person behave in such a way as to develop their own inner peace? This hardly needs an answer. A troubled state of mind is not a state we feel happy being in. Of course one would like to get rid of it. (You enjoy the headache?—Okay don't take the aspirin!) But what of others? Nagel puts the point in the following way:[26]

Do pleasure and pain have merely agent-relative value or do they provide neutral reasons as well? If avoidance of pain has only relative value [sc. to the agent], then people have reason to avoid their own pain, but not relieve the pain of others (unless other kinds of

[26] Nagel (1989), p. 158f.

reasons come into play). If the relief of pain has neutral value as well, then anyone has reason to want any pain to stop, whether or not it is his. From an objective standpoint, which of these hypotheses is more plausible? Is the value of sensory pleasure and pain relative or neutral...?

The objective standpoint is provided by the Net of Indra. From this perspective, there is no absolute duality between myself and someone else. My being encodes theirs, and theirs mine. Each plays north pole to the other's south. The value, then, is not relative to an individual agent. As far as peace of mind goes, my relation to your interests is the same as my relation to my own—or better: we both have an interest in our common interest. This is not, note, to say that I should be compassionate simply as a matter of self-interest (as, maybe, for Hobbes). The Net of Indra undercuts the very nature of the distinction between self-interest and other-interest.

15.10 Matters Socio-Political

Let me finish the chapter with a brief discussion of how all this bears on socio-political matters. For example: What kind of socio-political action does the ethics suggest? More grandiosely: what kind of socio-political system would this ethical system deliver?

Oddly enough, there is little discussion of such matters in traditional Buddhist literature.[27] Perhaps there are good reasons why. For a start, given the First Noble Truth, it would be entirely utopian (unrealistic) to design a society which was suffering-free. It would be utopian also in the Marxist sense. We do not have the liberty of constructing a society from scratch. We must start from where we are. Given the ethics, we should act in a compassionate way. That is, we should work to eliminate, or at least decrease, the disquietude in the world.

If one wants to do this in an effective way, one needs to understand its socio-political causes. What are these? Answers are, of course, contentious. And different kinds of causes may be local to different places. Racism, sexism, religious intolerance, for example, are more prevalent in some parts of the world than others. However, as one looks around the world at the start of the twenty-first century, it is hard to go past the thought that a major, perhaps the major, global cause of suffering is poverty—a poverty which results in hunger, disease, the inability to respond the natural disasters, and so on.

It is, in fact, an irony of the state of the contemporary world that we now have sufficient resources globally that no one needs to go hungry, everyone could have

---

[27] The various contemporary engaged Buddhist movements seem to be a major novel development in this regard. See, for example, the essays in Queen and King (1996). See also King (2005) and (2009).

decent health care and education, and many sorts of disease could be entirely eradicated. Why is this not happening? Clearly, because of the lop-sided distribution of wealth in the world. Most of this is concentrated in a handful of very rich countries—and within those countries in a handful of very rich people and corporations, whose major concern is to make themselves richer. At the other extreme is a vast mass of humanity who struggle to keep themselves alive, fighting hunger and disease. Clearly, what is needed is a redistribution of resources.

Of course, if this happened, the standard of living of people in the "advanced" capitalist countries would have to drop—though probably not by that much, given the enormous inefficiency and waste of these countries. For those of us in such countries to object on these grounds, could only be selfish—certainly not compassionate. Some might say that they deserve the wealth they possess since they have earned it. Not only is this blinkered: the single greatest determinant of one's wealth is the happenstance of where and when one was born; this is not a matter of desert at all; worse, given the ethics, it is *irrelevant*. Those with the most to give should be happy that they are in a position to do so.

The next relevant question is how this grossly uneven distribution has arisen, and how it is maintained. The answer to that is, however, obvious. It is a result of the development of capitalism in certain parts of the world, and, via the tendency of capital to agglomerate, to concentrate itself in a few hands. Given that such is a structural feature of capitalism, an inevitable consequence of the way it works, a simple corollary is that capitalism should be dismantled. As Marx noted, capitalism has been outstanding at developing the wealth in the world. But now that we have reached this point, it is time to do something other than just try to accumulate more of it. It might be said that if capitalism is dismantled, and resources are distributed more equally, global wealth will not continue to grow, and may even plateau. So be it. The creation of wealth is not a good in itself. It is a matter of what one can do with it. And there comes a point where its creation hits the law of diminishing returns—in spades. The difference between a $10 bottle of wine and a $40 bottle of wine is enormous. The difference between a $500 bottle of wine and a $530 bottle of wine is miniscule.

Add to this the fact that the creation of new wealth (economic growth) is currently in the process of playing havoc with the environment of the one and only world we have, and it would indeed seem time to say that enough is enough.

These are all the easy matters, though. They give us an idea of what sort of thing we ought be trying to achieve. They do not address the question of how best to go about achieving it. Sad to say, there is no magic bullet that is going to solve the problem. There is no single person or group which has the power to bring about these ends—and even if there were, it is a good bet that they would abuse it.

The socio-political movement required by the ethics I have described must be a grass-roots one, not easily corrupted by tṛṣṇā. Many kinds of social and political action can surely be helpful in this, but of central importance is undoubtedly education. People need to understand the nature of the world and how it works—and not just the grossly distorted view of the world that is foisted upon us by the popular media, advertising, and forms of political manipulation. Crucially, people need to understand how they are all dependent on each other. We need to break down the barriers of race, class, and gender, and of the vested interests of national governments and multi-national corporations. We need to realize our common inter-being. We need to understand the Net of Indra.

Having hearkened, not to me, but to the Word (Logos), *it is wise to agree that all things are one.*

Heraclitus, Fragment B50. [Graham (2011)]

Bibliography

[1] Aczel, P. (1988), *Non-Well-Founded Sets*, CSLI Lecture notes, Vol. 14, Stanford, CA: CLSI, Stanford University.
[2] Allard, J. W., and Stock, G. (eds.) (1994), *F. H. Bradley: Writings on Logic and Metaphysics*, Oxford: Oxford University Press.
[3] Allen, R. E. (1983), *Plato's* Parmenides, Oxford: Blackwell.
[4] Anscombe, G. (1966), 'The New Theory of Forms', *Monist* 50: 403–20; reprinted as ch. 3 of Anscombe's collected papers, Vol. 1: *From Parmenides to Wittgenstein*, Oxford: Blackwell, 1981.
[5] Ariew, R., and Garber, D. (eds.) (1989), *Leibniz: Philosophical Essays*, Indianapolis, IN: Hackett Publishing Company.
[6] Arlig, A. (2007), 'Abelard's Assault on Everyday Objects', *American Catholic Philosophical Quarterly*, 81: 209–227.
[7] Armstrong, D. M. (1989), *Universals: an Opinionated Introduction*, Boulder, CO: Westview Press.
[8] Artmann, B. (1999), *Euclid—the Creation of Mathematics*, New York, NY: Springer Verlag.
[9] Bacon, J. (1995), *Universals and Property Instances: the Alphabet of Being*, Oxford: Blackwell.
[10] —— (2008), 'Tropes', *Stanford Encyclopedia of Philosophy*, http://plato.stanford.edu/entries/tropes/. (Accessed April 2010.)
[11] Barker, S. (2009), 'Dispositional Monism, Relational Constitution, and Quiddities', *Analysis* 69: 242–50.
[12] Barnes, J. (ed.) (1984), *The Complete Works of Aristotle*, Princeton, NJ: Princeton University Press.
[13] —— (1987), *Early Greek Philosophy*, London: Penguin Books.
[14] Barwise, J., and Etchemendy, J. (1987), *The Liar: an Essay on Truth and Circularity*, Oxford: Oxford University Press.
[15] Baxter, D. (1988), 'Identity in the Loose and Popular Sense', *Mind* 97: 575–82.
[16] Bhattacharya, K., Johnston, E. H., and Kunst, A. (1978), *The Dialectical Method of Nāgārjuna: Vigrahavyāvartanī*, Delhi: Motilal Banarsidass.
[17] Bird, A. (2007), 'The Regress of Pure Powers?', *Philosophical Quarterly* 57: 513–34.
[18] Blumenthal, J. (2008), 'Śāntarakṣita', *Stanford Encyclopedia of Philosophy*, http://plato.stanford.edu/entries/saantarak-sita/. (Accessed January, 2013.)
[19] Bodhi, B. (1998), *Toward a Threshold of Understanding*, BPS Newsletter cover essays nos. 30 & 31. Accessed 15 Jan. 2007 from 'Access to Insight', http://www.accesstoinsight.org/lib/authors/bodhi/bps-essay_30.html.
[20] Boehner, P., Gál, G., and Brown, S. (eds.) (1974), *Guillelmi de Ockham: Summa Logicae*, St Bonaventure, NY: Franciscan Institute Publications.
[21] Borges, J. L. (2000), *The Aleph and other Stories*, London: Penguin.

[22] Bradley, F. H. (1922), *The Principles of Logic*, Oxford: Oxford University Press.
[23] Buchler, J. (1990), *Metaphysics of Natural Complexes*, 2nd, expanded, edn., Albany, NY: State University of New York Press.
[24] Bunt, H. C. (1985), *Mass Terms and Model Theoretic Semantics*, Cambridge: Cambridge University Press.
[25] Butler, J. (1849), *The Analogy of Religion*, Oxford: Oxford University Press.
[26] Cameron, R. (2008), 'Turtles all the Way Down', *Philosophical Quarterly* 58: 1–14.
[27] Candlish, S. (2009), 'Francis Herbert Bradley', *Stanford Encyclopedia of Philosophy*, http://plato.stanford.edu/entries/bradley/. (Accessed April 2011.)
[28] Chang, G. C. C. (1972), *The Buddhist Teaching of Totality: the Philosophy of Hwa Yen Buddhism*, London: George Allen & Unwin Ltd.
[29] Cherniss, H. (1957), 'The Relation of the *Timaeus* to Plato's Later Dialogues', *American Journal of Philology* 78: 225–66.
[30] Cohen, S. M. (2008a), 'Aristotle's Metaphysics', *Stanford Encyclopedia of Philosophy*, http://plato.stanford.edu/entries/aristotle-metaphysics/. (Accessed April 2010.)
[31] —— (2008b), 'Non-Substantial Particulars' (a supplement to Cohen (2008a)), *Stanford Encyclopedia of Philosophy*, http://plato.stanford.edu/entries/aristotle-metaphysics/suppl.html. (Accessed April 2010.)
[32] Cook, F. (1977), *Hua-yen Buddhism: the Jewel Net of Indra*, University Park, PA: Pennsylvania University Press.
[33] Copleston, F. (1961), *Aquinas*, London: Penguin.
[34] Cornford, F. M. (1939), *Plato and the Parmenides*, London: Routledge and Kegan Paul.
[35] —— (1957), *Plato's Theory of Knowledge*, 5th impression, London: Routledge and Kegan Paul.
[36] Cotnoir, A. (2010), *Non-Classical Mereologies and their Applications*, PhD thesis, University of Connecticut.
[37] —— and Bacon, A. (2012), 'Non-Wellfounded Mereology', *Review of Symbolic Logic*, 5: 187–204.
[38] Couturat, L. (ed.) (1961), *Opuscules et Fragments Inédits de Leibniz*, Hildesheim: Georg Olms Verlag Buchhandlung.
[39] Cowherds, The (2015), *Moonpaths: Ethics and Emptiness*, New York, NY: Oxford University Press.
[40] Crabbé, M. (2011), 'Reassurance for the Logic of Paradox', *Review of Symbolic Logic*, 4: 479–85.
[41] Cross, R. (1995), 'Duns Scotus's Anti-Reductionistic Account of Material Substance', *Vivarium* 33: 137–70.
[42] Curd, P. (2004), *The Legacy of Parmenides: Eleatic Monism and Later Presocratic Thought*, Chicago, IL: Parmenides Publishing.
[43] Dancy, R. M. (1975), *Sense and Contradiction in Aristotle*, Dordrecht: Reidel.
[44] Davidson, D. (1963), 'Actions, Reasons and Causes', *Journal of Philosophy*, 60: 685–700; reprinted in *Essays on Actions and Events,* Oxford: Clarendon Press, 2nd edn, 2001.
[45] Deguchi, Y., Garfield, J, and Priest, G. (2008), 'The Way of the Dialetheist: Contradictions in Buddhism', *Philosophy East and West* 58: 395–402.

[46] Del Punta, F. (ed.) (1979), *Guillelmi de Ockham: Expositio super Libros Elenchorum*, St Bonaventure, NY: Franciscan Institute Publications.
[47] Dennett, D. (1982), 'The Self as a Center of Narative Gravity', ch. 6 of F. Kessell, P. Cole, and D. Johnson (eds.), *Self and Consciousness: Multiple Perspectives*, Hillsdale, NJ: Erlbaum.
[48] —— (1993), *Consciousness Explained*, London: Penguin Books.
[49] —— and Steglich-Petersen, A. (2008), *The Philosophical Index*, www.philosophicallexicon.com. (Accessed January 2013.)
[50] Dipert, R. (1997), 'The Mathematical Structure of the World: the World as Graph', *Journal of Philosophy* 94: 329–58.
[51] Dodds, E. R. (1928), 'The *Parmenides* of Plato and the Origin of the Neo-Platonic "One"', *Classical Quarterly* 22: 129–42.
[52] Eames, E., and Blackwell, K. (eds.) (1973), *Collected Papers of Bertrand Russell, vol. 7: Theory of Knowledge*, London: Allen and Unwin.
[53] Edelglass, W., and Garfield, J. (eds.) (2009), *Buddhist Philosophy: Essential Readings*, Oxford: Oxford University Press.
[54] Edwards, P. (1996), *Reincarnation: a Critical Examination*, Amherst, MA: Prometheus Books.
[55] Fine, K. (1975), 'Vagueness, Truth, and Logic', *Synthese* 30: 265–300.
[56] —— (1999), 'Things and their Parts', *Midwest Studies in Philosophy* 23: 61–74.
[57] —— (2010), 'Puzzles of Ground', *Notre Dame Journal of Formal Logic* 51: 97–118.
[58] Forrest, P. (2010), 'The Identity of Indiscernibles', *Stanford Encyclopedia of Philosophy*, http://plato.stanford.edu/entries/identity-indiscernible/ (Accessed February 2010.)
[59] Foucault, M. (1988), 'Technologies of the Self', pp. 16–49 of L. H. Martin, H. Gutman, and P. H. Hutton (eds.), *Technologies of the Self*, Amherst, MA: University of Massachusetts Press.
[60] Frances, B. (1996), 'Plato's Response to the Third Man Argument in the Paradoxical Exercise of the *Parmenides*', *Ancient Philosophy* 16: 47–64.
[61] Fraser, C. (2011), 'Emotion and Agency in *Zhuangzi*', *Asian Philosophy* 21: 97–121.
[62] Frede, M. (1992), 'Plato's *Sophist* on False Statements', ch. 13 of R. Kraut (ed.), *The Cambridge Companion to Plato*, Cambridge: Cambridge University Press.
[63] Frege, G. (1892a), *Grundgesetze der Arithmetik*, Vol. 1; partial translation by M. Furth as *Basic Laws of Arithmetic*, Berkeley, CA: University of California Press, 1964.
[64] —— (1892b), 'On Sense and Reference', pp. 56–78 of Geach and Black (1952).
[65] French, S. (2010), 'Identity and Individuality in Quantum Theory', *Stanford Encyclopedia of Philosophy*, http://plato.stanford.edu/entries/qt-idind/ (Accessed February 2010.)
[66] Ganeri, J. (2001), *Philosophy in Classical India*, London: Routledge.
[67] Garfield, J. (1995), *The Fundamental Wisdom of the Middle Way: Nāgārjuna's Mūlamadhyamakakārikā*, Oxford: Oxford University Press.
[68] Garfield, J. (2002), *Empty Words: Buddhist Philosophy and Cross Cultural Interpretation*, New York, NY: Oxford University Press.

[69] —— (2011), 'What is it Like to be a Bodhisattva? Moral Phenomenology in Śāntideva's *Bodhicaryāvatāra*', *Journal of the International Association of Buddhist Studies*, 33: 333–57.
[70] —— Jenkins, S., and Priest, G. (2015), 'The Śāntideva Passage, *Bodhicāryāvatāra* VIII: 90–103', ch. 4 of The Cowherds (2015).
[71] —— —— (2003), 'Nāgārjuna and the Limits of Thought', *Philosophy East West* 53, 1–21. Reprinted as ch. 5 of Garfield's, *Empty Words*, Oxford: Oxford University Press, 2002; and ch. 16 of the second edition of Priest (1995a).
[72] —— —— (2009), 'Mountains are Just Mountains', ch. 6 of M. D'Amato, J. Garfield, and T. Tillemans (eds.), *Pointing at the Moon: Buddhism, Logic and Analytic Philosophy*, New York, NY: Oxford University Press.
[73] Gaskin R. (1995), 'Bradley's Regress, the Copula and the Unity of the Proposition', *Philosophical Quarterly* 45: 161–80.
[74] Geach, P., and Black, M. (trans.) (1952), *Translations from the Philosophical Writings of Gottlob Frege*, Oxford: Basil Blackwell.
[75] Gerson, L. (1986), 'A Distinction in Plato's *Sophist*', *Modern Schoolman: a Quarterly Journal of Philosophy* 63: 251–66.
[76] Gibbard, A. (1975), 'Contingent Identity', *Journal of Philosophical Logic* 4: 187–222.
[77] Gill, M. L. (1996), 'Introduction', pp. 1–116 of Gill and Ryan (1996).
[78] —— and Ryan, P. (1996), *Plato: Parmenides*, Indianapolis, IN: Hackett Publishing Co.
[79] Graham, D. W. (2011), 'Heraclitus', *Stanford Encyclopedia of Philosophy*, http://plato.stanford.edu/entries/heraclitus/. (Accessed April, 2013.)
[80] Grube G. M. A. (1992), *Plato: Republic*, Indianapolis, IN: Hackett Publishing Co.
[81] Gyatso, T. (trans.) (2002), *Guide to the Bodhisattva's Way of Life: a Buddhist Poem for Today*, Glen Spey, NY: Tharpa Publications.
[82] Haldane, E. S., and Simpson, F. H. (trans.) (1995), *Lectures on the History of Philosophy*, Vol. 2: *Plato and the Platonists*, Lincoln, NE: University of Nebraska Press.
[83] Halper, E. C. (2009), *One and Many in Aristotle's Metaphysics*, 2nd edn., Las Vegas, NV: Parmenides Publishing.
[84] Hamilton, E., and Cairns, H. (eds.) (1961), *The Collected Dialogues of Plato*, Princeton, NJ: Princeton University Press.
[85] Hanh, T. N. (1993), *Interbeing: Fourteen Guidelines for Engaged Buddhism* (revised version), Berkeley, CA: Parallax Press.
[86] Harte, V. (2002), *Plato on Parts and Wholes*, Oxford: Oxford University Press.
[87] Harvey, P. (2000), *Buddhist Ethics*, Cambridge: Cambridge University Press.
[88] Hawkes, T. (1977), *Structuralism and Semiotics*, London: Methuen.
[89] Hawley, K. (2009), 'Identity and Indiscernibility', *Mind* 118: 101–9.
[90] Heidegger, M. (1977), 'What is Metaphysics', pp. 95–112 of D. F. Krell (ed.), *Martin Heidegger: Basic Writings*, New York: Harper and Row.
[91] —— (1991), *The Principle of Reason*, trans. R. Lilly, Bloomington, IN: Indiana University Press.
[92] —— (1996), *Being and Time*, trans. J. Stambaugh, Albany, NY: State University of New York Press.

[93] —— (2002), *Identity and Difference*, tr. J. Stanburgh, Chicago, IL: University of Chicago Press.
[94] Hellman, G. (2001), 'Three Varieties of Mathematical Structuralism', *Philosophia Mathematica* 9: 184–211.
[95] Hick, J. (ed.) (1964), *The Existence of God*, London: Collier-Macmillan.
[96] —— (1970), *Arguments for the Existence of God*, London: Macmillan.
[97] Hilbert, D., and Ackermann, W. (1928), *Grundzüge der Theoretizchen Logik*, Berlin: Julius Springer.
[98] Hudson, H. (2006), 'Confining Composition', *Journal of Philosophy* 103: 631–51.
[99] Humberstone, I. L. (1987), 'Wanting as Believing', *Canadian Journal of Philosophy* 17: 49–62.
[100] Husserl, E. (1931), *Ideas: General Introduction to Pure Phenomenology*, London: George Allen & Unwin.
[101] Hyde, D. (1997), 'From Heaps and Gaps to Heaps of Gluts', *Mind* 106: 641–60.
[102] van Inwagen, P. (1981), 'The Doctrine of Arbitrary Undetatched Parts', *Pacific Philosophical Quarterly* 62: 123–37.
[103] —— (1990), *Material Beings*, Ithaca, NY: Cornell University Press.
[104] Ives, C. (2009), 'In Search of a Green Dharma: Philosophical Issues in Buddhist Environmental Ethics', pp. 165–85 of Powers and Prebish (2009).
[105] Jacob, P. (2010), 'Intentionality', *Stanford Encyclopedia of Philosophy*, http://plato.stanford.edu/entries/intentionality/. (Accessed, August 2012.)
[106] Jones, N. (2009), 'Fazang's Total Power Mereology', *Asian Philosophy* 19: 199–211.
[107] —— (2010), 'Nyāya-Vaiśesika Inherence, Buddhist Reduction, and Huayan Total Power', *Journal of Chinese Philosophy* 37: 215–30.
[108] —— (2015), 'Buddhist Reductionism and Emptiness in Huayen Perspective', ch. 6 of Tanaka *et al* (2015).
[109] Kahn, C. (2003), *The Verb 'Be' in Ancient Greek*, 2nd edn., Indianapolis, IN: Hacket Publishing Company.
[110] Kemp Smith, N. (trans.) (1933), *Immanuel Kant's Critique of Pure Reason*, 2nd impression, London: Macmillan.
[111] Kenny, A. (1969), *The Five Ways*, London: Routledge and Kegan Paul.
[112] Keown, D. (1996), *Buddhism: a Very Short Introduction*, Oxford: Oxford University Press.
[113] —— (2003), *Dictionary of Buddhism*, Oxford: Oxford University Press.
[114] —— (2005), *Buddhist Ethics: a Very Short Introduction*, Oxford: Oxford University Press.
[115] Keränen, J. (2001), 'The Identity Problem for Realist Structuralism', *Philosophia Mathematica*, 9: 308–30.
[116] King, P. (2010), 'Peter Abelard', *Stanford Encyclopedia of Philosophy*, http://plato.stanford.edu/entries/abelard/. (Accessed November 2010.)
[117] King, S. (2005), *Being Benevolence: the Social Ethics of Engaged Buddhism*, Honolulu, HI: University of Hawai'i Press.
[118] King, S. (2009), 'Elements of Engaged Buddhist Ethical Theory', pp. 187–203 of Powers and Prebish (2009).
[119] Koller, J. (2002), *Asian Philosophies*, 4th edn., Upper Saddle River, NJ: Prentice Hall.

[120] Koslicki, K. (2008), *The Structure of Objects*, Oxford: Oxford University Press.
[121] Kneale, W., and Kneale, M. (1962), *The Development of Logic*, Oxford: Clarendon Press.
[122] Kripke, S. (1972), 'Naming and Necessity, pp. 253–355 and 763–69 of D. Davidson and G. Harman (eds.), *Semantics of Natural Language*, Dordrecht: Reidel; reprinted as *Naming and Necessity*, Cambridge, MA: Harvard University Press, 1980.
[123] La Vallée Poussin, L. (ed.) (1970), *Mūlamadhyamakakārikās (Madhyamakasūtras) de Nāgārjuna, avec la Prasannapadā de Candrakīrti*, Osnabrück: Biblio Verlag.
[124] Ladyman, J., and Ross, D., with Spurrett, D., and Collier, J. (2007), *Every Thing Must Go: Metaphysics Naturalized*, Oxford: Oxford University Press.
[125] Leibniz, G. (1686), 'General Inquiries about the Analysis of Concepts and of Truth', pp. 47–87 of G. H. R. Parkinson (ed.), *Leibniz: Logical Papers*, Oxford: Clarendon Press, 1966.
[126] Lewis, D. (1968), 'Counterpart Theory and Quantified Modal Logic', *Journal of Philosophy* 65: 113–36.
[127] ——— (1983), 'New Work for the Theory of Universals', *Australasian Journal of Philosophy* 61: 343–77; reprinted as ch. 14 of Mellor and Oliver (1997).
[128] ——— (1991), *Parts of Classes*, Oxford: Blackwell Publishers.
[129] Linnebo, Ø. (2008), 'Plural Quantification', *Stanford Encyclopedia of Philosophy*, http://plato.stanford.edu/entries/plural-quant/. (Accessed May 2012.)
[130] Liu, M-W. (1982), 'The Harmonious Universe of Fa-tsang and Leibniz', *Philosophy East & West* 32: 61–76.
[131] Lopez, D. (1998), *Elaborations on Emptiness*, Princeton, NJ: Princeton University Press.
[132] Lowe, E. J. (2002), *A Survey of Metaphysics*, Oxford: Oxford University Press.
[133] Machina, K. (1976), 'Truth, Belief, and Vagueness', *Journal of Philosophical Logic* 5: 47–78.
[134] Mair, V. (1994), *Wandering on the Way: Early Taoist Tales and Parables of Chuang Tzu*, New York, NY: Bantam Books.
[135] Marshall, M. (2008), 'The Possibility Requirement in Plato's *Republic*', *Ancient Philosophy* 28: 71–85.
[136] McPherran, M. (1986), 'Plato's Reply to the "Worst Difficulty" Argument of the *Parmenides*: *Sophist* 248a-249d', *Archiv fuer Geschichte der Philosophie* 68: 233–52.
[137] Meinwald, C. C. (1991), *Plato's Parmenides*, Oxford: Oxford University Press.
[138] Mellor, D. H., and Oliver, A. (1997), *Properties*, Oxford: Oxford University Press.
[139] Miller, M. H. (1986), *Plato's Parmenides: The Conversion of the Soul*, Princeton, NJ: Princeton University Press.
[140] Minsky, M. (1986), *The Society of Mind*, York, NY: Simon and Schuster.
[141] Mitchell, D. (2002), *Buddhism: Introducing the Buddhist Experience*, Oxford: Oxford University Press.
[142] Molnar, G. (2000), 'Truthmakers for Negative Truths', *Australasian Journal of Philosophy* 78: 72–86.
[143] Nagel, T. (1989), *The View from Nowhere*, Oxford: Oxford University Press.
[144] Nehamas, A. (1982), 'Participation and Predication in Plato's Later Thought', *Review of Metaphysics* 36: 343–74.

[145] Nicholaus, M. (tr.) (1979), *Marx: Foundations of Political Economy*, London: Penguin.
[146] Nietzsche, F. (1969), *On the Genealogy of Morals and Ecce Homo* (trans. W. Kaufmann), New York, NY: Vintage Books.
[147] —— (2002), *Beyond Good and Evil*, ed. R.-P. Horstmann and J. Norman, Cambridge: Cambridge University Press.
[148] Nivison, D. (2000), 'Xunzi and Zhuangzi', pp. 176–87 of T. Kline and P. Ivanhoe (eds.), *Virtue, Nature, and Moral Agency in the Xunzi*, Indianapolis, IN: Hackett.
[149] Normore, C. (1985), 'Buridan's Ontology', pp. 189–203 of J. Bogen and E. McGuire (eds.), *How Things Are*, Dordrecht: Reidel Publishing Company.
[150] Parfit, D. (1984), *Reasons and Persons*, Oxford: Clarendon Press.
[151] Parkinson, G. H. R. (ed.) (1966), 'General Inquiries about the Analysis of Concepts and of Truth', *Leibniz: Logical Papers*, Oxford: Clarendon Press.
[152] Passmore, J. (1961), 'The Infinite Regress', ch. 2 of *Philosophical Reasoning*, London: Duckworth.
[153] Pears, D. (ed.) (1972), *Russell's Logical Atomism*, London: Fontana/Collins.
[154] Pelletier, J. (1990), *Parmenides, Plato, and the Semantics of Non-Being*, Chicago, IL: Chicago University Press.
[155] Pemberton, H. J. (1984), *Plato's* Parmenides: *the Critical Moment for Socrates*, Darby, PA: Norwood Editions.
[156] Petersen, S. (1996), 'Plato's *Parmenides*: a Principle of Interpretation, and Seven Arguments', *Journal of the History of Philosophy* 34: 167–92.
[157] Powers, J., and Prebish, C. S. (2009), *Destroying Mara Forever: Buddhist Ethics Essays in Honour of Dameon Keown*, Ithaca, NY: Snow Lion Publications.
[158] Priest, G. (1987), *In Contradiction*, Dordrecht: Martinus Nijhoff; second (extended) edn., Oxford: Oxford University Press, 2006.
[159] —— (1989), 'Primary Qualities are Secondary Qualities Too', *British Journal for the Philosophy of Science* 40: 29–37.
[160] —— (1995a), *Beyond the Limits of Thought*, Cambridge: Cambridge University Press; second (extended) edn., Oxford: Oxford University Press, 2002.
[161] —— (1995b), 'Multiple Denotation, Ambiguity, and the Strange Case of the Missing Amoeba', *Logique et Analyse* 38: 361–73.
[162] —— (1997), 'The Linguistic Construction of Reality', *Exordium* 11: 1–7.
[163] —— (1998a), 'Fuzzy Identity and Local Validity', *Monist* 8: 331–42.
[164] —— (1998b), 'The Trivial Object and the Non-Triviality of a Semantically Closed Theory with Descriptions', *Journal of Applied and Non-Classical Logic* 8: 171–83.
[165] —— (1998c), 'What's so Bad about Contradictions?', *Journal of Philosophy* 95: 410–26; reprinted as ch. 1 of G. Priest, J. C. Beall and B. Armour-Garb (eds.), *The Law of Non-Contradiction: New Philosophical Essays*, Oxford: Oxford University Press, 2004.
[166] —— (2001), 'Heidegger and the Grammar of Being', ch. 10 of R. Gasking (ed.), *Grammar in Early Twentieth Century Philosophy*, London: Rouledge; reprinted as ch. 15 of the second edition of Priest (1995a).
[167] Priest, G. (2002), 'Paraconsistent Logic', pp. 287–393, vol. 6 of D. Gabbay and F. Guenthner (eds.), *Handbook of Philosophical Logic*, 2nd edn., Dordrecht: Reidel.
[168] —— (2005a), *Towards Non-Being*, Oxford: Oxford University Press.

[169] —— (2005b), 'The Limits of Language' pp. 156–9 of K. Brown (ed.), *Encyclopedia of Language and Linguistics*, 2nd edn., Vol. 7, Dordrecht: Elsevier.
[170] —— (2006), *Doubt Truth to be a Liar*, Oxford: Oxford University Press.
[171] —— (2008), *Introduction to Non-Classical Logic: from If to Is*, Cambridge: Cambridge University Press.
[172] —— (2009a), 'Not to Be', ch. 23 of R. Le Poidevin, P. Simons, A. McGonical, and R. Cameron (eds.), *The Routledge Companion to Metaphysics*, London: Routledge.
[173] —— (2009b), 'The Structure of Emptiness', *Philosophy East & West*, 59: 467–80.
[174] —— (2010a), 'A Case of Mistaken Identity', ch. 11 of J. Lear and A. Oliver (eds.), *The Force of Argument*, London: Routledge.
[175] —— (2010b), 'Non-Transitive Identity', ch. 23 of R. Dietz and S. Moruzzi (eds.), *Cuts and Clouds: Vagueness, its Nature and its Logic*, Oxford: Oxford University Press.
[176] —— (2010c), 'Inclosures, Vagueness, and Self-Reference', *Notre Dame Journal of Formal Logic*, 51: 69–84.
[177] —— (2012), 'The *Parmenides*: a Dialetheic Interpretation', *Plato: The Journal of the International Plato Society* 12, http://gramata.univ-pavis1.fr/Plato/article120.html.
[178] —— (2013a), 'Between the Horns of Idealism and Realism: The Middle Way of Mādhyamaka', ch. 13 of S. M. Emmanuel (ed.), *A Companion to Buddhist Philosophy*, Chichester: Wiley-Blackwell.
[179] —— (2013b), 'Indefinite Extensibility—Dialetheic Style', *Studia Logica*, 101: 1263–75.
[180] —— (2014a), 'Speaking of the Ineffable . . . ', ch. 7 of J.-L. Liu and D. Berger (eds.), *Nothingness in Asian Philosophy*, London: Routledge.
[181] —— (2014b), 'Much Ado About Nothing', *Australasian Journal of Logic* 11: Article 4, http://ojs.victoria.ac.nz/ajl/issue/view/209.
[182] —— (2015a), 'The Net of Indra', ch. 5 of Tanaka *et al* (2015).
[183] —— (2015b), 'Compassion and the Net of Indra', ch. 12 of The Cowherds (2015).
[184] Prior, A. (1968), 'Time, Existence, and Identity', ch. 8 of *Papers on Time and Tense*, Oxford: Clarendon Press.
[185] Putnam, F. W. (2002), 'Televised Trauma and Viewer PTSD: Implications for Prevention', *Psychiatry* 65: 310–12.
[186] Queen, C. S., and King, S. B. (1996), *Engaged Buddhism: Buddhist Liberation Movements in Asia*, Albany, NY: State University of New York Press.
[187] Quine, W. V. O. (1953), 'Reference and Modality', ch. 8 of *From a Logical Point of View*, Cambridge, MA: Harvard University Press.
[188] Rea, M. (ed.) (1997), *Material Constitution: a Reader*, Lanham, ML: Rowman and Littlefield Publishers Inc.
[189] Reps, P., and Senzaki, N. (eds.) (1971), *Zen Flesh, Zen Bones*, London: Penguin Books.
[190] Resnik, M. (1997), *Mathematics as a Science of Patterns*, Oxford: Clarendon Press.
[191] Rickless, S. (1998), 'How Parmenides Saved the Theory of Forms', *Philosophical Review* 107: 501–54.
[192] —— (2007), 'Plato's *Parmenides*', *Stanford Encyclopedia of Philosophy*, http://plato.stanford.edu/entries/parmenides/. (Accessed May 2008.)
[193] Robinson, R. (1971), 'Plato's Separation of Reason from Desire', *Phronesis* 16: 38–48.

[194] Ross, W. D. (1924), *Aristotle's* Metaphysics: *a Revised Text with Introduction and Commentary*, 2 Vols., Oxford: Clarendon Press.
[195] Routley, R. (1980), *Exploring Meinong's Jungle, and Beyond; an Investigation of Noneism and the Theory of Items*, Canberra: Research School of Social Sciences, ANU.
[196] Rudder Baker, L. (1997), 'Why Constitution is not Identity', *Journal of Philosophy* 94: 599-621.
[197] Ryle, G. (1939), 'Plato's "Parmenides"', *Mind* 48: 129-51 and 302-25.
[198] —— (1960), 'Letters and Syllables in Plato', *Philosophical Review* 69: 431-51; reprinted as ch. 3 of Ryle's (1971) *Collected Papers*, Vol. I, London: Hutchinson.
[199] Schaffer, J. (2010a), 'Monism: The Priority of the Whole', *Philosophical Review* 119: 31-76.
[200] —— (2010b), 'The Internal Relatedness of All Things', *Mind* 119: 341-75.
[201] Scolnicov, S. (2003), *Plato's Parmenides*, Berkeley, CA: University of California Press.
[202] Selby-Bigge, L. A. (ed.), (1978), *David Hume: a Treatise on Human Nature*, 2nd edn., Oxford: Oxford University Press.
[203] Shapiro, S. (2000), *Philosophy of Mathematics: Structure and Ontology*, New York, NY: Oxford University Press.
[204] Sider, T. (1993a), 'Parthood', *Philosophical Review* 116: 51-91.
[205] —— (1993b), 'Van Inwagen and the Possibility of Gunk', *Analysis* 53: 285-9.
[206] Siderits, M. (2007), *Buddhism as Philosophy*, Aldershot: Ashgate.
[207] Singer, T., Seymour, B., O'Doherty, J., Kaube, H., Dolan, R. J., and Frith, C. D. (2004), 'Empathy for Pain Involves the Affective but not Sensory Components of Pain', *Science* 303: 1157-62.
[208] Smart, J. J. C. (1963), *Philosophy and Scientific Realism*, London: Routledge & Kegan Paul.
[209] —— (ed.) (1964), *Problems of Space and Time*, London: Macmillan.
[210] Spinks, L. (2003), *Frederick Nietzsche*, London: Routledge.
[211] Stevenson, I. (1997), *Reincarnation and Biology: A Contribution to the Etiology of Birthmarks and Birth Defects*, Westport, CT: Praeger Scientific.
[212] Szabo, A., and Hopkinson, K. L., (2007), 'Negative Psychological Effects of Watching the News in the Television; Relaxation or Another Intervention May be Needed to Buffer Them', *International Journal of Behavioral Medicine* 14: 57-62.
[213] Tanaka, Deguchi, Garfield, and Priest, K. (2015), *The Moon Points Back*, New York, NY: Oxford Unversity Press.
[214] Tanner, M. (1994), *Nietzsche: a Very Short Introduction*, Oxford: Oxford University Press.
[215] Thera, S. (2010), *The Kālāma Sutra*, http://www.katinkahesselink.net/tibet/kalama.html. (Accessed November 2010.)
[216] Unger, P. (1979), 'There are no Ordinary Things', *Synthese* 41: 117-54.
[217] Uzquiano, G. (2004), 'Plurals and Simples', *Monist* 87: 429-51.
[218] Vanderschraaf, P., and Sillari, G. (2007), 'Common Knowledge', *Stanford Encyclopedia of Philosophy*, http://plato.stanford.edu/entries/common-knowledge/. (Accessed April 2011.)

[219] Varzi, A. (2009), 'Mereology', *Stanford Encyclopedia of Philosophy*, http://plato.stanford.edu/entires/mereology. (Accessed April 2010.)
[220] Wallace, V., and Wallace, A. (trans.) (1997), *A Guide to the Bodhisattva's Way of Life*, Ithaca, NY: Snow Lion.
[221] Wasserman, R. (2009), 'Material Constitution', *Stanford Encyclopedia of Philosophy*, http://plato.stanford.edu/entries/material-constitution/. (Accessed, March 2011.)
[222] Watson, B. (trans.) (1964), *Chuang Tzu: Basic Writings*, New York, NY: Columbia University Press.
[223] ——— (tr.) (1997), *The Vimalakīrti Sūtra*, New York, NY: Columbia University Press.
[224] Weatherstone, B. (2009), 'The Problem of the Many', *Stanford Encyclopedia of Philosophy*, http://plato.stanford.edu/entries/problem-of-many/. (Accessed April, 2011.)
[225] Westerhoff, J. (2009), *Nāgārjuna's Madhyamaka*, Oxford: Oxford University Press.
[226] Wetelsen, J. (2002), 'Did Śāntideva Destroy the Bodhisattva Path?', *Journal of Buddhist Ethics* 9: 412–24.
[227] White, N. (1993), *Plato: Sophist*, Indianapolis, IN: Hacket Publishing Co.
[228] Whitehead, A. (1979), *Process and Reality*, corrected edn., New York, NY: Free Press.
[229] ——— and Russell, B. (1910), *Principia Mathematica*, Cambridge: Cambridge University Press.
[230] Williams, P. (2000), *Studies in the Philosophy of the* Bodhicaryāvatāra, Delhi: Motilal Banarsidass.
[231] Williamson, T. (1994), *Vagueness*, London: Routledge.
[232] Wittgenstein, L. (1953), *Philosophical Investigations*, Oxford: Blackwell Publishing.
[233] Wright, C. (2004), 'Intuition, Entitlement, and the Epistemology of Logical Laws', *Dialectica* 58: 155–75.
[234] Yaffe, G., and Nichols, R. (2009), 'Thomas Reid', *Stanford Encyclopedia of Philosophy*, http://plato.stanford.edu/entries/reid/. (Accessed, March 2011.)
[235] Yamada, K. (2004), *The Gateless Gate: The Classic Book of Zen Koans*, Somerville, MA: Wisdom Publications.
[236] Yi, B. (2005), 'The Logic and Meaning of Plurals, Part I', *Journal of Philosophical Logic* 34: 459–506.

Index

A

Abelard 58n, 93n
Allen, R. E. 119
anxiety 56, 211, 224
aporia 14, 51, 53
Aquinas, T. 184–5, 187
Aristotle xvii, 8, 12n, 15, 38–42, 44–5, 50, 58, 79, 81, 103, 104n, 109, 115, 121, 123, 125, 139, 141, 181n, 183n, 214, 221, 227
  Metaphysics 38, 40, 45, 81, 103, 104n, 109
Armstrong, D. M. 47n
Augustine 5

B

being xv, xvii, xxii, 5, 40, 42n, 48–54, 81, 83–4, 91–2, 128–30, 133, 135, 137, 140–1, 147–9, 167
Bird, A. 183n, 188n
Bodhicaryavatāra xxv, 228
Bodhidharma xxvii
Bradley, F. H. 10–12, 15, 80, 84
Buddhism xvii–xviii, 94n, 169–71nn, 174–5, 197, 210–5, 226n, 227–9, 231, 233
  Abhidharma xxiv, 175, 184n, 196–7, 228
  Chinese xxv–xxvii, 16n, 179, 204
  Huayan xvii, xxvi–xxvii, 80n, 168, 179–81, 193, 198, 205
  Indian xxiii–xxv
  Madhyamaka xvii, xxv, 16n, 168, 175, 184n, 193, 197–8nn
  Mahāyāna xxiv–xxvi, 228
  Sarvātivāda 184n
  Yogācāra xxv–xxvi, 197, 203–5, 208
Buridan, J. 10n

C

Cameron, R. 183n
Candrakīrti 201n, 202
characterization xxii–xxiii, 45–6, 90, 92, 230
Chengguan 180
compassion xviii–xxiv, 220–35
concept-senses 6–7, 9
Confucianism xxvi
conservation theorem 34
copula xv, 10, 53, 143, 148
Cornford, F. M. 85, 112n, 115n, 119n, 123n
cosmological arguments 184–6
Cotnoir, A. 90n, 95n
Crabbé, M. 74n

D

Daoism xxvi
Dennett, D. 170, 171n
dialetheism xviii–xxi, xxiii, xxvii, 71, 102–3, 104n, 137n
Dignāga 190n
Dipert, R. 175n
Dōgen xxvii
Donne, J. 225
Duns Scotus 40n

E

emptiness/empty xvii–xviii, xxv, xxvii, 33, 56, 91, 97–8, 100, 111n, 173–5, 177, 179, 180n, 181–4, 187–8, 190–4, 198, 201–4, 209, 221–2, 226, 229
Euclid 57
everything xvii, 54–6, 80, 100, 172n, 181, 201, 203
existence xxii, xxv, 14, 39, 49–50, 56, 64–6, 83, 87, 92, 148, 156–7, 168n, 169–70, 174, 180, 181n, 184, 198, 222, 228

F

falsity xix, 20n, 29, 34–6, 69, 79, 141–2, 144–5, 147–8, 150–3, 155, 161, 200n
Fazang xxvii, 179n
Fine, K. 40–1, 88, 187n
fission 66–8
forms 8, 9n, 28, 38–47, 86, 101–17, 119–21, 124, 127–8, 132–3, 137–42, 199
Foucault, M. 212
Four Noble Truths xxiv, 211–2
Frede, M. 148
Frege, G. xvi, 5–7, 9, 11, 53, 59, 61n, 142n, 143, 174, 199
function-sense 7
fusion 66n, 68, 90–2, 97–100

G

Gill, M. L. 101, 115n, 119, 121, 123, 127–8nn, 131n
gluons/gluon theory xvi–xviii, 5, 9, 11–12, 14–22, 24, 26–8, 31, 33, 37–8, 42–50, 51–53, 55–6, 60, 66, 68, 70–3, 79–81, 84n,

gluons/gluon theory (*cont.*)
 88n, 89–90, 92–4, 101, 104, 108–9, 114, 117–8, 125, 127, 133, 141n, 142–4, 154, 156, 159–61, 167, 168n, 177, 180, 194, 199–202, 205, 207, 209
 Prime Gluon Corollary 22, 32
Grounding Principle 106, 109, 111

H

Harte, V. 79n, 86n
Hegel, G. W. F. 55, 102n
Heidegger, M. xvii, 48–9, 51–6, 157, 159, 180, 200, 207–8
Hobbes, T. 221–2, 233
Huineng xxvii
Hume, D. 169–70, 214
Husserl, E. 157, 159

I

idealism xviii, 194–5, 197–8, 204
identicals/identity xv–xvii, xxvii, 5, 13–14, 17, 19–24, 26–8, 30–1, 36, 38n, 43–6, 49–50, 55, 57–74, 79–80nn, 89–90, 94, 96–7, 99, 109, 111, 114, 124, 143, 152, 161, 167, 169, 177–8, 179n, 181n, 190–2nn
 metalanguage 71–3
 object-language 71–3
 substitutivity xvi, 23, 30–1, 37, 57, 71–2, 96
 transitivity xvi, 17, 20, 23, 30, 66, 70, 72, 89, 181
 trans-temporal 177
Inclosure Schema xx, 200, 202, 208
inner peace 214–9, 221–2, 226–8, 230–2
instantiation xvi, 6n, 7n, 38, 45–7, 59, 84n, 110, 145–6, 172
intentionality xvii, xxii, 5, 15, 25–6, 60–1, 64, 79, 91, 95–6, 143, 149, 154, 159–61
interconnectedness 222
interpenetration xvii, 178–81

J

Jones, N. 94, 96–7

K

Kant, I. 14, 54, 116, 169, 183–4, 197, 204, 208
Keränen, J. 190n
Kneale, W. and M. 58n
Koslicki, K. 41–2, 88
Kripke, S. 25, 64
Kumārajīva xxvi

L

Leibniz, G. W. 20n, 22–3, 59, 173–4, 184
Lewis, D. 24, 67n, 91, 142n

Linnebo, Ø. 96n
locus/loci 172, 174, 175n, 176, 188–91, 193, 197n
logic xvi, xviii, xix–xx, xxii–xxiii, 18–19, 22, 28, 32, 36, 53–4, 57, 59, 64, 70–1, 73–4, 137n

M

Marx, K. 174n, 233–4
material substitutivity 31, 37, 71
McPherran, M. 140n
Meinong, A. xxii, 49, 91
Meinwald, C. C. 120, 127n
mereology xvii, 40–1, 56, 63n, 66n, 79–80, 88–93, 95, 97–8, 142–3nn
modality 25–6, 28, 35–7, 64–7, 70, 72, 92n, 146
Mūlamadhyamakakārikā xxv, 25, 172, 184, 202

N

Nāgārjuna xxv, 172n, 184, 202–3
necessity 14n, 25, 64–5, 83, 91, 200
Nehamas, A. 140
Net of Indra 167, 179–81, 193, 223–7, 233, 235
Newton, I. 173–4
Nietzsche, F. 62n, 216–7, 230–1
nihilism 91n, 132–4, 182, 184, 191–3
noema 157
non-being xxii, 91, 116, 130, 140, 141n
noneism xxi, xxvii, 45, 49, 55, 91, 149, 158, 171
nothing(ness) xvii, 47–8, 50, 54–6, 82, 83n, 91, 97–8, 172n, 180–1, 187, 195, 201, 203, 205, 207–9

O

object xv–xvii, xx–xxv, xxvii, 5–9, 11–24, 26–7, 29, 31–4, 37–56, 61n, 63n, 64–73, 80–1, 84n, 88–98, 105–9, 117, 119, 135–7, 141n, 143, 145–6, 149, 153, 157–61, 167–8, 171–92, 196–203, 205, 207–8, 225–6
 object-senses 6, 7
Ockham, William of 58, 61n, 92
one and the many, problem of the xv, xvii, 41, 63n, 94
overlap xix, xx, 18–19, 90, 98, 100, 151

P

paraconsistency xviii–xx, 153
paradox xviii, 195, 204–5
 Berry's 200
 debtor's 62n
 dependence 187n
 gluon 200–3
 identity 70
 inclosure xx, 200
 König's xxi, 200

INDEX 251

Nāgārjuna's 202–3
nothingness 207–9
Russell's xxi
self-reference xx
Sorites 68–9
Parmenides xvii, 15, 79–88, 97, 101–2, 104–5, 107–18, 120–3, 126, 128–30, 132–5, 137–9, 141, 147
parthood/parts xvi, 88–90
Pemberton, H. J. 119
perception 122, 130, 154–9, 161, 169, 197
personhood 42–3
Plato xvii, 9n, 45, 73, 79–80, 84, 88, 92, 94, 97, 101–4, 106, 115–21, 124–7, 130, 132–4, 136–9, 141–2, 147, 150–1, 153, 161
  Parmenides xvii, 9n, 101–3, 104n, 118–21, 132, 137–41, 161
  Phaedo 103n
  Republic 103
  Sophist 80, 81n, 84, 97, 140–1, 144, 154–5
  Statesman 103
  Theaetetus 148, 154–5, 158
Plotinus 50
plurality xxiii, 6, 9, 13–15, 41, 51, 84n, 85–6, 88, 94–6, 117, 131, 134
predicates xx, xxii, 6–7, 9–10, 20n, 23–6, 28–30, 31n, 32–4, 36, 39, 45, 46n, 50, 53, 58, 61n, 69, 73, 95, 99, 106, 129, 145n, 150, 207
Principle of Non-Contradiction (PNC) 15, 60, 81–4, 103, 139
properties xv–xvi, xviii, xxii–xxiii, 6–7nn, 15–16, 19–26, 28, 30, 36, 40, 43–4, 46, 49, 55, 61n, 65–6nn, 67–8, 70–3, 81–3, 85–9, 90, 93–4, 100, 102, 105–7, 109, 111–2, 114–6, 119–28, 130–3, 137–8, 140, 151–3, 156, 159, 171–2, 177, 183n, 201
property instances (pins)/tropes xvi, 43–6, 53, 108, 111n, 146, 152–3, 189, 190n, 196

Q

quiddity 167–8, 171–7, 180, 182, 186–8, 201, 222
Quine W. V. O. 65n

R

realism xviii, 24, 158n, 175n, 194–8
rebirth 212–4
regress xviii, 10, 11, 39–40, 45n, 109–11, 182–5, 187–8, 192, 193
  Bradley regress xvi, xviii, 9, 12–13, 16–7, 22, 42, 46, 84n, 186
Reid, T. 158
relations xxii, 10–12, 32n, 46, 72, 84n, 113–4, 172–5, 176n, 177–8, 181–2, 188–91, 198, 202, 225

representation 153–4, 157, 158n, 159–61, 175n, 197, 205–8, 224
Rickless, S. 102, 104n, 119, 120n
Ross, W. D. 38n
Rudder Baker, L. 65n
Russell, B. 10, 51, 59, 92, 95, 151, 183
Ryle, G. 120, 142n

S

Śāntideva xxv, 228, 229n
Sartre, J.-P. 225–6
Saussure, F. de 174
self xx–xxi, xxv, 27, 38n, 50, 99, 103, 107, 110n, 111, 120, 122, 167–71, 174–5, 180–2, 187n, 194, 197n, 200–3, 212–3, 228
  Self-Predication 107, 110n, 111, 116, 121, 123–4, 140n
Sider, T. 14n
simples/simplex 14n, 48, 49n, 56, 109n, 142, 184
Simplicius 104n
Smart, J. 196
Socrates 102, 104–15, 121, 124–5, 127, 133, 138–9, 148, 155–9
structuralism 172n, 174, 188, 190n
substance 38–40, 42–3, 45, 183–4
sūtras xxiv
  Astasāhasrikā Prajñāpāramitā 202
  Platform xxvii
  Prajñāpāramitā xxiv
  Vimilakīrti 204

T

tathātā 197, 203–5
Theaetetus 84, 140, 142–3, 145, 147–8, 150, 155–6
third man argument 9n, 109
time/temporality 48n, 62–7, 83, 172–4, 177, 185
truth xvii, xix–xxi, xxiii–xxiv, 6n, 18–19, 20n, 22–3, 25–6, 29, 31, 34–6, 46, 52, 59, 63, 66n, 67, 69–71, 80–1, 91, 97–8, 100, 106, 111, 140, 142, 144–53, 196n, 211
Tuxun xxvi

U

Unger, P. 14n, 24n
unity xv–xvi, 5–17, 22, 27, 38–44, 46–51, 53, 73, 79, 80, 84n, 86–8, 93–4, 96–7, 106, 109n, 116–8, 125, 127, 134, 138, 141–4, 153, 160, 169, 184, 186, 199, 203
universals xv–xvi, 8n, 38, 43–7, 53, 88n, 93–4, 101, 111n, 143, 145, 161, 229
Uzquiano, G. 14n

V

vagueness 68–70, 161
Vasubandhu xxv, 197
viciousness xviii, 9, 11, 16, 39, 45n, 46, 84n, 182–4, 186–8, 193

W

Whitehead, A. N. 51, 59
wholes xvi, 14n, 39, 57, 79–80, 84n, 85, 87, 94, 126, 134n, 140, 161

Wittgenstein, L. 152, 168, 200
  Investigations 206
  Tractatus 7, 153n, 199, 203–4, 206, 208
Wright, C. 60

Z

Zeno 104–5, 111, 115–6, 130, 138
Zermelo Frankel set theory 54, 71–3, 191

The manufacturer's authorised representative in the EU for product
safety is Oxford University Press España S.A. of El Parque Empresarial
San Fernando de Henares, Avenida de Castilla, 2 - 28830 Madrid
(www.oup.es/en or product.safety@oup.com). OUP España S.A. also acts
as importer into Spain of products made by the manufacturer.
Printed and bound by CPI Group (UK) Ltd, Croydon, CR0 4YY

20/03/2026

02075336-0008